THE ECOLOGY
OF STRESS

The Series in Health Psychology and Behavioral Medicine

Charles D. Spielberger, *Editor-in-Chief*

Chesney, Rosenman   Anger and Hostility in Cardiovascular
   and Behavioral Disorders
Elias, Marshall   Cardiovascular Disease and Behavior
Hobfoll   The Ecology of Stress
Lonetto, Templer   Death Anxiety
Morgan, Goldston   Exercise and Mental Health
Pancheri, Zichella   Biorhythms and Stress in the Physiopathology
   of Reproduction

IN PREPARATION

Byrne, Rosenman   Anxiety and the Heart
Hackfort, Spielberger   Anxiety in Sports: An International Perspective

THE ECOLOGY
OF STRESS

Stevan E. Hobfoll
Kent State University, Kent, Ohio

● HEMISPHERE PUBLISHING CORPORATION
A member of the Taylor & Francis Group

New York   Washington   Philadelphia   London

17873664

3-90

THE ECOLOGY OF STRESS

1 2 3 4 5 6 7 8 9 0   E B E B   8 9 8

This book was set in Times Roman by Hemisphere Publishing Corporation. The editors were Diane Stuart and Joanna Taylor, the production supervisor was Miriam Gonzalez, and the typesetter was Sandi Stancil. Cover design by Debra Eubanks Riffe.
Edwards Brothers, Inc. was printer and binder.

Library of Congress Cataloging in Publication Data

Hobfoll, Stevan E., date.
    The ecology of stress.
    (The series in health psychology and behavioral medicine)
    Bibliography: p.
    Includes index.
    1. Stress (Psychology) 2. Stress (Psychology)—Prevention. I. Title. II. Series.
BF575.S75H62   1988   155.9   88–11180

ISBN 0-89116-637-8 (hard)
ISBN 0-89116-845-1 (paper)
ISSN 8756-467X

To Ivonne Heras Hobfoll,
wife, lover, and friend, and to our children, Ari, Sheera, and Jonathan

CONTENTS

Foreword   xi
Preface   xiii
Acknowledgments   xvii

1   **The Stress Concept: Social and Psychological Perspectives**   1

Stress and the Human Experience   2
Psychosocial Stress: Founding Concepts   5
Stress Definitions and Models   16
Summary   22

2   **The Conservation of Resources: A New Stress Model**   25

The Model   25
The Investment of Resources: A Model within the Model   42
Emotions and Subconscious Processes: Role in Stress   48
Summary   54

3   **The Model of Ecological Congruence: Blueprint for Understanding Stress Resistance**   59

Models of Stress Resistance   61

Personal and Social Resources Fit to Environmental
Demand   70
Summary   105

4   Social Support and Stress: Searching for a Context   111

Environmental Bias in Understanding Strain   112
Social Support and Stress Resistance   118
Personal Relationships: The Process of Social Support   132
Summary and Conclusions   158

5   Personal Attributes and Stress Resistance   161

Personal Attributes and Psychopathology   162
Conceptualizing Health   164
Search for Stress Moderators   166
Early Perspectives on Personality and Well-Being   167
Early Work on Personality and Stress   170
Contemporary Research on Personal Resources and Stress
Resistance   173
Stress and Coping   187
Personal and Social Resources and Stress Resistance: Approach to
Ecologies   198
Summary and Conclusions   210

6   Stress Resistance during War: Applications of the Models of
Ecological Congruence and Conservation of Resources   217

Lessons to Be Learned from the Study of War   218
Review of the Models of Ecological Congruence and Conservation
of Resources   220
Civilians' Adjustment to War   225
Effects of War on Combatants   238
Implications for Understanding Stress Resistance   246
Summary and Conclusions   249

7   Stress Resistance in Times of Illness: Further Applications
       of the Models of Ecological Congruence and Conservation
       of Resources   251

       Importance of Study of Illness   253
       Coping with Threat to Life   256
       Adjustment to Complications of Pregnancy   261
       Reactions to Children's Illnesses   268
       Implications for Health Psychology, Behavioral Medicine, and
       Prevention   274
       Immediate versus Long-Term Stress Resistance   276
       Summary and Conclusions   278

8   Development of an Ecological Loss Theory of
       Personality and Intervention Efforts   283

       Theory of Personality Based on Avoidance of Loss   284
       Implications for Intervention   300
       Summary and Conclusions   319

References   327
Index   351

FOREWORD

This book is of special importance because of two outstanding features: its coverage and its original ideas. Its comprehensiveness is marked by a high level of scholarship, making it essential reading for anyone who wants a thoughtful survey of the current status of stress research. Health and illness, environmental processes, and extreme situations such as war are reviewed, and the major theories of stress are exemplified and analyzed.

Valuable for its comprehensiveness and up-to-date quality, the major achievement of the book is Stevan Hobfoll's integrative and theoretical contributions. He develops an interactional framework that supports both ecological-environmental factors and the personal resources of individuals. In so doing, he makes use of research in diverse areas and the writings of several key theorists. For example, he shows the relevance of recent work on social support, attachment, and Bowlby and Antonovsky's analysis of coherence in the attainment of health to the stress concept. Hobfoll makes clear that personality moderates responses to stress by creating the medium in which features of the environment are experienced. He offers numerous examples that support this point.

The portions of the individual's working models of self and of world that pertain to loss are an aspect of personality that Hobfoll sees as particularly relevant to stress and stress coping. He presents loss as a powerful factor in shaping personality because, as he sees it, experiences of loss represent personal crises and distress both at the time they occur and at junctures where cognitive templates are formed. These, in turn, lead to attributions, anticipations, and fears related to loss. If the loss experience is marked by strong unresolved emotions, a loss orientation may come to cast a pall over the individual's life.

This book will provide researchers and clinicians who deal with problems related to loss with clues to the achievement of positive adaptations to such phenomena as separation and rejection. Prevention and therapy are major foci of the book. Throughout his career, Stevan Hobfoll has had a strong interest in preventive, as well as clinical, interventions. In this book he develops a theory of stress that has important clinical and community implications, a theory that enables him to interpret much work on social support as a preventive aid and to refine his own concepts concerning the nature of social support.

The conceptualization of stress presented here might be viewed as involving a four-step process: (1) exposure to a particular task or situation; (2) stress arousal, that is, perceiving the situation or task to be challenging or threatening; (3) coping psychologically with the stress; and (4) adjusting to stress behaviorally, physiologically, and psychologically.

As Hobfoll makes clear, the way a task or situation influences an individual depends on his or her particular vulnerabilities, capabilities, and preoccupations. The preoccupation that is perhaps most central to Hobfoll's theory of stress is the individual's thoughts about loss. Developmentally, it is of great importance that people make strenuous efforts to avoid the burden of a loss orientation.

While the topics of stress and loss are not exactly cheery ones, this book approaches them in a constructive manner. Hobfoll is not just interested in talking about the terrible things that can affect a person's life. His emphasis on prevention strategies gives hope because people can learn to cope adaptively. Even when they fail to cope there are therapeutic techniques for overcoming unwanted stress effects. Stevan Hobfoll has given us a stimulating, useful, and wide-ranging analysis of the causes, treatment, and prevention of these unwanted effects.

Irwin G. Sarason

PREFACE

In planning this book I did not intend to spend much time or energy discussing what stress is, as I had naively assumed that the concept of stress was already clear in the literature. Rather, I planned to quickly present accepted definitions and models of stress and to proceed directly to the subject of *stress resistance,* that is, how individuals resist the potentially deleterious effects of stressors. Upon writing the book, however, I quickly became aware of how little progress had been made toward defining the parameters of stress.

Like many other researchers, I worked from the hazy premise that stress was an ubiquitous phenomenon that reflected an imbalance of perceived threat versus perceived ability to meet that threat. In other words, stress followed when perceived threat exceeded or was exceeded by perceived coping capacity. This book challenges that overly cognitive perspective, focusing on the contributions of both objective and subjective factors. In addition, the book questions the view of stress as an upset of homeostasis and argues that individuals innately seek to maximize growth, rather than preserve balance.

What emerges are two complementary models, one concerning the *causes of stress* and the second concerning the factors involved in *stress resistance.* Together, the two models fashion a comprehensive theory of stress phenomena. Both models emphasize culture, normative ways of responding, and psychosocial development. In so doing, they take a different tack than the idiographic and strictly personalogical perspectives that have recently dominated stress theorists' thinking. This volume also makes the point that stressors are not so much static events as they are evolving sequences of interactions between people and their environment.

One major thesis of the book is that because stress is such a profound and common aspect of life, people concern themselves with it even when no stressor is impinging on them. This view of stress is more proactive than prior models that have typically depicted stress as a reaction to outside events. Rather than be passive victims, individuals actively seek to prevent stress at some times and cause it at other times. Moreover, because this *tête-à-tête* with stress is so much a part of everyday experience, how people face, master, or succumb to it is seen as a principal shaper of who they are and how they view the world.

The first three chapters of this book are theoretical. The volume begins by focusing on the history of the stress concept, both in the way it has been conceptualized in the lay world and the progress in thinking about it in the social science literature. Chapter 2 develops a new model of stress termed the model of conservation of resources, which contends that people have a strong basic need to protect and enhance that which they value. When what is valued is threatened, stress ensues. The third chapter presents the model of ecological congruence. This model suggests that our success in combating stressors is a product of our resources, needs, environmental demand, time, perception, and values. It highlights the contribution of both the objective and the subjective world, emphasizing that the process of resisting stress involves an interaction of the person and the environment in a given culture at a given time in the person's life.

The fourth and fifth chapters involve broad reviews of the literature on stress and stress resistance. Chapter 4 focuses on research on social support and personal relationships and how they may limit or exacerbate stressors. Chapter 5 reviews the literature on personal resources, aspects of the self that affect stress resistance and presents the sparse, but important, research on the interplay of individuals' personal and social resources. Special attention is given to the more truly ecological research that examines the complex interaction of personal and social resources given contrasting environmental demands. This ecological work, in particular, is viewed as a cornerstone upon which future research should be built.

The next two chapters present research based on the model of ecological congruence, conducted by my colleagues and myself. Our research on the effects of war-related stressors on civilians and combatants in Israel is presented in Chapter 6. Chapter 7 presents research on stress related to physical illness. Both chapters emphasize the interaction of personal and social resources in countering the stress of contrasting demands. Whereas these studies were based on the model of ecological congruence, their results were seminal in the development of the model of conservation of resources.

In the final chapter, a new personality theory is conceptualized, based on what we have learned from research about stress and stress resistance. The theory focuses on counteracting loss as a principal shaper of personality. This in turn leads to a general blueprint for applications of stress research to interventions designed to prevent stress or limit its negative consequences. This final chapter criticizes superficial approaches to stress intervention, arguing that how people react to stressors and how successful they are in overcoming them are a function of deep-seated aspects of the self, complexly reflecting the interweaving of a person's internal and external resources. To be successful at aiding individuals in combating stress, interventionists are encouraged to appreciate that to change the way individuals react to stressors often requires changing very basic aspects of their selves. Furthermore, those aspects of the environment that might cause stress or that might function as potential stress moderators are often implacable, which suggests that only major efforts aimed at affecting people's environments are likely to be effective. If the difficulty of changing the course of stress is appreciated, interventionists will be less discouraged by certain limited effects of casual intervention programs. Meeting this challenge will be difficult, but the research reviewed in this book clearly points to directions of intervention that are likely to prove beneficial.

It is my hope that this volume will encourage new, more theory-based research and intervention efforts concerning stress and stress resistance. As I state early in the book, the goal of any theory is to lead to new research paths that in turn eventually lead to a body of information that bursts the seams of the theory. I have tried to conceptualize the stress literature in a new way that I hope better reflects current knowledge. It would be a great success if my approach to the stress phenomenon is heuristic and if it is eventually rejected in favor of a yet more sophisticated approach.

Finally, I have tried to write this volume in a fashion that will make it relevant to a broad audience. Many professionals are interested in stress today, including psychologists, educators, sociologists, nurses, physicians, social workers, epidemiologists, and business managers, to name a few. As a society we have become introspective of not only ourselves but our workplaces as well. There too we have noted stress and its marked effects. This book, I hope, crosses narrow disciplinary borders and has merit when viewed from each of these perspectives. It may serve as a worthwhile text for a stress course for advanced students from this same broad spectrum.

Because few books in this field develop theory and practical steps for intervention while also delving deeply into research, my goal has been to meet these objectives. There is no reason why they should be separated, and there are many good reasons why they should be integrated. In my estimation, the next generation of work on stress will attempt new and dynamic approaches to interventions in aid of stress resistance and improving quality of life. This volume makes one small contribution toward this important work by proceeding in an organized, data-based fashion.

Stevan E. Hobfoll

ACKNOWLEDGMENTS

I would like to thank the many people who helped with various aspects of the writing and publication of this book.

Perry London, Martin Covington, and Charlie Spielberger gave me encouragement to embark on the task and to allow myself to express what I thought and not what I perceived others wished to hear. Sheldon Cotler, Kenneth Heller, Rudolf Moos, and Sheila Ribordi read various chapters and provided insightful comments. I am greatly indebted to Leonard Jason who read the entire manuscript, provided detailed feedback, and knew how to mix humor with criticism when he needed to be very critical. Irwin Sarason read and provided feedback on the manuscript and was gracious enough to write the Foreword. Graduate assistants who worked on the project included Angela Bridges, Arthur Guidino, Kathy Long, and Vince Wisser. Special thanks are extended to Patricia John for editorial and secretarial assistance. My wife Ivonne and children, Ari, Sheera, and Jonathan, offered much needed love, affection, and support.

The publication team at Hemisphere was outstanding. In particular I thank Barbara Bodling, Christine Lowry, and Diane Stuart for their editorial assistance and attention to detail. I am particularly indebted to Kathleen Roach of Hemisphere for her confidence, support, and advice.

Finally, I thank my colleagues who collaborated with me on the research reported herein and to the many subjects who contributed their time and effort to our research.

I, of course, accept full responsibility for the contents of this volume. I hope that my contribution does justice to all the help and support others have provided in the course of its publication.

THE STRESS CONCEPT: SOCIAL AND PSYCHOLOGICAL PERSPECTIVES

If a man could see
The perils and diseases that he elbows
Each day he walks a mile; which catch at him,
Which fall behind him as he passes;
Then would he know that Life's a single pilgrim,
Fighting unarmed among a thousand soldiers.

(Thomas Lovell Beddoes, *Death's Jest Book,* 1798–1851)

Life is just one damned thing after another.

(Elbert Hubbard, *A Thousand and One Epigrams,* 1859–1915)

Before we can venture into a discussion of stress resistance it is imperative that we understand what we mean by stress. In reviewing the literature on stress, one is both impressed and overwhelmed with the amount of work that has been done. With all this material, one is nonetheless struck by the fact that researchers and theorists are still struggling for a clear definition of stress. A few favored definitions have been proposed and have been heuristic, but one finds each definition lacking in some way or form. This chapter will first make a case for the importance of the study of stress to humankind as expressed in the arts, literature, and religion. Then, a brief review of the development of the stress concept will be presented along with a discussion of the most well-accepted definitions of stress.

Rather than review the vast stress literature, then, this chapter will try to outline special areas of interest to stress researchers. Particular attention will be given to theories that have gained wide currency or that have been particularly influential in leading to the bridge from an interest on stress to a new focus on stress resistance.

STRESS AND THE HUMAN EXPERIENCE

The fact that no single accepted definition of stress has emerged is not surprising, as stress is one of the most complicated phenomena that can be imagined. It involves all the systems of the body—cardiovascular, endocrine, and neurological; all the systems of the psyche—cognitive, emotional, and unconscious; and occurs in all social systems—interpersonal, intrapersonal, small group, large group, and societal. It is evoked by such varied stimuli as minor daily hassles and the threat of star wars nuclear conflict. It involves our loves, hates, closest attachments, competition, achievement—indeed every matter in which humans are involved.

In a sense, stress is the most narcissistic area of study that psychology has undertaken. It is a reflection of ourselves and the things that concern us. It involves our worries, fears, goals, hope, and faith. Indeed, what more is human than these things?

When we examine religious writings, we see that the story of Job in the Old Testament is the story of every man and woman. Despite faith, caring, family, holiness, and righteousness, Job was tested by the Lord. In this story we see our fear that despite all our good deeds and intentions calamity may randomly or fatefully strike. For Job everything was lost: his children, his land, his wealth, and his health. Through what is perhaps the greatest of all stress resistance resources—faith—Job survived his ordeal. In this we express our own hope that despite life's many challenges and stressors, we will, or at least can, endure.

Another telling biblical example of stress as a test of people's mettle is found in the story of the 40-year wanderings of the Children of Israel following their escape from slavery in Egypt. Actually, the Jews arrived in Canaan some weeks after their departure from Egypt. However, when confronted with the information that Canaan was filled not only with milk and honey but also with powerful nations, the slave-minded Hebrews grew fearful and doubted their ability to conquer the land. For this lack of faith they were sent back into the desert until those who doubted died out and, most importantly, until a new generation could be raised. This generation would not be weakened by the helplessness of slavery, but would be strengthened by repeated tests of their ability in battle and in surviving as free men and women. They would later enter Canaan not as meek doubting slaves but as a self-assured warrior nation. Later in the book, when sense of mastery and stress inoculation are discussed, we will see that the lessons taught by this story form as sound a set of principles for stress resistance as stress researchers can offer today.

When we consider other religious works, legend, and mythology, we see repeatedly that they address the doubts in humankind concerning whether the stress of life can be overcome. Indeed, what is a religious testament, be it the Koran, the Old or New Testament, or the ancient Tao, if not a testament of faith, a prescription for how to withstand the stressors of life?

Literature, too, has expressed the theme of stress repeatedly. The works of Tolstoy, Dostoyevsky, Singer, Malamud, Steinbeck, and others revolve around the struggles of humankind. For Dostoyevsky, internal forces lead to the protagonist's ultimate destruction in the face of stressors that often only he perceives. For Steinbeck, individual courage and endurance aid the protagonists in their survival of the test of time. For Malamud, the stressors of life are the very stuff by which life is defined. And what is the adventure story, if not the expression of our wish to be the hero who overcomes fear against the greatest odds, winning love and glory in the end, withstanding terrible stressors where others falter? Nor is it any surprise that the most loved books of adolescence, such as *Catcher in the Rye* and *A Tree Grows in Brooklyn,* are about withstanding the terrifying stressors of coming of age.

Knowing nothing about literature except as a lover of books, I dare to say that what most great books have in common is the author's ability to depict the struggle of the individual against the multifarious and seemingly overwhelming demands of the environment. If Dostoyevsky's *Crime and Punishment* or Malamud's *Assistant* are only about madmen and afflicted souls, how is it that we so strongly identify with their characters? Obviously, we identify both with the individual's struggle and with what he or she is struggling against. Sometimes the struggle is concentrated within, as in the recent writings of Carlos Castañeda about the inner trials of a young American as posed to him by a Yaki Indian medicine man. Yet recall that even Castañeda's books were popularized as part of an escapist countercultural reaction to a way of life that produced Vietnam, consumerism, and the competitiveness of modern society.

Whether the battle is pitched as anxiety from within the self or as a challenge from the environment, we do not prefer a primrose path for our hero or heroine. Rather, we hope that our protagonists will withstand the tests before them and that, like Job, they will ultimately triumph. We are ever aware that fictional triumphs are like ours only when portrayed through enduring stressors great and small. *Catcher in the Rye* is the fantasy of an adolescent confronting identity crisis, sexual awareness, and independence. *Anna Karenina,* in contrast, represents an adult struggle to preserve esteem, love, status, and sanity amidst the vicissitudes of life's hard course. Each book appeals most to readers in the age group of its protagonist, but carries some meaning across generations, too.

The placement and context of this struggle often reflect the Weltschmerz of current concern. In film, the literature of Everyman, this is expressed in Chaplin's classic *Modern Times,* which so well illustrates the conflict between man and machine. The already classic *Swept Away* by Lena Wertmuller captures the struggle between the sexes, our attempt to define our roles as men and women through a period of rapid social change. Nor is it coincidence that Wertmuller's masterpiece is set against the backdrop of struggle between the classes, and that it follows her theme of fascism versus freedom, for these themes are on the forefront in Europe and Italy today. Back in the United States, Woody Allen's enormously popular sophisticated comedies express the anxieties of the New York genre of identity crisis, a product of the stress of relationships and the prolonged coming of age that today extends well into the fourth decade of life. Each of these films has in common the portrayal of our ability and fragility in withstanding the stressors of transition and life's demands upon us, expressed in terms and in context of the times.

I may be guilty of calling everything that is of interest to me stress. It could justifiably be argued, for instance, that Dostoyevsky is writing of an inner struggle, not a struggle between inner forces and external stressors. However, it is not by coincidence that in *Crime and Punishment* Dostoyevsky describes in great detail his protagonist's dire situation. We find Rashkolnikov to be hopelessly sunk in debt, embarrassed by his ragged clothes, and living in squalid conditions. Having recently left the university, he is unable to pay his rent and is confronted with having to pawn his last possessions. This state of affairs, accompanied by a weakening of Rashkolnikov's physical condition, leads him into melancholy and later to his crime of passion.

From this discussion, I have only hoped to argue the obvious: that stress is a complex phenomenon, that it concerns humankind's struggle for physical and existential survival, and that it is of interest to us because it is about us. I do not intend to make any special contribution to an understanding of religion, literature, or film. Rather, I have attempted as a psychologist to read into these works a framework that illustrates the importance an understanding of stress poses for humankind.

PSYCHOSOCIAL STRESS: FOUNDING CONCEPTS

As in literature and the arts, psychology has been interested in understanding and expressing human plight. Nowhere is this more true than in the work on stress. The modern concept of stress is an odd hybrid, borrowed rather loosely from the stress concept of physics and material science. Humans, it is argued, like metals may be subjected to stressors, a stressor being some outside force that is exerted on the metal. When stressors are of low magnitude, the metal returns to its original shape. Even when frequent stressors impinge on the metal, the metal retains its resilience and molecular integrity.

At some point, however, the stressors are too great, and the metal's strength becomes overburdened, resulting in a change in the molecular structure. The metal may look undamaged externally, but it loses resiliency. The result is that the metal either breaks or becomes brittle. These stressors may take the form of a briefly exerted extreme force, such as too heavy a weight on a bridge. Damage may also occur very slowly, as in the sun's effects on some plastics. In such cases, after a long period of wear the plastic may simply crumble under the slightest exertion. The analogy to humans is obvious, even if it is not exact. Indeed, one goal of this chapter is to point out the inadequacies of this superficially attractive analogy.

The Cannon-Selye Tradition

That the human body should react in a way that is even vaguely parallel to inanimate materials was perhaps first noted by Walter Cannon (1932). Cannon was concerned with the effects of cold, lack of oxygen, and other environmental stressors. He concluded that although initial or low-level stressors could be withstood, high-intensity or continued physical stressors resulted in a disturbance of homeostasis. When prolonged, this process could lead to a breakdown of biological systems.

Hans Selye, himself very much influenced by Cannon, dedicated a lifetime to work on the stress process. Selye saw stress as an orchestrated set of bodily defenses that reacted in the face of noxious stimuli. Selye was not interested in the psychological or emotional side of the stress reaction, but rather in understanding the physiological set of reactions created by such demands (Selye, 1950, 1951–1956). Using laboratory studies, he illustrated that organisms reacted to outside stressors, first via an alerting response, then with a resistance response, and finally with an exhaustion response when the system is overtaxed. So frequent and nonspecific was this response that he termed it the *general adaptation syndrome*. This sequence and Selye's general conceptualization remain of interest. However, his lack of insight into psychological phenomena accompanying stress and his lack of attention to individual differences that might be products of these psychological processes limit his relevance to current thinking on psychosocial stress.

Crisis Theory

Caplan (1964) and Lindemann (1944) introduced a much more psychological approach to stress. Both men were impressed with the crisis reactions of normal individuals who were subjected to extreme stress conditions. Caplan had lived in Israel following the birth of this new nation. His thinking was influenced by the effects of war and the massive immigration into the fledgling state. It is probably more than a coincidence that Lindemann's views were also shaped by the Holocaust to some extent; he was a Quaker who left Germany because of persecution and the impending war. Lindemann's thinking about crisis was further influenced by his experience working with the survivors and the families of casualties of the Coconut Grove fire in Boston. Caplan's and Lindemann's combined contribution represented a revolutionary departure from previous thinking. They argued that the characteristics of the stressful circumstances were as important as the individual and social characteristics of the affected persons in determining their distress.

Their thinking was especially radical when one considers the psychological climate of the times. Psychopathology was viewed as the product of early childhood experiences that molded the subconscious. Crises were considered intrapsychic, and outside events were at most triggers of inner conflict. Breakdown could thus only be the product of deep-seated neurosis or psychosis. In such a climate of thought, relating crisis reactions to outside events in adulthood was anathema. To suggest that during crisis personal and social characteristics of the individual played a tertiary role in the expression of crisis reactions and that environmental conditions were the principal determinants of these reactions was to go against the accepted grain of psychological thinking of the period.

More recently we (Hobfoll & Walfisch, 1986) have directly examined this question and provide evidence suggesting that Caplan and Lindemann probably overstated their case. However, in bringing their radical point into the arena of discussion they were only guilty of Bertrand Russell's adage, "What is worth stating, is worth overstating!" Clearly, individual characteristics do affect the expression of crisis reactions and the process of recovery, but it is the external circumstances that plunge the normal individual into reactions that may be so severe as to appear psychotic.

The circumstances of the crisis shape psychological reactions across a wide spectrum of people with very different personalities. Catatonic and conversion reactions, for example, were widely reported in response to shell shock during World War I. Today, breakdown in combat, termed combat stress reaction, rarely manifests itself in conversion reactions. Both then and now, individuals' personal traits may have contributed to breakdown, but it would seem that the typical symptoms of shell shock and of combat stress reactions are different enough that they are also products of the different types of stressors confronting soldiers in the two wars. Similarly, in a recent study we (Hobfoll & Walfisch, 1986) found that even though individual traits played a role, especially in recovery following crisis, more than half of the psychologically healthiest subjects showed signs of extreme depressive emotions at the time of crisis. So, whereas individuals' personal characteristics do influence crisis reactions, these reactions are common enough to suggest that they represent normal reactions to unusually stressful circumstances.

Working in the area of grief, Parkes (1970; 1972) identified loss as a key factor in provoking crisis reactions. Paykel (1974) also suggested that "exit" events—events that signify loss—are normally perceived as most threatening. Stressor agents are those events, or the anticipation of such events, that are interpreted by the individual as causing a significant loss to the self or the identity of self. These types of events tax psychological capacity to withstand stress, just as lack of oxygen or exposure to cold tax physiological capacity.

The different nature of responses to physiological demands and psychological demands also highlights a key departure from Selye's concept of universal responding. Loss is relative to the individual and is complicated by background, social norms, and culture. Consequently, the concept of loss implies that responding to events will be different for different individuals and between groups that have differing values. This will be reflected in both the type of event to which individuals will react and the intensity of their reaction.

Stress, Anxiety, and Cognition

In 1966 the formulation of the stress concept took a great leap forward with the publication of two books: Spielberger's *Anxiety and Behavior* (1966a) and Lazarus's *Psychological Stress and the Coping Process* (1966). Spielberger conceptualized anxiety as the response to stressful external events, but did not refer to the term "stress" per se. He outlined a process that included the cognitive assessment of information that the individual experiences as threatening.

He focused in this book and in later work on differences between physical threats and ego-threats, that is, threats to the integrity of the self. In this he departed from the seminal work of Cannon and Selye. Spielberger illustrated that although individuals react similarly to physical threat—the type of threat that generally interested Selye—they react quite differently to ego-threat. Whereas Selye saw a universal physiological human response, Spielberger saw a differential psychological reaction from persons whose personality traits differed.

In his classic experiments (Spielberger, 1972), subjects were presented with the threat either of physical shock or of failure. Subjects who differed in trait anxiety (the tendency to experience anxious reactions) did not differ in their reactions to the threat of physical pain. Specifically, subjects with high or low trait anxiety experienced a similar increase in state anxiety (the experience of anxious emotionality) under physical threat. In contrast, when confronted with ego-threat, which took the form of threat of failure, subjects with high trait anxiety experienced a greater increase in state anxiety than did those with low trait anxiety. Spielberger interpreted this as indicating that persons who tend to become more state anxious in more situations (those with high trait anxiety) respond to ego-threat as threatening. Individuals with low trait anxiety, in contrast, do not interpret these events as especially threatening. The actual event is the same for both types, but the interpretation or perception of the event is the active stress ingredient.

Perhaps because of his background in Hullian drive theory, Spielberger is one of the few stress theorists who has sought to gain insight into the motivational properties underlying the stress response. In this regard, he conceptualizes the stress process as being related to a Darwinian evolutionary development of human emotions (1986). Citing such emotions as anxiety, anger, and curiosity, he argues that these reactions developed as a means of ensuring progeneration and propagation of the species. Although these reactions are often maladaptive today, for men and women in the elements they were necessary components of survival. Curiosity ensured inquiry and experimentation, anxiety produced cautiousness, and anger facilitated defense of the family and physical self. Vestiges of these reactions reappear when people are exposed to conditions of extreme environmental stressors. This may be observed, for instance, in the hyperalertness of combat soldiers and in their ability to perform under conditions of extreme stress.

The implication of this evolutionary thinking is that we may be genetically preprogrammed to react to threat in a way that increases our survival ability. This line of thought is impossible to examine directly, but it is consistent with Darwinian reasoning and with certain data on the facilitative function of moderate levels of anxiety in test-taking circumstances (Spielberger, 1966b). There is support for such thinking in the finding that surgery patients may have better recovery and report less pain if they experience moderately high levels of presurgical anxiety than if they experience lower levels of anxiety (Auerbach, 1976; Janis, 1971). The stress reaction may prepare the body in some way for the physical and psychological assault of surgical intrusion into tissue and organs.

While Spielberger made great conceptual gains, Lazarus's work (1966) made an important conceptual contribution and acted as a catalyst for the popularization of what he termed *stress* and *coping*. Lazarus's major point was that stressors are a ubiquitous part of the human experience. We are all exposed to stressors large and small, hassles and catastrophes. However, what divides individuals' emotional reactions is their personal appraisal of the event's meaning.

Lazarus highlights the role of appraisal in the stress process. He and his colleague Susan Folkman (1984) clearly depart from Selye's tradition of a unifold response by all persons. They write:

> . . . extreme environmental conditions result in stress for nearly everyone, just as certain conditions are so noxious to most tissues or to the psyche that they are very likely to produce tissue damage or distress. However, the disturbances that occur in all or nearly all persons from extreme conditions . . . must not be allowed to seduce us into settling for a simplistic concept of stress as environmentally produced. Such extreme conditions are not uncommon, but their use as a model produces inadequate theory and applications. The main difficulties arise when we overlook the great variations in human response to so-called universal stressors.

> As one moves away from the most extreme life conditions to milder, more ambiguous ones, that is, to the ordinary garden-variety life stressor, the variability of response grows even greater.

What now is stressful for some is not for others. No longer can we pretend that there is an objective way to define stress at the level of environmental conditions without reference to the characteristics of the person. It is here that the need for a relational perspective is most evident, and where it is particularly urgent to identify the nature of that relationship in order to understand the complex reaction pattern and its adaptational outcomes, as well as to draw upon this understanding clinically. (From Lazarus & Folkman, Stress, Appraisal, and Coping *[New York, © 1984], 19, by permission of the author and Springer Publishing Company, Inc.)*

They go on to define psychological stress as "a particular relationship between the person and the environment that is appraised by the person as taxing or exceeding his or her resources and endangering his or her well-being (p. 19).

Having defined stress, they approach the stress phenomenon on what they see as two critical axes. They argue that the stress process is mediated by *cognitive appraisal* and by *coping*. Cognitive appraisal is the evaluative process by which individuals assess the stressfulness of their particular circumstances. Coping, in turn, is defined as the process by which individuals manage both the demands that are appraised as stressful and the negative emotions generated by this appraisal. These concepts and Lazarus's writings in general have had a seminal influence on the conceptualization and understanding of the stress phenomenon as well as the direction of much of stress research.

Lazarus's definitions of stress, appraisal, and coping emphasize the relationship between the person and the environment. They take into account, as did those of Spielberger, the characteristics of the individual, on the one hand, and the nature of the environmental stressor that is impinging on the individual, on the other hand. Lazarus emphasizes cognitive appraisal and makes a more general case than does Spielberger, who addresses with more depth the specific emotional reactions to stress. Spielberger also emphasizes personality characteristics to a greater extent than does Lazarus. Together they have formed a basis for much of the thinking on stress in the last 20 years.

The Stress of War and Catastrophe

Commanders and clinicians' observations of the effect of the extreme stress of combat on soldiers, have also had an impact on the development of an understanding of stress. I would argue that the impact of these observations has been much more profound than footnotes and references lead one to believe. Stress theorists often allude to references about the effects of combat on soldiers, but seldom detail the lessons that were learned from this man-made tragedy. Making an educated guess, I would suggest that the Vietnam War made the whole concept of war so unpopular to Americans that inferring that war could have any value became unacceptable. My argument here is twofold: first, society has a responsibility to attend to the soldier's wounds, be they physical or psychological, and second, war allows us the unfortunate opportunity to learn more about how people react under extreme stress and how to aid their adjustment in the face of these stressors. Because I see the study of war-related stress as making a special contribution to stress theory, I have addressed the topic here as a separate section.

Records from the American Civil War already indicate an awareness that insanity and stress responses could be differentiated. This may be inferred from the separate reporting of "paralysis" and "insanity" by medical staff during the war (Kellett, 1982). During the First World War the term "shell shock" was coined. It was believed that the bursting of bombs caused a reaction that looked like psychiatric illness, but that was a result of external forces and perhaps the noise of the explosion itself. This suggests that at a time when intrapsychic causes were increasingly seen as a cause of mental illness, physicians and psychiatrists were aware that the healthy personality could also be adversely affected by the intensity of modern combat.

The forward-looking insights of the American physician, T. W. Salmon, deserve special attention. From his experiences during World War I, Salmon (1929) developed a set of principles similar to those established in crisis and stress theory about 50 years hence. On one hand, Salmon observed that persons with preexisting mental disorders would be especially susceptible to the stress of combat. But he also saw that individual predilections to psychopathology were insufficient to explain the psychological reactions he observed. This resulted in his theory that all soldiers are liable to shell shock under extreme conditions.

Attesting to his understanding of the stress process, he proscribed four basic principles: soldiers experiencing shell shock should (1) be treated near the front line, (2) be treated immediately, (3) be given the expectation that they are experiencing a normal reaction from which they will soon recover, and (4) be ensured a psychological sense of community (Salmon, 1929). This, in fact, was found to be an excellent preventive approach to limiting what we know today as posttraumatic stress disorder. The importance he assigned to cognitions, situational determinants, and the urgency of treatment is remarkable considering accepted views in psychiatry at that time, and is quite consistent with Lazarus's and Caplan's thinking in this regard.

The very use of the term shell shock during World War I was an acknowledgment that an external stressor was a principal cause of psychiatric breakdown. World War I came prior to the great urban population influx. For rural lads the technological complexity of war, typified by the force of the modern shell, was both awe-inspiring and frightening. Few had ever before seen an airplane or a tank, and many had never before been away from home. The machines of modern warfare must have produced not just fright, but culture shock too.

In contrast, World War II was the "long" war. It was long not just in the sense of its length (there had been longer wars), but in the length of battles and time spent in combat. Already in the early years of the war it was observed that the best of the British, the Royal Air Force pilots, experienced psychiatric difficulties almost to the very last man. The stress of their endless missions led to what came to be known under the new rubric "combat fatigue" and "combat exhaustion." The concept of fatigue illustrated an understanding that persons became increasingly susceptible to psychiatric breakdown as they grew physically exhausted and when they were confronted with continued stress.

By this time a clear differentiation was made between exhaustion and true psychiatric problems (Kellett, 1982). It was illustrated that combat exhaustion occurred as a result of battle intensity, measured via casualty figures at a rate of about 5 to 7 percent. This rate rose under extreme combat conditions; as many as 20 percent of casualties were judged to be psychiatric during the Normandy landing.

Most recently, Solomon and her colleagues (1985) have embarked on the most ambitious and methodologically sound study of psychiatric breakdown under combat, basing their research on the experiences of Israeli soldiers during the Israel-Lebanon War. The term they employ is combat stress reaction or CSR. CSR implies that the exhaustion factor is not a necessary precondition of psychiatric breakdown. Modern warfare occurs so quickly, under such intense battle conditions, that psychiatric breakdown may well occur in the first hours of battle. Solomon and co-workers see combat as a highly stressful situation that threatens individuals' lives and bodies and during which performance levels must be at their maximum. Perception, prior training, prior psychiatric condition, family status, and other factors are seen as combining to contribute to the likelihood of experiencing CSR. Yet in studying CSR, too, it is obvious that individuals who are otherwise psychologically healthy may break down under the stress of war.

Major Events versus Minor Hassles:
Which Are the Real Stressors?

Lazarus and Folkman (1984) argue that more important lessons can be learned from studying everyday stressors (e.g., the minor hassles that confront people daily) than extreme environmental conditions because they see reactions to major stressors as being so uniform. I would strenuously argue otherwise. Everyday stressors may indeed teach us more than do catastrophic stressors about the appraisal component that is of central importance to Lazarus and Folkman, but this by no means indicates that they teach us more about stress and coping. The relatively low percentage of soldiers who break down in combat and the relatively few victims of natural disasters who sustain serious long-term psychological sequelae attest that reactions to massive stressors are far from uniform (Green, 1982). Moreover, because the catastrophic stressor is so clear and imminent, the opportunity to observe individual variations is set in a microcosm wherein a great deal of stress resistance activity occurs in a brief span of time and with a clear object.

I would further propose that because the appraisal component is less a factor during major stressor events, we can more easily study other individual and environmental differences under such conditions. Major injury is more universally stressful than a parking fine, but many personal and social factors nevertheless affect stress resistance capacity following major injury. Indeed, appraisal also plays a central role in interpreting the personal meaning of the consequences of the major stressor events and the method of adjustment people choose. The stress of combat allows one clear example of this diversity of human reactions. Certainly, nearly everyone has an initial fear reaction in such circumstances, but how they respond and how they recover varies widely.

There is even a danger in studying minor stress events, because at some point we cross the border from the *effects of stressors* to the *products of neurosis*. The neurotic may interpret the most positive event as stressful, but to understand such reactions we may benefit more from an understanding of psychopathology than of normal stress processes. This thesis has led some stress researchers to argue that the reporting of daily hassles and minor stress events may be so confounded with psychiatric symptomatology as to inhibit any clear study of stress (Dohrenwend, Dohrenwend, Dodson, & Shrout, 1984). Indeed, Dohrenwend et al. provide evidence to support the contention that the reporting of minor events is as likely to be a product of psychopathology as it is to be an antecedent of psychopathology.

In contrast, the work on major stressor conditions led to many of the earliest and most significant insights into the stress phenomenon, because during catastrophic circumstances the event and the reaction are unconfounded and therefore clearly distinguished. It is not possible to construe war, most serious illnesses, or factory shut-downs as *caused* by the victims. Nor is there a problem, as there is in the reporting of hassles, of misinterpretation of the reality of the event's occurrence. Thus any reactions following the event are probably due to the event and not vice versa. Nor are individual difference factors lost in the study of the most massive stressors. Even the German concentration camp experience provided evidence of the importance the victim's sense of meaningfulness in distinguishing between those who would psychologically succumb to this most massive of stressors and those who would not (Frankl, 1963).

As early as the 1930s, Horney (1937) made a similar proposal, having witnessed another catastrophic event, the Great Depression. She noted that pathological responses were common in men who had no preexisting psychopathology. She proposed the then-revolutionary concept that psychopathology may be a reaction to external events (i.e., a symptom) that is not a product of underlying neurosis. This observation has been verified during times of war and again illustrates that important understanding of stress can be gained in studying massive stressor events.

The study of massive stressors has also led to an understanding of a qualitatively different kind of stress reaction from the fight-or-flight reaction suggested by Cannon. Indeed, the fight-or-flight reaction is usually the only one referred to in discussion of stress reactions. Observations and physiological research point to the existence of a second, qualitatively different, kind of response to massive stressors, the *playing-dead* response (Folkow & Neil, 1971).

The fight-or-flight response is a mobilization of all bodily resources to directly oppose or to avoid the source of threat. Whether fight or flight occurs, metabolite-rich blood is shunted away from the vegetative organs and toward the organs involved in the response, for example, heart, brain, and skeletal muscles. The endocrine system also becomes activated, releasing hormones to stimulate the important structures. In contrast, the playing-dead response is a conservation-withdrawal response in the face of stress situations. This response may confuse predators. Autonomic and endocrine secretion are also reduced to minimal levels, allowing for savings of resources.

In a combination of the two mechanisms, a dual-axis stress response system can be visualized. As may be noted in Figure 1.1, the vertical axis is activity level, ranging from action to inaction. The horizontal axis, in turn, ranges from flight to fight. Thus four categories are outlined. In the

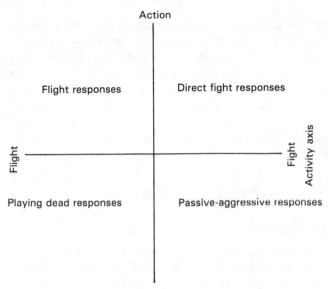

FIGURE 1.1   Dual-axis stress response system.

upper right quadrant are the direct-fight responses; in the upper left the flight responses; in the lower right, the passive-aggressive responses; and in the lower left, the playing-dead reactions.

Such a distinction is important because it highlights that any one of the four types of responding may be the preferred strategy depending on the situation and the response capacity of the individual. It is also suggested that this response system may have psychological as well as physiological correlates. By being inactive, for example, people may conserve psychological as well as physiological energy. One is immediately reminded here of the catatonic reactions of catastrophe victims, which often are followed by quick recovery. It is quite possible that continued exposure to the threat might have increased psychological damage and that the shut-off response is the psychological parallel of the playing-dead response.

My own bias is clearly that studying the major events is less confounded than studying hassles and offers insights into both internal and environmental aspects of the stress phenomenon. It should be added, nonetheless, that the distinction between minor and major events, itself, helps ferret out a number of important lessons about stress and stress resistance. Study of minor hassles focuses on cognitive processes, while study of massive stressors highlights the interactive role of the person-environment mix. One must take care when approaching either extreme, however. The study of hassles may be confounded with neurotic styles of reacting that are almost independent of the environment, and the study of massive events may lead to the wrongful conclusion that cognitions and individual differences are unimportant aspects of stress reactions. Clearly, we must develop more careful research approaches if we are to avoid these pitfalls and come to an understanding of how all levels of stressors affect people.

STRESS DEFINITIONS AND MODELS

Stress Terminology

At this point it is necessary to define some of the terms that will be used throughout this volume. Stress itself will be defined later on in the chapter. *Stressors* are those events occurring in the environment or in the body that make an emotional or task demand on the individual. *Strain* is the response to stress that is manifested by the organism. This may include psychological strains such as depression or anxiety, or biological strains such as disease. *Stress resistance* is the process of responding to stressors for the purpose of limiting strain. This should not be confused with *coping*, which is defined as behaviors that are employed for the purpose of reducing strain in the face of stressors. Coping then is just one specific domain of activities for resisting the vicissitudes of stress.

Stress resistance, in the sense I intend, includes our attempts to change stressful events or how we feel about the events, both of which are examples of coping. However, I would also include in stress resistance, such approaches as nonaction, by which we "wait and see" or allow intense initial physiological responding to subside. Stress resistance also includes regulating feelings about the self, independent of the event, such as belief in one's self and feelings about larger existential questions. Some have used the term coping in this larger sense, but items on the Ways of Coping survey (Lazarus & Folkman, 1984), for example, indicate that coping is measured in the more restrictive sense that I am implying here.

A Balance Model and Definition of Stress

Stress has been defined in a number of ways, but one of the leading and most useful definitions was presented by McGrath (1970), who defined stress as a "substantial *imbalance* between environmental demand and the response capability of the focal organism" (p. 17). This conceptual paradigm was stated along with a number of crucial qualifications.

The first qualification is that stress exists not in an imbalance between objective demands and objective response capabilities, but between subjective perceptions of these factors. This perception leads one to anticipate that one will not be able to cope with the situation. Thus Lazarus's cognitive appraisal of demand-resource imbalance is the necessary condition for psychological stress. McGrath's second qualification is that even if an imbalance is perceived, it will not be appraised as stressful unless the consequences of failure to cope are important to the individual. In this vein, stress is not merely the perceived failure to meet demands, but the expectation of adverse consequences stemming from such an occurrence.

Finally, McGrath qualifies his definition on two additional points concerning demand or "load." He argues that the quantitative and qualitative properties of the load need to be considered. A load may be too much for the individual to bear at any time or it may be too much of an additional load, given that resources may already be taxed, the proverbial straw on the camel's back. Obversely he argues that organisms may also be taxed by demand underload. He offers a guideline for judging underload: the state at which demands are less than capability. This state may generate boredom and a decline in function, just as might a state of overtaxed capabilities.

McGrath's definition of stress has been among those most favored by stress researchers. It has proved a good conceptual definition and along with the appraisal model of Lazarus has led to clearer thinking about the stress process. However, it suffers from a number of faults. First, it does not define the terms threat and demand, other than vaguely stating that demand is what is perceived as demanding and threatening. In other words, demand or threat cannot be counterbalanced by coping capacity. This is of course tautological and does not further a conceptual understanding of these two basic concepts.

Spielberger's (1972) ego-threat concept may be applied to sharpen the focus somewhat, if we add that threat is that which is threatening to the ego. However, this still does not explicate what is threatening to the ego. In fact, the distinction between physical threat and ego-threat becomes blurred outside of the laboratory; for instance, threat of illness or, say, the inability to withstand chronic pain is very threatening to the ego (Moos, 1977).

The second problem with McGrath's definition is that it does not distinguish resources, or what he terms response capability, from threat. That is, he implies that resources are those things that are employed to resist demand. Antonovsky (1979) does define resistance resources (he uses the concept of general resistance resources) somewhat more clearly in his adaptation of McGrath's model. He defines general resistance resources as characteristics of an individual, group, subculture, or society that are effective in avoiding or combating a wide variety of stressors. This may be a good definition for a few global resources, such as Antonovsky's sense of coherence, but how it may be applied to less robust resources is unclear. Is a resource anything that is "sometimes" effective in avoiding or combating some stressor? This would appear to be defining what might or might not be a resource by virtue of only one small property and would seem to include almost everything.

The third problem with McGrath's theory is the issue of how to weight the balance. What are threat-and-demand units and what are resource units? Is one demand unit equivalent to one resource unit? Are they both products of the same process of perception? Are the threat and response potential evaluated together or separately by the individual? Is the appraisal global, that is, "in sum where do I stand?" or point by point, that is, "where do I stand on this problem and that problem, on this hassle and that crisis?" The model offers a basic guide, but has no operational function on the applied level. It is not incorrect; rather it is skeletal.

Sociological Perspectives

Pearlin (1983) adopts a more sociological viewpoint that better defines what makes an event demanding. He argues that because people are socialized to invest themselves in their institutional roles (family, occupation, economy, education), when they encounter problems in these contexts they are likely to experience stress. This model, however, does not clarify what constitutes a "problem." When do individuals perceive that they are in conflict with their expected role or with meeting the demands upon them? One can spend a lifetime not meeting demands; which failures to meet demands are the ones that are stressful?

Menaghan (1983) describes a somewhat different condition in which stress may occur: when environmental opportunities constrain the satisfaction of individual needs. This notion is consistent with much sociological research on role conflict and role captivity and, as such, represents an important adjunct to the threat–resource balance model of McGrath. However, Menaghan does not state at what level we expect our current role to pay off, and so it is not known at what point the environment offers too little in the way of reward or comfort. In other words, the problem arises again as to what the nature of the threat is and why particular threat situations are viewed as important. How do individuals scale the satisfaction they expect to gain given their input?

Howard Kaplan (1983) presents a somewhat different approach, emphasizing values. He more clearly addresses what constitutes stress and how it comes about. Psychosocial stress,

> ... reflects the subject's inability to forestall or diminish perception, recall, anticipation, or imagination of disvalued circumstances, those that in reality or fantasy signify great and/or increased distance from desirable (valued) experiential states, and consequently, evoke a need to approximate the valued states. (p. 196)

This is a very complex definition of psychosocial stress, with many points to its credit. First, it states the basis for the occurrence of threat, that is, distance from valued experiential states. It also includes the pathway by which stress occurs, implying that stress is a product of cognitive processes. Most important, it sets an individual anchor point from which the distance to the desired state can be measured by indicating that individuals' have a valued state. It is implied that if they appraise a situation as enabling them to meet this state, they will not experience psychosocial stress.

Kaplan's value model does not, however, define a mechanism by which stress is counteracted. It is an excellent definition of an end state, but does not outline any dynamic properties of individuals for combating disvalued circumstances. Why individuals cannot "forestall or diminish . . . recall . . . or imagination of disvalued circumstances" is not addressed. This is a critical omission for a comprehensive stress theory. In addition, Kaplan's definition of stress lies entirely in the cognitive domain. It suggests that only cognitions may lead to stress and places emotionality and biological responses outside of the purview of the model.

One could combine Kaplan's and McGrath's definitions of stress and emerge with a rather complete model and definition. Such a merger might take the following form: *Stress is the state in which individuals judge their response capabilities as unable to meet the threat to the loss of desirable experiential states—states that are dictated by their values and expectations.*

Such a definition allows for a quantifiable, and therefore testable, operationalization (i.e., the translation of a concept into a measurable variable) of what constitutes threat. This quantifiability is provided by Kaplan's contribution to the merger, in which individual values, expectations, and desirable states may be measured. It would be possible, for instance, to develop questionnaires that assessed what individuals value and expect. The distance between the imagined valued state and the change in that state caused by the threat could then be measured. The definition also provides a mechanism for counteracting loss of desirable circumstances. This mechanism is the response capacity notion borrowed from McGrath's model. It implies that individuals are not simply pawns in the game of stress, but instead play an active coping role. The homeostatic, or balance, notion is also provided by McGrath. That it is the "judged" balance or imbalance that is important can be credited to Lazarus's and Spielberger's contributions to the stress literature.

Yet this definition also has a number of problems. First we are still left with two mechanisms, a response capacity system and a threat assessment system, and we are therefore again confronted with the problem of having to apply two qualitatively different scales if we are to test the model. One scale is necessary for measuring response capability, and one scale is necessary for measuring degree of threat. In addition, the problem of potentially confounding response capacity and threat assessment remains. This may be why Kaplan sidesteps the balance issue and moves directly to the total gestalt appraisal point in the stress process. That is, maybe he is correct in assuming that the balancing is done internally and as such can only be inferred to be occurring. If this is the case, the final appraisal, rather than a breakdown into its balance components, may be the best point of scientific departure.

Finally, it is paradoxical that whereas proponents of the balance model have emphasized the perceptual level of balance, the model is much easier to defend on the objective level. On the objective level the problem that threat could be confounded with resources does not occur. The degree of threat in an event may be judged objectively or assigned weights by large groups of people. Similarly, individuals' resources or coping capacity may be assessed objectively or at least by others who are blind to the degree of threat impinging on the individual. Such a strategy still does not solve the problems of finding comparable units for threat and resources (a point that will be addressed in greater detail in the following chapter), but does remove any confounding from the assessment of threat and resources. Unfortunately, researchers have rarely followed this more objective tack (Solomon, Mikulincer, & Hobfoll, 1987).

Ecological Models of Stress

Another direction that stress researchers have focused on is ecological models of stress, as opposed to personological or sociological models. Ecological models of stress have never been well elucidated. No single publication conceptualizes an ecological model of stress that is commonly cited by different writers and researchers interested in the stress phenomenon. Despite this fact, a number of those interested in the study of stress have adopted an ecologically based focus in their research (Hirsch, 1980; Hobfoll, 1985a; Mitchell & Hodson, 1986; Wilcox, 1986). All of these researchers point to the work of Rudolf Moos as seminal in their thinking.

Moos has published many articles, chapters, scales, and books that together have had a seminal effect on the stress field (see Moos, 1984, for a listing of publications). The main thread of Moos's work is that people are a part of social systems and any attempt to understand them outside of the context of these systems will produce a partial understanding that does not reflect the whole. Moos's contribution has been to illustrate that stress and coping occur within social settings, and the characteristics of these settings are as important as the characteristics of the individual.

To research these settings he and his colleagues have developed a plethora of scales to assess the particular stressors and supports relevant to specific settings. There are family environment scales, military environment scales, school environment scales, and work environment scales. The military company scale might, for instance, focus on buddy support and officer support, whereas the family scale might tap emotional expressiveness and family cohesiveness.

Moos's work reflects a more multidisciplinary understanding of stress than has been common in the approaches of others. Since understanding humans in their settings requires a background in anthropology, biophysiology, sociology, and psychology, the complexity of such a position may be one reason that Moos has refrained from presenting a guiding ecological model and has instead developed a general conceptual springboard based on ecological thinking. Nonetheless, Moos's influence must be acknowledged because of the special contribution it has already made to stress research and theory.

In the following two chapters, these ecological notions will be integrated into the general knowledge base around the study of stress, to develop first a new stress model and second a model of stress resistance. Hopefully, this will not only tie together what has already been said but will move toward a single, more comprehensive new theory of the stress phenomenon.

SUMMARY

This chapter began with a discussion of the attention that stress has been given outside of modern psychology. Stress has been a central theme of literature, film, and religion. Many of the most famous and popular films and books examine people's confrontation with the challenge of stress and their capacity to withstand the vicissitudes of life. It was proposed that people's interest in the topic stems from their identification with protagonists who succeed despite the great difficulties they encounter on life's hard course.

Following this, the development of the stress concept in modern psychology was presented. Beginning with the seminal work of Cannon (1932) and Selye (1950), stress was viewed as a universal response of organisms to an overtaxing of physiological systems. The work of Caplan (1964) and Lindemann (1944) expanded the concept of stress beyond the limited physiological context. They emphasized psychological reactions to psychosocial crises. Their work was especially important because it formed a basis for thinking that psychopathological reactions could occur among normal individuals in response to extreme circumstances. These concepts caused a mental health revolution, because prior to their work it was generally assumed that psychopathological reactions could only be manifested by individuals who possessed underlying psychopathology.

Next, the catalyzing effect of work on stress, anxiety, and cognitions spurred by such theorists as Lazarus (1966) and Spielberger (1966a) was discussed. These investigators embarked on an empirical study of stress-related cognitions and emotions, making important distinctions that many other stress researchers have adopted. Spielberger illustrated how personal traits interacted with physical threat and ego-threat in producing anxiety reactions. He noted that personal traits—trait anxiety in particular—did not affect the experience of physical threat, but that those high in trait anxiety were significantly more sensitive to ego-threat than those low in trait anxiety. Lazarus developed a model of stress that emphasized the role of appraisal and coping, showing that individuals' perceptions of events, rather than the objective qualities of the event, mattered most. Following appraisal, he has asserted that coping strategies play a central role in stress reactions. These concepts have remained central to stress research and have led to advances in the understanding of people's reactions to threatening life events.

The special contribution of the study of the stress produced by catastrophic events and war was also discussed. The examination of massive stressors enables researchers to focus not so much on the appraisal component of stress responding, but rather on the influence of factors relating to adjustment in the face of clear danger. In addition, the investigation of war and catastrophes illustrated as early as the Civil War that normal individuals are susceptible to psychiatric breakdown in the face of extreme or ongoing stressors. The study of extreme stressors also avoids the confounding of reporting biases and the confounding of event occurrence with psychopathology, because it cannot be construed that those exposed to calamities of this nature were exposed *because* of their psychiatric symptoms or that they falsely reported event occurrence.

Research on massive stressors and on physiological reactions to stress leads to the proposition that stress reactions are not simply fight-versus-flight responses, but that an action-inaction response system is also commonly evoked. A dual-axis model of stress responding was constructed based on this premise, and it was proposed that reactions to stress may be directly aggressive, passively aggressive, actively avoiding, or passively avoiding (the playing-dead reaction). The two axes were seen as related, but based on differing psychophysiological systems. Each type of responding was seen as functional, depending on the person-situation interaction.

A number of definitions of stress were presented next. Principal among these was the definition given by McGrath (1970), who defined stress as a substantial imbalance between perceived environmental demand and the perceived response capability of the organism in situations where the consequences of failure are judged as important to the individual. A more recent definition by Kaplan (1983) was also viewed as making an additional contribution to our understanding of the stress phenomenon. According to Kaplan, psychosocial stress reflects individuals' inability to forestall or diminish their perception of disvalued circumstances. This definition was seen as especially heuristic, because it parsimoniously defines what type of events are stressful, that is, those that lead to the perception of disvalued circumstances.

It was concluded that even when we synthesize these definitions a number of problems remain. First, the definitions suggest two mechanisms, a response capacity system and a threat assessment system, but each is defined in relation to the other. Stress is seen as the lack of balance between perceived stress, on one hand, and perceived response capacity, on the other. It is not clear, however, whether the perceptions of the two are not confounded with one another, whether the units of response capability are the same as the units of stressfulness, or how the balancing may be done. This is not to say the balance theories of stress will not continue to be helpful in guiding research, as they do provide a basis from which testable hypotheses can be indirectly drawn, even if the model itself can never be proven or disproven.

Finally, a more comprehensive ecological perspective on stress was considered, represented by the work of Rudolf Moos (1984) in particular. Moos has emphasized that humans are embedded in social contexts and that these contexts are as important in explaining stress responding as are the qualities of individuals. It was noted that a clear model of the ecology of stress has not been presented, but this was viewed as being due, in part, to the complexity of the social ecological viewpoint. It was argued that the focus on social systems will be a guiding force in future research on stress. One major goal of this book is to adapt the ecological viewpoint to a clear model and definition of both stress and stress resistance.

2

THE CONSERVATION OF RESOURCES: A NEW STRESS MODEL

In nature there are neither rewards nor punishments—there are consequences.

(Robert Green Ingersoll, 1833–1899)

If we must suffer, let us suffer nobly.

(Victor Hugo, *Contemplations: Les Malheureux*, 1802–1885)

THE MODEL

I would like at this point to introduce a new model of stress. Built on previous theory and definitions, this model seeks to be more accurate than previous ones, more streamlined, and more amenable to direct empirical test. The model is also comprehensive and is relevant to behavior under stressful and nonstressful circumstances. It is termed the model of *conservation of resources*. The basic premise is that people have an innate as well as learned desire to conserve the quality and quantity of their resources and to limit any state that may jeopardize the security of these resources.

From the model we derive a concise definition of stress: a reaction to the environment, in which there is either (a) *the threat of a net loss of resources*, (b) *the net loss of resources, or* (c) *the lack of resource gain following investment of resources.*

Resources are defined as (a) *those objects, personal characteristics, conditions, or energies that are valued by the individual or* (b) *the means for attainment of those objects, personal characteristics, conditions, or energies.*

Implied in this conceptualization of stress are the notions that there is nothing to stress besides gain and loss of resources and that people are centrally concerned with the conservation of their resources. In addition, that individuals evaluate their resources and how circumstances may affect their resources (i.e., they develop resource conservation strategies), and they expect a net gain in resources as time passes if they invest or risk resources.

The definition also implies a process by which stress occurs. Environmental circumstances often threaten our resources; they may threaten our time, our lives, our loved ones, our happiness, our self-esteem, our jobs, our homes, or many other entities that we perceive ourselves as "owning." These losses are important, not merely for their face value, but because together they define for us who we are (Erikson, 1968). It is the *actual* or *potential* loss of these resources, then, that threatens our identity or that which we prize and, in so doing, initiates the stress process.

Following either the threat of potential loss of resources or the perception of the actual loss of resources, we respond by attempting to limit the loss of resources and by maximizing gain of resources. To do this we must usually employ other resources (Schönpflug, 1985). However, we do so at a cost. The issue of resources will be discussed in detail in the following chapter. For now it is sufficient to indicate that some resources are more long-lasting than others, more replenishable, more accessible, and more valuable. Nearly all resources, however, decrease in some quality that we value when they are employed to counteract a threat, especially if used unsuccessfully.

Other stress models have not postulated what positive action occurs in response to stress. Instead, models such as those of Selye and McGrath describe only the breakdown response when stress occurs. Lazarus (1966) and Lazarus and Folkman (1984) clearly propose that individuals respond to stress with coping behaviors, but they do not define any particular direction coping takes. They define coping as all efforts taken to manage stress, thus suggesting a generic for the response to stress but not a general strategy of responding. The model of conservation of resources, in contrast, predicts that the state of stress initiates an action sequence, following the strategy of what in decision making is often called mini-max—minimizing loss, maximizing gain.

Let us consider an example. A student fails an examination, which represents for her a loss of several resources, some already in her possession and others that she expected to possess. She stands to lose self-esteem, a recommendation for graduate school, the opportunity to join a prestigious honors society, and the keys to her parents' car. The model of conservation of resources suggests that she will first perceive the loss of resources and will then act to limit her losses. She will do so by spending or investing other resources. She will spend some of what is owed her in social support by her friends to lift her self-esteem; she will invest some of her time in a make-up examination; she will spend some of her pride by pleading with her parents to give her a second chance.

Now that a general statement of the model of conservation of resources has been introduced, the details and implications of the model will be presented. The first requirement is to illustrate why the concept of loss is so central to stress.

The Concepts of Loss and Replacement

To state that threat only concerns a loss or potential loss of resources sounds like an overstatement at first. However, in a strict sense this is what is implied in the model of conservation of resources. The idea that loss is central to threat has been well stated by Lindemann (1944) and Parkes (1965). In the area of grief, which they studied, it is straightforward that the death of a loved one constitutes a loss that is threatening to the individual. It threatens how people see themselves, their economic and social status, and their social lives. It also results in a loss of love in two ways: The love relationship with the deceased is lost, and the feeling often arises that the capacity to love again is lost.

How an individual minimizes the net loss following the death of a loved one illustrates the process of compensating for deep loss proposed by the model of conservation of resources. The most profound example of this is the 40-year postwar experience of victims of the Nazi concentration camps. Many of these people lost their entire families during the war. It is common to have lost both parents, all one's siblings, and one's wife and children. How could such a loss be minimized?

Four domains of loss may be viewed as central to the Holocaust victim's experience: loss of loved ones, of home and security, of faith, and of personal integrity. The minimizing of net loss would, correspondingly, be expected to occur in similar domains. It is not surprising then that for these people building a new, postwar family has been of paramount importance. They tend to see their children as a rebirth of a lost world and even a rebirth of the part of themselves that perished in the death camps. Nor is it surprising that many came to rebuild a country for Jews in Israel and tenaciously support the Jewish homeland whether they resettled in the United States, Canada, or France.

If the model of conservation of resources is to be useful, however, it must be applicable to a much wider array of circumstances than loss of loved friends or kin. Specifically, it will be necessary to show that loss of resources and the tendency to minimize such losses are the core of stress in the widest spectrum of what we have come to see as stressful situations. In the following sections I will attempt to illustrate that the model is indeed robust and that loss is the essence of stress.

Undesirability of events and loss

Typically, studies have examined the degree of undesirability of an event and not the degree of loss the event represents. Brown and Harris (1978) define event severity in terms of the long-term or moderate-term threat to the individual. Others have classified events in terms of their cultural or social desirability as assessed by judges or researchers (Chiriboga, 1977; Ross & Mirowski, 1979). Holmes and Rahe (1976) suggested a more general approach in which a severe event was defined as one that required substantial readjustment. What is not clear from these approaches is why an event is viewed as threatening, socially undesirable, or requiring adaptation.

To seek the core characteristic of stressful events it is instructive to review the items of the Holmes and Rahe Social Adjustment Rating scale presented in Table 2.1. The judged rank order of event stressfulness is listed in the left column and the judged stress values are listed in the right column. As may be noted by reviewing the content of the events, almost all of the 25 most stressful events are obvious loss events. Typical of these are "death of spouse," "divorce," "marital separation," "fired at work," "retirement," and "foreclosure of mortgage or loan."

Other events are ambiguous as to their valence. It is not clear, for example, whether "business readjustment," "change in health of family member," or "marital reconciliation" are positive or negative events. Marital reconciliation may be a positive event or simply a measure of the storm and strife of some marriages. Researchers examining this scale and others like it find, however, that when the dimension of undesirability is partialled out of the correlation between the endorsement of event occurrence and outcome (e.g., depression, physical symptoms), the correlation drops nearly to zero (Mueller, Edward, & Yarvis, 1977; Vinokur & Selzer, 1975). In other words, undesirable events are stressful, whereas change itself is not. Consequently, if we view these ambiguous events as stressful only when they indicate the undesirable interpretation

TABLE 2.1 Social readjustment rating scale

Rank	Life event	Mean value
1	Death of spouse	100
2	Divorce	73
3	Marital separation	65
4	Jail term	63
5	Death of close family member	63
6	Personal injury or illness	53
7	Marriage	50
8	Fired at work	47
9	Marital reconciliation	45
10	Retirement	45
11	Change in health of family member	44
12	Pregnancy	40
13	Sex difficulties	39
14	Gain of new family member	39
15	Business readjustment	39
16	Change in financial state	38
17	Death of close friend	37
18	Change to different line of work	36
19	Change in number of arguments with spouse	35
20	Mortgage over $10,000	31
21	Foreclosure of mortgage or loan	30
22	Change in responsibilities at work	29
23	Son or daughter leaving home	29
24	Trouble with in-laws	29
25	Outstanding personal achievement	28
26	Wife begin or stop work	26
27	Begin or end school	26
28	Change in living conditions	25
29	Revision of personal habits	24
30	Trouble with boss	23
31	Change in work hours or conditions	20
32	Change in residence	20
33	Change in schools	20
34	Change in recreation	19
35	Change in church activities	19
36	Change in social activities	18
37	Mortgage or loan less than $10,000	17
38	Change in sleeping habits	16
39	Change in number of family get-togethers	15
40	Change in eating habits	15
41	Vacation	13
42	Christmas	12
43	Minor violations of the law	11

Source: From Holmes and Rahe, 1967:216, Table 3. Reprinted with permission from *Journal of Psychosomatic Research,* Pergamon Press, Ltd.

of the item (e.g., a negative change in financial state or a decline in the health of a family member), they too are loss events.

Still other leading events on this scale and other event lists may appear to be stressful because they imply change or readjustment that is not necessarily negative. It is likely, however, that these events too imply loss, and this will be considered next.

Transitions and resource loss

The idea that life transitions are threatening because they represent the loss or potential loss of resources is not as obvious as interpreting the death or separation from loved ones as loss. However, a key to why transitions result in loss and threat of loss is provided by stress researchers concerned with the stress of change. In this regard, Felner, Farber, and Primavera (1983) point out that transitions often follow loss events. They cogently illustrate that most loss events are not defined points in time, but rather are prolonged periods of process. Divorce (Hetherington, 1979; Wilcox, 1986), grief (Parkes, 1970; 1972), job loss Pearlin & Schooler, 1978), examinations, and many other loss events are best viewed as processes that make numerous demands over potentially long periods of time. It could be argued here that the demands, not the losses, are the source of stress. However, the demands are only present to the extent that individuals are concerned with minimizing losses or making gains (i.e., concerned with consequences).

However, this does not explain why positive transitions such as entering parenthood, moving to a new city, being upgraded to a higher status position, or entering college could result in a loss of resources. Yet these events may be very stressful. Felner et al. (1984) make a second point that addresses why positive transitions may be stressful, too. They describe how transitions tax the full spectrum of individuals' adaptive capabilities. I would argue that this taxing of adaptive capabilities results in an indirect loss of resources because it demands expenditures of resource reserves and energy (an important resource). During transitions people may spend savings, seek extra favors from friends, and expend great amounts of physical energy. No wonder people often feel physically and psychologically exhausted during transition periods. The physical expenditures in particular may engender exhaustion and render individuals susceptible to disease and injury (Thoits, 1983).

Loss also occurs because individuals are required to sacrifice resources to gain the new resource that is the goal of the transition. For example, they might need to part from family and friends, separate from colleagues, give up their old home and familiar environment, and bid farewell to their favorite hobby (hobbies often being climate related). Many transitions also mean having less leisure time; others may result in loss of responsibility (resulting in too much leisure time).

Expectation of future loss of resources is also common during periods of change. Because people are confronted with new tasks, they often develop feelings that they might not be capable of meeting the new challenges. One might fail at the new job and be fired, fail as a spouse and be divorced, fail in the new town and not make friends. In the best situations, people are in transition states because they succeeded. But will they now succeed as chief nurse or division manager? In the worst situations, people are in transition states because of prior failure. This, of course, only adds to the fear of future loss of resources. Thus, for example, even the seemingly positive event of marriage may represent a second or third marriage for many responders. What endorsers of this item may find stressful is not change, but fear of repeating mistakes and losing another chance at happiness.

Finally, I would add that some transitions do not beget loss or fear of future loss or else involve net gains when losses and gains are balanced. Such transitions would not be considered stressful, which is why change per se has not necessarily been shown to produce negative outcomes (Thoits, 1983). Only when change is accompanied by undesirable events—all of which I argue involve loss—is it associated with psychological distress (Thoits, 1983).

The Mechanism of Conservation of Resources

Now that the importance of loss of resources has been illustrated we need to define a mechanism whereby the loss and gain of resources are determined. Resources may be threatened, lost, or gained in a number of related social and biological systems. These systems add value to or "evaluate" raw resources.

First are the biophysiological systems. The absence of raw resources in this domain, such as food, liquids, vitamins, sunlight, or a healthful environment, may affect stress by causing a direct breakdown in physiological systems. These raw resources are not used directly by the body, but are processed by the biophysiological system into resources that are of direct use. For want of a better term I will call them *evaluated* resources, that is, resources that have added value by some process of conversion by the person. Throughout the book, however, the general term resources will be used unless it is important to distinguish between raw and evaluated resources.

The process whereby the evaluative systems add value to raw resources is illustrated in Figure 2.1. Food, for example, is a raw resource that is processed to become ATP, the evaluated resource that is the energy source of the body.

Raw resources may also be blocked or prevented from becoming evaluated resources. The presence of a pathogen, parasite, or other blocking agent may, for example, prevent an otherwise healthy system from benefiting from raw resources in the environment. The classic example of this may be described with a lock-and-key analogy. If a required raw resource is visualized as a key, it is only useful if it fits the lock *and* if the keyhole is unblocked. If a blocking agent fills this site, the raw resource is rendered ineffective.

At the next level are the cognitive systems. Information from the environment may result, for example, in loss of self-esteem, of the sense of mastery, or of hope. The individual may interpret lack of affection, say, to mean "I am unworthy of love." In each of these cases loss of a raw

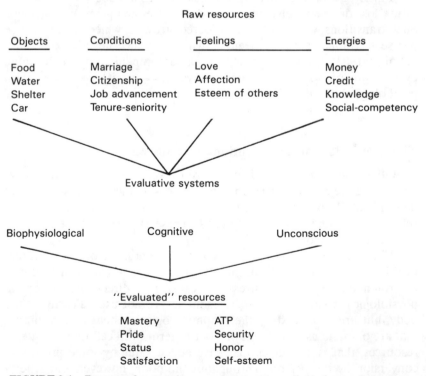

FIGURE 2.1   Process of converting raw resources to evaluated resources. Feelings tend to be translated to personal characteristics via evaluative systems.

resource (i.e., information and affection) is transformed into loss of an evaluated resource (i.e., self-esteem, the feeling of being loved).

In the biological system, health status determines how effectively resources will be gained and how quickly they will be lost. Similarly, the stability and efficiency of the cognitive system will depend on its health. Stability in this sense is the tendency to minimize loss of evaluated resources, given negative information or negative circumstances in the environment. Efficiency is the tendency, on the other hand, to quickly gain evaluated resources, given positive information or positive circumstances in the environment. A healthy system, then, will paradoxically be both stable and efficient, two almost contradictory characteristics.

Just how raw resources are evaluated in the cognitive system is also dependent on values. Values are essential yardsticks in determining the transformation from raw to evaluated resource. Whereas raw biological resources have equivalent value cross-culturally, the same may not be said for raw cognitive resources. Clearly, raw resources have different values within different societies and cultures. On the kibbutz, for instance, status must be obtained through hard work, leadership, and assignment to a productive segment of the kibbutz economy. Personal wealth is frowned upon. In some business environments, the privilege to have a key to the executive bathroom or to be invited to a certain cocktail party may be assigned great value.

Because the cognitive evaluative system is based on values and not on biological properties, this second system is also more flexible than the biophysiological systems. Values are fairly stable. Nevertheless, extreme events may beget a rapid reevaluation of seemingly fixed values. In our investigation of parents of ill children, for instance, we commonly heard parents say that all they had would be nothing if their child did not recover (see Chapter 7). Prior worries that had loomed large were relegated to the status of minor irritants, and what were thought to be major accomplishments were viewed with regret if they had, say, kept a father busy with his business and away from the child.

As in the biophysiological systems, the presence of some very negative message can block the acceptance of raw resources in the environment. For instance, children who have repeatedly been given the message that they are unloved at home may be incapable of accepting warmth and tenderness offered by a teacher or a foster parent. A child's capacity to utilize this resource is dependent on the ability to realistically interpret the offered resource. Negative cognitions may prevent such positive evaluations from transpiring.

The third evaluative system is that of the subconscious. The mechanics of the subconscious and their effect on loss of resources are decidedly more complex than the processes of the cognitive and biophysiological systems. I would posit that stimuli that symbolize early childhood experiences and very traumatic experiences in later life may trigger stress responses. Love, affection, limits, and adequate care are resources that have subtle effects on the psyche. The lack or excess of these or their bizarre or inconsistent application may themselves produce psychological disturbance. In addition, the experience of trauma may block or prevent the utilization of other resources in later life.

The influence of the subconscious becomes apparent when one examines this process of blocking the benefits of raw resources. For example, many men cannot achieve intimate relations because they were prevented from achieving intimacy in early childhood or because they were punished when expressing emotions for displaying a lack of masculinity. Later they find themselves handicapped when interacting on an emotional level, with no awareness that they have a problem (Doyle, 1983). Likewise, the experience of rape may be reawakened by vague stimuli long after the event, and victims of rape often have intrusive thoughts about the event that cause them to relive their trauma (Burgess & Holmstrom, 1979).

This inability to benefit from raw resources in the environment or the reawakening of previous trauma is greatest for the most seriously disturbed people. But it seems that many individuals who are generally psychologically stable sometimes experience these effects because of more circumscribed problems in their early childhood or because of specific traumatic experiences in their adult lives. Admittedly, there is very little stress research on this issue, but recent studies by I. G. Sarason, Sarason, and Shearin (1986) have found that the quality of early attachments is reflected in the social support reporting of adults. This suggests that at least one important resource is influenced by early childhood experiences as opposed to immediate environmental contingencies. Nor does it seem likely that the individuals knowingly linked social support to these early childhood experiences, because Sarason et al. examined early life experiences that are unlikely to be associated with social suport in awareness (e.g., parental over-protectiveness).

These evaluative systems also interact with one another. For instance, lack of a secure and loving environment may contribute to a breakdown in immunological systems that fight illness. Lack of exercise, in turn, can result in a sensitivity to negative information from the environment, to compound depression. Sensitivity to loss in one system may "leak" across to other systems. Tolerance for threat may, for instance, drop appreciably after long hours of wakefulness.

Recent stress theories have emphasized the cognitive component of stress. Most theorists recognize that physiological processes also result in stress, but such processes have generally not been integrated in major stress theories. Rather, they are presented as a separate class, governed by a separate set of rules. Subconscious processes have also been given little attention in stress research, but this does not mean they have been disproven. For the most part they have not been studied. Recent research in health psychology points to the need to consider the integration of cognitive and biophysiological systems (Feuerstein, Labbe, & Kuczmierczyk, 1986). I would add that empirical investigation of precognitive factors, avoiding issues that are not researchable, would further aid the development of strong predictive and explanatory models. This point will be discussed in greater detail later in this chapter.

The Expectation of Net Gain of Resources

Previous stress theories have not accounted whatsoever for the third stress route presented in the conservation of resources stress definition, which concerns the stress response to lack of return on investments. This route implies that individuals often act on their environment expecting to gain resources. They do so by risking or investing other resources. This obviously occurs in the financial realm, where people invest money in hopes of gaining more money or security (e.g., life insurance). I assert that a similar process occurs in all realms of life, across cultures. When net gain does not occur after considerable investment, people react much as they do to net loss of resources. Their loss is imagined in relation to their expectations of resources they would have had.

Let us take an example of a love relationship. A man invests his time at work to pay the bills at home. He exchanges his bowling night with his friends for a bridge night with his wife. He risks what he perceives as loss of manliness by sharing his fears with his wife. He moderates his need for control and supports his wife's desire to work. He sacrifices many things he values in order to gain intimacy with his wife. If his wife is aloof and critical, the situation will become stressful for him. This is because his investment and risk of loss of resources have not resulted in the expected gain of love, intimacy, and appreciation.

While this description may sound cold and calculating, this is not the intent of the model. People do not keep a written record of all that transpires in their relationships. Clark (1983), for example, illustrates that in intimate relationships a careful tit-for-tat accounting does not take place. Intimates are willing to make disproportionate investments without expecting a return in coin. However, even Clark implies that something is expected in return. That something is the expectation that if the situation were reversed the same giving, sharing, and helping would be offered with the same openness and generosity, and that other advantages are to be gained by the relationship.

What one expects from one's investment of resources is based on social comparison and personal characteristics. Our generation has learned to expect a great amount of leisure time and paid vacation. Our parents' generation expected one day off a week, and vacation was what occurred between jobs! If crystal goblets are set on our friends' tables, then we learn to expect our salaries to afford us similar status objects.

That payoff for investments is a process of social comparison becomes obvious when we examine the marketplace. If people's skills or expertise are highly valued they expect high reward for their investment. So, an attorney may expect a high fee for a consultation. The same attorney applies a completely different scale of expectation for gain in other domains of her life. Thus she expects another kind of return for the hours and years she invests with her children in coaching little league or serving as treasurer of the PTA. The committee that advised on the purchase of classroom computers for my eldest son's school read like the international advisory board of IBM, including professors of computer science and mathematics, corporate accountants and lawyers, business executives, and financiers. The return for their precious time will only be tallied in years to come when they see their children succeed in their own working lives and in some immediate feeling of satisfaction that they contributed to their children's well-being.

The influence of social factors in determining standards for what payoff is congruent with a given investment is also found on the macrosocial level. In Israel, one expects to pay a large portion of one's salary in taxes because of the security situation. However, one also expects safety, in streets that are relatively free of violent crime and rape (compared with the United States and most European nations). If this situation were to change for the worse, the effect would be stressful because people would not feel they were getting enough for their investment. The aversive stable situation, in contrast, is not necessarily viewed as stressful.

In many cities of the United States, movement is somewhat restricted by day and to a much greater extent by night because of criminal violence. Over the years citizens have come to expect a low payoff in personal safety for their investment in the society. When the situation gets worse (or when the media remind the public of the dangers of their locale) stressfulness increases. The situation, as bad as it was, was accepted as reasonable risk given investment, whereas the new situation is not.

Reappraisal of Resource Losses and Gains

I have emphasized the implications of objective loss and of shared social standards in the determination of loss. The model also proposes an important role for the individual's perceptions. In this regard, a flexible appraisal process may also aid or hamper the perception of conservation of resources if attention shifts from gains to losses or if the value of resources is reassessed. These processes will be considered next.

Shifting the focus of attention

Individuals can conserve resources by reinterpreting threat as opportunity or as challenge. Indeed, some people may display good stress resistance because they do just that (Kobasa, 1979; Kobasa & Puccetti, 1983). Such persons shift the focus of their appraisal from what they have lost to what they stand to gain. I have argued in a previous paper that this type of transition should not be romanticized as occurring for all stressors (Hobfoll, 1985a). Certain stressors and transitions are tragic and have little redeeming value. However, many everyday stressors may be interpreted as an opportunity to gain some resources. To the extent that resource gain can be viewed as outweighing resource loss, the individual will minimize the experience of stress.

The finding that positively framing the environment is beneficial has led to a renewed popularity of Pollyanna (Goodhart, 1985)! It would seem there is merit in her rose-colored approach to life. People who do not become depressed may actually read their environment less clearly than those who do become depressed. Depressive persons, in contrast, interpret events and transitions as risky, and they are. Marriage will lead to divorce—just observe the statistics—and children will have problems at every stage of development. After the children are raised, they will leave home and probably not choose to take you into their home in your old age. Depressive persons are not necessarily inaccurately assessing the stressors—the threat of loss—in their environment.

Those who interpret their situations in terms of what they have to gain may be deluding themselves. However, they are avoiding the feeling of stress and resultant disease (Kobasa, 1979). This, in turn, may contribute to a self-fulfilling positive prophesy. Minimally, by avoiding the feeling of extreme stress they avoid stress-related performance decrements. By remaining at the more optimum arousal levels of the state of challenge, they may even enhance performance, since a little stress often aids performance (Spielberger, 1966b). In this regard, it should also be emphasized that hardy individuals do not just refocus on the positive aspects of their circumstances, but also act to maximize their success (Kobasa, 1979). Simply focusing on the positive aspects of a situation, without acting to improve it, may even be self-defeating.

Reassessing the value of resources

In addition to refocusing their attention from aspects of circumstances that imply loss to those that imply gain, people may also limit stress by reassessing the value they assign to resources they have lost or expect to lose. A loss of money may be reinterpreted as having newfound *un*importance, when one's health is preserved. Individuals may reassess the value of the resources they have lost or gained, or they may make some overriding global evaluation of their total loss–gain picture without attending to an itemized list of details.

The global reassessing of the loss–gain picture practiced by individuals may be compared to a similar practice in business. Large corporations, say, in their yearly reports to shareholders, state that despite a loss of profits new research breakthroughs or modernization of equipment promises increased growth in the next fiscal year over that previously expected. Such perceptual hocus-pocus is probably effective to the extent that one wishes to believe the message. Even if the facts are correct, the shareholders are left with the problem of having to compare apples with pears (actual profits with future growth). Individuals are faced with the same types of problems, but in domains that are even more complex (e.g., health versus job security, time versus chance of advancement, current discomfort versus a statistical chance of better health).

Returning to our earlier example of the student who received a poor grade, we can see that she may choose to alter her perception of her net loss of resources. She may change her estimation of the value of the resource she lost or those she needs to invest in order to limit net loss. Such change in viewpoint actually follows quite directly from Lazarus's theory of cognitive appraisal, in which individuals are constantly appraising and reappraising their environment in order to determine the degree of threat around them.

I would suggest, however, that individuals first evaluate what they need to risk or invest in order to limit loss before they make such a reappraisal. My reasoning is twofold: first, because people tend to know when they are trying to fool themselves and second, because such devaluation risks a further net loss in their resources. In this particular example, our student has a considerable investment in seeing herself as competent and achieving, and if she devalues some aspect of this achievement, she may simultaneously be devaluating other related accomplishments. In other words, if this failure really isn't important, then her previous high grade point is also in jeopardy of losing value. This illustrates that reappraisal of the value of resources is not as simple and free of risk as it sounds.

If reappraisal itself potentially threatens one's identity, this implies that one's stable traits and beliefs will be good predictors of stress reactions. This follows because appraisals tend to remain congruent with individuals' identities. Naturally, these traits and beliefs operate in complex interactions with the environment, but we will see in later chapters that personality traits and values are robust predictors of stress response (see Chapter 5).

Two Possible Exceptions

Two possible exceptions to the model of conservation of resources need to be considered also. The first is sensation seeking, an instance in which stress is more complexly related to threat. The second exception is when stress follows directly from certain emotional states, antecedent to any sense of loss.

Gaining excitement: sensation seeking

The thrill and secondary gain of participating in risky behaviors may be a special case of refocusing attention or may be related to biological factors not dependent on the experience of loss. In this regard, some persons view physical stressors as exciting rather than stressful. Car racing, hang gliding, or experimenting with LSD is not only experienced positively, but life without such stimulation is viewed as boring and even stressful. Marvin Zuckerman (1976) calls these people sensation seekers.

The idea that some persons require stimulation that may entail considerable threat to life and find it enjoyable presents a problem to any stress theory. Why should threat be sought after? It might be that threat is a matter of perception and that sensation seekers are not interpreting skin diving or drug taking as threatening. This explanation is somehow dissatisfying, however. It does not add anything to say that an act is not threatening because it is not viewed as threatening. Why is it not viewed as threatening? This is the critical question.

Zuckerman (1976) explains by adopting a psychobiological model. He argues that high sensation seekers are probably biologically tempered to seek a higher optimal level of arousal than low sensation seekers. This implies that individuals require a minimum level of arousal, probably related to biological processes that are in part genetically determined and in part the product of early developmental processes.

As arousal increases, however, so does anxiety, as the source of danger is approached. When anxiety becomes more aversive than arousal is attractive, the individual moves away from the source of stimulation. At this point, even the sensation seeker will avoid the risky circumstances. Thus, Zuckerman provides a biological explanation for why physically threatening or dangerous situations may evoke positive emotions up to a certain point and for how biological and psychological factors may interact to determine the level of stimulation people seek.

Zuckerman's psychobiological dual-process model does not, however, preclude the possibility that sensation seekers may have other reasons for risky behaviors. It is presumed that arousal is the attraction for sensation seekers, but this may be only partially true.

How might the model of conservation of resources explain, in psychological terms, why relatively high levels of physical danger are not stressful for high sensation seekers? We may infer from the model that high sensation seekers transform the meaning of physically threatening events in a different way than do low sensation seekers. High sensation seekers may focus on resources they could gain by their participation in drug taking, sky diving, or fire fighting. Those who dare participate in such activities may gain a sense of self-esteem, virility, or individuality. A look at the items of the Sensation Seeking scale (Zuckerman et al., 1972) also indicates that high sensation seekers may be seeking popularity, friends, and even to belong with others like them. Existentially, they may also feel that they will lose something in life if they don't "do it all." One only has to look at how quickly a subculture grew up around drugs in the 1960s to see the gain in taking dangerous drugs. With drugs came friends, belonging, and identity, three of the most basic resources.

Such thinking is speculative, but it also highlights the value of the model of conservation of resources, because these speculations lead to straightforward testable hypotheses. Studies can directly investigate, for instance, what sensation seekers feel they have to gain by risk taking, or can include laboratory experiments in which potential gain is manipulated for high and low physical threat or exciting (e.g., through hypnosis) experimental procedures. Nor is the interpretation provided by the model of conservation of resources incompatible with the possibility that sensation seeking is based in part on a biological component. Many biological roots are affected by the environment, and interaction with psychological processes shapes how they are expressed. The model of conservation of resources may explain why persons with a certain biological temperament develop into sensation seekers.

Emotion as an exception to the model

The model of conservation of resources defines stress as a product of perceived loss of resources or the threat of such loss. Emotions may in some instances, however, represent a second instance of stress that occurs without the experience of such loss. It is possible, and there is some experimental evidence to support the premise, that emotions may cause cognitions (Isen, 1970; Nasby & Yando, 1982; Sarason, 1975). Stress reactions may be a physiological response to illness, say, even when the individual has no knowledge of being ill. The past is viewed with distress and the future with anxiety, irrespective of actual events. In such instances, stress is experienced prior to any awareness of conditions that signify loss.

Schacter and Singer (1962), in their classic experiments, illustrated how arousal states could be linked to a variety of emotions. In these experiments the cognitive interpretation of the emotion followed general arousal. Whereas general arousal is rather neutral and therefore open to positive or negative cognitive interpretation, other physiological states may be linked specifically to stressful feelings. Physical discomfort, lack of sleep, exposure to cold, or lack of liquids or food are likely to lead to edgy feelings. If prolonged, such conditions can engender even more intense aversive emotional states that are followed by similarly negative thoughts. These examples once again illustrate how emotions may precede cognitions.

If we could illustrate that the cognition that follows these physiological states involves a sense of loss it would fit the model of conservation of resources better, but there is no evidence suggesting this is necessarily the case. If it were shown to be true, however, it would merely suggest that the cognition was being attached ex post facto to the state of arousal—that the emotion was seeking an explanation, so to speak. Thus the following addendum needs to be added to the definition of stress: *Stress may also occur as a product of physiological processes that lead directly to aversive emotional states. When this occurs, cognitions and assignment of cause to an environmental factor evolve subsequent to the aversive feeling of stress or discomfort and may not be related to a sense of loss.*

THE INVESTMENT OF RESOURCES:
A MODEL WITHIN THE MODEL

Expending and Risking Resources

We mentioned earlier that people often have to expend or risk resources to minimize loss of other resources. Schönpflug (1985) has illustrated this in a number of experiments, where it was found that coping behaviors are themselves a source of stress. This point is well taken and must be accounted for by any stress theory.

The model of conservation of resources states that individuals experience stress when they experience a net loss or threat of loss of resources. To counteract this state, people act to minimize resource loss. They do so by expending, borrowing, or risking resources to offset potential or actual loss of resources. How then does one not fall hopelessly into a loss spiral? The answer is that people invest and risk resources of their own choosing when this is possible and do so using the strategy of minimizing loss and maximizing gain. So, for instance, they will tend to expend replenishable resources, ones that are evaluated as being less valuable than those they have to gain by their own risk or investment.

An example may help clarify this. A professor sells his large home and now finds himself with a great deal of money. However, the sale of the house is experienced as a very deep loss. The children grew up there, he and his wife loved each other there, he was a rising star there, he had fun there, and the house was a source of security. He may be seen as merely crying in his soup; after all he has all this money. However, the loss is a real one and signifies for him his age, his changed status, and the fact that he will no longer hear the young voices of his children calling out for Daddy as he lies in bed too early in the morning to be awoken.

The model states that he will try to compensate by spending other resources to minimize net loss. So, he will spend some of the money on creature comforts. This will counteract the loss of comfort experienced by selling the home. He will rent a luxury apartment, buy a fancy, sporty car, and not deny himself a few new shirts when he sees the price tag. He will use some of the money to visit his children and grandchildren, gaining closeness to them to counteract the loss of symbolic closeness that followed the sale of the house. He may also use the money to allow himself and his family to do some of the things that he wanted them to do.

He may also increase his evaluation of the freedom afforded him by the sale of the house. No more mortgage, weeds, mildew, repairs, or house-sitters to worry about. He can cut down on consulting and read more good books, owing to greater financial freedom and freedom of time that used to be spent taking care of the house.

In each of these instances he has risked or invested resources. He has had to spend money, change the way he sees himself, and alter some old habits. However, he has done this in a manner that was loosely designed to achieve net gain of resources. Perhaps he and his wife first decided what sum they wished to invest for their retirement before they considered which sporty car to purchase and how many trips to take. Given their values they chose a convenient apartment with plenty of room for visiting children and grandchildren, conducive to remolding a new life-style. If they are successful in applying their strategy, they will not regain what they lost in the house but will offset the negative balance between resource loss and resource gain.

Eustress: Accumulation of Resources

Previous models of stress either do not predict or are vague on what occurs if coping capacity exceeds threat. The McGrath model suggests that such a state will engender stress due to underload, but although people rich in resources may thrive from challenge, there is no evidence to suggest they are harmed by further gain in resources. Indeed, this point alone marks a serious weakness of the balance concept. The model of conservation of resources, in contrast, suggests that a surplus of resources is a desired condition. It may act in ways that both shelter a person from future stressors and beget *eustress,* a sense of control and positive association with the environment. These two responses to a surplus of resources are illustrated in Figure 2.2.

The accumulation of resources, as suggested by the model, allows the individual to exert positive energy toward further build-up of valued resources. This insulates the individual against future resource loss. One may become very loved, very wealthy, and very self-confident. Loss would have to be of particularly long duration and high intensity to alter such a state. Surpluses of resources also prevent negative chain reactions of loss. So, for example, loss of $1,000 for a blue collar worker may place his home and car in jeopardy. Loss of a proportional sum for the wealthy may be perceived quite painfully and indeed be stressful. However, it is unlikely that it will cause a chain of resource loss. So, too, losing one's sole friend is more traumatic than losing one of five close friends, even if both may be difficult losses to bear. Again this is related to chain loss, because with other friends one may still gain affection, esteem, a loan, help in moving, and other resources derived from these relationships.

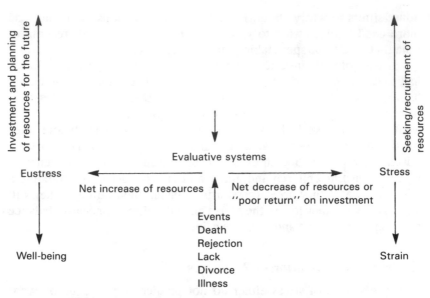

FIGURE 2.2   Effects of net gain and net loss of resources.

The loss of one's sole friend, in contrast, snowballs into loss of many other resources the friend provided.

The accumulation of resources also frees the attention and internal energies for creativity, play (not directed to a goal), and other endeavors that Maslow (1968) depicted as consistent with the self-actualized personality. Free of minor day-to-day hassles and stressors, people can focus on larger, more self-satisfying concerns. So, whereas net loss of resources leads to strain, net gain of resources leads to well-being.

The build-up of resources should not prove stressful if the model of conservation of resources is accurate. Why then are periods of rapid gain in resources sometimes experienced with emotional unrest? In this regard, the rapid change of events that may accompany a build-up of resources can be temporarily stressful for another reason. Specifically, such periods may result in overstimulation, which produces anxiety and may result in loss of sleep, changes in eating habits, and poor concentration. Thus the stress felt here is physiological. Possibly, it is attributable to prolonged reticular arousal and subsequent hormonal changes. Furthermore, such transitional periods may be physically exhausting resulting in additional physiologically based stress reactions (Thoits, 1983). These are testable hypotheses, and symptom-focused interventions such as relaxation techniques, physical exercise, or rest should be adequate to dampen such stress reactions. Nor can it be argued that this is what those who see "change" as stressful were intending, because related writings speak to the psychological and behavioral demands that change places on adaptation, not the transient physiological repercussions of such circumstances (see Felner et al., 1983; McGrath, 1970).

Little is known about the accumulation of resources. The only evidence that I may bring to bear on this issue is that positive events may act as an insulating mechanism against stressor events (Cohen & Hoberman, 1983). The experience of positive events either contributes to an emotional uplifting that is insular or marks the acquisition of further resources derived from the experience of personal achievements, successes, and good luck. Such thinking is also consistent with development of what Kobasa (1979) terms the hardy personality, an outlook on life that is fostered, in part, by a history of meaningful personal achievements. Studies that focus on the consequences of positive events will be of special interest, in this regard, if we are to understand how gaining resources affects individuals.

The Spiral of Resource Loss

Resource investment—the model within the model—also highlights the possibility of a very different sequence of events that may follow initial loss. In the case of the poor, some minority groups, many women, those with severe psychiatric problems, and other oppressed people, the options of resources that may be risked or invested are often very limited. Indeed, a good definition of oppression may be that state or condition in which resources are limited and in which the options to expand or invest resources are restricted.

Unfortunately, the types of stressors experienced by many poor or disenfranchised people are such that they frequently result in a negative spiral. Typically, the poor are confronted with chronic stressors or stressor conditions that eat away at resource reserves (Dohrenwend & Dohrenwend, 1981). Even if they originally possess resources, these are likely to be quickly exhausted. Other resources are risked with a slim chance of gain. This lack of resource reserves also compounds the effect of the initial loss, as preventive strategies are not at the disposal of the poor. Much of our time is spent insulating ourselves from potential stress. This is done by planning the investment of resources to make a kind of social-economic protective shield. This may take the form of insurance, advanced education, financial planning, moving to a neighborhood with high-quality schools and public safety, and so forth. The poor, in turn, must play out their options on a much more circumscribed field. Indeed, the most likely outcome is that one is constantly trying to minimize past loss of resources, with little hope of gaining equilibrium. Thus, the chances of achieving a protective posture are very low.

If this were not bad enough, an even more negative chain of events begins. The example of a poor woman can illustrate this process. Not only may she have no resources with which she can invest to minimize the loss, but she will often be forced into investing or risking highly valued resources to minimize the loss of other valued resources. The resources she must expend may even be more highly valued in the long term than those that are threatened, but she must survive the short term. So, for instance, to gain love she must swallow her pride and accept a relationship without marriage. To feed the child that comes out of this relationship, she may have to end her education and find poor-paying menial employment in a distant area of the city. To be closer to her child and meet her own social and sexual needs, she may involve herself in a new love relationship that holds little chance of success. So, she marries a man with little promise. The burden of the family is too much for him despite his genuine efforts, and the welfare system is structured such that it is preferable for her and the children that he leave. And the cycle continues. This process may be simply blamed on the victim; however, its prevalence suggests that it is a problem of a system that provides few resources while making excessive demands.

Perhaps the focus on stress since the 1950s comes from the luxury that choices afford the middle class—society has given people an increasing ability to exercise options, to invest and risk resources. In other words, interest in stress as a topic of study has increased at a time when a large segment of the population can do something to offset stressors. In addition, many stressors that affect the middle class are related to upward mobility and so are not likely to be as taxing as those confronting poor people.

It is no wonder that when the poor come to therapy they expect action and not insights. Changing the appraisal of their situation is most likely a strategy that could only lead to self-destruction or further demise, since their circumstances often demand immediate direct action. They come for help because they view their own resources as insufficient to offset more net loss of resources. The fine words and good intentions of the social worker may better serve the system within which the social worker enjoys a comparatively broad and valuable set of resources than they do the recipients of aid.

Mid-Term and Long-Term Behavior following Stressful Events

The model of conservation of resources also predicts future behavior subsequent to encounters with stressful circumstances. If, as the model states, people seek to minimize net loss of resources, we have a road map of what to expect of affected individuals. Specifically, people will continue to act in a way that will minimize net loss of resources. They will do so both in the immediate period following the event and in the distant future.

Lehman, Wortman, and Williams (1987) have shown, for example, that parents of children killed in auto accidents and widows of victims of auto accidents still experience significant emotional upset and psychological impairment many years after the tragedy. People do not ever totally recover from such major losses, and the process of recovery from more intermediate stressors may also require a prolonged period. This suggests that long after major stressful events there is a continued need for coping responses.

People often ruminate about stressful events, even many years after the event's occurrence. In their ruminations they frequently try to "correct" the occurrence by imagining a less traumatic chain of events than actually transpired. This, in fact, was discussed by Freud (1916–1917) and given as his explanation for obsessive-compulsive behavior. By ruminating, people can slowly change the recall of what occurred and convince themselves and others of their innocence, how they were victimized, or how little the loss really meant. The device can also be used to gain attention, an additional resource.

People will also enlist active coping behaviors to limit net loss of resources. Again they may do so long after the original experience. So, the professor in the above-mentioned example may continue to act to decrease the net loss of security he felt in selling his home. After being fired, an individual may deny any part in his own demise. It is likely, however, that he will nonetheless return to school nights in order to receive a higher degree so as to limit future losses of resources and enhance his sense of lost self-esteem. He may, alternatively, dedicate himself to raising his children, in order to minimize his job loss by increasing other resource gain. The greater the net loss, the longer and more pervasive will be the attempts to limit net loss.

The process of poststress action may also be applied on the macrosocial level. Sociologically, this model can be applied, for instance, to immigration. Immigrants tend to congregate in neighborhoods with others from their native land in order to limit loss of a sense of belonging. They are often also upwardly mobile, which can be seen as an attempt to compensate for their loss in status. It is also typical of immigrants to see their children's success as the quintessence of their sacrifice in coming to a new land. In this sense, their children's success compensates for their own pain and suffering.

EMOTIONS AND SUBCONSCIOUS PROCESSES: ROLE IN STRESS

Subconscious Loss of Resources

The perception of net loss of resources or the threat of such net loss may also occur on a subconscious level. This point was discussed briefly earlier in this chapter. Because the place of psychodynamic theory in the study of stress has not been well delineated, there is a need here to discuss in greater detail the possible implications of psychodynamic theory for the model of conservation of resources and for stress theory in general. It will be important to look objectively at the possible influence of subconscious processes in stress reactions and to determine if empirical study of the questions that will arise can be accomplished. Fanciful theories that have become associated with psychodynamic models must be avoided, and it may prove necessary to leave much of what cannot be empirically examined to the study of philosophy.

Emerging from community psychology, health psychology, and behavioral medicine, stress theory has evolved within the cognitively oriented models favored by these disciplines. Stress theorists have never disproved a psychodynamic basis for stress; they have simply side-stepped the issue. No serious effort, however, has been invested in comparing cognitive and psychodynamic models of stress or stress resistance. There are a few exceptions to the lack of attention, notably in the theoretical groundwork on stress and on social support of Caplan (1974) and in the delineation of the role of denial in coping purported by Breznitz (1983c) and Lazarus (1983). These, however, are clear exceptions and do not pertain to the issue of loss per se.

Psychodynamic theory also needs to be addressed in the presentation of the model of conservation of resources because the concept of loss of resources has been a central theme of psychodynamic theory from its inception, albeit couched in other terms. Generally, psychodynamic theory suggests that loss of loved objects in adulthood, or loss of emotional states linked to desired loved objects (i.e., security) leads to anxiety. This is because subconscious fears of losing a principal love object (especially mother) are reawakened. In 1905, Freud had already proposed that "anxiety in children is originally nothing other than an expression of the fact that they are feeling the loss of the person they love" (p. 224). Freud saw the infant and child as becoming anxious due to the feared loss of attainment of biological needs in the mother's absence. He linked this with the neurotic anxiety of adults and their fears that their needs would go unmet.

Whereas the anxiety is biological in its origin, Schur (1958) reasoned that at a later stage separation anxiety is learned. This occurs when the infant recognizes that an external object can cause or end a traumatic situation. Then it is no longer loss of biological fulfillment that constitutes danger for the child but the absence of the love object itself. Sullivan (1953) went still further. He posited that anxiety is learned when parents use anxiety-inducing sanctions, specifically restriction or denial (i.e., loss) of tenderness.

Bowlby (1973) combines biological and learned processes into his model of separation anxiety. He suggests that loss in adulthood activates anxiety from biological levels, early learned content, and later learned content. He also argues that there is an evolutionary component to this process, in that the species was furthered if organisms created and maintained close attachments at every period of life. While such conceptualization is difficult to prove or disprove, it is consistent with Darwinian thinking.

In general, then, psychodynamic theory posits that loss of loved objects produces anxiety in childhood. In adulthood, loss of valued objects or circumstances acts to reawaken these subconscious feelings. Such theorizing is difficult to operationalize, but may help explain why loss of resources is so particularly stressful. It also helps to explain why social support has been viewed as a primary resource during stressful circumstances. The role of social support in stress resistance and the importance of early attachment experiences will be discussed in Chapter 4.

The Stress-Distress Relation

Psychodynamic theory rests in large part on the assumption that behavior has a primal, instinctual component. This leads to an important question, namely, whether stress responses further the preservation of the species. This point is important to stress theory but has not been carefully addressed. The reason it is important is that it would explain why humans have developed psychosocial stress reactions, a type of response that is notably absent among other animals in their natural habitat. It would also indicate that on the evolutionary level, stress serves as a mechanism to preserve the system and prevent the loss of resources.

Thus the question is whether anxiety and other stress-related emotions have positive functional significance similar to that of pain, which is the alarm system for physical danger to the individual. I would propose that anxiety, in particular, is the psychosocial correlate of pain. Whereas pain is an internal alarm system, anxiety has both internal and external functions.

Internally, anxiety operates as a signal system for alerting the organism to psychological danger. Anxiety, for example, motivates people to seek psychological help. Similarly, moderate anxiety levels motivate people to stay in therapy. Anxiety also contributes to a heightened arousal state that may elicit other functional emotions such as curiosity and anger.

Higher levels of anxiety may also act as a switch system to reflexive reactions, such as the fight-or-flight reaction. Here it may be necessary to draw a distinction between anxiety and fear, because whereas it is obvious why fighting or fleeing is a functional response to fear (i.e., reaction to objective danger), it is not obvious why a system would evolve to ensure fight or flight from psychological threats. Such a response system may have evolved because of the distancing of humans from genetically encoded social responses observed in lower species. Because of their lower levels of prewired responding, humans would have had to develop a heightened sense of social reactiveness, hence the anxiety-fight-flight response system.

Still higher levels of anxiety may trigger a shut-off system at the point when significant losses of self-esteem and ego-integration would ensue, losses that would be difficult to recoup were there continued rises in arousal. Such a system represents a psychological parallel to physiological shock resulting from extreme physical trauma. Victims of catastrophes, for example, frequently exhibit temporary states of catatonia. Such extreme reactions are particularly common after exposure to extremely threatening circumstances such as evacuation of mutilated bodies (Taylor & Frazer, 1982). Most intriguing is that at this stage the physical threat to the survivor of the catastrophe has often ended. Although physical threat has passed, psychological threat remains. Psychological trauma casualties can return to high levels of functioning, often within a few days, if given proper care (Solomon & Benbenishty, 1986), again illustrating the functional contribution of anxiety. The shut-off system prevents a precipitous loss of resources and increases the possibility of later regain of resources.

Anxiety is different from pain, however, in that it also provides an external social function. Freud (1926), in fact, introduced the term signal theory. He suggested that in the absence of their mother infants and young children risk traumatic psychic experience. They correspondingly develop anxiety behavior as a device for signaling their need for attention and mother's presence. Developmentally, such early learning is likely to continue to be reinforced through childhood and into adulthood. Anxious reactions signal the need for help, a need that is often met by those who are sensitive to the individual. Thus, at a point in which the young of the species are relatively incapable themselves of preventing loss of resources, the stress reaction provides a signal for adults to provide this function (Bowlby, 1969; Wolff, 1987).

It is also possible to link the signal process to a more general social function. Just as the fear of one deer in the herd may signal the need to escape, the anxiety of the child may signal to the family that psychological danger is encroaching. Consequently, clinicians often find the child presented by the family as the identified patient. The parents have learned to cloak their anxieties and fears in rationalizations and avoidance behavior, but the child is more sensitive. Upon addressing the child's problems the clinician commonly finds that they are reflections of conflicts in the family.

Depression, another common response to stress, may serve a similar need. In the young child or infant, depression may take the form of distinctly decreased activity. This is often due to lack of stimulation. The child's inactivity signals to the parents that something is wrong, and they respond with increased care. Although the parents probably suspect a biological cause of this languidness, their response serves to meet the stress-related needs of the infant or child. Depression in adults may have a similar purpose. Specifically, depression occurs when active attempts to seek resolution of problems have failed. The state of helplessness is a regression to the earlier state when helplessness was a signal for help. In fact, often only when depression is marked will spouses, friends, and families respond with attention, loving, and attempts to address the depressed person's concerns.

In a sense, psychology and psychiatry represent the art and science of reading these stress reactions for the express purpose of understanding the underlying danger message. That this may occur out of the realm of the individual's own awareness may itself indicate its functional significance for the species (i.e., "help me even when I am unaware of my need for help").

From this argument we see that stress may have a functional significance as an alarm system that serves to prevent the loss of resources. No single experiment can prove or disprove this point. But the accumulation of research on Darwinian theory is consistent with thinking that something as integral to the human experience as the stress response must have evolutionary value. In addition to the psychodynamic implications, behavioristic interpretations of the function of anxiety and depression are also consistent, in that such behaviors would only be sustained if they had the kind of major reinforcement potential that is discussed above. If they were simply aversive states they would serve little good for the species and would be inconsistent with our understanding of learning principles.

Psychological Distress versus Psychopathology

This discussion of emotional, biological, and subconscious processes raises the issue of the distinction between stress reactions and psychopathology. This distinction sets limits on the model of conservation of resources by defining at what point we are observing processes for which the model is not applicable. At what point are researchers observing stress reactions to outside events and at what point are they observing psychopathological reactions to inner events? Is a paranoid's reaction to imagined goblins included in the universe of stress reactions? It would indeed be according to McGrath's and Lazarus's definition. That is, the individual is reacting to a par between his or her perceived resources, on one hand, and perceived threat, on the other hand.

I would argue that stress theories should restrict themselves to the universe of events that actually occur in the environment. I would thus restrict the implications of the model of conservation of resources to those events that have the objective potential of causing a loss of resources. When individuals' reactions are based on serious distortions of reality, the model of conservation of resources loses its predictive power. In such instances an understanding of individual psychopathology will lead to more accurate descriptions of process and predictions of outcome (see Monroe & Steiner, 1986, for a cogent discussion of this issue). No one doubts that people differ in their interpretation of the stressfulness of objective events, but to develop a strong predictive model we must begin from the standpoint that for many people the event would be stressful.

Implications for the study of stress

Separating the study of stress from the study of psychopathology has important implications for the method by which stress is examined. The investigation of objectively observable, potentially stressful events is typified in the life-event survey approach, by far the most popular strategy that has been used to study stress. This method was developed specifically because the reporting of such events was envisaged as a way of assessing actual events occurring in the environment. This method may, however, be incapable of achieving this end.

In the life-event survey method respondents are presented with a list of events that are judged by experts or peers to be stressful (e.g., Holmes & Rahe, 1967; Johnson & Sarason, 1978). Similarly, the Daily Hassles scale presents respondents with a list of occurrences that are minor irritations for most people (Kanner, Coyne, Schaefer, & Lazarus, 1981).

The life-event or hassle checklist methods would seem to meet the requirements stated above, since the events are thought to have actually occurred and are viewed by others as stressful. A serious problem arises, however, because rating that these events have occurred, verifying the cause of their occurrence, and recalling certain categories of stressful events are themselves related to psychopathology (Brown, 1974; Dohrenwend et al., 1984). Specifically, a large percentage of the items represent or are symptoms of psychopathology. This confounds the relation that researchers who use the scales are trying to establish, that is, that stressful events lead to psychological symptomology. Considering Dohrenwend et al.'s findings, it seems just as likely that psychopathology is causing stressful events or the reporting thereof.

One way out of this labyrinth is to study the temporal relation between these interlocking variables in cross-sectional slices of time, as first one variable and then another takes on the role of antecedent (Lazarus, DeLongis, Folkman, & Gruen, 1985). In this fashion causality may be teased out of the process. This is a scientifically "unclean" method, but may have the distinct advantage of most closely reflecting reality (which unfortunately is not designed to ease scientific experimentation). In reality, hassles do result in psychopathology and may be symptoms of psychopathology; psychopathology may, in turn, be implicated in the onset of stressors and the way people adapt to stressors.

Studying slices of time may be the only way to unravel these sequences. However, this method does not control for the fact that the more psychologically disturbed an individual is, the more the reporting of the data will be distorted and the more likely the occurrence of the events will be a function of pathology. In such instances the event is not antecedent to the psychopathology at any point. Therefore, any increases in psychopathology are related to prior psychopathology, not prior events.

Another research direction is to longitudinally examine reactions to a single known stressful event whose occurrence is out of the control of the study subjects (e.g., breast biopsy, large-scale job lay-offs) (Dohrenwend et al., 1984; Hobfoll, 1985b; Kessler, 1983; Pearlin, Lieberman, Menaghan, & Mullan, 1981). Out of the individual's control, the event cannot be construed as the result of individual psychopathology or personal traits. This approach also has the advantages of reflecting actual process and of being free of biases in reporting. Events can be chosen that are clearly stressful and for which there is no doubt that the event did occur.

The strategy of the single stressful event is being used increasingly, while the stressful-event list method is losing adherents. Integrating the information gleaned by both methods, however, will provide the fullest picture of the stress process, because each method has components the other lacks, and one method's strengths complement the other's weaknesses. Whatever model they use, researchers and theorists must pay closer attention to the issue of underlying psychopathology and be more careful in drawing the distinction between stress reactions and symptoms of psychopathology.

SUMMARY

A new way of conceptualizing stress was presented. The model of conservation of resources, based on previous models, was designed to be more accurate, more efficient, and more amenable to direct empirical test. The model is depicted in Figure 2.3. According to the model, *stress is defined as a reaction to the environment in which there is either* (a) *the perceived threat of a net loss in resources,* (b) *the actual net loss of resources, or* (c) *the lack of resource gain following investment of resources. Resources are defined as those objects, conditions, personal characteristics, or energies that are valued by the individual or that serve as a means for attainment of valued resources.*

The central importance of loss to the perception of stress was attributed to the viewpoint that people seek to preserve their identities and that which they value. Loss, it was argued, obviously follows death of a loved one or financial, health, or employment setbacks. However, it was further reasoned that even positive transitions may entail loss if they require substantial outlay of other resources. Indeed, the only negative sequelae of positive transitions may be in the physical health domain and have been interpreted as the consequences of exhaustion attributable to the massive expenditure of resources required during such periods (Thoits, 1983).

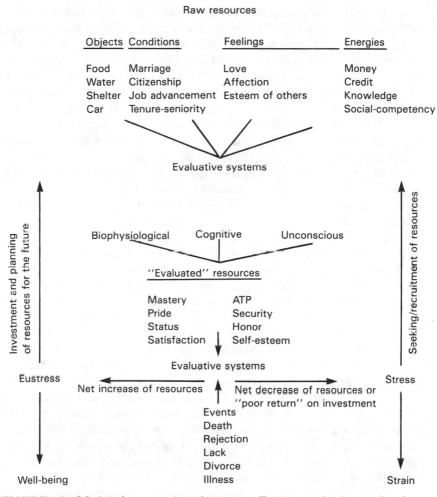

FIGURE 2.3   Model of conservation of resources. Feelings tend to be translated to personal characteristics via evaluative systems.

The model suggests that people are motivated to minimize loss of resources and that, given the perception that loss of resources might occur or has occurred, individuals will act to cognitively, physiologically, or behaviorally minimize this loss. Following loss, individuals will act or develop a belief system to regain lost resources, or their bodies will respond to recoup the losses. It was proposed that people will also invest resources to minimize loss of resources and maximize gain. It was further reasoned that to the extent possible, people will attempt to directly replace what was lost or to find some suitable substitute.

The chapter also considered the question that appraisal may alter the perception of stress. Two processes were considered. First, certain individuals refocus their attention from what they stand to lose to what they may gain from their circumstances. This Pollyannaish approach to life was seen as beneficial if coupled with a tendency to actively overcome the imposing threat. Alternatively, people may reassess the value of the resources they stand to lose or gain and in so doing minimize the perception of net loss. This strategy was seen as potentially detrimental, however, because it jeopardizes the system of values that has been adopted and may, if changed, threaten other resources.

The chapter continued by focusing on two instances in which the model may not apply. Sensation seeking, a tendency of some individuals to seek out threat, was viewed as one possible exception to the model, because threat is actually found to be attractive and not aversive. This tendency has been attributed to a biological need for arousal. However, it was argued that this may not go entirely against the model, because sensation seekers may also participate in risky behaviors to gain other valued resources such as friends, social involvement, and ego boosts.

It was also asserted that emotions may cause stress reactions in some instances, independent of the perceived loss of resources. Stress reactions may follow directly from emotional states, with no loss having occurred. Such reactions are most common following some physiological response.

The investment of resources was depicted as a model within the model. It was proposed that individuals develop strategies to build up resources. This prevents future net loss of resources and contributes toward eustress, a state of well-being that allows for energies to be invested more creatively. When individuals cannot make such investment or when the options for investment of resources following loss are constricted, a spiral of loss ensues. In such instances individuals are forced into self-defeating loss-minimization strategies in which they frequently must expend more valuable resources than the loss requires. This further depletes their resource pool and renders them more vulnerable to future stressors.

Psychodynamic theory concerning object loss was discussed to explain why loss is so central a human concern. This led to the proposal that human stress reactions made an evolutionary contribution to the species. It was argued that stress reactions act as psychological pain signals and have the additional social function of communicating to others the need for intervention to protect the organism or group.

Finally, the chapter addressed the need to separate the study of stress, which is based on reactions to objectively stressful circumstances, from the study of psychopathology. The use of stressful-event surveys may be inadequate for this purpose because they are likely to confound psychopathology and event occurrence. Instead, longitudinal investigation of reactions to known stressful events was recommended. Whatever method is employed, however, researchers need to apply strategies that distinguish between the consequences of exposure to stress and the consequences of psychopathology. Following the course of resource loss and investment may be one way of approaching this problem.

In the coming chapters I will frequently refer to the model of conservation of resources and use it as a framework with which to better conceptualize research findings. In the next chapter a complementary model of stress resistance will be considered, termed the model of ecological congruence. Together the two models represent the major theoretical thrust of this book and are intended to form a comprehensive stress–stress resistance theory.

3

THE MODEL OF ECOLOGICAL CONGRUENCE: BLUEPRINT FOR UNDERSTANDING STRESS RESISTANCE

Nature to be commanded, must be obeyed.

(Francis Bacon, *Novum Organum*)

We have defined the concept of stress and developed a new model for gauging stressfulness. In our model of conservation of resources, stress was defined as a reaction to the environment, in which there is either (a) the threat of net loss of resources, (b) the net loss of resources, or (c) lack of gain in resources following investment of resources. Underlying this model is the premise that individuals invest, expend, or risk resources in order to ensure net gain of resources, or, at least to minimize net loss of resources. The model of conservation of resources does not indicate what factors affect the choice of resources for obtaining the most positive outcome. Nor does it indicate the likelihood of success of a particular resource utilization strategy. It merely states that resource loss is stressful and that resources are employed to limit loss of other resources.

In the present chapter a second model, termed the model of *ecological congruence* is presented in order to move from a focus on *stress* to a focus on *stress resistance*. The model of ecological congruence forms a bridge whereby this transition is made, by defining and detailing the factors that affect the investment, expenditure, and risking of resources in the service of maximizing resource gain or minimizing resource loss. This model, with the model of conservation of resources, forms a comprehensive theory of the stress–distress link.

Surprisingly few models of stress resistance have been presented in the vast stress literature. Consequently, much stress research is either atheoretical or tied to a single repetitive paradigm. Such atheoretical work is difficult to integrate as studies accumulate. Moreover, to advance understanding it is advantageous if there are several competing conceptual frameworks from which counterarguments can be made. Lacking absolute measurement standards and exacting mathematical proofs, social scientists gain knowledge via comparisons of alternative explanatory mechanisms. The model of ecological congruence is offered as one such organizing structure from which hypotheses can be drawn and out of which sense can be made from individual empirical findings.

In this chapter the general parameters of the model of ecological congruence will be outlined and the terms of the model will be defined. In the remainder of the book the model will be used as an organizing system to aid the integration of findings of stress resistance studies. In Chapters 6 and 7 research will be presented that illustrates how the model was applied to guide my own research and that of my colleagues.

The first question that needs to be asked is, "Why is a model of stress resistance necessary?" The answer is that models guide research in such a way that comparisons can be made across different investigations for the purpose of *rejecting* the model. If a model is not rejectable it is one of two things: either a "fact" or an unscientific description of a set of variables. In the first case, facts do not require models, but rather, descriptions of their governing laws. Second, we have the case of an article of faith, something that is believed and not proven or disproven. Consequently, the second case is outside of the jurisdiction of science.

Of course, this does not mean that we create models that are obviously wrong (being summarily rejected is no great honor). Instead, science strives to create models that outline the underlying mechanisms that produce or explain a set of observed relationships between variables. It is also necessary, however, to be able to apply these underlying mechanisms to support or disprove the model, given a series of experiments or studies. When data accumulate, we either discard the model or incorporate it into more accurate and complex models.

Indeed, with any phenomenon that might be studied in the social sciences, it is doubtful that a model will ever be wholly correct and thereby gain the status of "truth." This is not because social scientists, or stress researchers in particular, lack creativity or insight, but because the things that interest them are so multidetermined. Consequently, the best models are only partial and can only be used to increase our ability to predict outcome.

Yet the goal of achieving partial answers should not be denigrated. Correlations of .20, if shown to be stable, are meaningful, even if they only describe 4 percent of the variability of the criterion. They are meaningful first because science is interested in understanding, and partial understanding leads to fuller understanding. Second, they are meaningful because increased predictability can have much greater impact than the simple correlation suggests; effects make additive and interactive contributions and may have cumulative pay-off over time.

In a recent study, for example, we interviewed women who were suspected of having a cancerous tumor in the hours prior to biopsy (Hobfoll & Walfisch, 1986). We found that among those women who had recently experienced three or more major stressful events, 100 percent reported levels of depression indicating they were at risk for clinical depression! In contrast, risk for clinical depression was noted in a relatively low 58.8 percent of the women who had experienced no major crisis event prior to biopsy. Yet the correlation between stressful events and depression scores was only .28. It would seem that knowledge of a biopsy patient's prior exposure to stressful events would be a very meaningful bit of information for any intervention, even if the magnitude of the correlation does not seem impressive.

I don't wish to belabor this point. Let it suffice to say that gambling casinos pay millions of dollars for a license to open an establishment that has only a 2 percent advantage on the bettor. They pay such prices because 2 percent is a significant advantage over time when one is dealing with many people. As social scientists, we find ourselves in similar circumstances as we too begin by confirming the general case. In the general case we are betting the predictive advantage we have gained through accumulated knowledge of the trends shown by large samples. Each gain in knowledge makes our understanding of the problem more comprehensive and increases our overall predictive accuracy. So too, as our knowledge grows, predictive models can become powerful enough to be used to plan individualized interventions.

MODELS OF STRESS RESISTANCE

Despite the widespread interest in stress and stress resistance, there are relatively few models of stress resistance. The models that do exist may be categorized into two broad categories: (a) models that outline a set of factors that affect stress resistance and a process by which these factors act and (b) models that imply that the degree of fit between person and environment determines stress resistance.

Factor-Process Models

Examples of the factor and process type are seen in the work of Lazarus and colleagues (Lazarus, 1966; Lazarus & Folkman, 1984) and of Kobasa and colleagues (e.g., Gentry & Kobasa, 1984; Kobasa, 1979; Kobasa, Maddi, & Courington, 1981). Reviewing the models proposed by these researchers will help illustrate the main points and limitations of such an approach.

Personality hardiness: a personalogical model

Kobasa's model is illustrated in Figure 3.1. She proposes that personality hardiness affects the interpretation of stressful life events in determining what she calls transformational coping. She derives the concept of hardiness from a phenomenological perspective that emphasizes a holistic world view with three components—a sense of commitment, control, and challenge. Transformational coping, in turn, refers to the translation of stressful events into messages that are meaningful for the individual and in ways that facilitate an orientation to action. Hardy persons, for example, tend to interpret stressful events as challenges and do not become alienated from their environment in the face of threatening circumstances. Hardy persons will also use other resources, such as social support, which is depicted here, more effectively than those who lack hardiness because they tend to rely on resource utilization strategies that enhance their health-oriented direction. Although Kobasa clearly sees hardiness as the principal personality resource, she does suggest that other personal resources (e.g., self-esteem, optimism) may also affect coping style and facilitate stress resistance.

Kobasa's model, viewed in its general form, suggests that there are a number of potential personality resources and coping characteristics that are given meaning through transformational coping. The former are the *factors* in her model and the latter is the *process*. She also emphasizes that constitutional factors and health behaviors will directly affect health outcome outside of the factor–process interaction. Indeed, she is one of the few researchers who has looked at the interaction of constitutional and coping resources in terms of their affect on health, and has illustrated the heuristic value of her approach with careful, creative research (Kobasa et al., 1981).

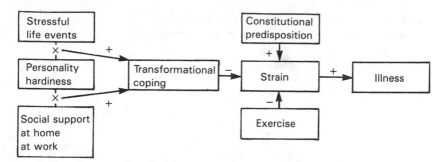

FIGURE 3.1 Model of validation of hardiness as a resistance resource. Reproduced by permission from W. Gentry (Ed.), *Handbook of Behavioral Medicine,* 1984, The Guilford Press.

Despite Kobasa's suggestion of the general applicability of her model, however, it clearly concentrates around the concept of hardiness. Thus it is not obvious what coping styles might follow from other personality resources or how some other personality resource might interact with external resources (say living in a closely knit community). In addition, Kobasa does not outline the limiting conditions of her model. Is hardiness likely to be beneficial in all circumstances? Are there some conditions in which hardiness might be a liability? Such questions are not considered in the model, and the concept of fit of resources to demands is not delineated. Given these concerns, Kobasa has offered an exciting direction for theory and research, but one that is too circumscribed for a comprehensive stress resistance model.

A cognitive-behavioral model

Lazarus and Folkman (1984) propose what they call a transactional model to explain stress resistance. This model is illustrated in Table 3.1. According to the transactional model two major processes are emphasized: appraisal and coping. Appraisal is defined as "the process of categorizing an encounter, and its various facets, with respect to its significance for well-being" (p. 32). Primary appraisal is the categorizing of the degree of threat inherent in an encounter. Secondary appraisal is the evaluation of what might and can be done to counteract the threat appraised in primary appraisal. Both forms of appraisal are ongoing and the terms primary and secondary do not refer to time of occurrence. Coping, in turn, is defined as "constantly changing cognitive and behavioral efforts to manage specific external and/or internal demands that are appraised as taxing or exceeding the resources of the person" (p.

TABLE 3.1   Transactional model of appraisal and coping

Time 1 encounter 1	Time 2 encounter 2	Time 3 encounter 3	... Time N ... encounter N
	Appraisal-Reappraisal Coping: problem-focused emotion-focused Social support: emotional tangible informational		

Used with permission from Lazarus & Folkman, *Stress, Appraisal, and Coping,* Springer Publishing Company, © 1984.

141). These processes operate on what Lazarus and Folkman call "causal antecedents," which are attributes of the individual or environment that affect outcome. So, the causal antecedents are the *factors,* and appraisal and coping are the *processes* in the transactional model.

Lazarus and Folkman further emphasize that to understand stress resistance one must study coping over time through the stages of the same event (e.g., a year of mourning) and in reaction to differing events. This underscores their emphasis on stress resistance as a process and not as a static event. This point also has broad clinical implications. Medical social workers, for instance, may be prone to extrapolate from how patients behave in the hospital to how they will behave at home. Reactions to illness, however, may have little in common with readjustment to work. In the first instance one may be observing coping reactions to the threat to life, and in the second case coping in face of controllable challenges. It would even be dangerous to predict coping efforts in response to illness that take place at home based on what transpired in the hospital, because, as Lazarus and Folkman point out in their model, reactions interact in a complex fashion with contextual factors.

One criticism of Lazarus and Folkman's model is that their distinction between coping and appraisal is difficult to justify. The tendency, for example, to appraise situations as nonstressful might be categorized as primary appraisal or coping. Likewise the lack of awareness of a threat in the environment (denial) is both appraisal and coping. It constitutes primary appraisal because it is the assessment of threat in the environment, and it is emotion-focused coping because it is used to modify the deleterious effects of this threat. Obviously, it is problematic when two basic components of a model are confounded in this way.

A comparison of the two factor-process models

On their surface, the Kobasa and Lazarus-Folkman models appear similar, even if they are couched in different terminologies. Both assign a role to antecedent variables, and both outline an important role for cognitive and behavioral coping efforts. The two models have a subtle difference, however, whose implication is critically important. Kobasa suggests that certain personality types (she is most interested in hardiness) are related to specific styles of dealing with stress. Her hardy personalities are typified by control, challenge, and commitment. Hardy persons' transformational coping then is typified by (a) interpreting threat as challenge, (b) responding by taking control and or interpreting many aspects of their environment and of the stressor as within their control or realm of partial influence, and (c) a sense of personal commitment. Thus, to know individuals' personality types is to know how they will react to stressors. This will in turn lead to improved prediction of outcome. This basic trait-oriented approach is also reflected in the work of several others (Lefcourt, Martin, & Selah, 1984; Johnson & Sarason, 1978; Sandler & Lakey, 1982).

Lazarus, in contrast, argues that coping processes tend not to be well predicted by coping style (Cohen & Lazarus, 1979; Lazarus & Folkman, 1984). According to this argument, hardiness would not predict behavior during stressful circumstances. According to Lazarus, coping is a complex amalgam of thoughts and behaviors, and trait conceptualizations underestimate this complexity. Lazarus emphasizes that good functioning in one sphere of life may be directly related to poor functioning in another, and people tend not to have consistent styles of coping.

Kobasa might counter these arguments in a number of ways. First, she might suggest that hardiness is a complex of three components that tend to be associated and so cannot be compared with the more circumscribed unidimensional trait models Lazarus is criticizing. Second, she might cite evidence that personality hardiness is related to a fairly consistent style of coping and world view (Kobasa, 1979). Finally, besides being related to coping style, hardiness has been empirically found to be a good predictor of health outcome. Consequently, if it does not predict the aspect of coping style associated with stress resistance, how could this relationship between hardiness and outcome exist? Hardiness must be related to coping style, which in turn is associated with outcome, even if this does not explain all of the variability of outcome.

Indeed, a substantive body of evidence supports the view that a variety of personality traits are related to stress resistance in the face of a wide array of stressors (for reviews see Cohen & Edwards, in press; see also Chapter 5). This strongly supports the contention that traits are related to fairly stable approaches to stressful circumstances. Because no one personal trait is considered all-important, it is also generally accepted that a combination of traits affects reactions to stressful conditions and ultimate outcome. Consistent with this viewpoint, Cohen and Edwards have encouraged researchers to examine multitrait models of stress resistance in order to increase the predictive power of the models and to examine the degree of overlap between related traits. Wheaton (1983) has even gone further by suggesting that good stress resistance is predicted by the very trait of flexibility in approaching stressful circumstances. These points are approached in greater detail in Chapter 5.

Lazarus and Folkman, however, make a valid point in arguing that researchers cannot assume that a given coping style necessarily follows from a personal trait in a given instance. Whether it does is an empirical question whose study will add detail to what we know about the actual stress resistance process. In fact, it will be illustrated in Chapter 5 that studies combining personalogical and coping perspectives are able to make especially valuable contributions to the understanding of how individuals behave when presented with stressful conditions. Such investigations may be seen as combining the most salient aspects of these two perspectives and building on the strengths of each.

Person-Environment Fit Models

French, Rodgers, and Cobb (1974) have proposed a different approach to stress resistance from the factors-process perspective. Their model has been termed person-environment fit theory, which they abbreviate P-E fit. Stress is defined as the lack of fit between the characteristics of the person and those of the environment. One may examine, for example, the fit of abilities, needs of the person, or performance levels with commensurate demands on the person from the environment. A number of studies, done in a variety of settings and cultures, have shown that P-E fit is a better predictor of strain than either P or E considered alone

(Harrison, 1978; French, Caplan, & Harrison, 1982; Kulka, Klingel, & Mann, 1980).

The P-E fit model emphasizes that both objective and subjective fit are important. In this way the P-E fit model diverges from the factor-process models noted above, which all but disregard the objective components of individuals' confrontation with stressors. In this way, a dual focus emerges. Specifically, in addition to individuals' perceptions of the fit or misfit between their abilities and the demands impinging on them, a second spotlight draws attention to actual degree of fit between the person and the environment. Objective measurement can be drawn from performance tests, observation, or reliable peer reports. Thus, stress is not just envisaged as existing in the eye of the beholder.

In a reconceptualization of the P-E fit model, Caplan (1983) now also emphasizes that past, present, and future expectations of P-E fit all affect strain. So, for example, depression may be the result of seeing past performance as poor (low P-E past fit). Alternatively, one may view current P-E fit as poor, but be hopeful because one predicts that future change will improve P-E fit. A woman may, for instance, be discontent with her job but optimistic because a new boss is taking over in a few months. That people are affected by past, present, and future conditions may appear obvious, but stress researchers have generally lumped these three perspectives into a single global assessment. The revised P-E fit model makes a wider contribution than just the concept of fit, as it also spotlights the importance of individuals' attention vis-à-vis time.

The P-E fit model leads to a very different set of predictions and investigations than do the factors–process models. In a recent study, for example, Caplan, Tripathi, and Naidu (1985) studied how subjective current, retrospective, and anticipated P-E fit would influence affective and somatic strain and well-being. To do so they administered self-report questionnaires to students preparing for annual academic examinations at an Indian university. The questionnaires distinguished between fit according to past, present, and future, in two categories: cognitive (e.g., meeting academic demands) and motivational (e.g., being capable of mustering and sustaining effort). They found that poor academic fit in the past and current frames was associated with greater strain. Poor motivational fit in the current and anticipated situations, in contrast, had the most salient effect on strain.

These findings suggested that in circumstances that people appraise as out of their control, the past time frame is most salient. If we cannot change our intelligence, say, or our ability to work with a certain colleague, we tend to predict future repetitions of similar situations based on past experience. Consequently, if we have failed in the past, we will experience strain when thinking about such future confrontations. In contrast, if the P-E fit is seen as subjectively controllable then we would tend to predict outcome based on future-focused assessments of P-E fit. For example, an executive has been unable to close a particular business deal but feels that at the next meeting she can apply some new sales skills she has learned. Anticipatory stress would be expected to be low in such a situation owing to her subjective assessment of her ability to improve her relevant skills. It would appear from this research that people do feel they can control their motivation, and if they feel they can improve their motivation they experience less stress.

The P-E fit model has not received widespread attention in research on confrontation with general life stressors, health-related stressors, or major life crisis. This may be because the model was originally conceptualized as relevant to occupational settings and work stress and the terminology (e.g., performance) was distinctly the jargon of organizational psychology and management. However, in the study detailed above and in the work of others, for example, on school crime and disruption as a function of poor student–school fit (Kulka, Klingel, & Mann, 1980), the model is certainly applicable to the person–environment interaction in other settings, too. In a sense, all confrontation with stressors can be conceptualized as performance. Since individuals perform consistently in all situations, merely focusing on traits will tell only a partial story. By focusing both on individuals and on their environments, P-E fit theory approaches a more realistic understanding of stress resistance.

The P-E fit model may also be usefully applied to findings of studies that were not generated directly from the model. Felner, Farber, and Primavera (1983), for example, found that changing the structure of the school day to encourage greater attachment of high school students to a core group of peers brought about school achievement and attendance gains. It may be inferred that the environmental change allowed a better fit between student needs and environmental resources. Furthermore, this rather simple change had profound effects on the students.

When we compare the P-E fit model with the factors-process models of stress resistance, a number of similarities and differences may be noted. The theories are similar in that individuals are viewed as having to adjust to stressors in the environment and cognitions are assumed important. They also differ markedly. P-E fit theory places greater emphasis on objective assessments than do the factor-process models and considers individuals' embeddedness in the environment as a more primary component of the stress-distress link. This is not to say that Lazarus and Folkman or Kobasa denigrate the role of the environment, but the high value they place on the role of appraisal overshadows environmental factors (see also the similar arguments made by Dohrenwend et al., 1984).

Because the environment is so important in the P-E model, measurement of the type of demand on the individual is likely to be much more explicit than in the factor-process models. Organizational psychologists have generally done this better than stress researchers in other areas. Work environment, for instance, may be described on a variety of parameters such as autonomy-control, democratic-autocratic, open communication-closed communication, and high performance pressure-low performance pressure. These parameters may in turn be rated in terms of their fit to individual characteristics (e.g., need for control, ability to work with low structure, introversion-extroversion). It is more difficult, however, to describe the characteristics of, say, a divorce environment. Some ideas may come to mind, such as amiable-conflicted, with children-without children, protracted-expedient, long marriage-short marriage, focused cause-diffused cause. However, there have been few attempts to follow such a course.

Because of the paucity of attempts to categorize environmental pressures we know little about social environments and the environmental parameters of stressful conditions. Typically, the environmental factor in the factor-process models are responses to aggregate lists of stressful events. This method, in which individuals check or rate all events that have occurred to them during a recent timespan, glosses over particular characteristics of the environment. It assumes that what is important is the general or sum total demand on the individual. It is thus probably the most unenvironmental environmental approach conceivable. A second strategy has been to focus on a single event over time. But single environments are difficult to characterize because we characterize by comparison. Consequently, we need to compare responses within a few circumscribed environmental circumstances or by following the course of a single event prospectively. This has only been done in a few instances, however (Hobfoll & Lerman, in press; Hobfoll & Leiberman, 1987; Folkman & Lazarus, 1984; Mitchell & Hodson, 1986; Pearlin et al., 1981; Ruch & Leon, 1986).

PERSONAL AND SOCIAL RESOURCES
FIT TO ENVIRONMENTAL DEMAND

Statement of the Model

In recent publications I have introduced a model of stress resistance termed the model of ecological congruence. This framework falls somewhere between the factor-process and person-environment models of stress resistance (Hobfoll, 1985a; Hobfoll, 1986b). The model of ecological congruence attempts to outline the major parameters involved in stress resistance and to outline the relationships between them. It is a factor-oriented model because it emphasizes personal and social characteristics of the individual. It is process oriented in that it proposes that cognitions, behaviors, biological links, and subconscious processes affect the interpretation, magnitude, and consequences of threatening events. The model also highlights person-environment fit, but goes further to suggest that there are general fit categories that are products of the natural properties of resources and environmental demands. It is further proposed that such fit is based, in part, on the common values of different social systems (i.e., cultures, subcultures, families). The model presented here has been slightly revised from its earlier form.

With the previously explicated model of conservation of resources, this model joins to form a comprehensive stress-stress resistance theory. The remainder of this chapter will introduce the model of ecological congruence and explain how it dove-tails the model of conservation of resources.

The model of ecological congruence is presented in Figure 3.2. The figure is read like a paragraph of normal text. It states that *resources* (among them social support, personality resources, flexible coping style, and financial resources) will reduce or increase *strain* (e.g., psychological distress, physical symptoms) or will have no effect on strain. This varies to the extent that the *resource complex* meets, does not meet, or interferes with *tasks, emotional* and *biological demands* made on the individual or group at a given point in time in relation to (a) the individual's own life and (b) the amount of time before or after the stressor event. This fit of resources with demands is influenced by personal values, cultural and family values, and value-dictated environmental constraints (e.g., prohibition on abortion or divorce). Fit will also be affected by perceptions of degree of threat, assessment of need, and perceptions of the availability and suitability of given resources as seen by the individual for a given situation.

The model outlines six *dimensions* critical in determining stress resistance: the resource dimension, the strain dimension, the need

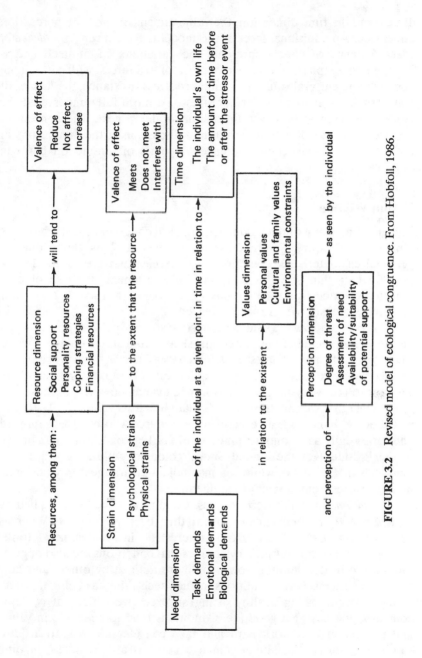

FIGURE 3.2 Revised model of ecological congruence. From Hobfoll, 1986.

Resources, among them: → will tend to →

Resource dimension
Social support
Personality resources
Coping strategies
Financial resources

Valence of effect
Reduce
Not affect
Increase

to the extent that the resource →

Strain dimension
Psychological strains
Physical strains

Valence of effect
Meets
Does not meet
Interferes with

of the individual at a given point in time in relation to →

Need dimension
Task demands
Emotional demands
Biological demands

Time dimension
The individual's own life
The amount of time before
or after the stressor event

in relation to the existent →

Values dimension
Personal values
Cultural and family values
Environmental constraints

and perception of → as seen by the individual →

Perception dimension
Degree of threat
Assessment of need
Availability/suitability
of potential support

71

dimension, the time dimension, the value dimension, and the perception dimension. An additional facet of the model is the concept of *valence of effect*. Valence of effect represents the parameter of fit itself and is included to emphasize that whereas fit of resources with situational demands and cultural values may enhance stress resistance, the lack of fit may actually contribute to further stress. To more fully understand the model, we describe these six dimensions in detail next. The concept of valence of effect will be interwoven in a discussion of the dimensions of the model, with particular reference to points of interaction between dimensions.

Resource Dimension

The first dimension of the model of ecological congruence is the resource dimension. Resources were defined in Chapter 2 as those objects, personal characteristics, conditions, or energies that are valued by the individual or that serve as a means for attainment of these objects, personal characteristics, conditions, or energies. In Table 3.2 the four basic types of resources are schematicized.

Objects resources are valued because of some aspect of their physical nature. These include food, water, air, shelter, and status objects such as sleek cars, split-level homes, and fur coats. They may have explicit or implied value. An automobile has explicit value because it gets us where we want to go. A crystal goblet has implied value, however, because it is not the fact that we can drink from it that gives it its value—a plastic cup would do. A diamond is an example of a resource whose value is implied and varies daily as a complex function of market conditions. The health of the President of the United States' colon may plunge the price of diamonds in Tokyo. So, while you may hold a 2-carat gem in your hand, its value varies from moment to moment.

Conditions may also be resources. Conditions have been studied by sociologists to a much greater extent than by psychologists. Whereas psychologists have been more interested in individuals' traits, sociologists have noted for many decades that conditions are also of great importance in determining how people are defined by others and how they define themselves. Conditions include such things as being married, being a parent, being healthy, being an executive officer of a major company, and having a good job. Conditions tend to be stable in value, and people tend to work hard and take considerable risk to acquire valued conditions. Sustaining valued conditions also requires ongoing investment of time, energy, and resources.

TABLE 3.2 Basic types of resources and their properties

Types	Examples	Special properties	Evaluative tendencies
Objects	Home Crystal glasses Sports car Car that operates	Achieve status Aid instrumental efforts Always external	Relatively easy to replenish Investable Degree of risk situational Vary in global value
Conditions	Marriage Parenthood Employment Seniority	Difficult to achieve Often require ongoing investment Often cause of stress Always external	Generally poor investability High riskability Difficult to replenish Highly globally valued
Personal characteristics	Self-esteem Mastery Optimistic outlook Hope	Part of self (mobile, robust, immediately accessible) Always internal	Difficult to replenish Low risk Limited chance of investing Highly globally valued
Energies	Money Credit Knowledge Social competency	Convertible to other resources No innate value May be internal or external	Investable Low risk Replenishable Vary in global value

One other feature that distinguishes conditions from the other resources is that sustaining them is a principal cause of stress. Obtaining conditions often requires many years of investment of other resources, but conditions may be lost overnight. A woman might work hard for years in her law firm, and after she becomes a partner the law firm may go bankrupt. Marriage is a constant source of stress for some people, notwithstanding that their marriages may be the fountainheads of their strength. For women, it is ironic that their partners may be the single most important resource but also a major contributor to stress if the relationship sours (Hobfoll, 1986b). We are often responsible for the demise of resource conditions, as when we do not invest enough effort in our marriage. In other instances, however, illness or fate may cause the loss of resource conditions that brings about stress. Thus a parent may lose a child to illness or accident, or the factory where one has achieved a senior position may encounter severe economic problems that lead to widespread layoffs.

This dual edge of conditions has led researchers to vacillate on whether to consider conditions as resources (see Thoits, 1982, for a discussion of the role of marriage as a proxy for social support). This vacillation is warranted. Given their stress-moderating and stress-producing capacity it will be necessary to look at the state and stability of people's conditions before we can determine the valence of their effect. However, resource conditions need to be researched because they are undeniably an integral aspect of the stressor–resource–distress chain.

Personal characteristics may be the most robust of all resources, most likely to be central to people's ability to withstand the demands made by threatening circumstances. I am referring here to trait characteristics and not to fleeting emotional or cognitive states.

I am using the term personal characteristics to include personality traits and stable tendencies and skills possessed by individuals. Personality traits such as sense of mastery, self-esteem, and private self-consciousness are examples of personality traits. Relational competence, solitude skills, and work-study skills are examples of skills that tend to be stable characteristics. Finally, an optimistic outlook, a pervasive feeling of happiness, and hope illustrate what I am implying by the term stable tendencies (the term "styles" is also used by some in such cases).

An example from learning theory may be used here to illustrate how personal characteristics may act as resources. Laura, a corporate officer, has a drinking problem. She drinks at lunch when she is under heavy business pressure. She does not drink often but she drinks when she most needs to perform at peak level, and this consistently interferes with her performance. One strategy she may use to control her own behavior is to focus on her sense of efficacy when she feels pressure in order to guide herself toward positive resolution of the demanding task at hand. Her sense of efficacy acts to elicit task-oriented behavior and inhibit interfering anxiety.

Personal characteristics may be particularly valuable resources because we carry them as personal baggage. They are part of us and so may be employed on a moment's notice. Object resources or social support, in contrast, may require acquisition time and may even be unavailable when required (Hobfoll & London, 1986). In contrast, self-esteem, sense of mastery, and optimism are mobilized whenever the individual needs them. Indeed, they may operate to offset resource loss without individuals actively employing them. In this regard, the way we view events in our environment is a product of how we feel about ourselves.

It is also important to emphasize the obvious here; namely, not all personal characteristics are beneficial. Whether a resource is an asset is situationally dependent. Some resources will be more robust than others, some more limited in their scope. Hopefully, the model of ecological congruence will guide research in identifying helpful traits and characteristics. However, it will also be necessary to isolate those resources that have limited positive roles, because these may be extremely important in particular circumstances. In any case, it is critical that we not repeat the situation that has occurred regarding the term "social support": that it must be supportive because it is called social support. Personal characteristics are resources if they are valued aspects of the self, but they are not always valued and do not always act in a salutary fashion.

Energies are the last resource category. Energies are states or objects whose value lies in their convertibility to desired objects or states. Without this convertibility they have no innate value. Money, credit, knowledge, and insurance are examples of energy resources. When needed, they can be exchanged or used to purchase valued resources that have explicit or implied value. Because they can lead to valued objects or conditions, energy resources may enhance power, confidence in taking risks, and ability to plan in order to facilitate the gain of other resources.

This convertibility makes energy resources especially valuable. Other types of resources are more fixed, but the flexibility of energy resources allows responses to situational needs. Money can be used to purchase an exercise machine or to pay the doctor's bill if we did not exercise. One can also opt not to use it and it still retains its value. In a sense, it loses value when it is converted because the quality of flexibility is lost. A good example is the case of knowledge in work settings. People who have knowledge can get things done. However, if they share their knowledge they lose part of their base of power, and this leads them to hoard information (Crozier, 1964; Pfeffer, 1981). Being owed social favors is another example of a nonfinancial energy resource. If one consistently helps acquaintances and colleagues in a way that does not threaten them, one may exchange the debt at a time of critical need (Walster, Walster, & Berscheid, 1978). In love relationships, too, the more one gives to one's partner, the more one may call on the partner to meet one's own needs. These should not be construed as tit-for-tat exchanges, nor is it likely that in intimate relationships a careful accounting is made (Clark, 1983). On the other hand, the debt accumulated in intimate relations has much greater exchange potential than the social debt between nonintimates. After years of investment in a relationship, partners expect fidelity, security, and even continued partnership in the case of job loss or physical infirmity.

Knowledge acts as a vitally important energy resource in two ways. First, it may directly lead to attainment of other resources. Doing well on a licensing examination leads to financial security and professional status, for instance. Second, it enables successful manipulation of other resources; knowledge engenders the making of sound choices in response to life's complex problems. This may be one reason that persons of higher socioeconomic status are more successful at confronting stressors than are persons of lower socioeconomic status (Dohrenwend & Dohrenwend, 1981). Specific knowledge may also engender better achievement of specific coping, such as when patients with complete knowledge about their medication were found to make fewer errors in drug use than their less well informed peers (Hulka et al., 1976).

Like personal characteristics, knowledge is a mobile resource that is carried with individuals wherever and whenever they go. An example of this on the broadest level may be seen in the experience of immigrants. Despite their arrival in the United States without money, possessions, or recognized education, since 1957 the Cuban community in the United States has made a quick and successful transition. What many of them brought to America from Cuba was knowledge and business experience. They quickly adapted this to their new surroundings. When one of the great violin masters was asked why so many refugees of Eastern Europe excelled in the violin, he is said to have responded, "it was difficult to move quickly enough with a piano!" I would say the same of knowledge, that it is cherished, in part, because it is mobile and cannot be robbed.

Social knowledge or competency is a very subtle kind of knowledge and may be used as a case in point. Michael Argyle, the well-known British social psychologist, has shown that there are complex rules associated with social relationships (Argyle, 1983; Argyle & Henderson, 1985). One obtains this valuable knowledge through years of social observation and modeling, because there are no published codes of social rules. Argyle and his colleagues illustrate that ignorance or short-cutting of these rules may lead to broken friendships and limited intimacy in marriage. Whether one is flying to Japan to close a business deal or entering the boardroom, culturally and situationally specific social rules apply and success will depend on one's degree of social acumen. In all these instances, social knowledge is used to manipulate other resources in the environment. So, if one wishes to receive such important resources as love, affection, a helping hand, or a pay raise, it is critical that one has knowledge of complex social processes.

Internal and External Resources

Another way of categorizing resources is to distinguish between internal and external resources. This distinction was introduced by G. Caplan (1974) and has been frequently used by others (Hobfoll & Leiberman, 1987; Kobasa & Puccetti, 1983). *Internal* resources are those resources that exist within the individual's self. These include aspects of individuals' personalities, stable personal styles, and ways of looking at problems. *External* resources are those resources that come from outside the individual. These include many aspects of social support, valued aspects of the physical environment, and material resources that are available to the individual.

A number of researchers have illustrated that the interaction of internal and external resources is a major determinant of stress resistance (Hobfoll & Leiberman, 1987; Kobasa & Puccetti, 1983; Lefcourt et al., 1984). It was shown that the positive effect of social resources is very much tied to how individuals utilize these resources, which, in turn, is a function of personal traits. At the current juncture it is important to point out that resources combine and interact and may even obstruct one another. The interaction of resources is obviously a complex issue and will be a major focus of coming chapters.

The internal and external distinction overlaps with the types of resources distinction. This may be illustrated in the case of the external resource "social support." Social support, for instance, has been conceptualized as the condition of marriage (e.g., Eaton, 1978), the giving of affection that leads to the feeling of being loved (Vanfossen, 1981), the giving of material objects (Gottlieb, 1978), the provision of advice and information (Gottlieb, 1978), and the loaning of energy resources such as money (Sarason, Levine, Basham, & Singer, 1983). Each of these types of support has been associated with improved emotional well-being in those who receive them, and there is clearly no one type of social support.

I will rely on both the "internal-external" and the "basic types" typologies in this volume because I see them each as exposing important properties of resources. In a sense, the two represent cross-sectional cuts at different depths of analysis. The internal-external focus has major advantages because it is simple and because it distinguishes between two categories upon which social scientists have traditionally focused. On the other hand, further breakdown of the properties of resources is also valuable because it provides more specific process information than grosser categorization schemes (cf. Gottlieb, 1978; Mitchell, 1982).

Value of Resources

In this discussion it has repeatedly been implied that different resources have different values. Breaking down resources into types may facilitate such an evaluation of resources. It may be recalled from the model of conservation of resources that stress ensues following perceived threat of net loss of resources or perceived loss of resources. When this occurs other resources are invested, expended, or risked for the purpose of minimizing further net loss of resources and for attempts at turning loss into gain.

One way of judging the global value of resources would be to have individuals or groups assess resources' contribution in preventing or offsetting resource loss. Just as researchers have had individuals and groups assess the degree of stressfulness inherent in a given stressful event (Holmes & Rahe, 1967; Johnson & Sarason, 1978), a similar strategy could be applied to the evaluation of resources. Of course, ratings must be relative, and one way that scaling may be accomplished is to assign the most valued resource a score of 100 and to allow individuals to rate other resources in relation to this. Such evaluation may be too general, however, because a given resource may have properties that lend themselves to stress resistance, that are irrelevant, or that cause greater stress, depending on the event. In addition, it would be necessary in such an approach to evaluate the global value of each resource separately because there are no further guidelines upon which to aggregate subclasses of resources. These problems lead to a need to devise some evaluative dimensions upon which the salient properties of resources could be articulated.

One crucial dimension on which resources could be weighed is in terms of their *replenishability*. Some resources, once expended, are not easily replenished. Other resources are quickly reinstated. Still others are not depleted whatsoever when used and may even gain in value when employed. Such is the case with successful use of sense of mastery. By employing sense of mastery, people are likely to enjoy success that, in turn, increases their sense of mastery. Meichenbaum (1977) and Meichenbaum and Jaremko (1983) have even used this as a therapy strategy. They asked people who have difficulty confronting stress to imagine successfully responding to the stressful situation. By achieving mastery in fantasy, they find that people can generalize this to new situations. Continued mastery leads to increases in one's sense of efficacy in meeting an increasing range of problems.

Investibility is another primary dimension on which resources might be evaluated. Some resources are given to investment, as opposed to outright expenditure. Investment is defined as the rendering of a resource to a third party or condition in which one retains ownership. However, premature recall of the resource usually results in a penalty. A simple example of this is lending a friend one's good dishes for a party, to repair previous bad feelings over an altercation. If one asks that the dishes be returned before the party, one receives the dishes and pays the penalty in the loss of a friend. The expression "to invest one's good name" is often used in this context; one does not actually give up one's name, but jeopardizes it as a kind of collateral. Indeed, the entire diamond industry is operated on this principle, with transactions not recorded but passed on the basis of honest reputation.

A more complex example may be drawn from the medical context. A senior surgeon disagrees with her colleague as to the correct medical procedure. She risks losing self-esteem in front of other colleagues if her arguments are defeated. At this time she may *invest* her esteem with a statement like, "In my 30 years of experience I have found that this is the best possible course." Now that the statement is public and she wins the argument, the investment is made. If the patient responds favorably, the surgeon not only receives her investment back, but also enjoys a gain in esteem. If, however, her recommendation causes further medical complications, then her investment is partially or wholly lost. She might have avoided the investment by saying, "I am not sure about this; let's consider all the options," or by calling for a third opinion. However, her motivation was the felt loss of esteem from having her opinion challenged as the treatment of choice and the felt need to make the investment to counteract further loss of this valued resource.

The last category that will be considered in the evaluation of resources is degree of *risk*. Resources may be expended with a varying degree of risk of gain. This differs from investment, because risk represents the likelihood that an investment will pay off. People usually only exercise high-risk options when they feel particularly pressed and, even then, usually after considering other strategies.

People often expend high-risk resources when they have limited resources. Neurotic individuals often risk their relationships in order to limit the repeated loss of esteem they feel when interacting with others, because they misinterpret interpersonal interactions. The poor or disenfranchised may frequently be forced to risk valued resources because of the absence of options, despite the low possibility of achieving a successful outcome. Often, middle-class mothers risk their relationships with their spouses, the approval of their parents, and their own sense of being a "good mother" if they choose to continue a career while their children are young (Aneshensel, 1986). Men are seldom placed in this dilemma. Forced risk of resources often turns into a dangerous spiral, whereby risk must be followed by greater risk in order to stave off failure of the original investment or expenditure. If the risk fails, major loss of resources is often incurred.

What emerges in the concept of risk is that some resources are not predisposed for use as leverage for gain of certain other resources. Marriage may be an effective resource for gain of self-esteem, affection, and security, but a high-risk resource when used to gain power or money. Similarly, friendship may be a low-risk resource when used appropriately, but it becomes a high-risk resource when we use it for the type of gain that may be interpreted by friends as exploitation. In this sense, it can be seen that risk is a product of the interaction of the resource and the circumstances in which it is employed. However, it should also be emphasized that some resources are so robust as to seldom or never be risky to use. Other resources may be risky to use in most circumstances, because their purpose is more circumscribed.

The value of any given resource is situational. Nonetheless, different types of resources have some stability in terms of their value along the above-mentioned evaluative dimensions. As may be noted in Table 3.2 objects tend to be investible, as we may loan them or offer them as collateral. Few resources are easy to replenish, but in contrast to the other resource types, they are relatively easy to replace. The degree of risk entailed in employing them to offset resource loss is variable, being a function of the resource–situation fit. Personal characteristics, in contrast, are very difficult to replenish when lost, but may be used with low risk. We are speaking of personal characteristics in a trait sense, not transient happiness or temporary self-satisfaction. Trait characteristics, by their nature, are relatively stable and withstand the stormy periods of people's lives (see Chapter 5). This is not to say that they are inalterable, but that they are robust. Because of this they tend to have high global value.

Conditions also tend to have high global value; after all, people work so hard to obtain them. However, conditions are best translated into feelings and used as resources such as pride in one's family or accomplishments, and they are very risky to employ directly to offset resource loss. Indeed, they are often not given to investment. In contrast, energies are easy to invest, relatively easy to replenish (again this is only relative), and are not risky to use. However, their global value varies considerably across situations.

It must be left to future research to determine the contribution that may be made by evaluating types of resources. The above-detailed schema is only a conceptual starting point. At this time, stressful events are frequently categorized and evaluated with a wide variety of yardsticks, but no such effort has been placed into categorizing and evaluating types of resources. I would not presume that the schema presented above will be the last word; rather, I hope it may be a first word that helps catalyze what I see as an important area of future research.

Strain Dimension

Strain is defined as the negative effects of stressful events, that is, the outcome of stress. In general, there are two types of strain, psychological and physical. More and more, however, research is showing that it is difficult to distinguish physical health from psychological health (Antonovsky, 1979; Feuerstein et al., 1986). Although we must recognize that any distinction between physical and psychological health is, in part, only a function of the questions we ask, the symptoms of the two are usually easily differentiated.

More complex is the question of whether strains are *general* system responses to stress or *specific* responses to particular types of stress. Researchers have generally studied psychological and physical strain using a nonspecific approach. So, for example, general measures of mental health or well-being (Wethington & Kessler, 1986; Wilcox, 1981; Williams, Ware, & Donald, 1981) or health (Kobasa et al., 1981) have usually been employed. Actually, these investigators would have little reason to look at specific strains, because most have looked at general life stress as measured by life-event scales. Consequently, if the stress is defined as general overload or an accumulation of many different stressors, a general response would be expected.

When investigating reactions to single events, some researchers have examined specific reactions. This is well represented in work on childbearing, where investigators have been familiar enough with the psychological and physiological impact of pregnancy and delivery to look at specific reactions that are common responses to this type of stress. So, for example, stress during pregnancy has been studied as to its relationship to eclampsia, hypertension, and difficulty in labor (Norbeck & Tilden, 1983; Nuckolls, Cassel, & Kaplan, 1972). In studies of psychological strain, difficulty at the time of delivery or during pregnancy has been related to depression (Hobfoll & Leiberman, 1987; Paykel, Emms, Fletcher, & Rassaby, 1980).

The measures of psychological and physiological strain in studies of pregnancy and delivery were not chosen by chance. Rather, by studying the problem empirically and through involvement in clinical work with pregnant and delivering women, a number of associations were made between certain types of stressors and strain. With more careful study, health psychologists and gynecologists have built increasingly sound predictive models of the relationship between stressors and strain in this population.

A few general models, rather than problem-specific (e.g., pregnancy, grief) models, for understanding how strain will emerge in stress sequences have been presented. Levi (1972) has proposed one such model to explain the occurrence of psychosocially mediated disease. Levi argues that any psychosocial change can act as a stressor that elicits a nonspecific biological response. However, individuals have a preexisting "psychobiological program" or propensity to react neuroendo-crinologically according to a person-specific pattern. In this way, the specificity is not a function of the type of stress, but of the propensities of the individual.

Minuchin et al. (1975) propose a different kind of model to predict the area in which strain will emerge. Their model suggests that particular kinds of familial stressors react with individual propensities to produce characteristic strains. They postulate that severe psychosomatic problems in children are a product of three necessary conditions: (a) a type of family organization that encourages somatization, (b) child involvement in parental conflict (lack of borders between parent and child domains of family knowledge and responsibility), and (c) physiological vulnerability. This model then suggests that the development of psychosomatic illness in general is related to a particular kind of familial stressor. The specific type of psychosomatic illness, in turn, is related to physiological vulnerability, that is, the propensity of the individual to develop a specific disease.

One of the major goals of this book is to illustrate the complex interaction of the dimensions of the model of ecological congruence in the prediction of person-situation-culture-specific reactions to stressors. The concept of strain will reemerge frequently in these discussions. In particular, later chapters will focus on how the model might be applied to different strains, including coronary heart disease, postpartum depression, and breakdown in combat.

I think the reader will be convinced that in studies of strains that are ecologically congruent with the person–situation interaction, more meaningful and interpretable results were gleaned. In contrast, in those studies that adopted a "shot gun" approach that captured any and all symptoms, I think it will be seen that the nature of the stress and stress-resistance processes remained more obscure. Ideally, theorists and researchers will develop and refine more general models of strain, such as those suggested by Levi or Minuchin and his colleagues. At the present time, however, it will be a clear step forward if researchers use common sense and experience to isolate particular strains that are congruent with the situation.

The Needs Dimension

The next dimension in the model is the needs dimension. *Needs* are defined as the internal biological, emotional, and cognitive requirements of the individual. These needs interact with stimuli from the environment, the interaction generating demands. *Demands* are defined as pressure to perform tasks in response to the interaction of events occurring in the environment with the psychological self and the biological self. *Tasks,* in turn, are defined as a complex of behavioral, emotional, and biological responses that are required to meet demands.

It would seem a misnomer to name a dimension in terms of needs when it focuses on demands. This is done to emphasize that environmental stimuli are only demands to the extent that they interact with individuals' psychological or biological needs. Food deprivation is only demanding because the body needs nourishment, and rejection by one's partner is only demanding because one needs love and acceptance. Nor is this interaction static. Physical and emotional requirements also change as a product of their interaction with the environment. In this way, being well fed (i.e., due to exposure to an environment rich in nutrients and calories) decreases requirement for food and so will delay the life-threatening demands of food deprivation. Similarly, love and affection from other friends (i.e., exposure to an enriching social environment) will limit the threat of rejection from a single relationship.

Threat and demand are often used interchangeably in the literature. To distinguish the two, threat may be said to be an attribution to an external event that either is perceived as having the potential to cause a loss in resources or has caused a loss in resources. Demand constitutes the response required by a threat placed on the individual. In a sense, demand follows from the perceived qualities of the threat.

A number of corollaries follow from this aspect of the model. The first is that the evaluation of stimuli as threatening is a function of the properties of the stimuli and the needs of the individual involved. Those who are socially anxious (with a high need for social reassurance), say, note events in their social environment that more callous individuals ignore. After noting the event's occurrence they are also likely to evaluate the event as threatening. Threat would not be an outcome if the event occurred to someone who was not socially anxious or if a different kind of event occurred to a socially anxious person.

A second corollary of the interaction of external stimuli and internal needs is that threat and response capacity cannot be completely separated. Those who have a high need for structure, for instance, will become aware of the absence of frequent feedback from their bosses and will interpret this as threatening. This need for structure also limits their response capacity. So, in this way, coping capacity interacts with environmental stimuli in determining the very noting of an event's occurrence, as well as the assessments of its stressfulness.

It might be argued that an awareness of one's environment is already a stage of adjustment or coping and in some sense this is so. Lazarus and Folkman (1984) consider this the stage of primary appraisal, when individuals evaluate the stimuli around them as irrelevant, benign, positive, or threatening. This would place primary appraisal before the coping stage (even if primary appraisal may recur following coping efforts). Moos and Schaeffer (1986), however, consider such appraisal as the first adaptive task demanded of individuals. In their treatment of the issue, they state that when individuals are confronted with events, the first task is to "establish the meaning and understand the personal significance of the situation" (p. 11). This conceptualization places appraisal as an important first step in the coping process.

Moos and Schaeffer's approach underscores the confounding here of coping capacity and appraisal of threat. It would appear that the very noting of threat is related to response mechanisms (e.g., appraisal, assignment of meaningfulness). Indeed some theorists see the assignment of meaningfulness as the very heart of stress resistance and the main focus of coping (Antonovsky, 1979; Frankl, 1963). Consequently, when theorists are discussing event occurrence and the degree such occurrences are threatening, they are already involved in the process of stress resistance. More succinctly, there is an immediate stage of stress resistance that occurs with the act of awareness of an external stimulus, and this stage involves both the properties of the stimulus and the needs of the individual.

What kinds of events are likely to be threatening? The needs dimension of the model of ecological congruence is also consistent with empirical evidence regarding the properties of threatening events. The question here is whether there are particular kinds of events that tend to be stressful for many people. Indeed, 20 years of stress research has concentrated on this question. In a careful review of this literature, Thoits (1983) sees some consensus that events that are undesirable, uncontrollable, and unexpected are the ones likely to negatively affect people.

Each of these categories illustrates the environment–person interaction reflected in the needs dimension because the desirability, controllability, and expectancy of events are to a large extent perceptual assessments. It is not change per se that is threatening, as originally thought, but the interpretation given to particular changes. This does not, however, negate that events have certain objective properties. As discussed in the preceding chapter certain events are more ambiguous than others, but many events have clearly distinguishable properties. Indeed, one successful research strategy has been to obtain normative assessments of these properties, indicating broad agreement as to their nature (Thoits, 1983). So, the extensive literature on stressful events supports the view characterized in the needs dimension that threat is a product of external stimuli and internal needs and cannot be fully understood when only one or the other of these facets is considered.

Finally, at least one issue cannot be resolved or addressed intelligently, because so few empirical data can be called to bear on the question. In this regard, it cannot be said which of the almost infinite things that go on around us constitute an event. It is not clear whether we appraise every single event in our environment to decide its personal meaning for ourselves, or whether we have some precognitive or subconscious alerting mechanisms to some special selected set of occurrences.

It is generally accepted that individuals have differential levels of *sensitivity* to events, signifying that sensitive individuals are alert to stimuli in their environment that others are not. We are all familiar with the experience of discussing with a friend the supposed rebuff he received at a meeting or party. We were there also, involved in the same conversation, yet we cannot recall any snub. Even when he tells us exactly what he thought happened, we argue that no rebuff occurred. Is this or is this not an event? Did we also note the event, but assess it as irrelevant for ourselves? Did we cope with the threat that was in the environment and did he not, because we do not feel rebuffed in such instances and he does? Or is the very occurrence of the event a product of his own construction? The answer to these questions awaits future research and will be very difficult to answer because of the speed with which humans survey and screen their environment.

All of these issues point to the interrelationship between events and needs in individuals' assessments of threat and even their very recognition that an event occurred. It is proposed that events make demands on people when three things occur: (a) individuals are sensitive to a particular set of events (i.e., they have certain needs), (b) they are aware of the event's occurrence, and (c) they have a need that will be threatened because of loss of resources that might occur or has occurred due to the properties of the event and their own situation. To further clarify the terms used here: *events* are objectively observable occurrences in the environment; *sensitivity* is a function of biological and psychological states of need; and *awareness* is a function of needs and attention (i.e., we may not be aware of an event if our attention is directed elsewhere).

The term tasks further belies a view of demands as creating an atmosphere that requires responding or performance. Originally, I had proposed that two types of tasks were possible, emotional tasks and instrumental tasks (Hobfoll, 1985a). However, in the revised model presented here, I would add biological tasks as a third and separate category. Emotional tasks require responding on the emotional level, instrumental tasks require responding on the behavioral level, and biological tasks require responding on the physiological level.

The same stressor event may require responding on all three levels. Such is the case, for example, with adjustment to mastectomy (Taylor, 1983). Women who undergo breast removal must meet the demands on their body in regenerating new tissue; they must meet demands on their psyche in how to accept their new disfigured body image; and they must meet the instrumental demands required by physiotherapy. Other events may make more circumscribed demands. A difficult academic examination may require primarily instrumental responding through studying long hours. Grief may at some stages make solely emotional demands. The nature and expression of the demands and the tasks that are required to meet them will also vary over time, and this will be considered next.

The Time Dimension

Time has too often been ignored in the study of stress and stress resistance. The time dimension of the model of ecological congruence focuses on time in two ways.

First, time is viewed in a developmental sense. Stressful events occur at different points in people's lives. Because individuals' needs and coping capacities change and develop over the life span, the impact of events is different depending on individuals' emotional and physical development (Datan, 1975). As time passes, people also find themselves in different roles and in interaction with different social institutions and practices (Pearlin, 1983). Psychology has been lax in its study of how institutions and social patterns associated with institutions affect people. Sociologists, in contrast, have made a clear case for the importance of these factors in determining people's roles over the life span.

Leonard Pearlin (1983) has this to say about roles:

> They [roles] are potent, I believe, because people usually attach considerable importance to role activities. Most roles are within such institutions as family, occupation, economy, and education; and because such institutions function for the maintenance of societies, people typically are socialized to invest themselves in their institutional roles. . . . Roles are also attractive to the stress researcher because they represent areas on which an array of social forces converge, with the result that they reflect properties of the broader contexts in which they are located. . . . Roles are thus excellent vantage points from which, if we turn in one direction, we observe aspects of broader social organization and, if we turn in the other, we observe the behavior of individuals. (p. 5)

Because much development along the life span is normative, we can predict how development will affect individuals' needs. For example, health generally follows an age pattern, getting worse as one gets older, and people tend to value security more as they age. Similarly, normative patterns can be found in the sequence of interactions with social institutions and practices. For instance, a social role sequence may be dating, marriage, parenthood, and empty nest, and an occupational role pattern might include school, college, entry into the workplace, seniority, and retirement. We must also respect the fact that some role development is ipsitive (individual). So, for instance, an individual may divorce and remain single or remarry, or, say, go back to school and switch occupations.

Whether development is ipsitive or normative it will interact with stressful events. It will do so in all facets of adjustment to events, affecting event recognition, appraisal of meaningfulness, availability and selection of coping resources, and breakdown. A young man may see a change in his company as a chance for advancement. An older employee may respond, in contrast, by feeling threatened by early retirement. A woman whose career is in good shape may feel ready to have children at the age of 35. A divorce is likely to change her feelings toward that possibility.

A second way to view time is to consider it in reference to an event's occurrence. In the study of grief, Silver and Wortman (1980) have illustrated, for example, that following important losses, individuals follow a sequence of reactions that may change their order and repeat themselves in the course of psychological adjustment to the loss. Others have also noted that the sequence of events following a stressful encounter is related to the demands that change over time (Folkman & Lazarus, 1985; Hobfoll & Leiberman, 1987). Breznitz (1967; 1983b) has also argued for increased concern for the role of anticipatory reactions that predate the event's actual occurrence. All of these approaches demand that attention be paid to the time of event occurrence.

How research is conducted

If we consider the dimension of time important, this will directly affect our research strategy. Those who emphasize that time is important when viewed developmentally or vis-à-vis the event have called on researchers to examine reactions to single events or to a few select events that may be compared (cf. Folkman, Lazarus, Dunkel-Schetter, DeLongis, & Gruen, 1986; Hobfoll, 1985a; Wilcox, 1986). Such events may be followed longitudinally so that normative sequences can be compared across individuals (that is, the group as the element of focus). Longitudinal study of events also allows for examination of ipsitive sequences, which can be compared using an intraindividual approach. In the intraindividual approach an individual is compared with himself or herself at other times. Rehm (1978), for instance, found that mood was influenced by whether the individual had more or less stress than on previous days, whereas overall stress levels were not predictive of mood.

Attention to the element of time leads to another serious criticism of the event-checklist method, since this method implies that time is unimportant. In the checklist approach respondents check all the events that have occurred to them in a given period of time. So, events that occurred one year earlier are aggregated with events occurring the day before. Events with special meaning for young singles are combined with events that have special meaning for married couples. By aggregating events in these ways any developmental information or differences that unfold following stressful events is averaged and thereby lost.

Kessler (1983) argues that as long as aggregate life-event measures are used, it will be impossible to develop specific models of adjustment. He suggests looking at individuals who are confronted by a common crisis in order to examine the events–response patterns that follow. In particular, he advocates use of case-control studies in which crisis victims are compared with individuals who have not experienced the crisis.

A good example of the case-control method can be found in a recent study by Davidson and Baum (1986). They investigated the long-term stress reactions of those exposed to events involving the accident at the nuclear power station at Three Mile Island. They compared Three Mile Island residents with residents of a similar community in nearby Frederick, Maryland, a town located some 80 miles from the reactor. Time in this study was tapped retrospectively, but we know when the accident occurred and therefore how much time had transpired. We also know that the same amount of time transpired for all respondents. Residents of Three Mile Island had more symptoms of chronic stress and of posttraumatic stress disorder compared with the Frederick residents. Residents of Three Mile Island were particularly bothered by intrusive thoughts about the damaged reactor. By considering the time element, Davidson and Baum are able to make the point that chronic exposure to a stressor can lead to mild symptoms of posttraumatic stress disorder. Previously, such disorders were attributed primarily to reactions following a major stressful event outside the realm of normal experience and not to exposure to chronic stressors.

Kessler also notes that a major problem stemming from the lack of attention to time in the aggregate model is that one cannot be sure to what extent events causally precede outcome or even follow as a consequence of prior strain. Lehman, et al. (1987) tackled this problem innovatively by comparing spouses and parents of auto accident victims with matched controls who had not experienced such a loss. They were very cautious to select cases with no recorded negligence on the victim's part. Time here is operationalized in terms of selection of subjects who experienced their loss four to seven years before the study. They were able to illustrate that even many years following such traumatic events individuals are still deeply affected by their loss. Their research design at the same time allowed them to clearly illustrate that the loss caused the strain and not vice versa.

In our own research we have tried to get as close as possible to the traumatic event and look at differences in adjustment at the time of the event itself and again some months later. This may be called a case-control longitudinal design. In addition, we have chosen events that occur more as a matter of chance than because of people's own doing, thus also limiting the possible confounding of event occurrence with strain. In one study, for example, we examined the reactions of women 24 hours before biopsy for suspected cancer and again three months later for those who were found *not* to have cancer (Hobfoll & Walfisch, 1984). In this way subjects served as their own controls, under high stress at the time of biopsy and under low stress three months later. In a second study (Hobfoll & Leiberman, 1987) we investigated the interactive effect of personal and social resources on the stress resistance of women immediately following delivery and again three months postpartum. In this second study, women were followed longitudinally and comparisons were based on whether their delivery was complicated or uncomplicated.

In both cases, interesting differences in the pattern of adjustment were noted. These will be discussed in detail later in the volume. What is relevant to the current discussion is that by looking at a time close to the actual threatening event and looking again after a reasonable period of recovery, we were able to effectively study high acute stress versus low stress. Prior to this, few investigations have examined immediate reactions to acute stress outside of the laboratory (Ruch, Chandler, & Harter, 1980) or compared the same individuals in high- versus low-threat conditions for stressors that are unlikely to be confounded with strain.

Resources, needs, strain, and time

Viewing those aspects of the model of ecological congruence that have already been discussed in reference to time, one may say that individuals who are at different developmental stages or who experienced stressful events at different times

1. will have different resources at their disposal and different role constraints,
2. will have different prior experience in utilization of resources,
3. will be susceptible to different strains,
4. will develop chains of related strains (e.g., divorce may be followed by severe emotional upset, leading to depression, leading to health-

impairing behaviors, and then stagnating in the form of long-term emotional distancing from the opposite sex), and
5. will have different needs that affect their primary evaluation of events and their chosen style of responding.

The concept of time will continue to be an important focus in future research. While earlier research and conceptualization of the stress phenomenon paid little attention to time in its developmental sense or vis-à-vis the event, there is already an impetus developing for a primary focus on the process of adjustment to stressful events whose properties and time of occurrence are known and a move away from focusing on general stress reactions to events viewed in their aggregate. At the same time there is increasing interest in the meaning of the event for people at different developmental stages.

The Value Dimension

The resource, need, strain, and time dimensions of the model that have been considered reflect the active components of the model. How they are interwoven, however, is determined by the value and perception dimensions of the model. These two dimensions interact to determine the valence of effect, the particular fit between resources and demands in the person-environment context.

The value dimension of the model of ecological congruence is the most complex because the concept of values is so ephemeral. Everyone seems to know what values are, but values defy being expressed in words. It is a critical facet of the model because values represent a basic set of standards that define the limits and constraints of the resource, need, and perception dimensions of the model and their interaction. Making matters more difficult, it is the facet of the model about which there is the least research. Theorists have been loath to even discuss the relationship between values and stress, although some studies allude to the issue of values as if what they meant by values were understood and clearly delineated. It is not. My intention here is to discuss how values affect stress and stress resistance and to outline how values are incorporated into the model of ecological congruence.

Values are the principal criteria or standards by which individuals measure themselves and their environment. These primary standards are the benchmarks that people use to make evaluations and comparisons. Values are more basic than attitudes, for example, and, as opposed to attitudes, values have no objects. A person may be prejudiced against blacks (an attitude). Blacks are the object of this prejudice. "White supremacy" might be the underlying value here. White supremacy has no object. Another person may dislike dirty hands at the table. Again, the attitude (disliking) has an object (dirty hands). The underlying value is cleanliness.

Robin Williams (1979), a sociologist, writes the following:

Values merge affect and concept. Persons are not detached or indifferent to the world; they do not stop with a sheerly factual view of their experience. Explicitly or implicitly, they are continually regarding things as good or bad, pleasant or unpleasant, beautiful or ugly, appropriate or inappropriate, true or false, virtues or vices. . . . All values have cognitive, affective, and directional aspects. Values serve as criteria for selection in action. When most explicit and fully conceptualized, values become criteria for judgment, preference, and choice. When implicit and unreflective, values nevertheless perform "as if" they constituted grounds for decisions in behavior. Individuals do prefer some things to others; they do select one course of action rather than another out of a range of possibilities; they do judge their own conduct and that of other persons. (p. 16; © 1979, Macmillan Publishing Company)

There is hardly room here to discuss the concept of values in great depth and for this the reader is referred to Rokeach (1973) and the many books outside of psychology on the philosophy of values. The model of ecological congruence includes three aspects of values that are particularly relevant to stress and I will address these here. These are cultural and family values, personal values, and environmental constraints. The three are interrelated because personal values are usually adopted from the society and family and because environmental constraints are the product of these values codified into law or some effective social or physical force (e.g., putting sinners in stocks in the town square; divorce laws).

Cultural and family values

These are the basic standards of the social unit, and they spring from two primary sources. The first source is some evaluation of what is considered to be a basic "truth." A belief in one God is an example. Such beliefs are so primary that they even preclude any apology to reason. If the true God commands sacrificing young lives in holy war, they will be sacrificed; if electric lights are not to be lit on the Sabbath because they constitute fire, which is forbidden on the Sabbath day, lights will not be lit; and if books are religiously censored, curiosity will be sublimated. I do not mean to criticize religion here; I myself practice some of these rituals. The point is that these actions are not based on logical rationales, but on belief. They are performed because we hold some very basic values.

The second primary source of values stems from concern for a greater good, and these values usually address aspects of our lives that we deem most important. This includes how we are governed, how we define the family, and how we interact with others. So, here we have democracy, family loyalty, and honesty. We appeal to these values in the light of reason, albeit capitalism and communism may both be extolled on the basis of rational argument.

Certain values are common to most members of a particular culture, but other values are particular to the family. We often hear such family values being reiterated in statements like the following. "We Smiths always stick together." "We Goldsteins are never prejudiced." "Your grandparents on both sides were fighters." Many family values, nonetheless, reflect those of the greater culture. Rokeach (1973) in his seminal work on values suggested that there is a basic set of values common to a society and that the family or individuals differ primarily in how they rank or order these values. This hierarchy or comparative rating of values is called the *value system*.

It is possible to gain great insight into what is stressful by understanding value systems. The most highly ranked values in Western culture, for example, include freedom, self-respect, a sense of accomplishment, family security, social recognition, and mature love (Rokeach, 1973). From these it follows that situations that threaten loss of independence, self-esteem, finances, status, and love will be the most stressful. Likewise, we can expect that these values will be reflected in individuals' needs.

Personal values

Another facet of the value dimension is the contention that personal values are also important in stress resistance. Individuals do not necessarily adopt all of the values of their society, social group, and family. Indeed, people change and create value systems that are very different from those around them. It is hard to say how original people are in expressing their personal value systems. Most likely people are influenced by exposure to books, charismatic leaders, or a subculture. In contrast to the greater society, beatniks were marching to the beat of a different drummer, but they shared many values with others of their subculture, following the lead of a handful of writers and musicians.

Likewise, those in Germany who rebelled against Naziism were likely responding to values they gained from family or a religious group. Nonetheless, at some point individuals must sort out their own value system and change their perspective in light of experience.

This leads to individual expression of resources, needs, and demands. Knowing the general values expressed by a culture or by a particular social group will yield information about how these resources, needs, and demands will find expression. Knowing individuals' personal values, though, will allow more exacting prediction. Both levels of analysis will be important. Let us consider examples of the predictive worth of understanding the society's and the individual's values.

Investigating students in a liberal college community comprising mainly nonobservant Protestants, one might assume a certain set of needs, resources, and demands concerning the issue of pregnancy and abortion. One might make predictions regarding how successfully incoming freshmen would resist sexual peer pressure, how they might respond to a counseling or sex education program, and how they would stand up to the stress of unintended pregnancy given their liberal background and their current environment. A different set of predictions would be called for if one were observing first-year students at a conservative Catholic university.

It would be dangerous, however, to apply this general approach to individual therapy at either institution. In such a context, learning about the individual's personal value structure would enable more precise prediction. Individuals may behave a certain way not because they are Jewish or Protestant but because of the particular way in which they have adapted the values underlying their background to other aspects of their selves. Nevertheless, it would still hold that sources of stress for the individual and the course of stress resistance will be tied in with values.

When values become constraints

Values may also affect stress resistance in a much more direct fashion than we have been discussing. This occurs when values become translated into societal constraints. Examples of this occur in societies where it is difficult to obtain divorce or abortions, in school systems that prohibit school nurses from counseling students about sex education, and in workplaces that pressure management into working long hours and Saturdays. Sometimes value constraints are codified into law, such as when divorce or abortion are made illegal. More often, though, the pressure is social rather than legal.

In many Middle Eastern countries only men may grant divorce. In the United States free clinics risked losing federal funding if they performed abortions, and during other periods abortion was strictly prohibited. These are obvious cases of value constraints. The corporate work ethic is a more subtle example. To succeed in business or law, for instance, executives and lawyers in prestige firms must work long hours during the week, take work home, and work on Saturdays. How does one use family resources if one hardly sees the family? How do young couples express their need to have children? Usually the wife stays home alone and frustrated by the lack of support she is receiving, or both spouses pursue their careers and indefinitely postpone plans for a family.

Alternatively, the wife may work and the husband stay home with the children. Imagine how much support he will receive from his family! Their values will influence him unless he is extremely committed to what he is doing. Then, when the time comes for him to reenter the workplace, he will be treated as a misfit for making this sex-role reversal.

I recently attended a preschool play performed for the proud parents. The boys portrayed the warrior heroes, and the girls fainted and swooned as their heroes returned home victorious! Many in this particular audience were liberally minded, dual-career families, who had taught their children equality between the sexes. These parents were taken aback, to say the least, at the implications of the script. Other more traditional parents failed to see the problem. The moral is that when individuals express values that are not well accepted in the general society, the sheer force of value constraints is felt. When one moves with the current, these constraints are hardly noticed.

Values, resources, needs, and demands

Values are integrally related to the resource, need, and perception dimensions of the model of ecological congruence. Personal resources such as control, hardiness, self-esteem, and hope, for instance, are all related to the values held by a society. Likewise, social resources such as social support and feeling part of a community are defined and operate within value systems.

How values affect other dimensions of the model can be illustrated in the study of a principal resource, control. Much research in North America has focused on personal resources related to control (Johnson & Sarason, 1978; Lefcourt et al., 1984; Kobasa et al., 1981; Sandler & Lakey, 1982). Israelis working in the area of stress have focused, in contrast, on hope (Breznitz, 1983a), resourcefulness (Rosenbaum & Ben-Ari Smira, 1986), sense of coherence (Antonovsky, 1979), and self-esteem (Hobfoll, 1985). It would seem that Americans value control and Israelis are content with survival.

Studies comparing Japanese and Americans have also shown that Americans rely on a direct form of control, whereas Japanese use more indirect forms of control (Weisz, Rothbaum, & Blackburn, 1984). This too is perhaps because American culture prizes results and the individual, whereas Japanese culture esteems respect and honor. Japanese executives will conduct a business deal by skirting the confrontive issues. Their American counterparts may want to "take the bull by the horns." These resource utilization strategies are determined and nurtured by the values of the different societies.

Values also affect and even define people's needs. We see this in changes in desired family size or the desire to marry and have children and in differences in attitudes about family size in different religions. Children raised in a religious environment may feel a life-long need for a closeness with God, especially when they are confronted by major stressors. Those whose parents emphasize secular reason may cling to rational thought during stressful periods of their lives and feel a need to avoid "being clouded by emotions." Women in one generation felt a need to stay home; their daughters feel a need for a successful career. All these needs are products of values.

Even such basic needs as the need for affection may be drilled out of individuals in societies that value stoicism and "manliness." There are probably serious repercussions when basic needs are repressed. Men, for example, have difficulty expressing emotions and disclosing their feelings (Lewis, 1978), skills necessary for fostering warm, intimate relationships.

Similarly, the demands that result from the interaction of outside events and internal needs are a function of values. How we respond to insult and loss of honor, sexual cues, and failure are examples. Few Europeans today challenge others to duels over insults to their fiancée; they felt obliged to do just that not long ago. Traditional Arabs feel obligated to avenge even the accidental death of a sibling; to Westerners honor does not demand such a response. Perhaps 20 years ago a woman may have accepted the role of making coffee at the office; today many women take issue with performing such role-demeaning tasks and with being cast in positions that include these as women's responsibilities. In each of these instances, values partially determine the demand characteristics that result from the interaction of external events and internal needs, the stressfulness of certain situations, and the limitations that are placed on the universe of potential responses.

In the coming chapters much more will be said of the relationship between the value, resource, need, and perception dimensions of the model of ecological congruence. Some research that my colleagues and I have carried out will also be brought to bear on the subject. Undoubtedly, the consideration of values will be troublesome for stress theorists, as it has been for those in other areas of psychological research. I hope to have made the point that, however troublesome, values deeply affect the stress process and stress resistance. I expect that this volume will, at best, raise questions concerning values for future research and will yield precious few answers. If the volume encourages the study of values in stress research, it will have made an important contribution.

Perception Dimension

The final dimension of the model is the perception dimension. Perception determines how resources are evaluated, the assessment of needs and demands in response to a given situation, and the availability and suitability of potential resources to meet assessed needs and demands. My contention is that both the objective environment and perception affect the process of stress resistance. Whereas perception is very important, I find its influence has been overstated by studies that see its influence as primary. Often when the data contradict the thesis that perception is the central phenomenon in the stress process, the objective elements of the situation are glossed over or ignored.

First, let us clarify the term perception. Perception in the stress literature refers to the influence of cognitive processes in the assessment of environmental events, resulting in individual interpretations of the personal meaning of an event. It is not simply information processing, which is perception in the more general sense. People in similar circumstances often respond differently. In reaction to examination stress, one student becomes depressed, another anxious, and another feels a numbing of emotions. Still another student responds as if there is little stress here at all, only an exciting challenge to show her mental prowess. These differences suggest that they are perceiving their situations differently.

Individuals assess their circumstances as to the degree of stressfulness, the strength of the resources they may employ to offset resultant loss of resources, and the fit of their available resources to the nature of the stress-related demands. If they assess the situation as unlikely to result in loss of valued resources, because either the stressor is minor or their resources are particularly well suited to the particular stressor, they will not be stressed.

In the eyes of the beholder?

Perception has come to mean more than this for some. Lazarus and Folkman's (1984) cognitive model, for example, pits perception against objective assessment of the environment. They argue that what occurs in the environment is not so important as the individuals' interpretation of the environment. In their model the role of environment is relegated to second-class status. This position is supported by findings that *hassles,* minor annoyances, are better predictors of somatic symptoms and psychological distress than are reports of more major life events (DeLongis, Coyne, Dakof, Folkman, & Lazarus, 1982; Kanner, Coyne, Schaefer, & Lazarus, 1981). The argument follows that if minor, highly subjective events are more important than major events in predicting strain, then individual perception of the meaning of the event must be the central axis of stress. The logic on which these conclusions are based has been questioned, however, leading to a very different interpretation of these findings (Dohrenwend et al., 1984). Specifically, it has been argued that minor events are strongly correlated with strain because the two are confounded; the measure of events itself assesses symptoms.

I would argue that both perception and actual events are important and that only in special instances does one or the other have dominant influence. Typically, what occurs is cyclical, without any dominant factor. A recent study, for example, found that stressful events only predicted concurrent levels of depression, and then only among those who were initially depressed (Hammen, Mayol, DeMayo, & Marks, 1986). Stressful events were not predictive of future depression. Moreover, initially depressed people were more likely than nondepressed people to encounter ongoing stressor events. A similar set of findings was noted by Goplerud and Depue (1985). Such findings lead to the conclusion that some persons cause stressful events to occur, are susceptible to interpret events as stressful, and respond with a particular stress-related emotion, in this case depression. However, the events are occurring, even if they happen more to people with a particular perceptual set and even if these people are causing their own demise.

This is illustrated in another way by the process research on depression that has been conducted by Coyne (1976) and Gotlib and Robinson (1982). These investigators have illustrated that depressed individuals press their environment such that they receive the social rejection they expect. They then experience depressive emotion in response to the rejection they invited. Again, however, they are responding to real events.

Perhaps, though, the question is whether this response is in the mind of the beholder (i.e., depressive personalities) or whether others would be susceptible to such rejection. If perception is more important than environment, then nondepressive individuals should be fairly resistant to such stressors. This is certainly not the case, however. Using a healthy student sample, for instance, Miller and Lefcourt (1983) used mild social rejection as a stressor. By simply not giving subjects feedback when they were talking about themselves, the researchers found that a consistent reaction was extreme agitation. It would seem that sensitivity to rejection is common not just among depressives and constitutes a stressor even in a contrived context.

Work on major stressor events also points to the importance of the objective nature of the event in determining stress reactions. In one study, we found that in the hours facing biopsy for suspected cancer, about 43 percent of women in the least high-risk group exhibited extremely high levels of depressive affect (Hobfoll & Walfisch, 1986). This represented about three and one-half times more risk for depression than the same group during a low stress period of their lives. Green, Grace, and Gleser (1985) have also noted that the objective levels of major stressors are good predictors of later stress responses.

In another study that illustrates this point, Murrel and Norris (1984) found that high exposure to stressful events resulted in the greatest increase in symptomatology. In contrast, moderate and low levels of exposure resulted in limited or no negative ramifications. Of special interest to our argument here is that even moderate levels of stressors were not necessarily detrimental. This suggests that individual differences would have an increased effect on outcome at these lower levels of stress, but at higher levels the events matter more. Another implication is that since most stressful event research has been carried out on student samples or relatively small community samples (of less than 200), few subjects can be truly categorized as falling into the high, recent exposure to stressor category. Consequently, any effect size would be attenuated by averaging truly stressful events with everyday events. Instead researchers would note effects likely to be the product of individual differences, including neurosis. This may well be what studies of hassles are depicting; the hassles noted may be a symptom of distress, not a cause of distress.

By no means do I wish to minimize the role of perception in the experience of stress. On the contrary, it is a major dimension of the model of ecological congruence. However, I do wish to emphasize that the objective components of stressful events and the objective resources of individuals may be overshadowed by methodological approaches that favor cognitive models. Moreover, I would argue that shared perceptions are more common in response to many stressors than are idiosyncratic perceptions.

It is consistent with the model of ecological congruence that differences in resources, needs, shared values, susceptibility to certain strains, and perception are all important in determining resultant stress resistance. Their relative importance differs from situation to situation depending on the complex nature of their interaction. Asserting that one aspect of the model has a dominant role only reflects research that preordains cognitions to be preeminent.

In general, it appears that the more major the stressor event and the clearer the objective threat, the greater the influence of the environment on outcome. In contrast, the more minor the event, the greater the influence of individual perception. However, care must be taken in the case of hassles and other minor occurrences, because at some point one begins to study intrapsychic neurosis, not a reaction to the current environment whatsoever.

The cautious emphasis on perception. In discussing the resource and needs dimensions of the model of ecological congruence we have already outlined many cognitive processes. Indeed, a number of the traits found to be important internal resources are cognitive orientations or ways of seeing the world and interpreting events. Among these are hardiness (Kobasa, 1979), control (Johnson & Sarason, 1978; Lefcourt et al., 1984), and resourcefulness (Rosenbaum & Ben-Ari Smira, 1986). Likewise, needs are often perceived on the cognitive level, and the same can be said for values and strain. Values all operate through cognitive systems, where individual differences are the key factor. Strains also are in part the product of the perception of the strain (e.g., reports of migraines or pain). So, the question arises: Why a separate dimension for perception? Perhaps, it would be more appropriate to include perception as an integral aspect of each of the other dimensions.

There are two reasons why perception is included in a separate facet of the model. The first reason is two-sided. On one hand, placing perception in a separate facet implies its great importance, over and above objective factors. A resource, say, may exist without the awareness of the resource, but perception of the resource also affects the resource's expression. And on the other hand, placing perception in a separate dimension highlights that objective factors are also important. So, alcoholism will affect the individual whether or not the person is cognizant of being an alcoholic.

The second reason for including perception in a separate dimension of the model is that perception functions in the model similar to connective tissue in living organisms. Perception is one of the three principal mechanisms that tie the separate facets of the model into a unified whole. This function of perception will be discussed next as it relates to the final facet of the model, valence of effect.

Valence of Effect: A Whole Greater than the Parts

The one facet of the model of ecological congruence that is not a dimension is the valence of effect. *Valence of effect* is defined as the directionality of the influence of the interrelationship between needs and resources. The relationship between needs and resources is affected by the inherent elements of these two dimensions in relation to time (developmental and vis-à-vis the event), values, and perception. This facet of the model highlights that the interrelationship between the dimensions of the model is relative and fluid and not fixed. It expresses the concept of fit that others have used (cf. French et al., 1982; R. Caplan, 1983), but does so within the special context of the model of ecological congruence. Thus the fit of resources with needs will either reduce, or not affect, or *increase*, strain to the extent resources meet, do not meet, or interfere with needs, respectively.

What is meant by "the inherent elements" of needs and resources? This belies the model's bias toward objective characteristics of the individual and the environment. Money may help whether or not we perceive it as helpful, say, by purchasing better medical care. Friends may provide support that helps even as we deny its importance and seek to isolate ourselves. Similarly, we may deny the need for water or for relaxation, but dehydration and breakdown will nonetheless occur. So, there is a fit that exists without the influence of perception or values. It exists because of the objective functional relationship between resources and needs.

Valence of effect is not fixed; rather it changes over time in relation to the stressor event and to the development of the organism. This was discussed in detail earlier. At this juncture it is important to emphasize that the fit of resources to needs bends and flows like a river, often repeating itself and often extending into new regions. A husband who nurtures his wife immediately after the death of her parent may be doing just what is needed (meeting needs), but six months later nurturance may inhibit her adjustment and foster dependence and adoption of a prolonged sick role (interference with needs). Young women after mastectomy may need preventive sexual counseling with their spouses (meeting needs) whereas elderly women may find this inappropriate and fear social isolation that comes with illness (not meeting needs).

Values also affect fit and so influence the valence of effect. If there is no value conflict in the fit between resources and needs, this may not be an issue. But when there is value conflict on the personal, societal, family, or constraint level, values will influence the fit. An individual may receive supportive advice of a parent, but feel the need to disregard the advice because it is a forced obligation (Tripathi et al., 1986). In this case, the acceptance of support is prevented because of the value of independence.

On the societal level too, individuals may be discouraged from using one resource or may be pressed into using a second resource. Both types of pressure may affect the valence of effect. Showing extreme sadness (the resource here is the ability to express emotions), for instance, may be the most efficacious response to death (Lindemann, 1944) where there is a need for catharsis. But, men are expected to be "strong" (another resource), despite the fact that such shows of strength may not meet the needs of grieving. So, men will tend not to show their emotions, and indeed they are less likely than women to cry hard or long (Doyle, 1983).

At still other times, individuals are constrained outright from employing their resources; for example, necessary sanctions prevent them from taking direct revenge after they or a loved one has been assaulted. In these instances potential meeting of needs is blocked. One may have the resources to exact retribution, but society forbids it. Victims of crime often attend trials, and there is a recent impetus to give them information on the progress of the trial so that they may indirectly fill their need for retribution. The biblical injunction of "an eye for an eye" is commonly misinterpreted as a spiteful attitude of Old Testament revenge. The intention, if one reads the full passage, was that victims or their families could exact payment commensurate with the worth of what was lost. Loss of an eye, a leg, or a life through negligence, for example, could thus be awarded a financial payment, but no more than proportional compensation could be demanded. In this way, people's needs for retribution were regulated to ensure meeting these needs and, at the same time, to limit excess.

Integrating the dimensions

Three mechanisms tie the dimensions of the model of ecological congruence into a unified whole, thus determining the valence of effect. These are perception, biological links (including instincts), and subconscious processes.

Perception is the first of three mechanisms to influence the valence of effect, as valence of effect is a product of the perceived degree of fit between needs and resources. In this regard, it is postulated that individuals judge the extent to which resources meet, do not meet, or interfere with needs. These judgments are based on past experience, knowledge of the current situation, or expectations as to the future. An important point here is that knowledge is always partial. Individuals are never privy to all the information they need until after the fact, hindsight being so superior to foresight. In part, the effect of stress itself may also limit perception because people may come to premature closure under stress before they have considered all the possibilities (Keinan, 1987; Kruglanski, 1980).

For example, people may select help from a friend in one situation and from a family member in another because of the perceived fit of one kind of support with a given situation. Individuals may also perceive help itself as threatening, and so may see it as not fitting their needs until they experience very high levels of threat of loss. Or a normally independent person may perceive it best to seek advice because of a recent rejection.

Recently, theorists have envisaged coping in terms of management strategies, an approach that underscores the importance of perception and decision making in determining and even altering the valence of effect. Thoits (1986), for example, suggests that individuals use coping strategies in their behavioral or cognitive attempts to ameliorate the effects of stressful encounters. She implies in the concept of management that they do so through a decision-making model based on their assessment of themselves and their environment. Perception helps them sort through the available information on resources, needs, and the particulars of the circumstances to design a strategy of good fit.

The second mechanism that organizes the fit of resources with needs is the biological responses that result from the interaction of demands and resources. These may be called hard-wired responses, although in humans they may be difficult to pinpoint. In this regard, many stress responses are preset biologically. The most basic of these links are the internal physiological responses to external stressors, which include reactions of the immunological system and responses to prolonged heat or extreme cold. These responses obviously occur outside of any awareness or direct behavioral control. The second class of these includes behavioral responses to physiological changes. When they are hungry, for instance, people become agitated and aggressive and seek food in their surroundings in order to alleviate stress.

Finally, it is likely that people also have instinctive behavior that organizes and activates resources in response to social threat. For example, people will react protectively against physical threats, often using resources they did not know they had. It is important to point out, however, that such thinking is based primarily on nonhuman research that was generalized to the human case (see Hinde, 1966; Tinbergen, 1951).

Spielberger (1986) suggested that anger, for example, may be a remnant of such a prewired response with particular functional correlates that affected evolution of our species. Bowlby (1973) also suggested that people may instinctually seek intimacy in the face of danger and that those who had this coded in their genes would have had a distinct survival advantage in evolutionary time.

The last mechanism that is viewed as linking and organizing the different dimensions is subconscious processes. An example of this is manifested in the all-or-nothing response in the case of psychological shock. In such cases as conversion reactions to combat exposure, for instance, the subconscious protects the ego by blocking recall of the traumatic event. Bowlby (1973; 1980) also argues that early attachment experiences are important in determining how we react to loss in adulthood and what we do to compensate for losses. For instance, individuals who experienced early loss may isolate themselves in response to threat of rejection. In similar circumstances, other individuals who had warm, consistent early attachments may seek social attachments. In either case, the valence of effect is influenced by early learned material.

Silverman and Weinberger (1985) illustrated in their unusual research the positive psychological effects of being exposed to subliminal presentation of the sentence, "Mommy and I are one." In a careful, replicated series of experiments, they showed that exposure to this stimulus provided emotional benefits, but exposure to other, similar cues did not (e.g., "Mother and I are one"). This suggests that the expression of oneness with the "good" mother of early childhood has a deeply rooted relationship with sense of well-being. The resource, mother, and one's inseparability with her seem to have a subconscious quality that aids individuals' adjustment. Obviously, we know less about what is occurring here than I am speculating, but the possibilities are exciting.

Many apparently subconscious mechanisms may be described in cognitive terms, but that does not mean that cognitions are the true determinants of behavior. I return to the thesis that psychodynamic theory has not been disproven and that the wholesale adoption of the cognitive model by many stress theorists is just as much a marriage of convenience as it is the product of empirical analysis. We need to study and compare psychodynamic and cognitive interpretations of stress responses if we are to achieve the answers to such questions. Theorists will need to include, as I do here, the possibility of such operating systems as the subconscious and the ego. My own bias favors the cognitive end of the continuum, but I feel that I would be academically overstating my case if I were a purist in this regard.

I would also like to propose a more cautious psychodynamic approach. On one hand, behaviorists and the new cognitive behaviorists have been disgruntled with the lack of objective evidence for many psychodynamic constructs. However, cognitive theorists themselves leave unexplained most of the variance in the outcomes they study.

What might fill this explanatory gap is emotion-motivated behavior. While we may never be able to measure some psychodynamic concepts, emotions can be studied. These emotions may be the products of cognitive processes, but it would appear that emotions may precede cognition (Zajonc, 1980; 1984). Moreover, emotions may override dominant cognitions, since people so often act against their own rational or irrational assessment of what they should do. To the extent that emotions precede or override cognitions in determining behavior, one may imply that internal dynamic processes affect individuals' thoughts and actions. I would therefore suggest that *emotiodynamics* be used as a provisional label for the motivational basis of behavior that rests in emotion. Only research on this topic will clarify whether such an approach is justified, but a mounting literature suggests that emotions play a substantial role in behavior (Zajonc, 1980; 1984).

SUMMARY

The model of ecological congruence was delineated. A model of stress resistance is important because a limited number of models have been presented and compared, and none of these models has been found wholly satisfactory. Two types of models have been presented previously. These are the factor-process models of stress resistance and the fit models of person-environment compatibility.

The factor-process models are seen in the work of Lazarus and colleagues (Lazarus, 1966; Lazarus & Folkman, 1984) and of Kobasa and colleagues (Gentry & Kobasa, 1984; Kobasa et al., 1981). According to Kobasa, personality hardiness and other personal traits (the factors) influence transformational coping (the process). In transformational coping individuals differ in how they interpret the meaning of events in their environment. More hardy individuals, for instance, tend to interpret events as controllable and as a challenge. Lazarus, in turn, sees the factors that affect outcome as situational and individual attributes;

he calls these causal antecedents. Appraisal and coping are the processes in his model that determine how these causal antecedents affect outcome. Appraisal refers to the evaluations of the nature of the stressor and its relevance to the individual. Coping refers to the cognitive and behavioral efforts to manage demands that are appraised as threatening.

Lazarus has argued that trait models like Kobasa's assume too much consistency in the relationship between personal traits and behaviors. He argues that coping is more idiosyncratic. Kobasa has argued that hardiness is related to a fairly consistent style of coping, and that as a multidimensional trait it predicts a wider constellation of behaviors than would any single trait. S. Cohen and Edwards (in press) also suggest that a number of personal resources would more likely predict a fuller set of stress responses than would any single trait.

Person–environment fit models of stress resistance have been less well delineated, but the proposed P-E fit model of French et al. (1974), revised by R. Caplan (1983), has been heuristic and shown to have moderate support in a wide variety of settings. This approach defines stress as the lack of fit between the person and the environment and emphasizes both the objective and the subjective nature of that fit. Most recently, R. Caplan has modified the model, arguing that persons judge their current, past, and future fit and that the combination of these judgments determines their stress resistance and efficacy.

Both factor-process and person-environment fit models of stress resistance envisage cognitions as important and emphasize that stress is a product of a mismatch between threat or demand and coping capacity. The P-E fit model places greater emphasis on objective factors and on the embeddedness of individuals in the environment than do the factor-process models.

A third model that, in part, combines properties of the factor-process and P-E fit models was presented—the model of ecological congruence (Hobfoll, 1985a, 1986b). This model outlines the major parameters involved in stress resistance and emphasizes cognitive, biological, and unconscious processes that operate in reactions to stress. The concept of congruence implies that resources, needs, strain, values, and perception interact to form either a fit, a misfit, or a lack of fit. This degree of fit determines the outcome of attempts to resist the detrimental effects of stress. Together with the model of conservation of resources presented earlier, it forms a comprehensive theory of stress and human behavior.

The five dimensions of the model were detailed next. Resources, the first dimension, were defined as those objects, personal characteristics, conditions, or energies that are valued by the individual or that serve as a means for attainment of these objects, personal characteristics, conditions, or energies. Objects are envisaged as material resources; conditions are the roles people fill (e.g., mother, partner, executive); personal characteristics refer to traits, stable tendencies, and skills; and energies are those states or objects whose value lies in their convertibility to desired objects or states (e.g., money, credit, being owed favors). It was proposed that the value of these resources is determined by their global worth as assessed by the individual or group, their replenishability if expended, their investibility to achieve more resources or more valued resources, and the extent of risk when they must be used to forestall or minimize loss of other valued resources.

Strain, the second dimension, was defined as the negative effect of stressful events, i.e., the outcome of stress. Two types of strain were delineated, psychological and physical; however, recent research suggests a broad overlap between the two. It was further proposed that particular strains may occur in response to particular types of stressors. Researchers have not generally tried to match strain with the type of stress under investigation, but where attempts to match have been undertaken significant progress in describing the course of stress resistance has been accomplished.

The third dimension of the model of ecological congruence is the needs dimension. It was reasoned that environmental events and internal needs interact to form demands on those experiencing stress. Whereas most stress theories have concentrated on external threats as the stimuli that tax individuals' resistance resources, the model of ecological congruence argues that threats only become actualized when they interact with internal needs. This approach led to two derivatives of the model. First, the evaluation of stimuli as threatening is a product of external events and internal needs. Second, threat (environmental) and response capacity (internal) can never be entirely separated, since the very awareness of a threat signifies the sensitivity of the individual. Seen this way, both the needs of the individual and the inherent properties of the event are assigned importance in an understanding of event stressfulness. Finally, the notion that demand refers to the requirement for some emotional or behavioral response to stress was presented.

Time is the next dimension of the model. Time was depicted both developmentally and in terms of the temporal distance from the stressful event. In the first instance, it was suggested that stress affects individuals differently depending on their stage of emotional and physical development. Elderly women will be affected differently by mastectomy than will young women, although the two groups will also certainly have some common reactions. In terms of time vis-à-vis the event, the needs of individuals were seen to change as time passes, both while anticipating and following a stressful event. In this regard, stress was seen not as a static single event but as an evolving transition to new circumstances.

The emphasis on time also led to a discussion of the need to conduct research such that time vis-à-vis the event can be delineated. The life-events list approach, which combines events that occurred over a broad span of time, was seen as obfuscating an understanding of the critical influence of time in stress resistance. Instead, it was proposed that research designs that compare individuals in different stressful circumstances and that follow individuals over the course of their adjustment will be more informative than the stressful-event list approach.

Values, the fourth dimension of the model, were seen as the most complex and least well-understood facet of the model of ecological congruence. Values were defined as the principal set of standards by which the individual measures the self and the environment. Three spheres of values were seen as influencing stress resistance: societal and family values, individual values, and societal constraints. Societal and family values affect how we define our world and how we will react to events in our lives. Furthermore, the resources we may use to counteract threat are limited by values. Individuals also create personalized value systems that must be understood if more precise prediction of outcome of the response of any given individual in a particular circumstance is to be achieved. The influence of values is most blatant when values are expressed as societal constraints. Examples of this include abortion and divorce laws, occupational standards, and sexist educational or business practices.

The final dimension of the model, perception, was defined as cognitive processes that involve the assessment of environmental events, resulting in individual differences in the interpretation of the personal meaning of the event. The model of ecological congruence sees perception as important, but also emphasizes that objective elements of the environment, properties of emotions, and biological factors are not to be ignored. It was argued that many theories may be overemphasizing the influence of perception and bending the evidence to support their case.

The five dimensions of the model of ecological congruence were seen as interconnected by three mechanisms to determine what was called the valence of effect. The three mechanisms were perception, biological links (including instincts), and subconscious processes. In this regard, the fit of resources with needs, and the influence of values and time on this fit, are determined at times by perceptions of the separate facets, at other times by fixed biological responses that emerge in the needs–resource interaction, and in other instances by the emergence of responses rooted in subconscious processes. The special role of emotions was discussed in this context.

In the coming chapters the models of conservation of resources and of ecological congruence will be used as an analytical backdrop to aid the understanding of research on social and personal resources. It should not be expected, however, that any given study will touch on all or even most of the aspects of the model, but I would argue that the more facets of the model reflected in a study, the better the investigation. Hopefully, the model will also be heuristic and encourage more ecological investigation of stress response in future years.

4

SOCIAL SUPPORT AND STRESS: SEARCHING FOR A CONTEXT

Thou wert my guide, philosopher, and friend.

(Alexander Pope, 1809–1849)

"If everybody minded their own business," said the Duchess in a hoarse growl, "the world would go round a deal faster than it does."

(Lewis Carroll, *Alice in Wonderland*, 1832–1898)

Social support is the focus of this chapter. Before entering into a critical review of the literature on social support, however, I will discuss the reason for a search for an environmental variable to explain the unexpectedly modest relationship between stressors and strain. I will argue that it is consistent with the scientific biases and world view of researchers that an environmental variable like social support is a catholicon that counteracts the deleterious effects of stress. Social support, in this regard, fits a number of expectations about the kind of natural resource that could succeed where psychotherapy and ego-strength have failed. Hopefully, by uncovering the roots of the interest in social support we can establish a broader and deeper theoretical and empirical base for future social support research. This will also help us understand what information is already at hand.

In uncovering the roots of social support the discussion will also lead to the greater context of personal relationships. If we forget that social support is essentially a function of personal ties, we are likely to lose sight of the fact that personal relationships, and therefore social support, engender both costs and rewards. In the perspective of personal relationships it becomes clear, as well, that social support interactions also have histories and futures and that they too are products of socialization and experience.

This connection between social support and personal relationships will also lead to questions concerning personal resources and their interaction with social support. People's social ties do not exist independently of their personal characteristics. The two are interactive and intercausative and when studied together contribute toward a fuller research approximation of the models that it is hoped this volume will develop.

In all of this discussion, the models of conservation of resources and of ecological congruence will be used in the search for a comprehensive stress-stress resistance theory. A central goal will be to tap these models with the aim of emerging with a holistic view of support that bridges from the diffuse nature of personal relationships to the circumscribed nature of the actual resources that serve the individual—the objects, conditions, personal characteristics, and energies that meet people's needs to offset and forestall loss.

The first section of the chapter addresses the stress-mediating role of social support. The chapter begins with an examination of the scientific and philosophical roots of the search for environmental explanations of behavior, which led to the excitement over the social support concept. This is followed by an historical account of the benefits of social ties during stressful times. Next, the modern study of social support is considered, and leading questions concerning the stress-mediating role of social support are discussed. The second section of the chapter addresses the role of social support in the context of personal relationships. Research and theory regarding intimacy, loneliness, reactions to victims of crisis, and sex differences in social support behavior are considered. Consistent with the viewpoint that depicts social support within the wider context of personal relationships, the negative side of social support is addressed next. Finally, the concept of social support is examined vis-à-vis the model of conservation of resources, in an attempt to uncover the active ingredients of social support.

ENVIRONMENTAL BIAS IN UNDERSTANDING STRAIN

Following the original work of Holmes and Rahe (1967) on the negative health sequelae of an accumulation of stressful experiences, there was an explosion of interest in the effects of stressful life events. Typically, however, researchers uncovered a much weaker relationship between stressors and strain than had originally been anticipated, seldom accounting for as much as 10 percent of the variance between the predictor and the criterion (Rabkin & Streuning, 1976). The failure of the data to meet expectations of the potency of stressful events provided impetus for the search for stress resistance resources, resources that might explain why stressors did not lead more precipitously to strain. Let us consider for a moment why these larger effects had been expected.

Psychodynamic Theory, Adult Experience, and Psychopathology

Since Freud, American and European psychodynamic psychology was motivated by a belief in intrapsychic causes of emotional disorder. Psychopathology was understood to be a product of crises in early childhood experience. Anxiety, depression, neurosis, and psychosis were (and still are) seen as rooted in early traumatic encounters. It was accepted that current events or events at any time in adulthood might exacerbate these disorders, but contemporary events were not seen as causing psychopathology. Events during adulthood were understood to act only as triggers that released underlying psychopathology. In fact, even the event was not envisioned as the active ingredient, but rather it was what the event symbolized vis-à-vis childhood memories.

A creeping belief that current events experienced during adulthood might cause psychological disorder can be seen emerging in the literature even in Freud's own work. Freud (1916–1917), for instance, related conversion reactions in soldiers to their war experiences, and he did report a few cases in which traumatic experiences in adulthood resulted in pathological symptomatology. Freud acknowledged in his lectures on these topics that psychopathology could follow stressful adult experience but noted that such instances were rare.

As mentioned in Chapter 1, Horney (1937) made much more of the effect of current experiences on psychopathology than did her contemporaries. Indeed, she was roundly criticized. On coming to America she was struck that many men who appeared free of early childhood trauma and whose past would not lead to the expectation that disorder would follow were, nevertheless, exhibiting symptoms of psychopathology. She noted that many of these men appeared depressed and showed signs of sexual dysfunction. She concluded that the great economic depression was having a devastating effect on their psyches. The confrontation with failure, unemployment, and loss of status that so many men were experiencing was undermining the ego-strength that had been gained in childhood.

Behaviorism, Environmentalism, and Social Equality

During this same period, American academic psychologists were beginning to adopt an environmental framework in their understanding of human behavior. Not only were they emphasizing environmental interpretations of behavior, they were deemphasizing any shared role of instinctual and internal constructs. This movement became known as behaviorism and by the 1960s was a strong contender for the allegiance of psychologists.

Behaviorism was, and continues to be, appealing on two planes. First, and foremost, it could be successfully studied empirically because all of the constructs involved are observable (Skinner, 1938). This met the emerging American need to place psychology in the realm of science and outside the realm of philosophy and faith. Such constructs as ego and repression were clouded in mystique and difficult to measure, but reinforcers and incremental increases in carefully described behaviors were clear and given to tight experimental study (A. A. Lazarus, 1971; Ulman & Krasner, 1969). Science is motivated by the will to understand causal mechanisms, and experiments could be conducted illustrating the causal relations between reinforcers and behaviors.

A second reason that environmental theories were gaining currency in America was philosophical. Behaviorism was anathema to the communist world, but it was highly congruent with the American Dream. This dream entailed the belief that any child could grow into "rich man, poor man, beggar man, thief" (Watson, 1928) given the right environment. Instinctual theories and frameworks that purport the primacy and immutability of early childhood experience are in many ways antiegalitarian. American liberalism, in contrast, allows that everyone should have a fair chance; it should not matter who one's parents were, into what class one was born, or from what background one came.

This philosophical bent was catalyzed by America's confrontation with Nazism in World War II. The returning psychologists and those who were to become psychologists were bent on proving that people were molded from their environment and that genetics did not explain superiority or inferiority. It is not surprising that the nature-versus-nurture controversies surrounding intelligence research (Jensen, 1980; Kamin, 1976; Loehlin, Lindsey, & Spuhler, 1975) were the most combative that psychology has ever known. Jensen proposed that intelligence was largely hereditary and that blacks and other ethnic groups were genetically inferior to whites. It is notable that his lectures were boycotted and that they were labeled on campuses as promoting neo-Nazi theories. Kamin, taking the nurture side of the controversy, countered Jensen and argued that any difference in intelligence could be explained by environmental factors. Most psychologists were clearly on the nurture side of this argument, as reflected in the clear predominance of nurture research in psychological journals of this period.

Add to these attitudes of fair chance the liberalism that emerged in the early 1960s. Psychologists were deeply involved in the ideals of John F. Kennedy and became active participants in the liberal programs of Johnson's Great Society that put the Kennedy principles into action. What was the basis of these principles? Clearly, it was that the causes of societal ills were environmental and that by changing the environment we could eradicate these problems. The problems spanned the continuum from individual to cultural, and the Great Society was to put an end to racism, poverty, and much of mental illness, too. These goals were reflected in the programs that evolved into national efforts through legislation and a substantial reapportioning of tax expenditures.

Psychologists and educators, who were very psychologically biased, entered in great force into programs such as Head Start, the Job Corps, and a comprehensive national network of community mental health centers. Indeed, Division 27 of the American Psychological Association, the Division of Community Psychology, was established precisely to aid these efforts, and its philosophy was deeply rooted in environmentalism as a cause of individual and societal ills and as the principal route to recovery. Many psychologists also became involved in the Society for the Study of Social Issues, which shared a similar ideology. Similar movements came into being in psychiatry, nursing, medicine, and applied sociology and anthropology.

Humanism: The Other Environmentalism

A second, very different, environmentally oriented approach was also emerging within clinical psychology during this time. Stemming from work by such theorists as Adler, Frankl, May, and Maslow, a new trend called humanistic psychology was on the upsurge. This approach was clearly represented by Carl Rogers' personality theory and client-centered therapy. Rogers' thesis was that people were basically good, if anything, and that their development depended on their interaction with "important others." If these important others loved and nurtured them and gave them "unconditional positive regard" then they would develop self-esteem and the ability to master life's tasks. If, on the other hand, people found that they were devalued by others, or valued only because of their acts and deeds and not because of who they were, they were likely to become depersonalized and psychologically alienated from themselves.

In Rogers' writings we find the seeds of a theory of social support. Rogers posits that social support consists of positive social interactions that validate a person's feelings, fears, and thoughts. It continues to do so throughout the life span, affecting the individual's ongoing development. Rogers' adaptation of this model to the context of psychotherapy was also evolutionary. Rather than an interpreter of dreams and a distant, neutral, analytical figure, the therapist was trained to validate people's sense of self and self-esteem.

Such thinking worked to demystify the therapeutic process, bringing it out of the hidden veils of psychodynamic theory. In fact, Truax and Carkhuff (1967) borrowed from Rogers' work to uncover the components of the "natural helping personality." The implication of their work, and what made it different from past thinking, was that the attributes inherent in the helping personality were not acquired over years of postgraduate training. Instead, these traits were found naturally in certain persons who exhibited empathy and communicated nonjudgmental positive regard of others.

This work, in turn, led to the use of paraprofessionals, the first "sanctioned" carriers of social support other than professional therapists (Mitchell, 1982). Interventionists were selected for their natural helping abilities, and a new type of mental health worker was born, one whose influence was attributed not to the ability to interpret childhood trauma but to the capacity to provide a healthful social environment for those who lacked this. Paraprofessionals could speak the language of the target population because they were matched with the population so as to increase understanding of the target group's problems.

This movement has important implications for the current discussion because it marks the transition from professional to nonprofessional helping and represents a change in the belief of mental health workers about the active ingredient of therapy. Professional therapists affected individuals by interpreting internal events and by understanding complex psychological concepts of therapy; these skills required long years of study and training to acquire. Paraprofessionals, in turn, influenced patients and clients by virtue of their empathy, presence, and fit with the characteristics of the client group, and did so equally as well as professionals (Durlak, 1979). Certainly, professionals could do this too, but empathy was not what was being taught in residencies and graduate schools. Such thinking spurred a pyramidal service model, wherein professional mental health workers functioned as supervisors, and paraprofessionals functioned as front-line workers (Seidman & Rappaport, 1974).

Gathering all of this into context, we can see that American psychology was moving away from instinctual and biological theories to explain personality and behavior and moving beyond a view of childhood as the shaper sine qua non of the self. Behaviorism, the liberal sociopolitical environment, and humanism formed a Weltanschauung that rejected the thesis that psychopathology was predetermined in childhood or birth and that once it emerged it was intransmutable. In this new context, environmental factors were viewed as the antecedents of behavior and personality, and all aspects of the self were considered to be malleable throughout the life span.

Social Support: An Environmental Answer to an Environmental Question

Findings that psychopathology and physical illness (Kobasa, 1979; Nuckolls, Cassel, & Kaplan, 1972), were products of environmentally occurring stressful events rather than of early childhood experiences or instincts, deeply resonated with this gestalt. It added weight to arguments against psychodynamic theory, which was already being attacked by the behaviorists because it was more philosophical than scientific and because traditional therapy did not alleviate symptoms any better than would occur by spontaneous recovery alone (Eysenck, 1952, 1961). It also was tremendously egalitarian. Everyone experienced stressors; they were a ubiquitous part of people's lives. It was a very fair way to see psychopathology and illness.

The methodology that became the standard paradigm for stress research was also quite straightforward. One could, it seemed, measure the events occurring in people's lives and correlate them with resultant psychopathology. Because this could be done with paper and pencil tests, it was also possible to gain large samples for relatively little cost. Fairly early on a few investigators were more cautious about this paper-and-pencil methodology (Brown, 1974), but hundreds of studies followed the paradigm.

Rabkin and Streuning (1976), in an important paper published in *Science,* reviewed the literature on stressful life events and came to the conclusion that the relation between stressful events and distress was modest, at best. This led researchers to realize what should have been obvious at the beginning: the stress process is complex. More specifically, it led to a search for variables that might mediate the stress–distress link:

resistance resources. The logic here was that although stressors have deleterious effects on some people, certain personal or social resources moderate the stress–distress link for others, thus attenuating this relationship.

SOCIAL SUPPORT AND STRESS RESISTANCE

In the previous discussion we saw that investigators were biased toward environmental explanations of psychopathology and, to some extent, of physical illness as well. Following the *Science* article and the publication of the landmark volume *Stressful Life Events: Their Nature and Effects* (Dohrenwend & Dohrenwend, 1974), in which many of the contributors came to the same conclusion as did Rabkin and Streuning, a great surge of research began in the search for such a resistance resource. Energy quickly focused on social support, which seemed consistent with what people felt about stress in their own lives. Friends and family helped during crises, and social ties were an important aspect of the cultural milieu of the 1960s and early 1970s. Recall the popular Beatles' tune that became the hallmark of a generation, "All you need is love."

As often occurs in research, the first work on social support was not very sound, methodologically. Nor was what was meant by social support rigorously measured. However, important theoretical groundwork was made by theorists who discussed the concept and proposed how it might moderate the stress-distress relationship (G. Caplan, 1974; Cobb, 1976; Dean & Lin, 1977). Before discussing empirical investigations of the effects of social support, it is instructive to review early thinking on the helpfulness of social ties during stressful circumstances.

Early Thinking on Supportive Benefit of Social Ties

Prior to the surge of social support research that occurred in the 1970s and continues today, those interested in stress had already discussed social support in fairly clear terms. In Jewish ritual following the death of a loved one, which was codified in biblical times, social support is obligated of family, friends, and bereaved. Burial must occur soon after death, but may be postponed so that close family can arrive, if they come with reasonable dispatch. Already, here, their participation in a social grief process is emphasized. The community is expected to prepare the corpse for burial, and every Jewish community is commanded to have a Sacred Society for this purpose. This is an excellent example of more distant support that typifies what S. B. Sarason (1974) called the "psychological sense of community." Following burial, close family come to the home of the grieved where the mourners congregate together, that is, decide on a common house of mourning. After the initial period more distant family and friends must come and pay their respects. It is also emphasized that social support may be detrimental to the bereaved and proscriptions that discourage dependency or adoption of a prolonged sick role are carefully detailed.

Social support has also been a part of military thinking throughout the ages. In the first century A.D., the Greek general Anasander advised the military commander to station "brothers in rank beside brothers, friends beside friends, and lovers beside their favorites" (cited in Kellett, 1982). The concept of troop cohesion as essential to military functioning has been reinforced over the centuries. Observations during the First and Second World Wars continued to confirm such thinking (Shils & Janowitz, 1948). It should also be noted that the negative side of social support is also defined in military thinking. Officers traditionally keep reasonable social distance from their men, and wounded who have social ties have often been separated to discourage a process whereby individual misery is combined into group malcontent.

Modern work that begins to look more empirical was carried out in an important paper on victims of severe poliomyelitis, published in 1961 by Visotsky, Hambur, Goss, and Lebovitz. They wrote,

> *Those patients who were visited quite early and often by reliable, warm, respectful relatives and friends were consistently among those who were best adjusted by any reasonable standard. The presence of such people did much to prevent the patient from being overwhelmed in the acute phase. (p. 427)*

They went on to say, "A patient's capacity to make friends with other patients and to be integrated into the patient group was an important variable in determining adjustment in the Respiratory Center (p. 434)." And speaking of adjustment to chronic stress they stated:

> *Now, perhaps even more than before, the depth of significant relations was tested, and the resourcefulness of those who meant a great deal to the patient had a crucial bearing on outcome. The sustaining qualities of interaction with family and close friends continued to be of great importance. (p. 436; © 1981, American Medical Association)*

Visotsky and colleagues were not blind, however, to the negative potential of social support. They discussed, for example, how friendships with other patients exposed people to the stress of others, which compounded their own personal grief. Family ties were also seen as potentially threatening because they highlighted the patients' doubts as to whether they could continue in their former role. Visotsky and colleagues further cautioned that supporters may be so busy meeting their own needs that they encourage mutual avoidance of threatening contingencies. In a specific example they cited family members who wanted so much to make the patient comfortable that they failed to encourage her to leave the tank and to attempt new steps.

Visotsky et al.'s key paper is seldom cited in the research on social support. However, it is clearly a critical paper in the development of an understanding of the complex effects of social support on stress resistance. Indeed, lessons these investigators learned from their polio patients were lost on the early research on social support, which we will see tended to ignore the negative potential of supportive ties. Like Jewish bereavement ritual and military strategists, however, Visotsky and colleagues were keenly aware of the positive and negative aspects of social support, even if their approach was mainly observable.

Modern Study of Social Support

Defining social support

Social support has been defined in nearly as many ways as it has been studied. In one sense, social support is a catchall term reflecting that "right stuff" that is gained by being socially connected. In another sense, social support consists of those interactions in which functionally meaningful support occurs between people. Whereas some have attempted to separate the two views it will be argued that there is broad overlap between them.

One of the original thinkers to discuss the importance of social support was Gerald Caplan (1974). He wrote that social support is helpful because it provides the individual with feedback, validation, and a sense that one can master one's environment. He added that social support provides material resources that individuals are lacking. Cobb (1976), another early theorist, argued that social support is beneficial because it provides information about being loved, esteemed, and valued members of a social network. Caplan's definition has functional as well as ego components, and this will be seen in the direction taken by some researchers. Cobb's model is essentially cognitive and, again, this is seen in the bias of other operationalizations of the social support construct.

A more action-oriented and specific interpretation of social support was introduced by House (1981). He reasoned that social support involves an actual transaction between two or more people in which emotional concern, instrumental aid, information, or appraisal transpire. Shumaker and Brownell (1984) also defined social support within an action orientation as an "exchange between at least two individuals perceived by the provider or the recipient to be intended to enhance the well-being of the recipient" (p. 13). This functional focus can also be seen in the work of Sheldon Cohen, who has carried out a number of reviews of the social support literature (Cohen & McKay, 1984; Cohen & Wills, 1985).

In a paper I coauthored with Stokes (Hobfoll & Stokes, in press), we argued that social integration and socially supportive interactions were two aspects of the general case of social support. *Social integration* should be viewed as the state of connectedness of individuals to significant others. Furthermore, Shumaker and Brownell's definition should be focused on defining social support *interactions* in particular and not social support in general. We thus defined social support as *those social interactions or relationships that provide individuals with actual assistance or that embed individuals within a social system believed to provide love, caring, or a sense of attachment to a valued social group or dyad.* Social support would then encompass both aspects of social support: social connectedness and supportive interactions. For the purpose of this chapter and the remainder of this volume I will rely on this integrated definition of social support.

Early research on social assets

Although it is important to define social support if we are to begin discussing related research, it should be emphasized that early research on the topic only vaguely followed the thinking represented in the aforementioned definitions. Even before attempts were made to define social support and to clarify how social support might mitigate the negative effects of stress, a milestone study was undertaken that asked searching questions on the topic. Nuckolls, Cassel, and Kaplan (1972) studied the moderating effects on stress of what they called "psychosocial assets." In a longitudinal study of pregnant women they were interested in how complications of pregnancy might be affected by life change and how the relation between life change and complications might be moderated by possessing psychosocial assets.

This study had a number of methodological flaws. There was appreciable attrition of the original sample, the subjects were all wives of men associated with the military, and the psychosocial assets scale contained items that tapped self-esteem as well as social support. Nonetheless, the results were novel and heuristic. The findings are presented in Figure 4.1, where the following can be noted: 1) life change was not directly associated with complications of pregnancy; 2) psychosocial assets were not directly associated with complications of pregnancy; but 3) the combination of high life change during and before pregnancy, when combined with low psychosocial assets, were associated with at least 34 percent more complications than exhibited by the next highest risk group.

The Nuckolls study focused on whether social support acts only as a resistance factor (i.e., buffering the adverse impact of exposure to stressors) or whether social support had a direct effect upon symptoms (i.e., contributing to well-being independent of stress levels). This became the central question in social support research, even to the point

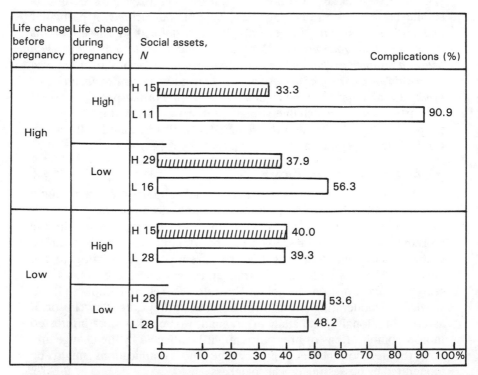

FIGURE 4.1 Effects of stressful events and social assets on pregnancy complications (expressed as percent with complications). High = ▨ ; Low = ☐

of disinterest in other equally important issues. It is instructive to consider examples of both the direct effect and the stress-buffering effect, and these will be presented in the next section.

Stress-Buffering and Direct Effects

A number of methods have been used to determine whether social support *directly* affects well-being independent of stress levels or *interactively* affects well-being, the latter termed a stress-buffering effect. The direct-effect hypothesis suggests that social support has an equivalent positive impact on well-being under high and low stress conditions, stemming from the overall salutary effect of healthy social relations on individuals. The stress-buffering effect, in contrast, suggests that social support has greater positive impact under high stress than under low stress conditions. Stress buffering would occur, accordingly, because under high stress people are especially likely to call on and respond to attempts at aid and the sustenance provided by close ties. Furthermore, it is reasoned that under high stress, supporters would be increasingly likely to offer aid and to provide intensive levels of helping.

One could graph these relationships by placing stress level on the horizontal axis and strain level (e.g., depression, physical symptoms) on the vertical axis. Our third variable (social support) is depicted by two separate lines, one for high social support and one for low social support (usually split at the median halfway point). The direct effect, then, would look like two parallel lines, as may be seen in Figure 4.2a. This is because those with more social support react with less strain than those with low social support, *at all levels of stress*. The high social support group has no increased advantage over the low social support group at high as opposed to low stress levels. We could say that the advantage of the high social support group over the low social support group is constant (hence the parallel line).

A stress-buffering effect would be represented, in turn, by two diverging lines. The high social support individuals react with only limited strain as stressors increase (hence a moderate slope). The low social support individuals react with a steep increase in strain as stress increases (hence a steep line) seen in Figure 4.2b. Statistically, this emerges as an interaction effect.

Researchers discussing the stress-buffering effect have suggested that only the above interaction denotes a true stress-buffering effect (Cohen & Edwards, in press). However, a stress-buffering effect may take place with parallel reactions among high and low social support groups. This has seldom been noted in the literature (Hobfoll &

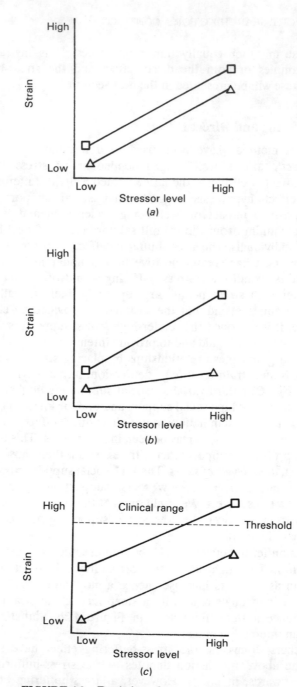

FIGURE 4.2 Depiction of stress-buffering versus direct effects. Low social support = □ ; high social support = △).

Walfisch, 1986), but is theoretically possible. This type of stress-buffering effect is illustrated in Figure 4.2c. Although the high and low social support groups react similarly to increasing levels of stressors, the high social support group begins from a lower initial point. Consequently, if we can conceptualize some danger zone or threshold beyond which higher levels of strain enter into the "clinical range," where we would have a diagnosable disorder, say, then the low social support group crosses this line at lower levels of stress than the high social support group. Indeed the high social support group may not enter into the danger zone at all. True to the stress-buffering hypothesis, what we have here is a case with no differential effect noted for high and low social support groups under low stress levels (both were below the threshold). However, under high stress only the low social support group passed the critical levels of distress. One might argue that no clear threshold or danger zone exists. Clearly, however, there are levels of distress below which individuals continue to function and above which they do not, even if these levels are not finely demarcated.

Direct Effect and Stress-Buffering Effect: Research

Few controversies have catalyzed more research than the question of whether social support directly contributes to well-being or differentially aids those experiencing high stress more than those with low stress. The question is important both because science seeks the "truth" and because finding one or another effect to be true holds implications for design of intervention. Direct effects would suggest the need to generally enhance social support, for example, whereas stress-buffering effects would indicate a need to target groups at high risk for exposure to stress. To clarify some of these issues an extended example of a study that supports each of the proposed models will be presented.

A direct- or main-effect view of social support has been found in a number of studies (Andrews, Tennant, Hewson, & Vaillant, 1978; Aneshensel & Frerichs, 1982; Lin, Ensel, Simeone, & Kuo, 1979). Let us look closely at the study by Williams, Ware, and Donald (1981) because it has a number of methodological strengths.

Williams and colleagues gathered data from 2,234 persons living in Seattle, Washington. The study sample generally represented the Seattle population. Questionnaires were sent on two occasions, approximately one year apart. They were self-administered, and return rates exceeded 90 percent.

Two measures of environmental stressors were assessed: physical limitations and unfavorable life events. Social support was assessed using a brief measure that tapped the availability of close personal ties and community attachments (e.g., religious participation). Strain was measured with a scale that assessed anxiety, depression, and positive well-being over the past month.

Social support was found to directly contribute to better mental health. No significant interaction of stress and social support or physical limitations and social support on mental health were observed. When this model was tested on the second half of the sample for purposes of cross-validation it was confirmed.

A plot of the mean mental health scores for nine groups differing in levels of social support and life events is presented in Figure 4.3. In this figure there is no crossover of the lines and their slope tends to be parallel. These are good indications of direct rather than stress-buffering effects, because the latter are interactive and hence either crossover of lines or unequal slopes would be observed.

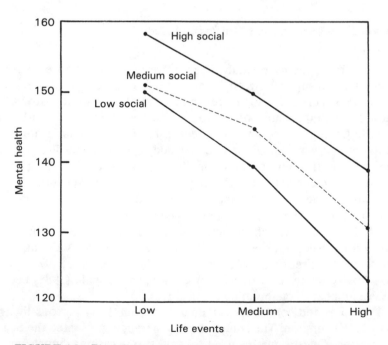

FIGURE 4.3   Plot of mean mental health scores for nine groups differing in levels of social support and life events. (Used by permission from Williams, Ware, & Donald, 1981.)

Reviewing this study's findings one can see that social support contributes to well-being, but that it does not aid individuals more if they are experiencing more extensive stressors than if they are experiencing less extensive stressors. The large sample size, careful prospective methodology, and cross-validation support the validity and generalizability of the findings. It is also important that initial levels of mental health were controlled and that stressors attributable both to stressful events and to physical limitations were examined.

Other studies, however, have found stress-buffering effects of social support (Brown, Bhrolcrain, & Harris, 1975; S. Cohen & Hoberman, 1983; Paykel et al., 1980; Henderson, 1981; Pearlin, Leiberman, Menaghan, & Mullan, 1981; Wilcox, 1981). A particularly interesting study by Norbeck and Tilden (1983) will be detailed to illustrate this model. This study uses a particularly sound methodology and gives an example of how physical health complications may be studied.

Norbeck and Tilden sampled pregnant women between the ages of 20 and 39 years who were free from a history of pregnancy-related health problems, free from other major health problems (e.g., diabetes, cardiac disease), and currently free from severe maternal malnourishment or drug abuse. Women were at between 12 and 20 weeks of gestation at the time of recruitment into the study. Subjects completed an initial questionnaire, a follow-up questionnaire, and consented to a review of their medical charts.

Norbeck and Tilden measured undesirable life experiences, social support, and emotional distress. Pregnancy complications were scored from careful chart review. Complications included gestation complications; labor, delivery, and postpartum complications; and infant complications. Such complications occur in somewhat over 50 percent of women.

Only direct effects were found for social support on emotional distress. Focusing on pregnancy complications, however, revealed that the interaction of life stress during pregnancy and the tangible support factor was significant for each type of complication. For both gestation and infant complications, the interaction was consistent with the stress-buffering hypothesis, the interaction accounting for between 5 and 9 percent of the variance in the criterion.

Two factors make this study a model for future research. First, it is important that different assessment techniques were used to assess independent and dependent variables. By measuring predictors using self-report and the health criteria using medical records, a spurious association between independent and dependent variables owing to commonality of method of measurement is avoided. Second, focusing on psychological and health factors guards against the problem that predictor and criterion variables might be correlated merely because they are two aspects of the same construct. Low self-esteem, for instance, may not be so much a predictor of depression as it is an aspect of depression. Infant complications, in contrast, cannot be construed as being another way of looking at social support. Both of these factors contribute to our ability to infer causal ordering of the variables.

Which Effect is the True Effect?

There has been much ado about whether the direct effect or the stress-buffering effect represents the true contribution of social support. Recently, however, the focus has shifted to differential contributions of social support, depending on the type of social support being measured and the fit of support to the stressor at hand. Here, there is increasing consensus that direct effects and stress-buffering effects both occur, but at what point they occur depends on an interaction, as yet not determined, of individual, kind of social support, and environmental conditions.

Cohen and Wills (1985) noted two trends in their thorough review of the social support literature. First, when social support measures tapped social embeddedness, direct effects of social support were found. Studies of the structure of social networks (e.g., network size, network density) are examples of such parameters. Cohen and Wills reasoned that social integration engenders feelings of stability, predictability, and self-worth and acts against a sense of isolation. These are general effects, then, that occur independent of stress level and do not aid specific coping efforts.

The second trend is for measures of supportive functions or presence of an intimate tie to lead to stress-buffering effects. They suggested that in both cases actual supportive interactions occur that increase feelings of self-esteem and self-efficacy and aid the combating of stressors. So, under high stress, individuals have an increased need for support because they are likely to feel negatively about themselves and their ability to master the obstacles before them. Support that addresses these needs would therefore be especially effective. When stress levels are low, in contrast, there is no need to mobilize support and so no effect of social support is noted. For instance, under low stress conditions, support systems may remain dormant because neither the supporter nor the potential recipient of aid feels there is a need to activate latent support.

Kessler and McLeod (1985) concur with this general premise, but suggest that stress buffering occurs not so much as a product of the actual function of social support as in the perception that one's network is ready to provide aid. When this supposition was tested, the perceptions of support were more important than received social support and the effects of received social support were moderated by perceived social support (Wethington & Kessler, 1986). The distinction between Cohen and Wills' and Kessler and McLeod's conclusions is a subtle but important one. The former argue that social support's effect is a product of its functional contribution, whereas the latter suggest that it is the belief that such help exists that is significant.

Fit, Ecological Congruence, and Social Support

Cohen and McKay (1984) also suggest that stress-buffering effects are most likely to occur when the measured functions of social support are consistent with the needs of the individual. They join Kessler (1983) and myself (Hobfoll, 1985b) in arguing that aggregate stress measures (e.g., life event checklists) obscure the specific stress-support linkages that may clarify the stress-buffering process. Aggregate measures of stressors, such as the one used in the study by Williams et al. discussed earlier, average all of the demands made on the individual for the different events in a fairly broad period. Social support in this context is likely to be weighted in favor of direct effects because what is being studied is the general adjustment of the individual, not the specific reaction to a stressful event.

If the buffering effect requires that a rally of social support takes place around a stressful event (Gore, 1985), then it is also unclear what aggregate measurement is tapping in terms of social support. Is the implication that over a year's time persons who possess high social support will receive a continued mobilization of functional aid? It is possible that, as Kessler and McLeod argue, they will feel they are likely to receive such aid but it is highly unlikely that continued functional support could be offered over such long periods and for such varied events.

Why specified stressors may be more illuminating is exemplified in the pregnancy complications example above. It appears that pregnant women are especially helped by tangible support. Most women probably receive emotional support during this period, but not every husband, for instance, will translate his emotional backing into housework and caring for the children. Women who are not so aided may neglect their own health and become overworked and overtired. This, in turn, could lead to poor health.

The theoretical and methodological advantages of fit theory apply to studies of psychological outcome as well. In this regard, psychological stress-buffering links have also been noted in studies of the role of social support and specified stressors such as job loss (Pearlin et al., 1981); proximity to a nuclear accident (Fleming, Baum, Gisrel, & Gatchel, 1982); economic, homemaking, and parental stressors (Kessler & Essex, 1982); and war-related stressors (Hobfoll, London, & Orr, in press).

The model of ecological congruence goes beyond fit theory, however, in predicting the actions of social support in stress buffering. If we consider the actual ecology of the stress–social support interaction, it is of paramount importance to consider time. As events unfold, two things we know about social support will work against its usefulness.

First, support takes time to mobilize (Hobfoll, 1982). This process is depicted in the five-stage model in Figure 4.4. Initially, individuals often need to recognize their need for aid. Next, they need to act to recruit support, or their supporters must spontaneously decide that they wish to offer support. Then supporters must respond to the request or to their own desire to help, but of course there will be times when they cannot or will not. They may be busy with their own lives or may themselves be involved in the crisis at hand. Even if support is received, it may not be what was needed, and the recipient may need to further cue the supporter. Finally, recipients of aid must provide feedback to their supporters and often must also respond by supporting their supporters in later situations when roles change.

Viewing the process of support vis-à-vis the model of ecological congruence highlights that the positive effects of social support can best be achieved when there is time to mobilize support and when circumstances are congruent with supporters' desire and ability to be supportive. This brings us to the second point we wish to emphasize about the model of ecological congruence: desire and ability to be supportive are not static but change with time. Supporters may initially wish to help, but they usually need to return to their own problems. Intensive support is time limited. The supporter's involvement with the recipient of support and with the event may also quell the desire to help or bring about a sense of hopelessness that depletes continued motivation. These points will be considered in more detail later in this chapter in the discussion of factors that limit the effectiveness of social support.

The model of ecological congruence also emphasizes the importance of values. A major value in Western society is that individuals should ultimately be independent. Consequently, the supporter might limit support after a time because more support could lead to dependency on the part of the recipient (Hobfoll, 1985a). In a sense, the most supportive act at some point may be to refuse further support and to demand that

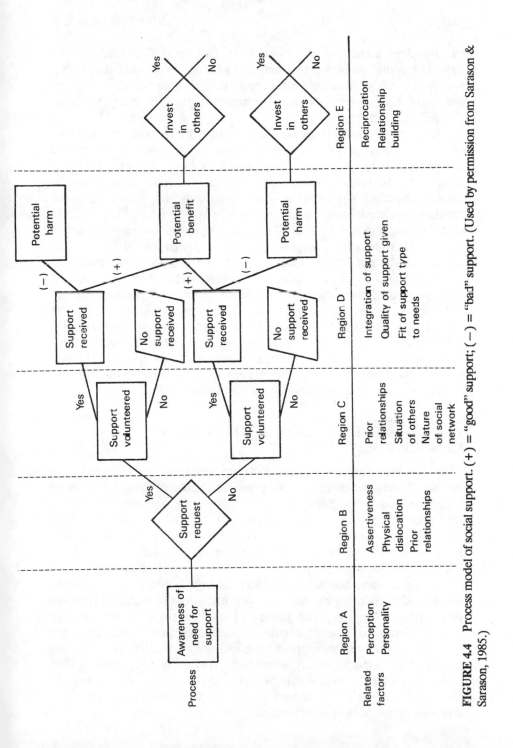

FIGURE 4.4 Process model of social support. (+) = "good" support; (−) = "bad" support. (Used by permission from Sarason & Sarason, 1985.)

the recipient stand on his or her own two feet. This leads to the supposition that social support may not produce stress-buffering effects for chronic stress situations; supporters may tend to withdraw support too early and to presume quicker recovery than is likely to occur (Wortman & Lehman, 1985).

In summary, stress-buffering effects may be most likely to occur when the social support measure taps perceptions of functional components of support that aid coping efforts. In this regard, it is not yet clear which is more important, the perception of the support or the actual functional contribution. Any stress-buffering effect, however, requires that circumstances be consistent with the type of support and that the situation not be so brief as to prevent effective mobilization of support nor so long as to cause an ebbing of supportive efforts.

It should be noted, however, that few studies have measured specified events, and consequently the importance of fit of social support with the type of stress can only be tentatively inferred. Because the vast majority of studies rely on aggregate event scales to measure stress, the issue of fit is lost in the averaging of different events, occurring at different times, to people of differing personal needs. Future research will want to focus to a much greater extent on a few specified stressor events, occurring at known points in time to more homogeneous groups of people (e.g., nurses, young-old versus old-old, middle managers).

PERSONAL RELATIONSHIPS: THE PROCESS OF SOCIAL SUPPORT

There has been surprisingly little work on social support, outside of the stress-buffering versus direct-effect question. Indeed, progress in social support research may have been held back by the perseverance around this question. Recently, however, several researchers have begun to examine the process of social support and to examine its correlates and mechanics (Hobfoll et al., 1986; Sarason et al., 1986; Stokes, 1983; Wortman & Lehman, 1985).

To understand how social support works it is helpful to examine a number of related topics that turn the focus to the study of personal relationships. There is a rich history of work on personal relationships that is relevant to an understanding of social support. In addition, the study of personal relationships emphasizes the qualitative, as well as the quantitative, aspects of relationships (Duck & Perlman, 1985). Highlighting the qualitative side of social support will do much to enrich the understanding of the functions and mechanisms that occur in the stress-social support-distress puzzle.

Among the topics that fall under the general rubric of personal relationships and are relevant to social support are (a) intimacy, (b) relational competence and loneliness, (c) reactions to victims of life crisis, and (d) the study of sex differences in the give and take of social support. In addition, (e) focusing on personal relationships raises the point that social support is not necessarily supportive and, indeed, may itself lead to further stress and distress. However obvious this point seems, it was disregarded in all but the most recent work on social support. These topics will be considered in the following pages.

Intimacy and Social Support

A number of studies have used the presence of a confidant or intimate relationship as the indicator of whether a person enjoys social support (Brown et al., 1975; Hobfoll & London, 1986; Hobfoll & Leiberman, 1987; Paykel et al., 1980; Warheit, 1979). Possessing such a relationship implies the availability of esteem support, informational support, and instrumental aid in meeting stress-related and everyday goals. However, it should also be pointed out that intimate ties are of utmost importance because they have been reinforced developmentally from earliest childhood. Such thinking is beginning to emerge as part of the first comprehensive theory of social support, and an attempt will be made here to explicitly present this line of thought.

Intimacy and a theory of social support

Much of psychodynamic theory rests on the central importance assigned to the intimate relationship between mother and child and, to a lesser extent, between father and child. Clearly, the major sources of neurosis and most psychoses are attributed in this literature to problems that occur in this attachment (Freud, 1926; M. Klein, 1932). This suggests that there is some primacy in the attachment of the young child to the parent or primary providers (Bowlby, 1969). Missing someone who is loved and longed for, Freud writes, is "the key to an understanding of anxiety" (pp. 136–137, Freud, 1926).

Intimacy can be seen as having instinctive underpinnings. No human infant could have survived in early development of humankind without a deep-seated tendency on its part or on the part of the mother to cling and form an attachment. We see the primacy of this in Harlow's (1961) work on monkeys and in reports of bonding in various animals. While we are phylogenetically more complex than these organisms, it is unlikely that we are so very different in this respect.

Leaving instincts aside for the moment, learning theory would also predict a strong bond between the infant and the provider of nourishment, warmth, and protection. It can be seen that the child has many physiological needs and if a parent-figure meets these needs, the baby becomes attached to that figure. Of course, attachment works both ways, and a successful attachment is also reinforcing to the mother, who feels satisfaction, release of tension, and sensual stimulation upon breast-feeding. Learning theory is not, however, incompatible with biologically based developmental theory (Bowlby, 1973). It is not accidental that the same breast-feeding that pleases mother and child also causes the uterus to contract to its original size. The biological and the behavioral aspects of attachment have been linked for millions of years, and fortuitous relationships between the two are unlikely to be passed on among the fittest.

Early attachment also has functional benefit for the protection of infants and the meeting of their needs because it enables communication between the infant and primary caregivers. As mentioned earlier in this volume, Freud (1926) termed this signal theory. He theorized that the infant-mother attachment served the purpose of creating a strong communication link through which infants make their needs known. In learning theory terms this would have very rich reinforcement potential because the infant is a poor communicator of specific needs and desires. A strongly attached primary caregiver will be the most likely other to work through the frustrating sequence of trial and error necessary to find out just what the infant requires. This is reinforced many times a day and continues as the child grows.

Intimate ties continue to receive reinforcement as the child grows. Parents and siblings are often sources of solace after a bruised knee or ego. Who could so often praise a child for things that every child has done for ages than the parents? So too, the touching and holding that children continue to need and enjoy are most likely to be provided and to be deemed acceptable within the family. Later, when the children's needs grow to include need for money and transportation, intimates are most likely to be the ones who provide what the child requires and desires.

The research on social support has avoided the sexual side of intimacy. Sexual intimacy, however, is probably an important aspect of social support. Sex is an important way to show caring and love, especially when it is within an emotionally and personally satisfying relationship. When sex meets both partners' needs and desires it is likely to act as a bond between them. It also relieves tension that has built up, providing further reinforcement. Just how sexual intimacy aids stress resistance, however, is open to speculation. An intimacy scale developed by Vanfossen (1981) is one of the few support measures to contain even one item on sex, but this would obviously give only the most superficial information. Recent theorizing about the functional aspects of social support in adulthood has begun to emphasize the role of intimacy in adulthood and the link between earlier attachment experiences and the needs of the adult. In speaking about the importance of intimacy Sarason, Shearin, Pierce, and Sarason (1987) say the following:

> *The function which social support plays in a young adult and an adult's life is likely an extension of that played by attachment experiences in infancy. While supportive attachment experiences in childhood foster a sense of personal worth and provide the child with a secure base from which to explore his or her surroundings, supportive relationships in later life maintain and improve the individual's sense that he or she is valued and loved. This support continues to promote "exploratory behavior" in which, throughout the life span, tasks are undertaken which are meaningful to the individual and are in the pursuit of his or her goals.*

> *Social support is often communicated through such "supportive behaviors" as loans of money, advice, and shoulders to cry on. Yet the offer and receipt of these provisions does not constitute social support. Nor should each of these supportive behaviors be viewed as conceptually distinct categories of support. Individuals who value and care about us are willing to do for us what they can. Though "supportive others" differ in their ability to provide money or communicate love, it is knowing that others love us and would willingly do for us what they can that is the essence of social support. (pp. 44–45)*

This says a number of important things about the relationship between intimacy and social support. First, it places social support and adjustment in the face of crisis in the developmental perspective; what is true for the child is true for the man or woman. Second, it suggests that in adulthood as in childhood intimacy acts to increase self-esteem and a stable base from which to explore the fullest repertoire of behaviors required in the adjustment process. Finally, Sarason and colleagues postulate that it is not what the supporters *do* that enhances health but the fact that we are loved and esteemed that is the core of social support's power.

Research on intimacy

Let us examine whether the research backs these contentions. In an early study by Brown, Bhrolcrain, and Harris (1975) a sample of women from the working-class Islington borough of London were studied. Brown and associates were interested in examining the social correlates of depression. Using a careful, in-depth interview format, they found that women with young children were especially susceptible to clinical depression. Also the presence of even a single confidant buffered the effects of severe negative life events. Most of the confidants were boyfriends or husbands; confidants other than these failed to provide protection from stressors.

Also in England, Paykel et al. (1980) found that presence of an intimate spouse was especially important in buffering the postpartum stress of mothers. A measure of confidants other than spouse did not show an interaction effect with stress, but did show a main effect. Hobfoll and Leiberman (1987) also found intimacy with a spouse to be related to better stress resistance among women following delivery. In addition, they noted that intimacy with family was related to dissatisfaction with support received if women lacked intimacy with their spouse or a close friend (Hobfoll, Nadler, & Leiberman, 1986).

Pearlin et al. (1981) also found that possessing a confidant buffered the effect of stress on mastery and self-esteem caused by unemployment. Furthermore, the buffering effect of confidant support on depression was not significant when the effects on mastery and self-esteem were partialed out. This supports the Sarasons' contention that intimacy works through mastery and self-esteem. Pearlin and associates' measure of intimacy was composed of a three-point measure of intimacy with spouse; an additional point was added if there was an additional confidant. Consequently, although this measure is weighted heavily with spouse support, this alone did not account for the effect. However, Pearlin et al. suggest that spouse support was especially salient.

Other studies of the effect of intimacy on emotional distress tend to support the contention that intimate ties, especially with one's spouse, make a special contribution to stress resistance (Habif & Lahey, 1980; Husaini, Newbrough, Neff, & Moore, 1982; Kessler & Essex, 1982). In fact, no other area of social support research reports such consistently positive findings. This gives credence to the belief that intimate ties with a few significant others are critical for adults as well as for children. Most remarkable, just as the attachment of parents is primary for children, the receipt of further intimate support over and above one or two primary ties makes a limited additional contribution to adult well-being.

It is important, however, to note that these studies did not examine what actual support was given. Intimates may have provided functional support, and indeed this is likely, but it is also possible that the mere existence of cherished ties was comforting. This leads to two possible explanations of the data. Either the functional support provided by intimates is of special significance, or the presence of the intimate tie itself is meaningful. Clearly, much of what is behind the positive effects of social support will be discovered in further study of intimacy, its determinants, and its subcomponents.

Relational Competence, Loneliness, and Social Support

If intimacy is a central ingredient in the stress-social support-distress chain, then the absence of intimacy may be an important factor in understanding the process of social support. Hidden behind the findings that one or two confidants may make the difference between healthy stress resistance and breakdown, is the fact that the total absence of intimate relationships may lead to illness and psychological distress. It is not so much the presence of a confidant that combats other stressors, but rather that having no such ties, or having conflicted ties, is a critical additional stressor.

Loneliness is defined as the distressing feeling that one's social relationships are deficient such that one has a sense of isolation and anomie. Sullivan (1953) saw loneliness as the outgrowth of the failure of the individual to meet the need for human intimacy. Peplau and Perlman (1982) found that as many as 10 percent of the population fail to have such needs met and suffer from severe, persistent loneliness.

It is important to point out at this juncture that most people experience loneliness at one time or another. However, the loneliness most likely related to a lack of intimacy is chronic or prolonged loneliness. Being lonely means both that no intimate others are around to buffer the effects of stress and that the individual has a continuing experience of aversive social deprivation. Rook (1985) makes the point that the absence of social support is not, in itself, aversive. The absence of close ties, however, is a deeply aversive state that may lead to depression independent of other stressors. Furthermore, lacking close bonds, lonely individuals are deprived of important social cues that intimate others provide. Thus the lonely lack others to remind them of the need to take their medication, carry an umbrella, and behave in a socially acceptable manner. Those who live alone may be more likely to engage in risky and self-destructive behaviors because they lack others who might moderate their behavior (Hughes & Gove, 1981).

Lonely individuals are in many ways unlike those who do not report chronic loneliness. Many of these differences have been implicated as causes of loneliness, and it is here that we find a link between interpersonal behavior and the acquisition of supportive personal relationships. Jones (1985) points out that many people are predisposed to relational failure because they are deficient in social skills or lack social confidence. Also, the same personal characteristics that have been linked to lack of social support have been associated with relational failure that ends in loneliness. Examples of these characteristics include lack of self-esteem, shyness, introversion, and lack of assertiveness.

Jones has suggested the usefulness of a concept he calls *relational competence*. Relational competence is seen in persons with high self-esteem and assertiveness, who are not shy or socially anxious. It is not just that those low in relational competence are lonely because that is the way they feel about themselves. They also seem to behave in a way that makes them unattractive; others find them less friendly, less warm, and less open than those higher in relational competence (Jones & Briggs, 1983). These behaviors distance others and contribute to an environment lacking in the close social contacts that people need.

Hansson (1986) provides an interesting example of how the study of social support and relational competence might be integrated. He compared samples of "young-old" subjects (60–72 years) with those of "old-old" subjects (73–94 years) to examine how the two groups might be affected by social support and relational competence. Adopting an ecological perspective, Hansson predicted that relational competence and social support would be related to better morale for the young-old. For the old-old, however, there is less social role involvement and greater chance of emotional pain, rather than positive pay-off for social relationships. The social roles of the old-old become increasingly restricted, and they occupy symbolic roles that are often void of actual social participation. They also have fewer opportunities to replace lost relationships, such that their social involvement may be in their memories with those who have died rather than with the frequently unfulfilling interactions with friends or family.

The results of a series of studies by Hansson were consistent with these assumptions. The young-old tended to have better adjustment the greater their social competence and the more satisfied they were with their personal relationships. Among the old-old, in contrast, health, income, resolution of the relationship with the deceased spouse, and a satisfactory relationship with God were most important. It is also interesting that the one important health variable for the young-old was hearing, a critical determinant of the ability to coherently engage in social interaction. Hansson did not provide information as to whether relational competence affected social support, but the studies do suggest that the two follow similar patterns of relationships with outcome. This may mean that relational competence and social support are interrelated, but just how remains an empirical question.

In summary, theory and a modicum of data suggest that those who lack relational competence may also lack the skills necessary to create and maintain effective support systems. This may result in a social environment that fails to provide them with help when they need it and that leaves them with a chronic sense of social isolation. Consequently, their psychological health suffers both because they are exposed to stress without the buffering support of close ties and because lacking such ties is itself a major source of stress. Their physical health may also suffer because prolonged stress produces negative health consequences and because they are not privy to the social prodding toward health maintenance that close associates provide.

Obviously, much more needs to be done on the question of the relationship between social support, relational competence, and loneliness if these suppositions are to be confirmed. The study of and theory about loneliness are already providing a more comprehensive picture of how social support affects individuals. The positive effect of social support may not be just a product of how it aids people; it also reflects that the absence of support and attachments is a deeply aversive state for humans from childhood until early old age.

Reactions to Victims of Life Crisis

The study of social support may be seen as the investigation of people's reactions to others with whom they have personal relationships who are in crisis. Most research, however, has focused on the consequences of receiving social support, not on the determinants of that support. Furthermore, empirical work on social support has focused on the recipient of support, and the important role of the provider of support has been ignored. If social support is a social interaction, which it obviously is, then attention must be paid to all those involved in the interaction. Because almost no work has been directed at this key issue, information and theory borrowed from related areas of study will be integrated and focused to provide a few answers and many new questions.

A model for research on reactions to significant others in crisis is provided by the classic work of Latene and Darley (1970) on the "bystander effect," which examined how strangers reacted to the plight of victims who appeared to be in need of help. Study of the bystander effect demanded sophisticated and creative study designs that appeared natural, for example with confederates feigning illness on public transport so that the behavior of witnesses could be observed. Study of supporters' reactions to those in crisis with whom they have an ongoing relationship are more complex. However, just as *victim, environment,* and *help-provider* variables were each integral to solving the puzzle of bystander behavior, so will these components be important for deciphering the interactive social dance that accompanies social support behavior. Until now, however, research has focused almost exclusively on victim variables and the victim's assessment of the social environment.

Why supporters help

A starting point is to consider why potential supporters would help. There are three reasons for the motivation to help. First, people help because they care and wish to see that things go well for the other member of a relationship. In particularly close relationships, such as between parent and child, the caring may be so strong that crises occurring to the child are more painful for the parent than are the parent's own problems. It follows that if a close friend or family member can intercede to limit the detrimental effects of a crisis, they will do so.

Studies of persons in close relationships suggest that they will help one another because they value the relationship and are empathic with the other's needs. Clark (1983) calls these communal relationships. In communal relationships people are not so much motivated by what the other has done for them recently; rather, they have a holistic view of their part in the relationship. This implies that close relationships engender a feeling of responsibility for what occurs to the other, based on a sense that those involved are mutually affected by what happens to each member of the relationship. This may be contrasted with more distant relationships in which helping may be ruled by laws of tit-for-tat and by a "what have you done for me lately?" attitude (Walster et al., 1978).

A second reason that people help is that they themselves benefit by helping. This is perhaps a selfish reason. Nevertheless, much of the glue of personal relationships is based on the fact that the closer the tie, the more likely those involved are to sink or swim together. If a woman is depressed because she feels that her family obligations are interfering with her career aspirations, her crisis will affect her husband, children, and job. Her boss may fire her without undue suffering, but her husband will suffer if he does not help to alleviate her crisis. He may not treasure cleaning floors and toilet bowls or missing work to care for an ill child, but he may feel threatened by the consequences of not helping. He may lend a hand not because he empathizes with her plight but because he fears divorce or dreads the prospect of living with a disgruntled wife. Thus it may serve the selfish interests of supporters to alleviate the burden of those with whom they have a close relationship who are victims of crisis.

Such behavior should not, however, be judged too harshly. Had there not been mutual caring and commitment, as in the case of the woman's boss, the husband might well have sought divorce or offered a confrontive ultimatum to his wife. Furthermore, selfish behavior may add strength to a relationship because, despite the real motivation, people may reinterpret their selfish motivation by reframing attributions to reflect how they want to be seen (e.g., "I helped because I cared"). Such reframing, in turn, may act to increase their commitment to the relationship. Receivers of support may also make positive attributions about the supporters' motivation because they want to view their relationship in the best light.

The third reason people help those with whom they have close ties stems from a sense of role obligation. Supportive interactions have definite structural roots in the social roles around which people interact, or role sets (Merton, 1957). Social roles frequently include an obligation to help others in times of need, even if helping is aversive to the help-provider (e.g., "rich or poor, in sickness or in health"). There is indication that this sense of obligation may sometimes be aversive to the provider (Stein & Rappaport, 1986; Kessler, McLeod, & Wethington, 1985), but it is nonetheless a critically important social practice that is one of the pillars of organized society.

All three factors that press persons to provide support to close others are consistent with the emphasis on values in the model of ecological congruence. Much supportive behavior is prescribed in values. This becomes obvious when we examine differences between men and women in their provision of social support (Vanfossen, 1981; Hobfoll, 1986a). It is uncommon for men, say, to move for their wives' career advancement, decrease their working hours substantially to become the major provider of childcare, or take over the care of elderly parents. Women do so frequently. Husbands do not define these behaviors as consistent with their roles and they would likely receive negative sanctions from work and family if they were to make these sex-role reversals. Yet, this lack of concession may be why the wives are finding their own stress levels intolerable (Aneshensel, 1986; Vanfossen, 1986).

Women, in contrast, may feel guilty if they do not make these sacrifices. The issue of sex differences in social support will be addressed in detail later; the point here is that the provisions and limits of social support behavior are products of commonly held values.

Why people are unsupportive

There are at least three reasons why people may respond to loved ones undergoing crisis in ways that are unsupportive (Wortman & Lehman, 1985). First, people often hold negative feelings about others who are suffering or distressed even if they are bound by a close relationship. Confrontation with another's problems may engender feelings of helplessness or resentment because one is in the uncomfortable position of being expected or obligated to help. The greater the problem, the more likely these feelings may occur, paradoxically rendering those in most need of support least likely to receive it (Dunkel-Schetter & Wortman, 1982).

Second, Wortman and Lehman suggest that support-providers are often placed in delicate circumstances for which they have little expertise. This elicits a fear of making the wrong move or saying the wrong thing and consequently of making matters worse. Finally, Silver and Wortman (1980) argue that we often hold misconceptions about how people should react in the face of crisis. To the extent that these misconceptions differ from what actually constitutes normal reactions to crisis, providers of support are more likely to act inappropriately.

Wortman and Lehman (1985) provide a preliminary test of their assumptions about why people respond to victims of crisis unsupportively. They interviewed two groups of subjects. The bereaved group consisted of individuals who had lost a child or spouse in a motor vehicle accident four to seven years earlier. The control group included people carefully matched with the bereaved group, who had not lost a loved one. This design allowed for a comparison of how the bereaved recall others responded to them, with how the control subjects imagined they should help based on their expectations of the bereaved persons' reactions to aid.

They found that approximately 60 percent of a sample of bereaved individuals reported that others had behaved unhelpfully. The four most common support tactics judged to be unhelpful were giving advice, encouraging recovery, minimizing the magnitude of the problem or forced cheerfulness, and attempting to identify with feelings (e.g., "I know how you feel").

The responses of the control subjects, in turn, illustrated that it is not out of ignorance that people provide inappropriate or unhelpful support to the bereaved. Indeed, control subjects overwhelmingly knew how they should react, and their responses mirrored the responses of the bereaved as to what they thought was the right way to react. Controls commonly expressed that they would be there for the victim, that they would show concern, and that they would provide an opportunity for the victim to discuss his or her feelings. These types of responses were judged by the bereaved to be the most helpful. The gap between what supporters feel they *should do* and what they are *perceived as doing* seems to be related to distortions that are caused by the actual confrontation with the bereaved. Whether the factors cited above or other factors account for these distortions must be confirmed by further research, however.

Supporting the earlier arguments about why people are motivated to help, this study also indicates that in most cases others do provide effective support. Fully 70 percent of the bereaved judged that someone in their support network had provided especially helpful support. Given the strong aversive factors that Wortman and colleagues propose as leading to the offering of ineffective support or abandonment of the victim, one may infer that close social bonds are generally resilient to these negative pressures. The positive interpretation of these findings is that 70 percent of the bereaved received helpful support despite the obstacles that occur during major crisis.

The results of this study suggest that people are motivated to help loved ones who are victims of crisis and that they have a good sense of how they should help. When confronted with the task of helping, however, many people provide ineffective support. Nevertheless, perhaps owing to people's commitment to loved ones, sense of obligation, and role functioning, most victims of crisis do receive helpful support. Future research that compares how people think they should act with how they actually do act with victims of different kinds of crises will be valuable.

Sex Differences in Social Support

Nearly all we know about the socialization of individuals vis-à-vis the giving and receiving of social support is inferential and is based on the study of sex differences in social support. Only a limited number of studies have examined sex differences in social support. These studies, however, are quite consistent and provide important insights into the process of social support between those in personal relationships (Hobfoll, 1986a; Hobfoll & Stokes, in press).

In one of the early studies on social support, Hirsch (1979) found that female college students reported spending more time with others in their social network than did males. They also tended more than male college students to share feelings and personal concerns, a fact that suggests that they were also interacting on a more genuine and personal level. Burke and Weir (1978) also report that adolescent females are more willing than adolescent males to disclose personal problems with peers. Together these two studies suggest that women may be more open to the types of interactions that foster supportive exchanges, even if that was not what was directly measured in either case.

Other researchers who more closely examined actual exchange of social support also find that women receive more social support than do men (Burda, Vaux, & Schill, 1984; Cohen, McGowan, Fooskas, & Rose, 1984; Rich, Sullivan, & Rich, 1986; Stokes & Wilson, 1984). These differences appear most apparent when emotional aspects of support are studied. It is interesting that college women also find their families to be more cohesive and expressive than do college men (Rich et al., 1986). It would be valuable to know whether daughters actually contribute to cohesiveness and expressiveness in families or whether this was merely a perception of these women. This could be studied by comparing the ratings of young men and women from families that have equal numbers of male and female children.

Several studies have reported that women's social networks are larger than those of men. As Kessler et al. (1985) point out, women are more comfortable than men saying "what happens to you is important to me." This also engenders costs, as these investigators note, because the openness to others also exposes women to greater stressors than confront men. They find that men tend to underreport more minor network crises and events that occur to people at the edges of their social networks. They further illustrate that women are not more distressed than men in response to serious personal events (e.g., divorce and income losses), but that they are much more deeply affected by death of a loved one other than a spouse. These differences account for much of the psychological vulnerability noted in women as compared with men (reports, for example, for depression of women compared with that of men range from 1.6:1 to 2:1 [Weissman & Klerman, 1977]). It would appear that they are not more vulnerable to stress than are men, but that they are exposed to more stressors through their social network (Kessler et al., 1985).

A fair amount of evidence indicates that women consistently report greater support and greater satisfaction with support than do men (Sarason, Sarason, Hacker, & Basham, 1985). This is likely to be a product of socialization differences in the raising of girls and boys. Boys from early on may be reluctant to acknowledge difficulties or to admit their need for help. Fausteau (1984) and Lewis (1978) also suggest that men are uncomfortable with intimacy and that they tend to foster shallow relationships. Little girls, in contrast, are from an early age socialized to express emotions and warmth. The feminine sex role may also encourage greater interpersonal competence than masculine sex roles, as women are seen as the social conduits of the society (Sarason et al., 1985).

If women are more socially competent and more comfortable with intimacy than are men, it is likely that they also benefit more than men from supportive interactions. Looking at mortality figures, Berkman and Syme (1979) report that both men and women benefit from attachment to social institutions and contact with friends and relatives, but that these associations are more pronounced for women. Examining psychological correlates of stress, a number of researchers have also noted that women benefit more than men from intimate support (Henderson, Byrne, Duncan-Jones, Scott, & Addock, 1980), social support from spouses (Husaini, Newbrough, Neff, & Moore, 1982) and confidant support (Cohen & Wills, 1985).

Reis, Senchak, and Solomon (1985) report, somewhat surprisingly, that men are not less capable than women of creating intimate relationships. Rather, they are more selective in their choices of persons with whom they are willing to hold intimate ties. One reason for this is that both males and females find relationships with females to be more satisfying than relationships with men (Wheeler, Reis & Nezlek, 1983). Women have the advantage of varied levels and types of relationships with other women, whereas men may seek a single sexual relationship with a woman and feel that relationships with men have little to offer them outside of superficial activities and colleagual assistance. One should be careful in generalizing these findings beyond college students, however, as they may not be true among older or less educated samples.

There is also a feminist side to these sex differences that emerges within marriages. Men have nurturant wives to support them when they encounter major stressors or daily hassles. Women, however, have unsupportive husbands! Bernard (1971) has similarly argued that wives are disadvantaged in marriage because they are less likely than husbands to receive the social support they need from their spouses. Bernard states that the provision of social support has been socially inscribed as the dominant role of women. However, while they fulfill their role by tending the ills and raising the status and esteem of others in the family, women receive little in return. Thus, although Husaini et al. (1982) do note that women benefit more from spouses' support than do men, this indicates that they are more sensitive to it when they receive it, not that they receive more of it.

Parsons' (1949) functionalist theory proposes that the traditional division of labor in families, based on reproductive roles, delegates to men the role of aggressor and provider and to women the role of nurturer and raiser of children. Vanfossen (1986) further suggests that women receive less social support for their social role because of the devaluation of femininity and the female's role in the male-dominant culture. In investigating sex differences in the provision of social support, however, Vanfossen found only a modicum of evidence for differences in perceived support from spouse for men and women. This suggested that it was not support, in general, that women were lacking.

Aneshensel (1986) did find, however, that women who felt that their husbands were nonaccepting of their behavior and of the type of person that they were, were especially likely to experience marital role strain. Similarly, women who reported receiving inadequate rewards for their work were likely to experience job strain. Aneshensel notes further that women who work outside the home are liable to be exposed both to added stressors and to conflicting demands (e.g., demands on the same period of time from both work and home). She concludes that women are increasingly confronted with dual roles (home and work) and that rewards may be hard coming in both domains. On the positive side, however, those women who did receive support from their spouses were significantly more stress resistant than women who did not.

Combining these findings, it would appear that women are especially likely to be inadequately supported if they choose nontraditional roles. This may be because they are "sanctioned" by their spouses and families for working outside the home. It may also be partially attributable to the increased need for support when one is working both in and outside of the home and having to meet the consequent added and conflicting demands of these dual roles. However, when they do choose such nontraditional roles and are supported, they enjoy enhanced stress resistance.

This line of thinking indicates a number of directions for intervention. It appears that men may need to be sensitized to their own views toward their wives' roles both in and outside the home. To the extent that they fail to esteem these roles, they are likely to fail to provide the support their wives need. Some of the required support they should be encouraged to provide, in this regard, will be emotional, and some will be a more basic sharing of mundane responsibilities of the household and the important responsibilities of childcare. In the work setting, it will be important that women also get the support they deserve for their contribution and access to the kinds of jobs that intrinsically provide such rewards. Interventions in the workplace, consequently, may take the form of sensitizing and educating employers and colleagues about sexist practices in the distribution of rewards, assignment of tasks, and praise.

Finally, environmental changes that lighten potential stressors and add built-in support should also be considered. Examples of such strategies include changing to flexitime (variable work schedules), providing on-site quality daycare, and considering the need of both fathers and mothers to leave the workplace when, say, a child is ill or must be transported. It may be noted here how such *research-based* approaches to intervention coincide with the emphases of the *theoretically based* model of ecological congruence, both highlighting multiple sources of internal and external resources, settings, and underlying values. These points will be more carefully detailed and integrated in the final chapter of this volume.

Obviously, the role of sex differences in social support will continue to be an important area of research if we are to uncover the working mechanics of social support and how best to intervene to enhance the quality of support in people's lives. It will be important for future researchers to conduct developmental and process studies on this topic, however, as the data are very suggestive of process but do not directly address this issue. Such studies may take the form of cross-sectional or longitudinal investigations of males and females in different developmental age groups (e.g., preteens, teens, young adults, etc.). They might also tap the style of social interaction for these groups and changes in these styles as males and females mature. Nor is it too early to attempt model intervention studies for dual-career families or at work sites. The study of sex differences has already led to important insights about the commerce of social support and may prove to be one of the keys to understanding support phenomena.

The Negative Side of Social Support

The term social support may have led to some of the early misconceptions about the role played by social support in stress resistance. The term implies that the social interactions in question are in fact supportive. This presumes a positive outcome that may not evolve, even from the best social intentions. In the rush and excitement over social support, researchers and theorists sidestepped information from social exchange models (Blau, 1964; Homans, 1961) clearly suggesting that social interactions involve both benefits and costs for the provider and recipient of support. A blind eye was also turned to family systems theory, which illustrates how close personal ties may provide destructive kinds of support even with the most positive intent (Minuchin, 1974).

In this section the negative side of social interactions will be presented. It is important to include such a discussion in a chapter on social support because many social interactions that have positive intent are actually detrimental. Also, intentionally destructive interactions may be mixed with social support because many relationships involve both helpful and harmful components. Thus to discuss social support without discussing the negative side of social interactions is to deny the true nature of personal relationships.

Following a discussion of the effects of negative social interactions, factors that limit the positive contributions of potentially effective social support will be presented. These are especially interesting because they are less obviously problematic than are overt negative interactions. But they are important because they are likely to be very common.

Negative social interactions

Social input may directly lessen one's sense of well-being. Rejection, criticism, exhausting demands, unwillingness to provide help, violation of privacy, and social exploitation are all examples of such interactions (Rook, 1985). Unfortunately, a close relationship is paradoxically more likely to include such negative input than is a more distant relationship, because if a more distant relationship is negative we have the option of terminating it or, at least, of strongly protesting or exacting some consequences (e.g., refusing to cooperate with a colleague). Obligations, investment, and fear of being alone prevent people from evoking such sanctions in their close relationships. This is one principal reason why some people feel that obligated relationships are negative and not supportive (Stein & Rappaport, 1985). Perhaps because loss of loved ones is such a major stressor some people are even willing to accept extreme abuse from their most intimate relations.

Supporters may also choose to support unhealthy behaviors or feelings. This is the case when husbands encourage dependent feelings in their wives, for example, by suggesting that their working will "only increase the family's tax burden," or that "it will barely pay for daycare," and anyway "you're doing such a good job raising the children." Hirsch (1980) suggested that one reason that support from friends who are unconnected to family is important is that such supporters are more likely to consider women's best interests and not what is best for the family. Friends who are linked to the family, for instance, might be torn between the wife's and the husband's interests. Mitchell and Hodson (1983) give empirical support to this supposition. They found that battered wives whose friends were connected to their husbands were more likely to receive responses to their help-seeking characterized by avoiding the issue or minimizing its seriousness than were battered wives whose friends were unconnected to their spouses. Those connected to both the wife and husband were acting less as advocates for the battered wife than those who were connected primarily to the wife.

Supporters may also promote unhealthy behavior because it is consistent with group membership. Drinking buddies encourage drinking, cults encourage dogmatic conformity to the group's norms, and families support behavior consistent with the implied norms of the family. Minuchin (1974) argues that deviant family patterns are subtly upheld by family members who encourage behaviors and attitudes consistent with the deviancy. Sometimes this is as blatant as scapegoating, but it often appears supportive, such as in the case of the "support" that is really the parents' attempt to control an anorexic adolescent daughter.

Rook (1984) found that elderly women experienced both negative and positive social exchanges with important others. This finding is unusual because it represents one of the few attempts to examine both positive and negative interactions simultaneously. Rook further noted that negative interactions were more detrimental than were positive interactions beneficial. Others have also noted that being upset with social network interaction was strongly associated with increased depression and decreased network satisfaction, whereas helpful aspects of the social network bore little effect on outcome (Pagel, Erdly, & Becker, in press). These findings emphasize that social support research should be more holistic and consider social climate more fully. Future research would do well to follow Rook's and Pagel and colleagues' lead in this regard.

Factors limiting effectiveness of potential aid

Now that it is clear that social support is not always supportive, it is important to look at what factors might limit the beneficial effects of social support. In an earlier paper I argued that three factors limit the effectiveness of social support (Hobfoll, 1985a): (a) situational factors that obstruct the positive transfer of support; (b) personality factors that interfere with the interpretation of support and how support is provided; and (c) the interaction of stigmatized events and certain individual characteristics.

Limiting situational factors

The first case whereby situational factors obstruct the positive transfer of support is structural, that is, related to the characteristics of the event. This highlights the importance of the ecology of the event as demonstrated in the model of ecological congruence. During crisis, for instance, social support may not be available to individuals because crisis events often occur unexpectedly, and, indeed, unexpected crises are especially stressful (Thoits, 1983). Consequently, supporters are often physically distant from the crisis victim or involved in tasks from which they cannot extricate themselves. So, no matter how good the intent to help, the sudden unexpected nature of crises often imposes structural limitations on the transfer of supportive acts.

Typical expectations about independent functioning also color supporters' reactions to the victims of crisis and thus limit the support given. Western values are consistent with the expectation that people should quickly "get back on their own two feet." Vachon (1979) found, for example, that women with breast cancer are expected to quickly resume their normal functioning once medical intervention has been completed, despite the fact that many women are severely distressed long after successful surgery. Walker, MacBride, and Vachon (1977) also found that widows frequently report that loved ones expect them to limit their grieving, even a few days after the loss.

When stressors become chronic, supportive resources may also dwindle because supporters eventually must return to their own responsibilities. Support providers may take off from work or neglect other responsibilities for a time, but they are expected and they expect themselves to return to daily routine. Even intimates such as a spouse must continue to support the family and care for children. Indeed, the burden on those closest to the victim is likely to increase following crisis, further limiting the ability to be supportive. Undertaking these additional burdens is a central aspect of support, but crisis victims may nevertheless feel that they are being ignored in the process.

A third situational factor that limits the positive effect of social support is that many stressful events occur during transitional periods (Felner, 1985). When a youth moves to college, when a family relocates in a new town, and when a woman rises to a senior company position, they are all likely to confront stressors for which they lack coping experience. At such critical times they are also likely to be physically distant from traditional support providers. In our own study of women undergoing biopsy we did not find any protective effect of long-distance telephone support; indeed, many instrumental kinds of support cannot be provided long-distance.

Another situational factor that typifies many stressors is that few such events concern a single individual. Stressful events more commonly directly affect an entire family, say, than one member of the family. Consequently, job loss, death of a loved one, or illness characteristically tax all the individuals within the social unit. This may provide the opportunity for mutual provision of support; however, those involved may be too psychologically devastated to provide effective support to each other. It is interesting that the church or community historically took responsibility for burial arrangements, as the bereaved are so often too incapacitated to take on this additional burden. What support intimates do provide one another may also be based on faulty judgment because of the effect of stress on decision making (Janis, 1983).

In a study of the effects of war on women whose loved ones were mobilized, Hobfoll and London (1986) found that possessing greater intimates and receiving more recent support were related to more, not less, psychological distress. The findings were interpreted as a "pressure cooker" effect, whereby those who had greater social support were more privy to rumors and to constant confrontation with the reality of war through their interaction with others in similar circumstances than women who had less-intimate ties and less social support. In fact, groups of people are known to interpret information more extremely than are individuals (Myers & Lamm, 1976). Because this study was cross-sectional we cannot be sure about the direction of the relationship, but it is consistent with the thesis that individuals with a common crisis may compound their distress by interacting with each other.

There is also indirect evidence of this phenomenon in the observations of military psychiatrists, who have noted that groups of soldiers often break down in combat (Marlowe, 1979). Rather than behave as a buddy providing support to those who begin to develop crisis reactions, the crisis victim may pull others down who are teetering on the edge of their own ability to withstand the immense stressors about them. This may be one reason why the army buddy system ostracizes those who are judged as weak, to ensure psychological distance between the weak individual and the competent group (Grinker & Spiegel, 1945).

Limiting personality factors

Personality characteristics of the support provider and receiver may either limit or enhance the provision of support. In the following chapter the personality of the recipient of support and how personality affects the receipt and utilization of support will be discussed in detail. For now it suffices that many personality characteristics cause individuals to reject or denigrate the support they are given, such that even objectively effective support is rendered useless or counterproductive. Let us now focus on the characteristics of the support provider and how they might limit the effectiveness of support.

Giving aid requires much tact and diplomacy. The help provider who is insensitive to the threat involved in the receipt of support or who is motivated by the power that may be gained by giving aid may not provide effective assistance. It is a tradition in the Middle East not to look into the face of beggars when offering them charity so as to not embarrass them further. During the depression, my grandfather would give fresh chickens to poor families by asking them to do him the favor of taking the chicken off his hands so that it would not become spoiled in his store. Even with loved ones, caution must be exercised on the part of the provider so as not to accentuate the diminished capacity of the recipient.

Work on exchange theory (Walster et al., 1978) illustrates that people suspect that the offering of aid may be a strategy designed to enhance the provider's power. Research by Fisher, Nadler, and Whitcher-Alagna (1982) also suggests that the support provider may be viewed as in the socially desirable position, as the provider is seen as strong and effective whereas the receiver is weak and ineffective.

Taken together, exchange theory (Walster et al., 1978) and information on helper–helpee dynamics (Fisher et al., 1982) may be used to imply that support providers need to be careful lest their help be judged as oneupmanship. This may be another reason why intimate ties are so important. In such relationships trust is built up and one may be sure that attempts to help are genuine and carry no negative ulterior motive.

Another characteristic of help providers that may limit the effectiveness of their attempts to assist is their role vis-à-vis the recipient. For example, help from a colleague at work may immediately place her in the position of expert and the recipient of help in the position of novice. For this reason, the colleague may turn down her offers of assistance. Similarly, if a wife thinks her husband wants to provide her more material aid so that he may gain dominance in the relationship, she may reject this support. In the first case if the help was from someone in a different role, say a friend, and in the second case if the husband had fulfilled a different role in the past, say one supporting equity, then the aid offered might be interpreted more positively.

Work on social support has often exclusively tapped recipients' assessment of the support they received. From this section it becomes obvious that the intentions of the supporter and the characteristics of the provider may be critical determinants of whether support is effective, benign, or detrimental. It would seem that, just as social support researchers presupposed the positive contribution of support, they designed studies that would tend to mask or average the negative contributions of support due to the negative attributions about the support provider (Hobfoll & Stokes, in press). Much more work needs to be done on this topic as while the anecdotes I present on the topic have the ring of truth, they do not have direct empirical backing.

Both objective and subjective assessments of the support provider will be of interest. Hobfoll and Stokes (in press) theorize that the perceived intent of the support as seen by the recipient is one important perspective. If recipients have strong positive or negative feelings about the provider of support they will tend to interpret the aid positively or negatively, respectively. The actual quality of the supportive act may hardly matter. A cup of tea may have little functional value but a substantial effect if the intent is interpreted as an act of love. A large financial gift may, in contrast, be very functional but have a negative effect because it is interpreted as an attempt to gain influence. When the recipient has less-polarized feelings about the support provider, on the other hand, the actual functional qualities of the support may be most important. Here the attributions about the intent are more vague and will not color the interpretation of the supportive behavior.

Stigmatized events as limiting factors: individual-event interaction

The model of ecological congruence emphasizes that individual personal traits only have functional significance in specific contexts. Certain personality traits may limit the effectiveness of social support and certain environments may inhibit the efficacious passage of aid. The model of ecological congruence also highlights that personal and social traits interact with the environment, at times inhibiting social support's effectiveness. One principal class of such interactions occurs around stigmatized events.

Being ill is one of the most ubiquitous stigmatized events. It is perhaps surprising that illness is often accompanied by embarrassment or self-consciousness and a concomitant sense of failure (Moos, 1977). Even though we know that our sickness is no one's fault and despite the fact that we would seldom blame others for their illnesses, we do not seem to be so understanding of ourselves. Perhaps because some people are especially sensitive to negative self-attributions the sick role is particularly avoided by them.

This interaction between personal characteristics and illness has complex implications. Rejection of the sick role and its concomitant support is good because people will push themselves to recovery and avoid exploiting their malady to gain from their illness. In addition, early denial of the sick role is helpful because it limits anxiety (Gentry, Foster, & Haney, 1972). Accepting the sick role begets feelings of helplessness and danger of becoming ingratiated to those who provide support. The sick role, however, is an important stage in recovery, and avoiding it may have grave consequences if the individual is truly ill (Croog, Shapiro, & Levine, 1971). Social sanctions are implied in the sick role that permit the ill individual to accept help and to temporarily exit from normal role responsibilities.

Another example of the interaction of personal and situational characteristics is common in the case of shyness. Shy individuals have been found to have weak support systems and difficulty receiving social support (Jones, 1985). Such impairment is all the more magnified by embarrassing social events. Job loss, divorce, unwanted extramarital pregnancy, and even death of spouse (widows having depleted social status) all have degrees of stigma attached. Shyness, and indeed any trait that is related to a sensitivity to failure, may interact with stigmatized events to inhibit the likelihood of receiving and benefiting from social support. At such times shy individuals are likely to avoid affiliation and retreat.

Another critical ecological point may also be made at this juncture. The social position of the individual may interact with situational constraints imposed by the society for continuation of the status quo. Social support systems have multiple allegiance: to the supportee and to the system. When individuals' needs are in conflict with the social order, support is likely to be offered sparingly or in a manipulative fashion that serves the needs of the group. A study of Dressler (1985) illustrates this point.

Using an ecological analytic strategy, Dressler noted that young black women in a Southern community were not aided by kin support, although they were a particularly needy group. Dressler argued that to the young women support meant coming under great scrutiny with an expectation that they would closely follow the advice of their elders. For the men studied, in contrast, social support from kin validated their high-status social role in the traditional structure of the black community. This, in turn, reduced the restrictions placed on their behavior. Structurally, social roles and situational characteristics interacted so that support ensured continuation of the accepted social order.

In summary, it appears that positive and negative social inputs are often provided within the same relationship. In addition, even social support that could potentially have a positive effect may not be transmitted or may be transmitted such that its efficacy is attenuated depending on personal and environmental factors and their interaction. Social support research will obviously need to examine closer how social support is transferred, the personal characteristics of those involved in the supportive interaction, and the ecological context in which the transaction takes place.

Social Support and the Model of Conservation of Resources

The discussion of the process of social support leads us to question what underlies this process. Perhaps this is the chemistry or mechanics of social support. While the research begins to untangle some possible pathways for the process of social support, it does not address what active ingredients enable the support to be beneficial.

The relationship between loss and stress as presented in the model of conservation of resources suggests why social support is such a potentially valuable resource. Social support may operate in two ways. First, social support widens people's pool of potential resources. It helps by replacing lost resources or those that are otherwise lacking. Second, social support acts not by replacing resources that are lacking, but by reinforcing resources that have been weakened by external circumstances. Here, social support enhances people's ability to translate raw resources into actual or usable resources—cutting and polishing the diamond in the rough.

In the first case, social support widens individuals' resource pools because supporters by definition are offering goods and services and boosts to esteem that fill some deficiency in the recipient of support. When an individual needs a loan or help in moving, supporters respond to meet these needs. In the second case, when I say that support helps people translate raw resources into actual resources I am implying a much more subtle process. In its most effective form social support helps people actualize parts of their selves that they are having difficulty expressing. In this regard, the most important aspect of social support may be that it helps people recognize what they already know about themselves but lost sight of during stressful times. If they did not themselves possess these resources the effect of social support could only be to provide a temporary inoculation (Hobfoll, 1985b). Social support cannot substitute for a deeply engrained positive self-concept or sense of mastery. This point will be empirically demonstrated in Chapter 7, which presents the applications of the model of ecological congruence to research on illness. A case example I came across will be used here to demonstrate this point.

A young physician has received consistent positive feedback about her excellent work in surgery. As a senior resident, she is capable and efficient, shows excellent judgment, and feels confident in her abilities. On two consecutive evenings on call, young children who are close in age to her own die while she is operating on them. Although she continues working she becomes anxious that another child will be sent to the emergency room while she is on call. She has lost her self-confidence and her sense of efficacy and imagines the future loss of her children. She tells herself that she is incapable at work and that by working she is missing watching her own children grow up. "They could die, too," she tells herself. Sharing this with her husband, he reminds her of all her achievements, of how good she is with the children, how much free time she has managed to find despite her career commitment, and how she really does have the ability to make it through this temporary crisis. He also calls a respected colleague to have a talk with his wife to give a friendly but professional reinforcement of her sense of confidence. Within a few days, with continued tender care, and with her own willingness to confront her fears she is again feeling positive about herself and her work.

This may be compared with a case in which the individual lacks a positive sense of self notwithstanding the current stress situation. An executive who generally feels that events are out of his control, who is alienated from his environment, and who lacks a strong feeling of commitment returns home following a significant failure at work. Imagine how hollow would be the positive social support his wife might provide. She could tell him that he really is capable, in control of his future, and an integral part of his company. Indeed, she may temporarily convince him that this is so. However, how long could such a message last before his basic sense of self reemerges? These traits are not transient (Kobasa & Puccetti, 1983) and so are not easily dismissed. Such support might have the important effect of brunting crisis levels of stress, but it is doubtful that it would continue to be efficacious.

Indeed, he is more likely to receive social support consistent with his self-image, which will reinforce his self-defeating posture. When he returns home, then, his wife will agree with his view that his failures are the fault of others and will encourage him perhaps to take a few days off to regather his strength. In this regard, intimate relationships tend to reinforce whatever self-image the support recipient possesses (Swann & Predmore, 1985). Perhaps Goffman (1959) stated it most clearly when he argued that individuals use intimate others to reinforce however they wish to be seen.

That social support may act by reinforcing personal resources rather than creating them clarifies some otherwise puzzling findings. Coyne, Aldwin, and Lazarus (1981) found, for instance, that depressed women are not well served by social support even though they receive more of it than nondepressed women. The support here fails to replace the woman's negative self-image. In contrast, Lefcourt et al. (1984) and Kobasa and Puccetti (1983), for instance, both report that social support is more likely to help those who possess a positive view of their own efficacy than those who feel that they are not the masters of their fate. It would appear that social support can do little more than actualize a sense of self that is perhaps only temporarily weakened. It would seem that social deficits, on the other hand, need to be offset by addressing both supportive behavior and the underlying personal characteristics and competencies of individuals (Jones, 1985).

All other factors being equal, support is most effective when it meets the functional requirements of the individual (Cohen & McKay, 1984). Object, condition, personal characteristic, and energy resources may be provided or boosted by such interactions. Receiving money, for instance, may have no benefit after the loss of a lover or even a job, if the individual perceives self-esteem and a sense of belonging as the central losses to occur. Money may increase total resources, but is not the key to the current experience. As proposed in the model of conservation of resources, individuals seek to replace losses. This concept of replacement is the key fit. Whenever possible, people will attempt to directly replace what was lost or reinforce what has been diminished. When it is not possible to replace in kind, attempts will be made to approximate the lost resource. When this is not possible a period of prolonged mourning is likely.

Loss of an intimate friend or kin

If loss is the central component of stress, as the model of conservation of resources would have it, then loss of an intimate other, with whom there has been a positive relationship, is especially destructive. By losing a loved one we lose the source of our most valued resources and the one provider of resources who can most effectively help us replace the loss and reinstate the sense of fallen self-esteem and self-efficacy that accompanies the loss.

Other sources of social support may help but are dependent on individuals' dependency on the lost individual and their degree of sociability. The more independent or more gregarious woman, for instance, is more capable of making peer attachments that will help her recover from bereavement than the woman who was dependent on her spouse, especially for social direction (Bankoff, 1986). In any case it is not surprising that loss of a spouse heads many stressful life-events lists as the most stressful. Even six or seven years after the loss the bereaved are likely to continue to show significant psychological distress when compared with people who have not suffered such a loss (Lehman et al., 1987).

SUMMARY AND CONCLUSIONS

This chapter began by giving an account of the trends in psychology and in stress research that led to a search for stress resistance variables in the environment rather than within the individual. The psychodynamic model depicted psychological distress as a product of internal conflicts. Behavioral and humanistic models, in contrast, argued for a more environmental interpretation of all behavior and internal states (e.g., feelings and cognitions). In addition, it was argued that the social and political Weltanschauung was consistent with environmental rather than biological or inborn interpretation of behavior. Social support, then, as an environmental resource, was congruent with trends in science and society and as such was met with a favorable early reception by stress theorists.

It was also pointed out that social support is not a new concept. Indeed, its roots are seen in the ritualized grief practices of Jews for thousands of years and in military strategy, which has emphasized troop cohesion for a similar period of time. More recently, work that predates the modern conceptualization of social support was reported by Visotsky and colleagues (1961), who emphasized the supportive as well as harmful role of social relationships throughout the stages of rehabilitation for polio victims.

Following this historical account, definitions of social support were considered. A definition was settled upon that emphasized the aspects of both social embeddedness and transfer of aid intended to assist the recipient. Specifically, *social support was defined as those social interactions or relationships that provide individuals with actual assistance or that embed individuals within a social system that is believed to provide love, caring, or a sense of attachment to a valued social group or dyad.*

Research was considered next on whether social support has a direct effect on well-being or has a stress-buffering effect. In the first instance, a direct effect is evident when social support is related to well-being independent of levels of stress. A stress-buffering effect, in contrast, takes place when social support is associated with less psychological distress or illness under high stress conditions, but has no relation to psychological distress when stress is low. Some researchers have argued that the stress-buffering occurs when social support is measured in terms of functional contributions of supportive others (i.e., actual transfer of aid), but not when support is measured in terms of social embeddedness. Others, however, have argued that stress-buffering occurs when individuals perceive that their social networks have the potential of providing support when they are in need. Although the concept of fit is appealing, few studies have examined specific stressor events, and consequently the evidence supporting this interpretation was seen as promising but far from conclusive.

The second part of the chapter focused on the process of social support within the context of the study of personal relationships. First, intimacy was considered because intimacy may be the key to understanding the process of social support. Intimacy was envisaged as providing both functional support and the sense that individuals are loved and appreciated. Such a viewpoint was seen as congruent with a biological and developmental interpretation of the importance of attachment in the human experience.

If intimate ties are central to healthy functioning, then the next avenue to explore would be the state of absence of intimate ties. Following this logic, research on loneliness was considered. Loneliness was discussed in terms of environmental and personological factors that contribute to it. From the discussion of loneliness emerged a viewpoint that relational competence may underlie both loneliness and social support. Seen this way, social support is the product both of its availability in the environment and of individuals' capabilities of tapping these social resources.

Also in relation to the process of social support, the sparse research on reactions to victims of crisis was considered. Supporters were depicted as motivated to help others with whom they had personal ties because they care for these individuals, because they have a sense of obligation, and because they may also benefit themselves. However, they are potentially impeded in providing aid owing to (a) negative feelings that may be engendered by confrontation with crisis and those involved in crisis, (b) their general lack of expertise in dealing with the complex reactions of victims, and (c) common misconceptions regarding the course of recovery.

Research pertaining to sex differences in the utilization and benefit of social support were also reviewed. Women were found to be more comfortable with the process of social support and to benefit more than men from its receipt. This engendered a cost, however, as women were also found to be more likely to be exposed to the troubles of others in their larger, more intimate supportive network.

The next section of the chapter considered the negative side of social support. Personal relationships were argued to have both positive and negative components, and a view that emphasizes one or the other is misrepresentative of what actually occurs between people. Situational and personal factors and their interaction may limit the effectiveness of social support. It was emphasized that the ecology of the event must be considered if we are even to predict when positive attempts to help will prove effective.

In the final section of the chapter, the active ingredients of social support were considered within the model of conservation of resources. Social support was depicted as providing lacking resources or reinforcing diminished resources. It was argued that social support is most likely to be effective when it bolsters diminished resources existing within the recipient. Whether replacing or reinforcing resources, the fit of the resource provided by social support to the particular resource lost or diminished was highlighted. The closer the fit, the more likely and positive the adjustment. Where fit is especially poor, prolonged adjustment problems unfold. This may be why death of a loved one is so devastating. In such instances support can, at best, provide only a partial substitution for what was lost.

In the next chapter internal resources that aid stress resistance will be considered. Then an attempt will be made to integrate the social support literature with the literature on internal resources. This will move us closer to research that more fully reflects an ecological model of stress resistance.

5

PERSONAL ATTRIBUTES
AND STRESS RESISTANCE

Envy and wrath shorten the life.

(*Ecclesiastes*)

This chapter will focus on the role of personal attributes in stress resistance. The relationship between personal attributes and stress has only begun to receive research attention, but exciting trends are already emerging. Because the self has been of central interest to psychology, there is good groundwork for interpreting why certain characteristics interact with stress as they do. Hopefully, this background will promote an understanding of how personal attributes affect individuals confronting stressful circumstances and will bridge the gaps in knowledge that still exist. In the final analysis, people's reactions to stress must ultimately depend on themselves, who they are, and how they perceive the world.

In this chapter I will begin with a discussion of why interest was drawn to the influence of personal attributes on stress reactions. Following this I will review some empirical studies that have examined key personal traits in terms of their relationship to stress. Emphasis will be placed on developing theoretical insights that explain the influence of certain personal characteristics. As in the previous chapter on social support, the findings will be considered in terms of the constructs and concepts developed from the models of conservation of resources and of ecological congruence. This will lead to a consideration of the combined contribution of personal attributes and social support to stress resistance, a step that will bring us closer to what occurs in the real world, where the self and the environment are in continual contact.

Three aspects of the self will be considered. Taken from the theoretical work of the existential viewpoint, these are the three simultaneous aspects of being in the world (May, 1958). They are *Umwelt*, which literally means "world around" and can be understood to mean the self vis-à-vis the environment; *Mitwelt*, literally the "with world," the self vis-à-vis others; and finally the *Eigenwelt*, or the "own world," the sense of relationship with one's self. While stress researchers have been more atheoretical than this, it will be seen that this trichotomy encompasses the investigative trends concerning the relationship between the self and stress and, in the end, facilitates a more integrated analysis of the research findings. These three aspects of self also occupy a circumplex that begins with the self and encircles the phenomenological world, which preoccupies the self and reflects back on the self. In this regard, individuals will be affected by stress as a product of the way they view themselves, their environments, and their social interactions. How they view these domains will, in turn, result in reactions from the environment and social realm that will affect them.

PERSONAL ATTRIBUTES AND PSYCHOPATHOLOGY

The interest of clinical psychology and psychiatry in the role played by personality has had a negative bias throughout much of the modern history of these disciplines. Attention was oriented generally toward how personal traits affected psychopathology and illness and seldom toward a study of mental or physical health. Especially in the study of clinical issues, researchers and theorists were biased toward consideration of how certain traits contributed to breakdown, neurosis, psychosis, or psychosomatic illness, and not to well-being or health.

This point is well illustrated in the psychiatric view of the personality of adolescents. Psychological disturbance is considered a normal concomitant of youth (A. Freud, 1958; Ackerman, 1958). Adolescence is viewed as a state of storm and strife characterized by distressing and turbulent thoughts, feelings, and actions. Those who do not display such erratic thoughts and feelings are not spared, however. Not only is the display of pathology considered pathological, but the lack of display of pathology is also considered pathological! Beres (1961) suggests that adolescents who do not experience these traits are likely to have suffered from premature crystallization of their response patterns. Anna Freud (1958) similarly argued that teenagers who conform to societal strictures and fail to display their certain unrest are likely to develop deviant adult personalities.

The problem with these conceptualizations is that they take for granted that adolescence is a particularly tumultuous period and that displaying bizarre behavior is the norm. This is not necessarily substantiated by research, however (Bandura, 1964). Most adolescents conform to their parents' and society's wishes, and rebellion usually takes the form of an occasional outburst and a passion for some genre of music that their parents would prefer at a lower volume. Most teenagers stay in school, seek work, socialize with their friends, and have a rising interest in the opposite sex. This is not to say that families with adolescents do not experience storm and strife, but the blame for this is best attributed to the transition that both children and parents are making. Their roles are changing as the adolescents conform to society's demands by becoming increasingly independent and therefore autonomous of their parents' rule.

Because psychiatry and clinical psychology have based their ideas on work with abnormal populations, the tendency to develop personality theory from knowledge of the pathological personality has clearly dominated the literature, at least until the late 1950s (Jahoda, 1958). One could argue that pathology or psychopathology were also looking at how personality was associated with *not* breaking down or *not* developing psychopathology or disease. However, the absence of neurosis is not mental health and the absence of asthma is not physical health. We can see that this is obviously the case if we depict health and illness on a continuum and not as dichotomous variables. As illustrated in Figure 5.1, the population under normal conditions is represented by the right of the two bell-shaped normal curves. Interest in pathology then is concerned with the left-hand tail of this curve. Indeed, the type of pathology usually indicating hospitalized or outpatient groups is fairly uncommon and therefore couched well into the left tail of the distribution. Obviously, not everyone who does not fall in this area of the distribution on a given trait is healthy; they may be marginally ill, have yet undiagnosed symptoms, or have another malady altogether.

This raises another point about pathology and psychopathology: they are typically studied in terms of a given disorder. It is common to find reports of, say, lung cancer, or all forms of cancer, or clinical depression, or schizophrenia. It is uncommon, on the other hand, to find studies of all mental illnesses or all diseases. Studies that even approach such questions would very likely be chastised for being scientifically muddled, as the causes of these different diseases are so varied. Indeed, one of the principal purposes of diagnosis is to provide a means for

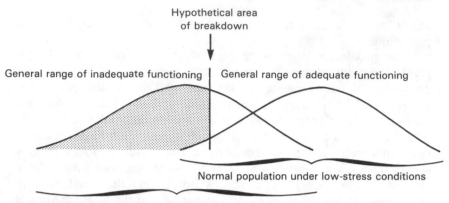

FIGURE 5.1   Statistical representation of stress-health-breakdown model.

distinguishing the antecedents of one disorder from those of another. Whereas this is a valuable goal, differential diagnosis and specialization in medicine obfuscate the greater gestalt of factors that contribute to breakdown, instead favoring the more circumscribed question of what contributes to a given disease (Antonovsky, 1979).

CONCEPTUALIZING HEALTH

Health, in contrast, is more difficult to define. If the etiology and correlates of pathology are best illustrated by extreme groups at that end of the continuum, then it might follow that the same principles can be applied in examining the etiology and correlates of health. Thus, health might be represented by those persons who fall in the right tail of the figure which reflects those who have positive health profiles. In terms of physical health, Olympic athletes in the prime of their youth may be thought of as models of superior health. In the psychological realm, the self-actualized individual may epitomize positive mental health. Few individuals, however, are so blessed and, consequently, a study of health that focused on the right-hand tail would also be very restrictive.

Another problem emerges when one tries to define health. As already mentioned, when an individual has even one significant symptom of pathology he or she is categorized as ill. Being highly anxious or depressed and having elevated systolic blood pressure or an abnormal white cell count indicate illness. That the anxious individual is functioning at work or that the hypertensive has good lung capacity is generally not of interest. At best these factors would be considered secondary in defining the individual's status. If an individual is healthy on nine traits and unhealthy on a tenth, then he or she is said to be ill, not well. The upshot is that few individuals are healthy in this sense.

At any one time a majority of the population may be characterized by some morbid condition in the realm of physical health (Antonovsky, 1979), and an even higher percentage may display significant psychological problems (Srole, Langner, Michael, Opler, & Rennie, 1962). Even the percentage of individuals who suffer from severe, marked, or incapacitating mental impairment has been reported to be as high as 23 percent of the population (Srole et al., 1962). Pathogens and stressors are so ubiquitous it is a wonder that anyone is healthy.

Research on stress, however, makes possible another approach for studying health. If the normal distribution depicted in the right-hand bell-shaped curve of Figure 5.1 represents the status of health of the general population at a time of low stress, then the distribution illustrated by the curve on the left reflects this same population under conditions of high stress. As may be observed, the number of individuals who fall to the left of the hypothetical area of breakdown becomes larger, as many of those who lacked pathological symptoms prior to the exposure to stress producing conditions now break down. At the same time, of course, the number of persons who do not display symptoms of illness or breakdown becomes relatively smaller.

The conditions that produce stress thus provide another perspective on the question of health and illness. By challenging the coping capacity of individuals, one may identify false positives (those who were thought to be healthy but were actually only marginally so). This opens the way for a distinction between three groups: *the reasonably healthy, the ill or unwell,* and *the marginal.* This marginal group is represented in Figure 5.1 by the shaded area, which is the difference between that portion of the population in the area of illness who were not in that area prior to stressful conditions but who entered that area after exposure to these conditions.

Although this three-part distinction does not represent the full continuum of health and illness, it does mirror our real-life concerns. Few people expect to be professional athletes or self-actualized souls. For most people just remaining in a reasonable state of health despite life's multifarious threats and challenges is as much as may be expected. Such a distinction also meets the needs of health care providers and policymakers. It distinguishes between those currently in need of treatment, those likely to need treatment if stressors occur (say, pollution levels were to rise), and those who are likely to continue to function independently.

A number of theorists have arrived at criteria for health and illness continua that are consistent with such relativistic thinking, but they express the above points conceptually rather than statistically. Fanshel (1972), for example, states that people are well to the extent that they can carry out their daily activities and they are in a state of dysfunction when they cannot. Antonovsky (1979), as I read him, suggests that health is represented by a continuum from "ease to dis-ease" that is dependent on four facets: pain, functional limitation, prognostic implication, and action implication. Within this schema, health and illness are relative. However, he distinguishes between those who are moderately or severely incapacitated and those who are only mildly incapacitated or not at all incapacitated. Jahoda (1958) expresses this perspective most distinctly in the psychological domain when she defines mental health as success or adaptation in six areas of human functioning: ability to love; adequacy in love, work, and play; adequacy in interpersonal relations; efficiency in meeting situational requirements; capacity for adaptation and adjustment; and efficiency in problem-solving. These theorists share in their view of health an emphasis on reasonable functioning given the constant challenges that people face.

Focusing the study of personality on the prediction of who will adapt to life's hard course exposes psychology and psychiatry to new questions. The relevance of personality theory is extended to a much wider segment of the population, for it concerns virtually everyone and not deviant individuals alone as in studies of pathology. Moreover, it changes the orientation from looking at a single disease to the overall functioning of individuals. Finally, it draws attention to questions of central concern to stress; namely, which aspects of personality allow individuals to function at acceptable levels amidst the constant hassles and stressors and occasional catastrophes that accompany life.

SEARCH FOR STRESS MODERATORS

Earlier I made the point that stress researchers were concerned with the reason stressors did not have a more pervasive impact on the self (Rabkin & Streuning, 1976). The argument was that the environmental bias pressed researchers and theorists to expect that exposure to stress would have a profound impact on mental and physical health. When health outcome was found to be only modestly affected by stressors a call-to-arms was made to search for factors that might modify this relationship (Dohrenwend & Dohrenwend, 1974). The logic for this was based on the supposition that stressors do result in distress, but that some individuals are shielded from these deleterious effects because they possess certain resistance resources.

We argued further in the previous chapter that attention was quickly directed to the study of social support because as an aspect of the environment it fitted the *Weltanschauung* that sought an environmental explanation for mental illness. If an environmental cause, embodied in stressors, did not largely contribute to psychological distress, then at least a combination of environmental factors, namely stressors and social support, might. As the previous chapter illustrates, there was some merit in this approach. Social support has been found to be associated with well-being and may buffer the impact of stressors when there is good fit between the help provided by social support and the requirements of the situation (Cohen & Wills, 1985; Gottlieb, 1981; Hobfoll, 1986a; Sarason & Sarason, 1985). Without deprecating its appreciable contribution, social support has not lived up to initial expectations that it is a social catholicon that would solve the stress distress puzzle.

As is often the case in research, when new solutions do not meet optimistic early expectations, the pendulum swings back to reexamination and reframing old solutions. This can be seen in a flurry of fresh and interesting attempts to reevaluate how the self may influence stress resistance. Jumping ahead a bit, one might say that these fresh attempts could be called personality revisionism, in that they revise the view of self from something that contributed to ill-being to something that might explain stress resistance. Before reviewing some of the key attempts to investigate this revisionist stance, the roots of this position will be examined.

EARLY PERSPECTIVES ON PERSONALITY AND WELL-BEING

One of the earliest perspectives on personal attributes and well-being was that of Adler (1929). Adler postulated that two principal factors led to the healthy personality. The first was an active stance; activity allowed for moving toward mastery and away from feelings of inferiority. The second factor was social attitude, *Gemeinschaftsgefühl*, translated as "social interest" or "social feeling." Children's observations of family interactions, parental patterns, and societal practices were viewed as leading to a social attitude encompassed in the personality on a continuum from antisocial to prosocial. Placing the two factors together we see that Adler envisioned the healthy personality as one that incorporated an active, prosocial structure. Although both the seeds of humanism and an understanding of self that was based on mastery lie within his construction of personality, Adler still insisted that the primary drive was a negative one, the inferiority complex. This divides him from later humanist theorists.

World War I spawned a search to understand the evils of humankind through art, philosophy, and psychology. Modern world warfare was a shock to Western culture, a culture that at the turn of the century had hoped that technology and liberalism were foreshadows of an age of advancement and wisdom. Perhaps the most well-known example of this disillusionment is Picasso's *Guernica*, which depicts the bombing of a small Spanish town in the extreme abstract form of modernism. This painting symbolizes crisis and despair beyond the boundaries of human control. It is also of interest that Freud's publication of the theory of Thanatos, the death wish, followed the First World War (1920).

The Second World War, however, brought horrors beyond those ever imagined in the first war. Society no longer expressed hopes that technology was the key to a new era of peace and wisdom. Nazism showed the extent to which science could be exploited in the death camps, and the atomic bomb foretold of an age of potential world destruction. Perhaps most disconcerting, Nazism had sprung from one of the most sophisticated cultures in the history of the human race. Germany prior to 1933 was a country of democracy and liberalism and a wellspring for the arts, sciences, and humanities.

Perhaps in reaction to this horror, people needed to search for new hope and to place what had occurred in perspective. Following the Second World War there was a surge in psychology to understand the two aspects of the self: that which is healthy and that which would bend to the will of a Hitler, Goebbels, or Mussolini. The latter aspect is illustrated in the work on dogmatism, conformity, aggression, and authoritarianism that followed the war (Adorno, Frenkel-Brunswik, Levinson, & Sanford, 1950; Bandura, Ross, & Ross, 1961; Rokeach, 1960; Sears, Maccoby, & Levin, 1957), but this is of less concern to my argument here. The early postwar effort to understand the healthy aspect of the self, in contrast, may be seen as the progenitor of the search for personal attributes that explain the human ability to resist the taxing qualities of major life stressors.

Out of the fires of the concentration camp itself emerged the theories of Victor Frankl (1963), who forged his existential psychiatric perspective during more than seven years in Hitler's death camps. Despite overwhelming circumstances, he witnessed some individuals emerging from the camps with a heightened sense of self. He theorized that people must fulfill *creative values* through productive endeavors and *experiential values* through enjoyment of that which is beautiful and pleasurable. When the routes to creative and experiential fulfillment are blocked, as they were in the concentration camp, individuals are left with a search for meaning. Those who find a purpose in their suffering and death resist hopelessness and despair. In terms of stress resistance, Frankl posited that people must create new meanings for existence when older, cherished meanings have lost validity.

Maslow (1968) became a major proponent of the viewpoint that men and women are positively motivated and growth oriented. Maslow postulated that neurosis emerges when wishes for safety, for belonging and identification, for close love relationships, and for respect and prestige are thwarted. Given fulfillment of these needs, however, humans would naturally move progressively along the steps of psychic growth. Maslow's theory, however, should not be confused with a theory of adjustment. Whereas he did think that mentally healthy individuals are particularly capable of adjusting to their environment, he placed still greater emphasis on the autonomous character of the healthy personality. This autonomy allowed self-actualized people to choose whether they would adjust to society, resist society, or ignore society. It is this independence from the environment, however, that is the key to their heightened mastery. Because self-actualized individuals act relatively independently of their environment, they possess great stability in the face of deprivation, challenge, frustration, failure, and loss. With autonomy comes an enhanced sense of self with which one can withstand the vicissitudes of life and remain strong in the face of hardship.

This humanistic existential trend finds favor in the writings of many other theorists of the early postwar period, including Rollo May, Carl Rogers, and Erich Fromm. Together their work reflects a view that people are capable of overcoming adversity, are basically good, and possess the ability to choose freely among the myriad choices that confront them. Their optimistic work moves psychology away from psychodynamic theory's negative view and behaviorism's neutral view. Most important to this discussion, these positive theories demand that a distinction be made between mental health and mental illness. Health, like illness, is defined by a certain set of symptoms. The traits of health include positive self-regard, mastery, autonomy, self-knowledge, and sense of meaningfulness. Socially, they include a feeling of belonging and the ability to love, coupled with a lack of dependency.

EARLY WORK ON PERSONALITY AND STRESS

A number of practical areas of inquiry have also contributed to our thinking on personal attributes and stress resistance. The influence of personal characteristics on withstanding combat pressures has long been of interest to military strategists. During World War II and the Korean War, psychologists and psychiatrists applied their knowledge and techniques to the question of what factors affect psychiatric breakdown in battle. The insidious erosion of men in moderately intense combat that characterized World War II suggested that breakdown was not related to personal characteristics. The fact that such a high percentage of carefully selected soldiers broke down after prolonged service in active theaters of fighting, suggested that situational contingencies, not personal attributes, were responsible for soldiers' reactions. Records showed psychological casualty rates ranging between about 10 and 50 percent of total line strength, with averages of about 25 percent. Such a high percentage of breakdown far exceeded the contemporary understanding of psychopathology, which was believed to occur at much lower rates.

The following quotation from the report of a military psychiatrist serving in Europe typifies the leading perspective of the day (quoted in Marlowe, 1979). Reporting on a period of heavy fighting the psychiatrist writes:

On 16 September the incidence of exhaustion casualties began to increase and by 27 September had reached an alarming figure. On that date 71 men were admitted for treatment. Some of the best men in the division became exhaustion casualties, including a high percentage of non-commissioned officers of the first three grades.

Two points can be drawn from this quote: increasing numbers of men broke down as stress continued, and the best men seemed to be as vulnerable as others. The conclusion that extreme or prolonged stressors affect everyone equally has subsequently been shown to be invalid (Milgram, 1986). On the other hand, a progressive step had been made in the conceptualization of stress; namely, given enough stress, anyone can break down.

Despite certain misconceptions, the large group trends noted during the war are instructive because they give us insights about the marginal health group discussed earlier. After an initial bout with acute anxiety, soldiers entered into a period of peak performance four or five days after exposure to combat. This peak period continued until an average of about 28 days after entering the war zone. The incidence of combat exhaustion rose precipitously following this period, even to the point of reaching over 100 percent of troop strength (i.e., not everyone breaks down, but, including reinforcements, more break down than are in the field at any one time) (Marlowe, 1979). This testifies to the presence of a broad marginal band of individuals who withstand fairly high and extended stressor situations, but who are likely to succumb to particularly intense or prolonged stressors. It also suggests that virtually any individual is susceptible to breakdown if the stressors are sufficiently extreme.

Whereas individual characteristics were not thought to be related to breakdown in combat, observations of group characteristics led to some interesting insights about the role of personal resources in breakdown. Prior experience with stress was viewed as a principal factor in breakdown. Inexperienced troops tended to have high rates of neuropsychiatric breakdown and injury proneness. Morale was judged to be another significant factor; the stigma of failure and incompetence had a devastating effect. The 24th Division, which had been responsible for the defense of Oahu during Pearl Harbor, for instance, experienced high numbers of psychiatric cases and, interestingly, unusual amounts of reported homosexuality throughout its deployment. Perhaps the latter was a reaction on the part of men to their extreme malaise.

In contrast, more well trained troops who had a strong belief in their military competence experienced exceedingly low levels of neuropsychiatric casualties. The 442nd Regimental Combat Team, composed of Nisei (Japanese-Americans) from Hawaii and relocation centers, was heralded for *esprit de corps*. It was the most decorated unit in the U.S. Army, saw intense combat, and had almost no psychiatric casualties (casualty information obtained from Marlowe, 1979). Well-trained Airborne divisions also had low rates of breakdown, again despite their continued exposure to intense combat.

One of the first careful studies of combat-related stress was undertaken by Basowitz, Persky, Korchin, and Grinker (1955), who extensively investigated soldiers undergoing paratroop training. They identified two different aspects of anxiety, one associated with fear of or fantasized dangers of jumping and the other associated with sensitivity to the shame of failure. Basowitz et al. concluded that the fear of failure, possibly a reflection of poor self-esteem and low sense of mastery, was often more pervasive than fear of bodily injury.

Despite the fact that this study of Basowitz et al. is seldom quoted in the stress literature today, its findings and methodology are instructive. In discussing the work with me, Shelley Korchin related how the research staff labored to achieve questionnaire, behavioral, and physiological data, always attempting to gain access to soldiers as near the time of the jump as possible. The practice of stress researchers today to distribute questionnaires principally to college samples who have vague exposure to stressful circumstances cannot achieve the level of exactitude that this more in-depth method can. Nor can it provide nearly as much information about the stressful characteristics and phases of external events.

The classic study of patients' reactions to poliomyelitis undertaken by Visotsky et al. (1961) also deserves mention. Visotsky and colleagues were concerned with personal attributes that facilitated keeping stress within manageable limits, generating encouragement and hope, maintaining or restoring a sense of personal worth, enhancing physical recovery, and improving future prospects (interpersonal, social, and economic). The personal attributes associated with recovery in this broad sense were "determination to improve," "acceptance of disability," and "hope." In addition, Visotsky et al. attached great importance to adopting a stance that progressed from initiative to mastery. Finally, the ability to seek and accept help was an attribute that aided the prolonged recovery process, and those who had a "long-standing, intense need for independence had considerable difficulty in accepting the help essential to furthering their recovery" (p. 443).

Their study represents a pioneering attempt to understand the nature of the stress process and was published well before such research became popular. No data were presented, however, to buttress the conclusions of the authors, and it is possible that the findings are confounded with stereotypes and expectations of the staff based on the behavior of a few prominent patients. Nonetheless, the report is insightful and points to a number of areas where more controlled research should venture.

These early studies are notable not only because they laid the groundwork for future research but because they were conducted at a time when psychologists and psychiatrists were looking at personality variables per se, and not the role of personality as an aid to stress resistance. The Zeitgeist of interest is illustrated by the publication of volumes that aimed to experimentally and theoretically define the limits and nature of personality traits, such as Mowrer's (1950) Learning Theory and Personality Dynamics, May's (1950) The Meaning of Anxiety, and

Eysenck's (1957) *The Dynamics of Anxiety and Hysteria.* As we examine current research endeavors it will become apparent that these forward-thinking stress researchers helped lay the groundwork for an area of research that is integral to any comprehensive understanding of stress resistance.

CONTEMPORARY RESEARCH ON PERSONAL RESOURCES AND STRESS RESISTANCE

Self vis-à-vis Environment

Contemporary stress research on personal attributes has focused, for the most part, on the self in relation to the environment. Aspects of the self that pertain to control have received particular attention. Variables that exemplify this trait include internal locus of control, mastery, and personality hardiness. It is no accident that Western psychologists have concerned themselves so extensively with control. Control is central to Western conditions and biases based on the Protestant ethic, a philosophy that assumes a fixed relationship between actions and reactions and esteems independent accomplishment.

Control expectations

The study of the relationship between locus of control and stress resistance has interested a number of researchers. When persons believe circumstances are within their own control they are termed internal in their locus of control. When they believe outside factors determine what happens to them, they are categorized as external in their locus of control. It follows that "internals" should be active copers, because they assume that their own efforts will increase the likelihood of success.

One of the first studies to test this hypothesis was reported by Johnson and Sarason (1978). They collected retrospective data on stressful life events and current self-perceptions concerning locus of control, anxiety, and depression among a sample of college students. They found that only "externals" were significantly negatively affected by stressful life events. This finding, along with similar reports by others (Lefcourt, Miller, Ware, & Sherk, 1981; Sandler & Lakey, 1982), has been interpreted as indicating that internals do not see their fate as solely determined by external factors and tend to view themselves as capable of overcoming environmental stressors. Externals, in contrast, are likely to feel that stressful events lead to negative outcome because they are incapable of counteracting powerful outside forces.

Little is known about the kinds of stressors that are best met by mastery orientations. Lefcourt et al. (1981) noted that internal locus of control had buffered the effect of stressors in the more distant past, but that both internals and externals were similarly negatively affected by more recent stressful events. These authors interpreted the results to mean that negative life events have an immediate impact on nearly everyone, but that personality factors may affect how long these deleterious effects are manifested. Wheaton (1983) examined the effect of a subset of locus-of-control variables that indicate fatalism on the impact of acute and chronic stressors, but failed to find a differential effect of fatalism on these two kinds of stressful events. He did find, however, that low fatalism decreased susceptibility to schizophrenia and depression. The moderating effects noted in the case of schizophrenia and depression were substantial. Obviously, these results are preliminary and may be related to specific sample or situational characteristics rather than to the interaction of a control orientation with situational demands.

At least two studies of locus of control did not find stress-buffering or main effects (i.e., directly related to outcome, not interacting with stress level) attributable to an internal control orientation (McFarlane, Norman, Streiner, & Roy, 1983; Nelson & Cohen, 1983). Both studies relied on prospective analyses, but did not find locus of control directly related to outcome, or that it interacted with stressful events to affect outcome.

Cohen and Edwards (in press) have suggested that stress-buffering effects have been more consistently noted when the well-known Rotter measure of internal-external locus of control is used than when other measures are employed. The two studies just mentioned, for example, did not use the Rotter scale. Also, Krause (1985) suggested that buffering effects emerge more clearly if response set is controlled (e.g., the tendency to acquiesce).

However, the data appear to be much more complex than this. One significant difficulty has been the repeated use of stressful-event lists, which are fraught with reporting problems and which mix many different kinds of events that occur over varying time periods. I would suggest that the data indicate that internals have some advantage over externals, but that this research renders any analysis of fit impossible. Internal locus of control may be a poor resource indeed when one is faced with a continued sequence of objectively uncontrollable events and an excellent resource when one is confronting business challenges. At this time, however, this is open to conjecture and awaits situation-specific research. The research on how control orientation interacts with social support, which will be reviewed later in this chapter, will shed some light on this issue.

Personality hardiness

Hardiness is another orientation of the self vis-à-vis the environment that has aroused interest among stress theorists. Hardiness actually comprises three related characteristics: (a) control, which refers to belief in one's ability to successfully affect the course of events, (b) commitment, exemplified by an interest in one's surroundings and a sense of meaningfulness, and (c) challenge, which refers to the belief that change is part of life's course and stimulates development (Kobasa, 1979; Kobasa et al., 1981). Kobasa proposes that persons who possess the trait of hardiness are more stress-resistant owing to their belief in their efficacy, their resistance to feelings of alienation, and their concentration on what they can gain and how they may grow from stressful circumstances. Accordingly, hardy individuals interpret events positively, which leads to goal-directed behavior and avoidance of regressive coping (e.g., withdrawal, avoidance).

In a prospective study of middle- and upper-level managers of a large utility company, Kobasa et al. (1981) examined whether hardiness reduced the negative health sequelae that follow stressful life events. The results indicated that stressful life events and constitutional predisposition increase the propensity for illness, whereas hardiness decreases the chance of illness. Only direct effects of hardiness on health were noted, but the pattern of means has been interpreted as a stress-buffering effect for hardiness (Cohen & Edwards, in press). In fact, when constitutional predisposition was dropped from the analysis, the interaction of stressful events and hardiness was significant, attesting to a stress-buffering effect.

Other studies have also found hardiness to be associated with better psychological and physical health (Ganellen & Blaney, 1984; Rhodewalt & Agustsdotter, 1984; Wiebe & McCallum, 1986), although questions remain as to which aspects of hardiness are most important and whether they may be viewed separately or should be considered as a greater whole. In a prior publication I also questioned the applicability of the hardiness concept to cultures other than those shared by American managers and affluent college students. However, Kuo and Tsai (1986) have since found that Asian immigrants who exhibited personality hardiness were less likely to experience stressful life events, financial worries, and adjustment difficulties than those low on hardiness. Furthermore, hardiness was significantly associated with lower levels of depression in this sample. Path analysis, a method designed to determine the causal relationships between sets of variables, further suggested that hardiness both directly limited depression levels and indirectly acted on depression by reducing adjustment difficulties and encounters with stressful happenstances.

In a different study, Westman (personal communication) has found that Israeli soldiers who possess hardiness are more successful during rigorous training than those who lack it. This study is notable because performance data are available from independent judges concerning behavioral measures and so may not be explained by biased self-reports on both hardiness and outcome. It is also of interest because Westman concentrated on a circumscribed series of clearly stressful events that make emotional and performance demands on individuals beyond their normal day-to-day experience.

Tests on samples that are characterologically or culturally different from those on which measures were normed are exceptional examinations of the validity of a concept because the results are unlikely to be attributed to response sets or stereotypical patterns of responding. Unfortunately, the stress literature is plagued by repetitive studies using college students and middle-class samples. The findings of Kuo and Tsai and Westman are exceptional in this regard. Whether hardiness directly affects individuals or reacts interactively with stressful events remains to be seen; however, this may not be the most important question in the long run. What is important is that hardiness appears to be a robust trait that gives adaptive advantage to those who possess it. Just how it does so and whether it is a stable constellation of traits will be important questions for future research.

Type A behavior, anger, and stress resistance

Another aspect of the self in relation to the environment revolves around the concepts of type A behavior and anger. The type A behavior pattern is exemplified by impatience, competitiveness, hostility, and accelerated speech and motor movements. It is contrasted with the type B pattern, which is defined as the relative absence of these behaviors, a more relaxed attitude toward life (Friedman & Rosenman, 1959). It was originally proposed that the type A was more likely than the type B to experience intensified behavioral and physiological reactions to stressful environmental conditions, which lead to heart disease and other pathology (Glass, 1977).

Rhodewalt, Hays, Chemers, and Wysocki (1984) examined whether type A was associated with poorer stress resistance in a small sample of university administrators. They found that the extreme type A, who reported more job-related stressors and general life stressors, was more susceptible to physical and psychological problems than the moderate type A and type B who experienced similar stressful circumstances. The type A and type B who experienced lower levels of life or job stress did not report differential levels of stress consequences. Although this is a cross-sectional study, the authors do illustrate the specificity of the events noted, adding confidence to the findings. Specifically, moderately controllable events were found to be the most difficult for the type A, a fact consistent with theoretical notions regarding the difficulty such individuals have with ambiguous circumstances. Secondly, health consequences were only noted in respect to cardiovascular disease, the health problem thought to be most clearly associated with the type A behavior pattern.

In a second study of type A behavior, this time relying on the self-reports of a large sample of undergraduates, Rhodewalt and Agustsdotter (1984) also noted that type A personalities were especially vulnerable to events that were not fully under their control. The specific vulnerability of the type A to events for which degree of personal control is indeterminable was noted in another student sample by Suls, Gastorf, and Witenburg (1979).

The cross-cultural validity and gender specificity of the type A construct has also been examined. In a study of employed women, Kelly and Houston (1985) found the type A pattern to be associated with greater feelings of stress and tension. Among working married women, type A was also associated with poorer physical health, but this was not found for divorced, widowed, or single working women. In a fascinating study, Cohen, Syme, Jenkins, Kagan, & Syzanski (1979) looked at the relationship between type A behavior and coronary heart disease in Japanese-Americans living in Hawaii and found only a moderate relationship. In this cohort, men who scored high on the "Western" dimension of type A behavior—hard-driving, competitive, speedy, and impatient—had heightened rates of coronary heart disease. But two other aspects of type A behavior, hard work and commitment, were not associated with heart disease in this sample. This might suggest that Japanese-Americans and other Americans are differentially affected by stressful circumstances, or it may indicate that hard work and commitment are culturally tied to type A behavior but are not that aspect of type A that is disease-producing.

Two studies have failed to find any association between type A and stress resistance. In the first, Somes, Garrity, and Marx (1981) measured type A using the structured interview technique. A problem here may have been the difficulty of categorizing subjects as type A or type B because of the very subjective interview format. In the second study, however, the self-report method also failed to find a stress-reducing affect of type B behavior (Kobasa, Maddi, & Zola, 1983).

Such irregularity of findings is frustrating for readers, and it is easy to begin to search for the "key" that will resolve the inconsistencies. Further skepticism is warranted because journals view studies showing no significant effects or lacking interaction effects as less "interesting" and so these studies are often left unpublished. Consequently, reported results are biased toward type-I error, false rejection of the null hypothesis. Type A seems to be associated with stress resistance, but again, the lack of studies looking at specific circumstances blurs any discussion of the mechanisms by which the type B person gains advantage over the type A. Once again, applying the fit concept will be necessary if future research is to clarify this issue. Furthermore, type A persons may differ from type Bs primarily in their expression of anger, and investigation of this more basic component of personality in anger-producing circumstances may be the most productive direction for future research (Spielberger, Johnson, Russell, Crane, Jacobs, & Worden, 1985).

Views of events and stress resistance

A broad category for an aspect of self vis-à-vis the environment that includes a number of different constructs pertains to the way in which persons view events occurring in their environment. This is a general catchall category and clear distinctions have yet to emerge from it. Let us consider some of the promising leads.

In an early study Bulman and Wortman (1977) examined how the coping of 29 accident victims who had been paralyzed related to their attributions of blame for their plight. Victims were defined as coping well if they had "accepted the reality of their injury and were attempting to deal positively with the paralysis. Patients who had a positive attitude toward physical therapy, who were motivated to work toward improvement of their physical abilities, and who reflected a desire to be as physically independent as possible were considered to be coping well" (p. 355). Those prone to blame others or feel they could have avoided the accident tended to exhibit poor coping, so defined. Blaming oneself, in contrast, was a successful predictor of good coping. These complex findings were interpreted as indicating that people are comforted by seeing an orderly world in which events do not just occur randomly. If their accident occurred during the normal course of events, say, as a result of their usual behavior (i.e., following an orderly world), this was more acceptable than if the accident occurred because they were engaged in a one-time behavior (i.e., a world in which chance and fate rule). Such insights are consistent with existential viewpoints of Antonovsky (1979) and Frankl (1963), which express the importance of people finding meaning in life, especially when tragedy strikes.

Another approach is to examine "affect intensity" and its relationship to reactions to life events (Larsen, Diener, & Emmons, 1986). In prior research, Diener, Larsen, Levine, and Emmons (1985) found affect intensity to be associated with experience of emotions, such that those high in affect intensity experienced more extreme emotions than those low in affect intensity. Diener et al. attributed this to factors that affect the excitability of the nervous system (e.g., hunger, caffeine, fatigue) and to stable individual differences in arousal, reactivity, or excitation potential. Studies indicate a tendency on the part of those high in affect intensity to respond more strongly to events than do those low in affect intensity. Thus temperamental characteristics may be more closely associated with stress responding than most environmentally oriented investigations have suggested. However, the extent to which affect intensity may be learned and the extent it is inherited and developed during the earliest periods of life have yet to be determined.

Another aspect of affect intensity is the degree of anger expressed in reaction to stressful events and the way the anger is expressed. When individuals who tend to hold stress-related anger inside themselves are confronted with stressful conditions, they have been found especially susceptible to elevations in blood pressure (diastolic) (Chesney, Gentry, Gary, Kennedy, & Harburg, 1984). The elevation in blood pressure was not noted for those who tend to withhold anger when under low stress conditions. Outward expression of anger, in turn, had a stress-buffering effect, such that those who displayed their anger were shown not to experience blood-pressure elevation, even when faced with greater exposure to stressors. This trend was noted for job and family stressors (Chesney et al., 1984) and for the stress caused by internal racial hostility (Kennedy, Chesney, Gentry, Gary, & Harburg, 1984), suggesting the robustness of this trait in stress resistance.

All of us have been encouraged at one time or another to "look on the brighter side" and to recall that "every cloud has a silver lining." Such admonishments are often rejected as too syrup-sweet, too unrealistic. Recent data on college students, however, suggest that persons who focus on the positive implications of stressful events are less negatively affected than those who are more realistic. Goodhart (1985) found that viewing the outcome of stressful events as positive was associated with positive aspects of well-being (e.g., self-esteem, life satisfaction). Viewing events as negative, in comparison, resulted in a diminished sense of well-being and increased sense of psychological distress (e.g., negative affect, psychological symptoms). A second important finding by Goodhart was that negative thinking had an enduring incapacitating effect, whereas a positive viewpoint made a short-term, positive contribution. Furthermore, those who took a negative stance were more likely to encounter future stressful events.

These findings suggest that people who take a negative stance are unable to reconcile the event with positive views of the self and the world. However, a second possibility is that negative thinkers are attempting to reconcile the world with their enduring negative view of self. These individuals may have a stake in a world view that places them in the role of martyr and helpless victim of circumstances. For negative thinkers, the negative view is a *primum mobile,* freeing them of the need to attempt to change the future. A positive viewpoint, in contrast, seems to require continued responsibility, as one interpretation of this Goodhart study is that a positive viewpoint does not, in itself, alter future perceptions or result in a primrose path. Instead, positive thinkers do well with current circumstances and must sustain their attitude to ensure future well-being.

Another series of studies that looked at a positive view of the self vis-à-vis the world illustrated the beneficial effect of a different aspect of self, learned resourcefulness. Rosenbaum and Palmon (1984), and Rosenbaum and Smira (1986) define learned resourcefulness as the "ability to employ various cognitive and behavioral skills to minimize the emotional impact of stressful events and to ensure the smooth flow of target behavior." Epileptic patients who exhibited moderate or low seizure frequency became less depressed and anxious if they were high in resourcefulness than if they were low in resourcefulness (Rosenbaum & Palmon, 1984). The performance advantage of more resourceful individuals was illustrated in a second investigation of dialysis patients in which high resourcefulness was associated with better past adherence to stringent fluid-intake regimes and with a more positive evaluation of future success in following medical demands (Rosenbaum & Smira, 1986).

Overall, research on variables that measure aspects of the self vis-à-vis the environment clearly indicates that the way individuals view themselves interacting with the environment affects their stress resistance. It would appear that feeling in control is most advantageous when (a) one is confronting a moderately stressful experience and (b) the need for control is not so great as to cause distress during events that are not controllable (as in the case of the extreme type A). Seeing meaningfulness and order and having an enduring sense of one's own resourcefulness may be especially important when the ability to gain control is tenuous, and a tendency to find meaning in tragedy may be especially important following exposure to catastrophic stressors. Finally, reactiveness appears to have at least two dimensions, intensity and valence. Regarding intensity, a tendency to react to events with extreme positive or negative emotions has been found to vary among people. There is also preliminary evidence that expressing anger in reaction to stressful events is beneficial and suppressing anger may result in increased blood pressure. Regarding valence, persons who adopt negative interpretations of events, or who withhold their anger, appear more prone to emotional upset and to encounter further stressful circumstances. This is clearly an exciting area for future research and may contribute to forming a conceptual bridge between environmental and personological perspectives.

Self Faces Self

Much less research has been undertaken in the domain of *Eigenwelt,* how the self views the self and the effect of this on stress resistance. This should not be surprising if my argument that stress researchers have been primarily concerned with environmental perspectives is correct. Existentialists and existential psychiatrists, who tend to be European (May, 1958), have preoccupied themselves with the *Eigenwelt.* It is the "I" of Buber's "I and Thou," the "I" that must be understood if the relationship to others is not to lack "power and the capacity to fructify itself" (May, 1958, p. 65). Such thinking revolves around abstract notions of self-knowledge and self-appreciation that are difficult to investigate empirically. Nevertheless, attempts have been made to identify the self vis-à-vis the self using normative measures and to examine whether such self attitudes affect individuals' capacity to adjust to stressful conditions.

Self-denigration, for instance, was studied by Kaplan, Robbins, and Martin (1983) in an exceptional 10-year follow up of 1,633 individuals first interviewed in the seventh grade. Adolescents who felt higher self-denigration were particularly vulnerable to greater psychological distress if they experienced greater numbers of bad events, failure events, and events that signified changes in routine. This was not, however, attributable to the fact that self-denigration led to more encounters with stressful events; rather it is best explained by the way such individuals interpret how environmental occurrences reflect on themselves. Stressful events may confirm their feelings of being lacking and unworthy.

Cronkite and Moos (1984) investigated the role of self-esteem in stress resistance, focusing on depressed mood, physical symptoms, and alcohol consumption. This study was unusual in that it relied on reports from married couples, whereas most studies have only examined individuals. Using a longitudinal design, Cronkite and Moos found that self-esteem was related to lower subsequent depression. The alleviating effect of self-esteem on depression was stronger yet for those whose spouses were also high in self-esteem. They also noted that greater self-esteem in wives occurred when husbands drank less alcohol, but surprisingly, greater self-esteem of husbands was related to wives drinking more. Self-esteem was not related to physical symptoms in either men or women. Men who were high in self-esteem also utilized more approach coping (i.e., directly facing their problems), whereas men who were low in self-esteem used more avoidance coping. Examination of the interaction of stressful life events with self-esteem failed to indicate any stress-buffering of self-esteem on outcome. This suggests that self-esteem contributes to more favorable outcome independent of stress levels.

Cronkite and Moos's prospective design, their controlling for prior levels of outcome, and their examination of married partners make this an exceptional contribution to our understanding of the role of self-esteem in the stress-illness relationship. It also highlights the complexity of the issue. Important information would have been lost if the effects of partners on each other had not been examined. Such an approach is consistent with that of the model of ecological congruence, because it more fully depicts the ecology of the individual's life space. But this is not surprising, since Moos has been a leading proponent of the ecological approach (see also Chapter 1).

Still another aspect of the self vis-à-vis the self was studied by Suls and Fletcher (1985), who examined the effect of "private self-consciousness" on adjustment to stressful circumstances. They argue that private self-consciousness results in greater awareness of the effects of stress on the self. This awareness "serves as a prerequisite for engaging in appropriate health seeking behavior" (p. 469). Interestingly, this coincides with existential theory that the individual is unable to cope with life's challenges without a heightened understanding of *Eigenwelt* (May, 1957).

Only a modicum of evidence supports Suls and Fletcher's notions, however. Nor is it clear whether lacking private self-consciousness plays a negative role akin to denial or whether the ameliorative effect of high private self-consciousness plays a positive role by fostering an active coping posture. In addition, what research there is has a number of inconsistencies, which leave some doubt about just what was found. There appeared to be some problem related to a globally positive response set, and the data were unstable from one wave of the study to the next (Suls & Fletcher, 1985). The construct of private self-consciousness nevertheless remains of considerable conceptual value, and these data will hopefully pique the interest of other researchers studying the actual process of thinking implied by Suls and Fletcher.

This early work on characteristics of the self vis-à-vis the self is encouraging. It suggests that the principles of mental health and ego-integration discussed by Maslow and others have validity when one differentiates between people who adjust to difficult life circumstances and those who do not. Those who appreciate and know themselves have a decided advantage over those who denigrate their personal worth and who avoid self-investigation. Faced with life's challenges their enduring positive sense of self stays them and helps preserve their psychological well-being.

Theoretically, the self vis-à-vis the environment evaluates itself on the basis of success. The self vis-à-vis the self, in contrast, is like Rogers's unconditional positive regard, if positive and strong it accepts without reference to outer events; this makes it potentially more enduring than the self that reflects the environment. Indeed, this may be the major advantage of such traits as self-esteem, because they are not tested by each attempt at mastery and each confrontation with the environment. The same principle, however, applies to self-denigration; despite objective successes it would tend to be implacable. Certainly these aspects of self are not entirely invulnerable to outside influence, but theoretically they should be comparatively resilient. Research that addresses such theoretical formulations will be of enormous interest and will facilitate a richer understanding not just of stress resistance but of personality itself.

Self vis-à-vis Others

The third aspect of the self that stress researchers have considered is the *Mitwelt,* the self vis-à-vis others. This aspect of the self is important to stress resistance, because humans are social animals. We live in dyads or families, nested in larger groups, which are part of greater societies. From birth we are dependent in some fashion on how others see us, and we consequently tend to adopt a view of ourselves that represents our link with others.

Returning to Adler's key concept of social interest, *Gemeinschaftsgefühl,* Crandall (1984) developed the proposition that those who are high in social interest have an advantage in dealing with stressors over those low in social interest. As I understand his argument, social interest results in people having a more active approach to life. Indeed, Crandall cites evidence for a positive relationship between internal locus of control and social interest. In addition, those high in social interest are likely to possess supportive ties and to find life meaningful. Furthermore, social interest is related to a decreased self-centeredness that results in a wider range of interests. This too, he argues, facilitates stress resistance, because it leads to a sense of challenge when one confronts some stressful events. Finally, he argues that those high in social interest tend to deemphasize their personal problems and, thus, maintain a more balanced outlook when faced with hardships.

Crandall examined his hypotheses in a study of two samples of students who completed questionnaires concerning social interest, encounter with stressful events, trait depression, anxiety, and hostility. He found that high social interest was associated with encountering fewer stressful events over a year's period. Also, subjects who were low in social interest were more negatively affected by stressful events than those high in social interest. Furthermore, those high in social interest had less intense symptoms of anxiety. These findings generally support Crandall's hypotheses. Unfortunately, he did not control for initial levels of symptoms, thus limiting the causal statements that might otherwise follow from this study. Nevertheless, his lead will be promising if those high in social interest are, in fact, shown to manifest the styles of coping that he suggests typify this trait. Otherwise, it is more parsimonious to suppose that social interest may merely represent a positive response set that measures the tendency of people to positively evaluate themselves and their surroundings. If social interest merely reflects the wish to appear in a socially desirable light then it has little value.

The moderating effect of anomie, alienation from society, was examined in a study of the relationship between stressful life events and psychiatric symptoms in a sample of air traffic controllers (Jenkins, 1979). This sample is of special interest because of the high levels of job stress they encounter. Anomie could exacerbate vulnerability by isolating the individual from social support and by contributing to a sense of meaninglessness. Jenkins prospectively followed a large sample of air traffic controllers who were initially free of clinically significant psychological problems. Analysis over a 27-month period failed to reveal any stress-buffering effect of low anomie on the dependent variable, impulse control problems.

Two other aspects of self vis-à-vis others were studied for their stress resistance potential by Cohen, Sherrod, and Clark (1986), social anxiety and self-disclosure (the willingness to share information of a personal nature). Cohen et al. were interested in determining whether these factors might underlie the stress-buffering effect that has been attributed to social support. The logic was that stress-buffering effects of social support might be shadows of characteristics of the self that affect the process of attainment of aid and intimacy. They measured perceived stress rather than event occurrence as their independent variable and depression as their dependent variable. Focusing on college freshmen they found a stress-buffering effect only in the case of social anxiety. Students with lower social anxiety were less negatively affected by high perceived stress than those who were high in social anxiety. The researchers failed, however, to find any three-way interactions (e.g., stress × social support × social anxiety or self-disclosure). So, no evidence was found for the thesis that the stress-buffering effect of social support might be a reflection of underlying social anxiety or self-disclosure. Their data are unclear on the extent to which social anxiety and self-disclosure had direct effects on depression. Process information was revealed, however, such that students who reported greater self-disclosure and lower social anxiety received more social support. Also, those reporting greater self-disclosure increased the number of their friendships over the 22-week interval studied.

Unfortunately, Cohen and associates' measure of stress is exceptionally confounded with depression. Other scales examine event occurrence or level of stressfulness of an event. But the particular measure used by Cohen et al., the Perceived Stress Scale (Cohen, Kamarck, & Mermelstein, 1983), taps "the degree to which subjects find their lives to be unpredictable, uncontrollable, and overloaded, and it includes a number of direct queries about current levels of experienced stress" (p. 965). Thus the measure is akin to measures of strain, not stressors. Such an approach will produce artificially high correlations between stress and distress, because the measures are almost one and the same. Further, it is difficult to see what interactions of perceived stress with resources are actually assessing. In a sense, this study measured the interaction of three personal variables, not two personal variables (social anxiety and self-disclosure), and an environmental variable as perceived stress reflects individual tendencies, not environmental exigencies.

Finally, I would call the reader's attention to the previous chapter on social support and to arguments promulgated by Sarason et al. (1986). Specifically, these authors provide evidence that much of what is thought to be environmentally based social support is actually an individual difference variable. They see social support comprising three components: environment contingencies, social competence, and ways of seeing the social world. The last two aspects are very much linked with the self as it relates to others rather than to the environment. In the previous chapter I chose to include social competence in the discussion of social support, but this was to make the point that social support is associated with aspects of the self. It would have been equally logical to place the discussion of social competence in this chapter.

Like aspects of the personality, social support tends to be stable over long periods of time and during periods of transition (Sarason et al., 1986). In addition, its perception is largely a product of underlying feelings about the self rather than of environmental occurrences (Coyne et al., 1981). Therefore, much of the stress-moderating effect of social support lies in these stable, underlying qualities. This calls into question some of the basic assumptions of social support researchers and theorists about the meaning of reports of receipt of aid and satisfaction with such receipt. Future investigations that differentiate between the "trait" of social support and the response to the acquisition of environmental support will be required to clarify this critical issue.

At this time only limited generalizations can be made from these studies. A modicum of evidence suggests that individuals who are motivated and comfortable about being in a world with others are more likely to resist the deleterious effects of stress and to feel a sense of well-being. However, it is entirely unclear whether this stems from the behavioral consequences of their attitudes toward themselves or directly from their self-evaluations. It is also possible that the self vis-à-vis others directly aids stress resistance or that it contributes to other factors such as social support that, in turn, buffer stress and enhance well-being. Perhaps the most exciting aspect of this area of research is that it remains so unexplored. Much further inquiry is required.

As can be seen, there have been many more attempts to examine the self vis-à-vis the environment than vis-à-vis the self or vis-à-vis others. Western psychology is probably only guilty here of reflecting Western values, which focus on independence as a keystone. Independence means being in control of the environment, not a "pawn in the game" or dependent on others. Furthermore, independence requires no self-understanding; Western society does not revere the Buddhist-like practice of peeling the levels of self to approach the core of one's needs. Yet, when these variables have been studied they have been no less powerful as predictors of stress resistance than is control. Prior to such evidence it may have been possible to argue that these aspects of self are irrelevant to Western society and adjustment to Western stressors, that they have poor fit with environmental demands. However, this does not appear to be the case.

Methodologically, the studies cited above can be faulted on a number of grounds. Cohen and Edwards (in press), for example, suggest that only when interaction terms were directly tested can stress-buffering effects be verified. Others have noted that measures of internal variables are often poorly constructed. The more recent studies, however, are usually longitudinal, and they control for initial levels of distress and appropriately test direct and interactive effects. The preliminary results of these investigations are robust, even if it is yet premature to make final judgments; certain personal characteristics are associated with well-being and stress resistance and those who possess these traits have a distinct advantage over those who do not.

What is lacking is an integration of the meaning of different traits. What does self-esteem have in common with mastery and how are the two related to social interest? Almost all of these studies draw their hypotheses from the variable itself, not from the concept behind the set of variables. Future researchers have a formidable challenge before them to understand the bridges that exist between the different aspects of self, which together make up the personality of the individual. Most likely there is considerable redundancy in the various aspects of self, despite their different names, and there are also likely to be independent facets of the self. What these are, how they aggregate, and how they affect stress resistance are exciting questions for the next generation of research.

STRESS AND COPING

Until now I have been discussing how *who we are* affects stress resistance. A second important focus of research addresses *what we do* in the face of stressors and how this affects outcome. This area of research falls under the general rubric of *coping,* which recent researchers (Mitchell, Cronkite, & Moos, 1983) have defined as "the cognitions and behaviors that people use to modify adverse aspects of their environments as well as to minimize the potential threat arising from such aspects" (p. 435) or, similarly (Lazarus & Folkman, 1984), as "constantly changing cognitive and behavioral efforts to manage specific external and/or internal demands that are appraised as taxing or exceeding the resources of the person" (p. 141).

There is not space here to fully address the topic of coping, which, although it is only one facet of stress resistance could easily fill an entire volume. Those seeking greater detail and depth are referred to other sources that have dealt primarily with coping (cf. Lazarus, 1966; Lazarus & Folkman, 1984; Meichenbaum & Jaremko, 1983). My more circumscribed goal is to examine how coping may be tied to personal resources that affect the stress resistance process. I view this as the most promising direction for research and intervention. This is the case, I would argue, because by identifying personal traits associated with coping styles or by identifying characteristic coping styles, investigators can discover why people tend to adjust well in certain situations and not others. Such an approach also enables researchers to identify which styles or traits are generally successful or generally maladaptive.

Two common misunderstandings should be clarified at the outset. First, in everyday language coping is often used to imply outcome; for example, someone who says he is "coping with the situation," means that he is successfully adapting to the problems confronting him. The generally accepted meaning of the term coping in stress research, however, carries no implication of valence or direction of success. Coping merely refers to the set of behaviors we use in our *efforts to manage* stressful situations, regardless of whether such attempts are beneficial. Second, coping should not be equated with mastery, since coping can include escape, avoidance, and denial, as well as efforts to directly overcome stressful circumstances (Lazarus & Folkman, 1984).

Lazarus and Folkman (1984) have promulgated a two-part distinction in the major forms of coping. These are emotion-focused coping and problem-focused coping. Emotion-focused coping includes efforts to cognitively regulate emotional reactions to stressful circumstances. Problem-focused coping, in turn, consists of those efforts aimed at directly managing or altering the source of distress. In the former case, the individual may consume alcohol or fantasize about better times in order to limit distressful emotions. In the latter case, the individual might search for a new job when unhappy with current employment or perhaps study harder to counteract anxiety over an upcoming examination.

It should not be assumed that one kind of coping is better than the other. There is an overwhelming Western bias toward taking action, especially in the way men are socialized. Action orientations have even been equated with mental health, whereas passive orientations have been equated with mental illness. Such a viewpoint, however, is more the product of stereotypes and inculcated beliefs than of research, which is only beginning to unravel the complex nature of these relationships. Attempts to reduce interfering emotional reactions may be particularly well suited, for instance, to situations in which control is impossible or where the event has already transpired. Problem-focused coping, in contrast, may prove most efficacious in approaching resolvable problems where there is a reasonable likelihood of success.

The model of conservation of resources further suggests that "reasonable likelihood of success" is a critical axis on which the appropriateness of choosing emotion- or problem-focused responses is weighed. As stated in the model and as emphasized by Schönpflug (1985), coping requires expenditure of resources, and it would be self-defeating to continually attempt a quixotic strategy of direct attack. Attempts to calm emotions or even stir them further may prove advantageous if their cost in terms of resources is low. If, as I suggest, individuals adopt a subjective, often emotional, cost-benefit approach to the problem, they will be likely to consider the price that must be paid for different coping scenarios in relation to the potential chance of gain and the value of what is to be gained in the offing.

Prior Experience and Coping

Before we consider the research on coping, a word should be said about "experience" and how it indirectly taps coping. Coping and experience are intimately tied with one another, even if this tie has not been highlighted by coping researchers. When a military unit is looking for a combat veteran or when a company hires a job applicant with management experience, they are implying that personal traits and theoretical knowledge may not fully predict behavior under the actual situational pressures that will occur. This expresses the lay belief that experience is a coarse test of coping strategies and also performs a weeding process whereby those whose coping skills are inadequate for meeting real-life demands can be identified.

Yet it should not be assumed that experience is necessarily predictive of future success. Experience has been indicated as having a facilitating effect on confrontation with new stressors (Burgess & Holmstrom, 1979; Hinkle, 1974) or, precisely the opposite, as having a debilitating effect on such confrontation (Holmes & Rahe, 1967), depending on whether one adopts a stress-inoculation or life-event model (respectively).

More recently, a U-shaped model has been suggested, in which lack of exposure to stressors and too much exposure are considered detrimental, but where a modicum of exposure is viewed as beneficial (Ruch et al., 1980). This is based on the thesis that lack of exposure to stressful events denies individuals the chance to test their fortitude and develop mastery and competency. Confrontation with a few stressful events, in contrast, allows time and energy to be devoted to mastery, thus enhancing a sense of efficacy for later stress resistance. This is akin to Meichenbaum's stress-inoculation approach. Confrontation with more severe or additional stressors, however, tips the balance such that the debilitating effects of past events outweigh any positive experiential component. Rather than feeling mastery and hope, individuals may already feel overwhelmed when new threats or challenges emerge and consequently may fail to meet the additional challenge. A modicum of evidence supports this U-shaped model (Ruch et al., 1980; Wildman & Johnson, 1977).

In our own research (Hobfoll & Walfisch, 1986) we studied the interactive effect of experience and mastery on depression among women awaiting biopsy for potential cancer. We failed to find any facilitator effect of exposure to prior stressful events (experienced in the past year) at the time of biopsy. The experience of as few as one or two recent stressful events increased the odds of depression by about 30 percent over those for women who had no recent encounters with stressors. Furthermore, even those who were high in mastery reported greatly increased levels of depression on the day prior to biopsy if they had experienced two or more recent stressful events. They still felt high in mastery, but this did not limit their depressed feelings. Only those women who were high in mastery and who had experienced *no* recent stressful events, or only one such event, had decreased risk for elevated depressive feelings.

We also followed up those women who were *not* found to have cancer in order to obtain information about the speed of their psychological recovery following the threat of cancer. Those with no recent stressful events (other than the biopsy) dropped precipitously in depression over the next three months and women who had encountered few stressful events dropped appreciably, albeit to a lesser extent than those who had experienced no recent stressful events. Women who had experienced many stressful events, however, remained at high levels of depressive affect.

What excited us the most was the next finding, however. Women who had a high sense of mastery decreased markedly in depression no matter what their recent experience with stressors. Women low in mastery also showed appreciable decreases in depressive affect if they had encountered few recent stressors. For those low in mastery, in contrast, exposure to recent stressors continued to be associated with elevated depression levels. This suggests that any facilitating effect of mastery may be accumulated in the long term, after individuals have been able to recuperate from prior stressful encounters and have had time to make personal sense of experiences and integrate them into their view of self. It is not the experience that is beneficial; indeed it tends to be detrimental. Rather it is the way the self emerges from the experience that is important, and this is a product of personal resources that probably existed going into the event.

Comparing our work with that of Ruch et al. and Wildman and Johnson, one can see that they found only marginal curvilinear effects of exposure to stressors. Furthermore, their studies examined the adjustment of young adults for whom experience with a few stressful events may indeed be critical in order to test their mettle. For our older sample, we doubted whether exposure to recent stressful events would add much to their sense of mastery. We suspected that it would not and that the primary effect of increased exposure to stressors for adults is likely to be more detrimental than helpful. Two other studies that examined the U-shaped model also used mature adults (Cooke, 1981; Cooke & Green, 1981), and they too failed to find evidence for curvilinear effects. Based on this limited research, it appears that some experience in coping with stressful circumstances may build mastery, but it is the mastery that is important. Unsuccessful experience that damages mastery or that occurs to those with a weak sense of mastery, even if it is only a single event, is likely to increase psychological distress.

Research on Coping and Stress Resistance

Lazarus, more recently joined by Folkman, and their colleagues have been instrumental in identifying research directions on coping. Their pioneering work has uncovered important questions, and they have approached the most complex issues. In my opinion this research area is the least well developed of all the stress areas that I have considered up to this point, but this is not owing to lack of sophisticated efforts to address critical problems. The transactional approach proffered by Lazarus and Folkman predicts that all aspects of the self, the environment, and behavior interactively affect one another and that causality is only valid in the sense of one limited space in time. This follows from their notion that feedback loops constantly occur and that appraisal and coping are constantly changing in reaction to the dynamic environment that is itself changed by the individual. In addition, statistical tools are still fairly rudimentary, and the model suggested by these theorists often seems to outstretch state-of-the-art techniques for ferreting out interactive and recursive mechanisms. Such handicaps should never discourage theory, but they often frustrate scientists who wish to receive answers to critical questions.

I wish to focus on one aspect of their model, the relationship among personal characteristics, coping, and outcome. Lazarus and Folkman see personal characteristics as antecedents to coping efforts, but they suggest that wide variability is left even after controlling for trait characteristics. Establishing this point would be a marked contribution to the literature, since the studies of personal traits and stress resistance have typically assumed that personal traits are linked with particular styles or approaches to coping. As may be noted in the material already reviewed in this chapter, however, such assumptions have seldom been tested. Correlations between, say, hardiness and psychological distress do not prove that those scoring high on hardiness *behaved* in a hardy manner. They may not have acted committed, nor felt challenged, nor employed problem-focused strategies when confronting stress. If the ecology of the person–situation fit includes the interaction between individuals and their environment, it must include investigation of the coping processes that follow from personal resources.

Personal characteristics and coping efforts

Whether personal characteristics are antecedent to coping efforts was empirically tested in a study of community residents (Folkman & Lazarus, 1986). Depressive symptomatology was assessed monthly for five months. In addition, the degree of investment people felt they had in different encounters was measured, along with the ways people chose to cope. It was found that persons with depressive symptoms felt they had more at stake and used more confrontive coping, self-control, and escape-avoidance. They also accepted more responsibility and responded with more disgust, anger, worry, and fear than those low in depressive symptoms.

It is interesting that the unexpected combination of increased confrontiveness and escape-avoidance was exhibited by those with depressive symptoms. Because they feel especially vulnerable, depressives may practice a revolving-door coping strategy, likely to frustrate any resolution of the problem. This revolving-door strategy is typified by episodes of confrontation, followed by avoidance, followed by confrontation. This interpretation is supported by the fact that depressives also felt that they had to hold back from responding when faced with events. In this way, they avoided either detaching entirely from unresolvable problems or confronting problems that were potentially resolvable until a favorable solution was reached. At the same time depressed individuals felt particularly responsible for their plight, while not capable of changing it. This study failed, however, to relate depressive symptomatology to the outcome of encounters (e.g., "unresolved and worse," "resolved to your satisfaction," etc.), which is puzzling because outcome is assumed in their model to follow from the different coping efforts, which themselves follow personal characteristics. This failure to find a relationship is not sufficiently explained by the authors.

Billings and Moos (1984) also showed that depressive disorder is related to coping style. Employing a large sample of depressed patients and a sociodemographically matched group of nondepressed controls they examined whether stressors, social resources, and coping responses were associated with severity of patients' depressive symptomatology and whether these relationships held for both men and women. They found that problem-solving was associated with less severe dysfunction. Emotion-focused coping, in comparison, was more complicatedly associated with adjustment. Specifically, attempts to see the situation in a more positive perspective or escape through other activities or focus on the future were associated with less-severe disorder. In contrast, attempts to discharge emotions (e.g., "take it out on other people") or reduce tensions through eating, drugs, or alcohol were related to more-severe disorder. This latter style was more common among women than men.

Each of these studies illustrates that unsuccessful coping may lead to depression but that depression is characterized in turn by particular styles of coping. Lazarus and Folkman would suggest that the "cause" and "effect" in this chain could be only artificially separated and that the link is part and parcel to the ongoing interchange between the self and the environment.

Style of coping as a personal characteristic

By trying to outline a transactional model of coping, Lazarus and Folkman and their colleagues have deemphasized the role of coping traits, arguing that coping traits are not good predictors of actual coping behavior (Folkman & Lazarus, 1984). Others, however, have been interested in precisely this direction.

Two early attempts to characterize coping styles or traits yielded only negative results. In these two studies, Andrews, Tennant, Hewson, and Schonell (1978) and Andrews, Tennant, Hewson, and Vaillant (1978) attempted to categorize individuals according to their "coping maturity." They assumed that behaving charmingly to people one does not like, suppressing anger, and generally avoiding stress by distraction and withdrawal were traits that characterized "mature" copers, whereas passive-aggressive responding and showing anger were "immature." No evidence was found for a palliative effect of mature coping. However, what is described here as mature has been interpreted by others as avoidance coping (Billings & Moos, 1981; Lazarus & Folkman, 1984) and regressive coping (Kobasa, Maddi, Donner, Merrick, & White, 1984). Indeed, both mature and immature aspects of coping are loaded with what have since been found to be the more stress-increasing forms of coping.

A study by Wheaton (1983), discussed earlier in another context, explored reactions to acute and chronic stressors in a sample of randomly selected adults from a mid-sized American city. He found chronic stressors and an inflexible coping style to be related to greater anxiety, depression, and schizophrenic symptomatology. A flexible style of coping was found to display a stress-buffering effect in the case of schizophrenia and depression, but not in the case of anxiety. The stability of this coping trait was highlighted by the finding that flexibility was especially important in reducing symptoms related to chronic stressors, which suggests that it had some ongoing ameliorative effect. Wheaton suggested that flexibility "allows for a wider choice of strategies and therefore more changes in strategy" (p. 220). In this way the coping trait of flexibility is depicted as a kind of guiding trait for more specific coping efforts.

Dispositional optimism is another coping style that has been depicted as fostering effective stress resistance, doing so in a manner consistent with optimist expectancies (Carver & Scheirer, 1983). Specifically, people who expect positive outcome are likely to continue goal-directed behavior despite obstacles or disruptions. In an empirical test of this hypothesis, it was predicted that among a college sample those with generalized positive expectancy about outcome (optimists) would be more likely to engage in problem-focused coping than would those who had negative expectancy about outcome (pessimists) (Scheier, Weintraub, & Carver, 1986). It was also predicted that optimism would be related to emotion-focused coping that facilitates problem-focused coping and emphasizes the positive aspects of relationships, whereas pessimism would be related to denial.

As predicted, optimism was positively associated with problem-focused coping, seeking social support, and positive reinterpretation, and negatively associated with acceptance and resignation. In a finer analysis of whether the event was controllable or uncontrollable it was noted that optimists used problem-focused coping and positive interpretation in controllable situations, but they actually relied more than pessimists on acceptance and resignation in uncontrollable circumstances. It is most interesting that optimists are generally less likely than pessimists to disengage, but more likely to do so in uncontrollable circumstances, a coping strategy that may act to preserve their optimism. I see this research as especially important because it emphasizes that emotion-focused coping does not necessarily act in the service of minimizing negative emotions. Rather, it acts to maximize ultimate loss and gain and preserve an important resource, optimism. This is consistent with the model of conservation of resources, in that attempts to produce positive outcome are abandoned to preserve a valuable resource.

Is Coping a Trait or Situation-Specific Behavior?

Perhaps the most important question that emerges from comparing Lazarus and Folkman's notions with those of researchers who have partially adopted their model is whether coping is a trait-like style of reacting or constantly changing effort that reflects the moment-by-moment person-environment interaction, as was originally proposed. I see this as a false dichotomy, however, as both sides have research support and only together can a complete picture emerge. This is illustrated in research and theory on the use of denial.

The use of denial or avoidance was traditionally thought to be a symptom of neurosis. Ego psychologists (Menninger, 1963; Haan, 1969) saw denial as a primitive form of coping and de facto a sign of unsuccessful coping. But the model of ecological congruence and Lazarus and Folkman's model would advocate that such a hierarchical viewpoint might be the product of generalization and even tautological thinking. That is, in a viewpoint that places denial on the bottom of the hierarchy, those using denial will be seen in a pejorative light.

Early empirical work on denial by Janis (1958) and Lindemann (1944) confirmed that denial leads to more severe reactions to stress. Janis called this "the work of worry" and suggested that thinking about and dwelling upon a threat helps individuals work through their anxieties and achieve better outcome. Lindemann observed a similar process when studying reactions to loss of a loved one and coined the term "grief work." He, like Janis, found that denial leads to more severe reactions at some later date, even if the initial response is less severe. Indeed, the lack of severity of initial reactions was interpreted as a strong sign of ineffective coping.

Breznitz (1983c) suggests that this is a narrow view that concentrates on the most severe form of denial, denial of reality. He suggests that there are more functional levels of denial that may aid coping, such as denial of part of the information, denial of urgency, and denial of personal relevance. He presents a new notion that I have not seen empirically examined, that persons only choose the more ineffective, detrimental, and severe forms of denial when less severe forms have failed to help coping efforts. Indirect support for his thinking appears in studies that have tapped less extreme forms of denial and found them to be related to positive outcome (Cohen & Lazarus, 1973; Hackett, Cassem, & Wishnie, 1968; Rosentiel & Roth, 1981). This underscores the importance of carefully outlining what behaviors lie under a general rubric such as denial; different measures or samples may be focusing on very different traits or behaviors, which are nevertheless called by a common name.

If, however, we wish to average across situations, the tendency to repeatedly rely on denial is probably detrimental in the long run, even if it is effective in certain situations. It prevents adopting action efforts or escape and generally leaves people in a continued, unresolved negative state. These points are illustrated in a recent investigation by Cronkite and Moos (1984). This unusual study was detailed earlier; it may be recalled that they looked at the interaction of coping with depressed mood, physical symptoms, and alcohol consumption in marital partners. Wives who used avoidance coping were more susceptible to exposure to stressors and developed more physical symptoms and consumed more alcohol, in particular, than those who did not use this style of coping. The interaction of spouse's depression and avoidance and spouse's physical symptoms and avoidance were both also associated with greater depression in husbands and greater alcohol consumption in wives. When both partners used avoidance coping, the relationship between stressors and outcome was further exacerbated. This suggests that using avoidance is consistently injurious and approach coping is consistently salutary.

Somewhat surprisingly, however, Cronkite and Moos also found that when both partners utilized approach coping, this exacerbated the relationship between stressors and distress when a partner is faced with the stress of the other's physical symptoms. In a complex way this may reflect the importance of flexibility, because in the face of physical illness a head-on approach may be self-defeating or require too many resources to directly attack the sources of stress. When action-focused coping is the preferred strategy of both partners, the couple is locked into a coping posture that fits poorly with the ecological demands of intractable situations. In contrast, if one member of the couple has more avoidance tendencies this might press the couple to adapt one of the less severe forms of denial that Breznitz suggests will be helpful when unmanageable stress occurs.

Using denial then as a general example, one may argue that coping styles or traits do exist, have some stability, and predict outcome when long-term or summative reactions to stressors are considered. In any situation, however, a given coping style can only be evaluated for its fit to situational demands and congruence with the person's needs and values. Rather than concentrate on traits versus situational distinctions, I would instead like to add another dimension that I have not seen mentioned in the literature: *how well does the individual employ the coping strategy?* This dimension of coping makes obvious that stress management strategies may be efficient, sophisticated, and creative, or they may be inefficient, naive, and ineptly applied. Carefully titrating levels of denial, for instance, implies a high level of coping ability. Coping adeptness is a personal characteristic that probably has some generalizability but also varies, because individuals are not equally effective in coping with all situations or in the use of all kinds of coping strategies.

This concept of adeptness in stress management further suggests why traits or styles of coping emerge. I speculate that the reason most people manage their stressful lives reasonably effectively is that they adopt a style of coping that is comfortable for them. They may originally try a coping technique by happenstance or because they saw another use it. They eventually find themselves comfortable with a given repertoire of coping efforts and perhaps a coping philosophy to go along with it (e.g., "I am a cautious person" or "I believe in a head-on approach to problems"). They practice this over years. Trait studies of coping styles suggest that people use a "shotgun" approach to given situations, applying their general style to a broad array of circumstances. Perhaps only when these initial attempts fail are alternatives chosen that are oriented to the particular circumstances.

Such thinking is also consistent with recent cognitive theories that people normally evaluate only a circumscribed portion of the situation before them (Kruglanski, 1980; Tversky & Kahneman, 1974; 1981). It is also indirectly supported by findings that persons attend to portions of their environment that fit their own model of self and their preferred view of situations (Goffman, 1959; Swann & Predmore, 1985). Finer, in-depth analysis is only likely to follow after such reflexive attempts have proved unsuccessful. When they do, depth and breadth of coping abilities are truly tested. It is fascinating to consider how well people manage stressors when pressed to use their nonpreferred style. These questions await future research, and I would suggest that comparative analysis of how people who possess certain personal characteristics react in contrasting situations (e.g., those who have good fit with their resources and coping styles and those who do not) will be especially significant. They would also be excellent applications of the model of ecological congruence.

PERSONAL AND SOCIAL RESOURCES AND STRESS RESISTANCE: APPROACH TO ECOLOGIES

I would like to look now at studies of the interaction of personal and social resources. Such approaches are a first step toward the ecological study of stress resistance, because they catalyze comparative thinking about the effects of different domains of resources and encourage consideration of the fit of resources to situational demands. Because science usually proceeds by comparison, adopting even a dual-resource model, rather than a single-resource model, exhibits a qualitatively more complex side of the resource–stress resistance picture.

Referring to the model of ecological congruence, one may recall its emphasis that resources interact with one another to foster or inhibit stress resistance. Actually, examining any two resources would suffice, but, as mentioned earlier in this and earlier chapters, personal resources tend to overlap with other personal resources and social resources tend to overlap with other social resources. Because of this, it is difficult to untangle additive and interactive effects of different resources from the same domain. Where, for example, does the effect of mastery end and that of self-esteem begin? When resources are examined from different domains, however, this problem is largely overcome, because their separate contribution is conceptually distinguishable. So, for instance, the effects of self-esteem and social resources or paid employment and marital intimacy can be differentiated.

One could adopt a maximalist view that the entire model of ecological congruence must be applied to each investigation in its entirety for research to be considered ecologically valid. However, this is not my intention. Portions of the model may be considered separately. Indeed, it would be impossible to examine all aspects of the model in any single study. The model pleads for analyses of stress resistance that are above the level of single-variable research based on correlational associations between that variable and outcome. Instead, the model advocates two basic principles. First, two or more variables from one or more facets (e.g., resources, values, time) should be considered together.

Second, the predictions should be based on processes that are congruent with the ecology of the samples' needs and situational demands.

Studies described in this section move closer to the model because they follow the first principle. The first studies we will review in this section, however, are still not good representatives of the model because they tend to follow the second principle post hoc when interpreting findings and also ignore facets of the model other than the resource domain. I will refer to them as "interactive, pre-ecological" approaches. These studies are actually methodologically sound, but they fail to directly or fully address the ecological perspective.

I could be charged here with hubris if I implied that these research and theoretical efforts are deficient because they fail to follow my model. However, I would argue that they fail to meet their own standards. In the research reviewed in this and the previous chapter, it is a rare study indeed that does not apply ecological concepts post hoc in interpreting the findings. The concepts of fit, interaction of different domains, needs, perceptions, values, and situational constraints are acknowledged in nearly every discussion of study findings; seldom, however, are they stated at the outset and incorporated in the study design or in the logic supporting the hypotheses.

Typifying this paradigm, Ganellen and Blaney (1974) examined the effects of social support and hardiness among college students. In presenting their logic they cite the frequent associations of social support and hardiness with healthy outcome in the face of stress. They even ask if one plays "a more important role in buffering the effect of life stress than the other" (p. 158). However, they give no reasoning as to how the two might interact, why one might be better than another, in what situations one might be preferable, or the process by which they act together. In discussing their results, however, they consider how different aspects of hardiness may overlap with social support, possible causal directions between the two domains, and the implications of the different needs of their sample with that employed by others. These aspects of the ecology are necessary to make sense of their data. One final point that they never consider, however, is that their college students may seldom experience the type of stress that requires hardiness. This is glaringly obvious, however, when one reflects on the nature of hardiness and the type of stressors that it may buffer.

This study is typical in that it considers post hoc only those aspects of the ecology that fit the data. I have singled it out, but it is no worse (and indeed a lot better) than many other reports in the literature. If these ecological factors are important, they must be considered at the outset, incorporated in the hypotheses, and discussed vis-à-vis the findings. Ecologies are complex and nearly any outcome can be "explained" by appealing to ecological processes. This capitalizes on chance and inhibits a progressive understanding of ecologies, because the hypotheses that are confirmed or rejected do not themselves concern the ecology. Ecologies thus are used to explain inconsistent results, the predictions concentrating on the "pure" effect of the variables *sans* ecology.

In the second set of investigations, the few clear ecological studies beyond those that directly apply the model of ecological congruence will be detailed. These studies examine resources from different domains, given various situational demands, and focus on the process of stress resistance. They also consider sample characteristics. The interactive and ecological factors that are envisioned as affecting outcome tend to be incorporated in the studies' designs and theoretical development, and the analyses follow ecologically relevant principles. I will refer to them simply as ecological approaches. They differ from research carried out by my colleagues and myself only in that they do not relate specifically to the model of ecological congruence. This model, however, is only one possible ecological vantage point, and there is no evidence to prove that it is more or less valid than the approaches of these other studies. Instead, they complement one another. I hope I am justified in suggesting that the model of ecological congruence is more comprehensive, because it states the complete set of parameters that affect stress resistance rather than focusing on the situation-specific case.

Study of Personal and Social Resources

Interactive pre-ecological approaches

The interaction of personal and social resources has been examined in reference to control expectancies and social support by a number of investigators (Husaini et al., 1982; Kobasa & Puccetti, 1983; Lefcourt et al., 1984; Sandler & Lakey, 1982). Each of these studies used aggregate measures of recent exposure to stressful events. Sandler and Lakey first took the logical step of contemplating how control expectancies might affect social support in contributing to stress resistance. They cited past research showing that internal locus of control is associated with taking action, seeking information, and remaining task oriented and showing that social support includes information, task assistance, and emotional support. They reasoned that this implied that internals should be more likely than externals to seek and profit from social support. They pointed out, however, that since people tend to affiliate under stress, the more distressed externals might also have increased motivation to seek support.

Hardiness, it will be recalled, also has a central control component. Looking at hardiness and social support, Kobasa and Puccetti went considerably further than Sandler and Lakey by suggesting that hardy individuals not only make the best use of social support but also exploit modest levels of social resources to their benefit. Those low in hardiness, they suggested, might actually be further harmed by social support when faced with stressful circumstances. For them, social support might be a shelter in the storm, which encourages their escapist propensities and which they will fear leaving. Kobasa and Puccetti do not describe what kinds of situations this pattern will be manifested in, however, implying that it is a stable principle, independent of specific situations.

Sandler and Lakey found that externals did receive more social support than did internals but that only for internals was social support associated with improved stress resistance. This highlights two aspects of the person–situation interaction: first, feeling that external factors determine outcome leads to seeking external aid in the form of social support, and second, internals most effectively utilize the beneficial aspects of social support. Kobasa and Puccetti did not find hardiness to be related to family support. As in the case of control, however, hardy individuals who encountered high levels of stressors did benefit more from family social support than did those low in hardiness. Those low in hardiness, moreover, had considerably higher levels of reported illness if they had high perceived social support, as was predicted. For them social support was misused in some way that led to greater debilitating effects.

This reversal effect of social support for persons lacking personal competencies was also noted in the study of rural adults undertaken by Husaini et al. Their measure of personal competency emphasized the mastery component, which is similar to the control aspect of hardiness and to internal locus of control. Comparing the value of internal and external resources in stress reduction, they found that personal competency was more salient than social support.

Lefcourt et al. (1984), in considering the findings on control expectancies and social support, suggested that control may have a more modest effect on outcome than had earlier been thought. They concluded that the combination of an internal orientation and effective tapping of social resources collectively contributes to effective stress resistance. Furthermore, the inclusion of control and social support variables by Lefcourt et al. (1984) highlighted the need to consider the focus of control, since they had conflicting results for *achievement* locus of control and *affiliation* locus of control. Moreover, studying two domains simultaneously forced the authors to consider the underlying properties of each of the variables and their interplay with the environment, both perspectives having been treated more superficially in most single-domain research.

Ecological approaches

A more ecological approach was adopted in the study of self-esteem and social support of Murrell and Norris (1984), who recognized the importance of combinations of social and personal resources. They also considered the physical health of the individual a resource. Furthermore, their research is important because it is longitudinal and concentrates on older adults. They found that combined personal and social resources reduced depression more for individuals with high perceived stress than for those who reported low *perceived stress*. This stress-buffering effect was not found for those exposed to a higher number of stressful events, as opposed to a lower number, however, suggesting the importance of perceptions. Unfortunately, the ecological points to be drawn from this study are limited because the authors combined the different resources into a single score in both reports of the study with which I am familiar (Norris & Murrell, 1984; Murrell & Norris, 1984). These studies did provide information on the process of stress resistance, however, indicating that resources dampen perceptions of stressfulness of events and have salubrious effects even when people perceive their recent past as very stressful.

Self-degradation, another component of self-esteem, and social support were studied in terms of their interrelated stress-resistance capacity by Kaplan et al. (1983). This study was discussed earlier when the personal facet alone was examined. The authors consider the process of self-degradation and its relationship to social support, suggesting that self-degradation and deprivation of social support are spirally related. Appreciating the nature of this overlap, they nevertheless predict that these two variables have separate and independent relationships with stress resistance. They also suggested that continuing deprivation of social support would bring about distressful self-rejecting feelings.

In a study sample of seventh-grade students, they found self-degradation, peer rejection, and family rejection were interrelated, as predicted. Nevertheless in a 10-year follow-up, self-degradation, peer rejection, and family rejection had each independently predicted psychological distress. This is one of the few confirmations that social support has an effect on psychological distress independent of personality characteristics, a major question emerging from the earlier chapter on social support. Kaplan et al. also found that low self-degradation had a stress-buffering effect, being most helpful under high stress conditions, whereas social support made only direct effects on subsequent psychological distress. Unfortunately, the interaction between the personal and social domains was not reported.

By outlining an ecological context in their introduction, however, the authors move comfortably into a discussion of the inconsistencies of their findings and draw ecological points about the comparative contribution of self-derogation and the meaning of social support. They point out that self-derogation has a stress-buffering effect on psychological distress 10 years hence, even though their subjects were initially tested in adolescence, a time when personality is still in flux. In comparison, social support probably does not possess this same stability, especially in the case of more mercurial peer relations. In addition, Kaplan et al. point out that when social support fails, individuals may seek other supportive relationships, so that the effect of social support may be most apparent when specific support is examined. These factors, they argue, may explain why social support only had a direct effect on later psychological distress. Had they not adopted an ecological stance at the onset, this discussion of the interactive properties of social support and self-degradation would have been contrived.

A few studies of the process of women's adjustment to stressors have adopted a particularly ecological bent. An unusual study of combinations of resources is reported by Parry (1986), who investigated the effects of paid employment and social support on psychological distress. Parry studied working-class mothers of young children in England because of the high risk of this population for psychological distress. First, attesting to her ecological bias, she predetermined the composition of contrasting study groups (e.g., employed–unemployed, high instrumental support–low instrumental support) to ensure true comparisons of genuinely contrasting groups. Typically, a given sample is collected and then divided at, say, the median into high and low social support groups, neither necessarily high or low in any absolute sense on social support. The nature of the stressor for matched groups was also carefully broken down into subcomponents that would be consistent with the model of ecological congruence; type, severity, and months since occurrence. An ecological approach was also followed in examining the relationship between type of stressful event and distress, revealing that the occurrence of a single severe event was a critical factor in producing psychological distress. Parry further showed that the effect of employment extended beyond the financial advantage it begat. This suggests that being employed says something to women about themselves and is not only valuable for its functional properties.

Paid employment, considered in isolation, was not related to psychological distress. Women who had experienced a severely stressful event did benefit, however, if they were employed *and* received emotional support (see Figure 5.2). As the figure shows, employed women who experienced a severe stressor and did not receive emotional support had higher levels of psychiatric symptoms than all other groups. Thus, for women with young children who experienced a severe stressful event, employment was an additional stressor if they did not receive social support, but was a stress buffer if they did receive support. These results would not have emerged from the data if the meaning of work, motherhood, social support, and stressful events had not been carefully considered for this particular group. Nor could results of this type be convincingly explained if a nonecological approach had been adopted, because the reader would then have been justified in wondering if the author was not on a "fishing expedition," massaging the data for whatever could be found.

In another study of women's adjustment in the face of more specific stressors Mitchell and Hodson (1986) noted that those women who had nontraditional attitudes toward women (e.g., husbands and wives should be equal partners) were more likely to utilize active behavioral coping in the face of increased marital violence, whereas women who had more traditional values used less active behavioral coping as violence increased. Applying an ecological comparison, Mitchell and Hodson found these tendencies did not occur for nonviolent stressful situations. Social support had a more mixed effect, however. More supportive ties, on one hand, were associated with less avoidance responding. But when the content of support encouraged avoidance, as it often did, this reinforced avoidance strategies.

Vachon (1986), studying both mastectomy and bereavement following the loss of spouse, found that in both cases dissatisfaction with social support was related to poorer adjustment. She also noted that social support evolved to affect different demands as time since the event transpired. Her work emphasized the prolonged interactive process of stress resistance and the similarities and differences of contrasting situational demands. In contrast to the robust effects of social support, Vachon found only a circumscribed role for personal resources. This may be attributed to her use of a general personality inventory that does not necessarily focus on traits that have been associated with stress resistance. Personal resources might have proved more valuable if she

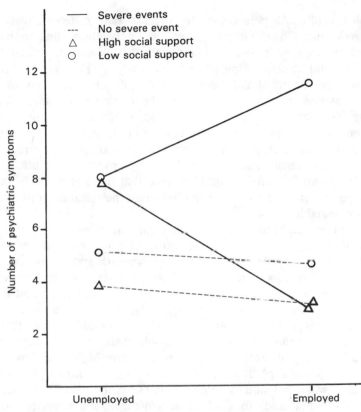

FIGURE 5.2 Effect of employment, severe life events, and social support on psychiatric symptoms. (Used by permission from Parry, 1986.)

had selected personal characteristics that particularly fitted the demands she was studying.

Vachon's approach also supports the model of conservation of resources; she finds the loss components of mastectomy and bereavement and ties the two events together despite their otherwise disparate demands and qualities. She finds similarities in adjustment to the two situations at each stage and notes that similar natural and professional interventions are effective in each case. It is possible, on the other hand, that these two events are similar, but that loss is not central to other major events.

Moos and colleagues (Holahan & Moos, 1986, 1987; Billings & Moos, 1982; Mitchell, Cronkite, & Moos, 1983) have also used a complex ecological perspective to suggest that different resistance resources may have different effects depending on individual characteristics, gender, and the individual's life space (e.g., work-related stress, marital stress). Using prospective analyses, Holohan and Moos observed the combined and separate contribution to stress resistance of self-confidence, an easy-going nature, the tendency to use avoidance coping, and family support. This is one of the only studies of the differential effect of personal resources, coping style, and social support. They do not, however, predict a priori how they expect these variables to interact with each other or what they expect their differential contribution to be. But it could be argued that in early stages of theory development it is best to simply observe the relationships among different variables.

Holohan and Moos (1986) find that the personal resource of self-confidence and the coping resource of possessing an easy-going nature are each related to few psychosomatic symptoms and less psychological distress under both high and low stress conditions, which supports the direct effect. They note that avoidance coping and family support, in contrast, are more strongly related to outcome under high stress conditions than low stress conditions. I would suggest that the former two variables are used on an ongoing basis, such that they are not tapped in a significantly different way under high and low stress conditions. Social support and avoidance coping, in contrast, are likely to be sought when individuals confront stress. When there is nothing to avoid and no wounds to bind, then avoidance and support are not meaningful. These comparative processes were masked when they considered the combined effect of all these resources, because the different direct and stress-buffering effects aggregated to show only the direct effect.

One might also expect the home environment, and particularly parents' resources and strain, to be associated with children's psychological and physical health. Holohan and Moos (1987) found parental risk factors (negative life events, depression, physical symptoms, and avoidance coping) related to greater psychological and physical distress in their children. Maternal dysfunction was the strongest risk factor for children. Family support, however, was related to less psychological and physical distress in the children. Although parents provided the information on their children's functioning, this does not appear to confound the results, since parents rated their children's distress similarly even if one parent was clinically depressed and one was not. Children were affected more by current parental distress than by parents' personal characteristics or past conditions. In discussing the home environment's effect on children, Holohan and Moos infer that children are especially affected by current conditions but may be fairly resilient to past circumstances. If such a claim can be substantiated by further research, it would constitute a major change in developmental thinking about the etiology of emotional distress and stress-related physical illness in children.

When the type of stressor and nature of the sample are added to the examination of the ecology of stress, even richer information emerges. In another study by Moos and colleagues (Mitchell et al., 1983), depressed patients were found to experience more stress, to use less problem-focused coping, and to perceive less family support than matched nondepressed controls. Spouses of patients used more problem-solving than their partners but experienced more chronic stressors and lower family support than did matched controls. Also, patients' spouses felt less depressed than their partners, but more depressed than the matched nondepressed controls. Such analyses enable us to infer an interactive process, whereby the patient is at a disadvantage at each point in the stress process and the spouse seems to be depending on personal resources (e.g., problem-focused coping) to deal with the increased strain. It is also tempting to infer that the spouse's lack of social support is a by-product of the fleeing of social ties from the ongoing strain engendered by the psychiatric disability of the patient. As suggested in Chapter 4, social support is likely to wane under such conditions.

Mitchell, Cronkite, and Moos report other important findings as a product of their ecological approach. Comparing patients with nonpatients they find that both groups are negatively affected by ongoing stressors and a lower proportionate use of problem-focused coping. Patients were less negatively affected than nonpatients by discrete stressor events (as opposed to ongoing events) and less positively affected by family support. Both ongoing and discrete stressors increased psychological distress, but each made significant independent contributions. Few studies have included ongoing stressors in their analyses and this may be one reason why the stress–distress relationship has been shown to be only modest.

A major contribution of the Mitchell et al. study is the initial consideration of how ongoing stressors may attenuate family support, which then acts to limit effective stress resistance. When reading their report, one gets a sense of the family climate of depressed patients and of the detrimental and palliative processes at work. This study is exemplary in that Mitchell et al. apply their ecological model at the design stage, in constructing their hypotheses, and in analyzing the data. Such an effort should be a standard bearer for future research.

One additional, especially thoughtful study deserves special attention, "The Stress Process" by Pearlin et al. (1981). While I analyze the study in terms of the model of ecological congruence and the model of conservation of resources, it should be clear to the reader that this study preceded my formulation of these models and, moreover, was particularly influential in the development of my thinking on stress resistance. Pearlin and associates adopt a truly ecological approach and go well beyond most other studies in elaborating on their predictions and findings. They hypothesize that stressful events result in chronic stressful conditions that tax individuals' stress resistance capacity. They also predict that stressful events and the chronic stressful conditions they create are most likely to cause psychological distress when they result in a diminished sense of self, particularly in loss of mastery and self-esteem. Consistent with the model of conservation of resources, they reason that "the protection and enhancement of self . . . are fundamental goals after which people strive" (p. 340). They describe a process beginning with exposure to a stressful event or events, leading to chronic stressful sequelae, which, in turn, lead to decreased sense of mastery and self-esteem and finally resulting in increased psychological distress.

Consistent with the model of ecological congruence, Pearlin et al. also consider the fit of resources to particular events and the process of stress–distress that stems from differing circumstances. Thus they choose a discrete kind of event for study—"disruptive job events"—rather than choosing aggregate measures. They apply their model to this kind of event, hypothesizing that disruptive job events lead to increased ongoing economic stressors and a drop in income. These, in turn, are predicted to contribute to faltering mastery and self-esteem, which then contribute to increased depression.

Their focus on depression is justified based on criteria very similar to those recommended in the strain dimension of the model of ecological congruence detailed in Chapter 3. Specifically, they argue that depression is "especially well suited to studies concerned with social and economic antecedents . . . depression may be especially sensitive to a distinctive kind of experience that is both enduring and resistant to efforts aimed at change" (p. 342). In an even greater convergence with the congruence model, they go on to interweave the event with the type of strain and the process of loss of self-esteem and mastery. They state, "It will be recalled from our discussion of mastery and self-esteem that these are the very kinds of experiences we also consider to be especially erosive of positive self-concept. The diminishment of precisely these kinds of self-concepts, in turn, has been associated with vulnerability to depression" (p. 342).

Both coping and social support resources were considered. Again the choice was not based, as in most prior research, solely on the previously observed association of these resources with stress resistance but on their particular stress-attenuating capacity in this instance, as well. In terms of social support Pearlin et al. reasoned that such major stressors are best met by intimate support in relations that exhibit deep trust. Coping, they felt, is also most relevant when warranted by specific demands. For economic stressors following job disruption they posited that making positive comparisons with others and with past or future circumstances is one especially useful strategy. One can make positive assessments of one's relative condition in relation to those who are worse off, and one may look positively at the future or compare one's plight with a previous worse experience. Coping under this kind of pressure may also be beneficial if individuals realign their values to see economic resources as less important than, say, health or family. These two types of coping are consistent with the breakdown outlined in Chapter 2, wherein it was suggested that loss may be minimized by transformational coping or changes in values.

In analyzing their longitudinal data, drawn on a large community sample, Pearlin and colleagues note that the process they predicted was borne out. Disruptive job events were shown through path analysis (a technique designed to address causality) to lead to negative changes in income and increased economic strain, both of which led to greater levels of depression. Loss of self-esteem and mastery also followed the events and, in turn, also commonly led to depression.

The model of ecological congruence further points to the importance of comparing events that have different ecologies, and Pearlin et al. did just that to illustrate the process by which job loss contributes to depression. They reasoned that loss of mastery and self-esteem were not inherent and inseparable symptoms of depression itself. Rather, they envisioned mastery and self-esteem to be independent states whose loss *leads* to depression. To show this independence they searched for a kind of stressful situation that makes demands resulting in a rise in depression without concomitant decrease in self-esteem and mastery. Analyzing the effects of events appraised as a consequence of blind chance (death of a child and physical illness), not attributable to the self, they showed that such events led to depression without commensurate loss of self-esteem and mastery.

In this way they uncovered two separate processes leading to psychological distress, and provided insight into the factor that determines which process will be followed. Events that are perceived to be of one's own doing result in psychological distress via loss of self-concept. Events that are perceived as occurring outside of the control of self, however, lead more directly to depression. Further, these processes follow from the objective qualities of the events; they did not analyze individuals' perceptions of the events, but rather the structural nature of the events. This ecological point should not be lost, since stress researchers have been quick to leave the environmental level and depend on perceptions sine qua non.

Both coping and social support produced stress-buffering effects. By comparing the two, the authors were able to show that social support behaved in a more specialized fashion. Its effectiveness was exclusively a product of limiting loss of self-esteem and mastery. In this manner social support indirectly limited depressive emotions. This finding further supports the model of conservation of resources; social support acts not to limit depression but to militate against a heightened sense of loss of other resources.

The study of Pearlin and colleagues is well cited in the literature. However, their method of deductive and inferential analysis has not been followed. My only explanation for this is that American psychology has adopted a determinist model that identifies associations between variables and avoids underlying issues, feedback loops, the nature of the sample, and situational considerations. It values clear tests of causality, curious statistical interactions, and theories that do not cross interdisciplinary boundaries and vague borders between the self and the environment. Obviously, some of these biases are the very strength of American empirical psychology, but clarity can be gained in more complex investigations when study design is applied creatively and appropriate cautions and controls are exercised.

SUMMARY AND CONCLUSIONS

This chapter focused on the role of personal attributes in stress resistance. It was suggested that stress research initially led stress investigators away from the concept of self, but failure to find social resources that explained substantial portions of the variance in stress resistance may have led back to the contribution of self. When searching for stress-reducing aspects of the self, those interested in the stress resistance value of personal resources borrowed from health-oriented rather than illness-oriented models. By moving away from abnormal processes, they could explore the palliative effects of personal traits.

Humanistic theorists, it was noted, proposed some of the earliest health-directed approaches to stress resistance. Examples of this include work by Adler on the social self, by Frankl on concentration camps, by Maslow on the self-actualized personality, and by existential theorists such as Rollo May. Jumping back to earlier chapters, one may also find it interesting that Gerald Caplan and Eric Lindemann both pioneered stress resistance perspectives, and both were witnesses to the horrors wreaked by Nazi Germany, Caplan in Israel after the war and Lindemann as a refugee from German in the 1930s. It may be said that both theoretical and historical stress resistance research has had a humanistic profile following from these early contributors.

Another point made in the chapter was that early work on war-related stress led both to insights and to misconceptions about the role of the self in withstanding the vicissitudes of combat. On one hand, observations of combatants suggested correctly that stressors could mount to a point at which many more persons would break down than were thought to have premorbid psychopathology. On the other hand, an incorrect conclusion was drawn that premorbid factors were unrelated to combat stress reactions such as combat exhaustion. Nevertheless, there was a general belief that military units possessing a sense of mastery and readiness were less likely to break down than others without these positive views. Early work on polio victims by Visotsky and colleagues (1961) also laid the groundwork for a more experimental approach to these questions. Many of their observations were well ahead of the current *Zeitgeist* in drawing attention to a number of personal traits that contribute to improved stress resistance.

Following this theoretical and historical groundwork, contemporary work on the self was reviewed. It was helpful to divide this research into three aspects of the self delineated by existential theorists: *Umwelt*, or the self vis-à-vis the environment; *Mitwelt*, the self vis-à-vis others; and *Eigenwelt*, the self vis-à-vis the self. The majority of work has been directed at the first dimension, typified by the study of expectancies for control of the environment. A number of such studies found that an orientation toward the self, which is characterized by feeling capable of controlling future outcome of events, helps stress resistance and is generally associated with well-being. Another trend suggests that people's style of reacting to events also affects their stress resistance. Early evidence suggests that optimism, expressing anger, and more moderate affect intensity may all be related to better adjustment in the face of stressors.

The self vis-à-vis the self has received some limited attention in the investigation of the stress-reducing role of self-esteem and private self-consciousness. The early work on this dimension of the self was encouraging and suggested that persons who have a more positive and deeper sense of their personal worth are more resistant to stressful events than those who lack these qualities. Finally, the self vis-à-vis others was discussed. There is relatively little research on this domain of self, but a few innovative studies have shown that well-being is associated with feeling interested in others, integrated with others, and comfortable in their company. There are further hints of improved stress resistance among people who possess these traits, but too few studies have been reported to draw any clear conclusions beyond the general association with well-being.

Next, the topic of stress and coping was addressed. Coping was defined as efforts to manage external and internal demands that are appraised as taxing or exceeding the resources of the person, after Lazarus and Folkman's model (1984). A number of researchers noted that coping style is a function of personal traits. Depressives and pessimists were found in separate studies to use more emotion-focused coping; optimists used more emotion-focused coping when success was perceived as untenable. It was further noted that a single, inflexible coping style, rather than a more situation-specific approach, was likely to lead to more anxious, depressive, and schizophrenic symptoms. In a final note on coping, it was argued that research on coping should continue to follow both trait and situational perspectives, because both are related to stress resistance. Indeed, future research should study how individuals depend on coping styles and what occurs when these styles fail. In this regard, one would ideally have an effective style of general coping but be able to transfer to a less preferred array of efforts when the situation demanded.

When personal and social resources were studied together, much greater insight into their workings accrued. Although some of these studies only considered ecological concepts and the issue of fit post hoc, they were much more likely to critically evaluate the person-situation interaction than were single-resource studies. Feeling in control of the environment was found to be linked with more effective use of social support and lacking this personal resource was even shown to lead to misuse of social support. It may be deduced that people who feel in control of their destiny are most likely to build effective support networks and to exploit them in a positive way when stressful circumstances occur. Those lacking in a sense of mastery, in contrast, are likely to be ineffective at building mutually beneficial relationships and might tend to favor dependent relationships that are counterproductive in stressful situations.

Studies of self-esteem also show that a positive view of self is associated with less psychological distress, independent of the contribution of social support. There is some indication that personal traits may have a more generalized effect on well-being, whereas social support's contribution is more situation-specific. Only a few studies have compared the relative effectiveness of personal and social resources, however, so it would be premature to come to even a preliminary conclusion in this regard.

Finally, a few key studies by Moos and colleagues and Pearlin and associates, and by a handful of researchers studying stress resistance among women, vividly illustrated how an ecological perspective can aid in formulating hypotheses relevant to the event at hand and how the particular mediating processes and reactions follow from an ecological model. They further illustrated how comparing events, processes, and stress resistance resources leads to a complex interactive understanding of the stress process. While their studies were more complex than most earlier efforts, their ability to outline and analyze a very complex person-resource-environment model was a conceptual and methodo-logical leap forward.

In analyzing these studies in terms of the model of conservation of resources and the model of ecological congruence, a number of points are highlighted. First, it appears that preserving a positive view of self is an important resource. Whereas stressful events tend to press individuals to focus on their loss, personal resources counteract this effect by calling attention to self-worth, the ability to effect positive outcome in the future, a sense of meaningfulness, and a sense of attachment. These reflections may place the sense of situational loss in a circumscribed perspective that does not encroach on the highly valued territory of the self. When individuals lack such personal resources or when stressors are too massive or too prolonged, the situational loss is magnified by a feeling of loss of personal efficacy, self-esteem, and sense of attachment. Bulman and Wortman (1977) have pointed out that events that deprive individuals of their sense of meaningfulness and order are most devastating of all.

Interestingly, there is converging evidence that those with positive traits may have a better sense of when to disengage from confronting the stressor. This allows them to admit temporary or situational defeat but to reserve resources in the long run. Those who lack personal resources, in contrast, may see such defeat as too devastating and so prolong the event beyond any chance of successful resolution.

Personal resources also seem to forestall loss by acting to rally social resources. Thus, when individuals are unable themselves to counteract the threat of loss they may tap the strength of others to come to their aid, act on their behalf, or militate against second-order stressors that follow in the wake of the principal event. This may have the joint effect of decreasing the amount of threat of loss and of allowing individuals to shore up their own defenses, regain their composure, and prepare for further confrontation with stressors.

The models of ecological congruence and conservation of resources show the difficulty of interpreting aggregate measures of stressful events. Precisely what is being lost, what is being challenged, what strains are likely to evolve, and any attempt at fit are obfuscated. Some attempts to compare chronic stressors with more acute ones have been an intermediate step; these investigations have generally revealed richer insights than studies utilizing aggregate measures. With the concept of fit becoming increasingly accepted as a major axis for the examination of stress resistance, an increasing number of investigations will be likely to adopt single-event paradigms or will compare discrete numbers of events (see Kessler, 1983, for an in-depth methodological analysis of this course of research), but very few studies have followed this course to date.

The research on multiple resources from separate domains illustrated the benefit of applying the principles of the model of ecological congruence. Studies that focused on situational fit, the likelihood of a particular kind of strain, the evolution of the event, the developmental needs of the sample, and perceptions were more likely to emerge with meaningful results than investigations that concentrated on only one of these facets. As argued in this chapter, it would be an act of certain hubris to judge all this research against my model. However, the researchers themselves consistently discussed their research along complex ecological lines, while designing their studies and analysis without regard to the specific needs of their samples or the particular situational demands. Indeed, the model of ecological congruence was derived in large part from an analysis of the facets that researchers and theorists discussed as being most important in explaining their results.

In Chapters 6 and 7, I will present some of the research that I and my colleagues have conducted. A central goal in this research was to outline facets of the ecological congruence model from the outset and to design and analyze the results with the model in mind. Chapter 6 will focus on research involving the stress of war for civilians and soldiers. Chapter 7 will address the model in terms of illness-related stressors. Many of the studies reviewed in this and the previous chapter are as sound as those that I and my colleagues have undertaken. The point that I hope to make is that in following the model of ecological congruence a richer harvest is possible from all of these studies, and a deeper understanding of the process of stress resistance is uncovered.

6

STRESS RESISTANCE DURING WAR: APPLICATIONS OF THE MODELS OF ECOLOGICAL CONGRUENCE AND CONSERVATION OF RESOURCES

There never was a good war or a bad peace.

(Benjamin Franklin, 1706–1790)

The next greatest misfortune to losing a battle is to gain such a victory as this.

(Arthur Wellesley, Duke of Wellington, 1769–1852)

In this chapter I will present research on stress resistance among civilians and combatants during war, applying the models of ecological congruence and conservation of resources. The model of ecological congruence was a guiding framework in the design, analysis, and interpretation of this research, which was carried out by my colleagues and myself. The model of conservation of resources, in turn, emerged from the results of my own thinking about the findings of these studies, as well as from the work, of others. The goal of this chapter is threefold—first to illuminate how individuals react to the massive stressor of war, second to illustrate how the model of ecological congruence may aid the study of stress resistance research, and third to evaluate the utility of the model of conservation of resources in the interpretation of the studies' findings.

LESSONS TO BE LEARNED
FROM THE STUDY OF WAR

There has been little research on stress during war and even less is methodologically sound. There are several reasons why this is the case. One principle reason for an absence of recent research on war is that just when interest in the topic of stress was advancing, American psychology and psychiatry were aligning with liberal elements of the society who were against the war in Vietnam. This had the unintended side-effect of limiting the attention paid to returning soldiers and to the families of soldiers who did and who did not return (Figley, 1978; Figley & Leventman, 1980). Indeed, American society in general tended to isolate Vietnam veterans and to ignore their plight (Star, 1973).

Military psychiatrists in the Vietnam era also tended to minimize soldiers' psychiatric problems in the field. They cited the frequent removal of soldiers to safe zones and the one-year rotation in combat as factors that attenuated the psychiatric sequelae of exposure to combat (Marlowe, 1979). The attitude was, at best, myopic, and possibly part of a general military attitude that avoided any negative sanctioning of the war effort. It is possible that military mental health professionals were misled owing to the masking of symptoms by soldiers' frequent use of illicit drugs (Figley, 1978), but this itself should have been diagnosed as a symptom of the severe underlying distress that soldiers experienced.

The lack of research on stress and war does not in any way reflect the importance of this topic. Stress during war is a key area of research on how individuals are affected by massive stressors. Massive stressors occur in many other areas of life as well, but although research on war is difficult to conduct, it is often even more difficult to examine people's reactions to natural disasters and private tragedies. Natural catastrophes tend to produce such chaos that most attempts to study them are frustrated until well after the disaster has ended (Green, Grace, & Gleser, 1985). Private tragedies are also difficult to study because they occur to persons who are scattered among the general population. In addition, it is unethical in many situations to immediately approach those who have undergone massive stress (Ruch, Chandler, & Harter, 1980; Hobfoll & Walfisch, 1984). Consequently, even most grief research begins well after the time of the loved one's death.

These factors have led to a paucity of research on a primary class of stressors. The study of war has ramifications for the understanding of such diverse stressors as rape, divorce, bereavement, victimization to violence, victimization to transportation accidents, cancer and other life-threatening diseases, natural disasters, and nuclear accidents. If we are to wait for an accumulation of information about reactions to each of these specific problems, interventionists will simply have to operate without the benefit of empirical reports that may shed added light on possible directions for intervention efforts.

Even if we were to wait for evidence to accumulate on each of the above-mentioned stressors, the data could ironically be more confounded than those produced by the examination of war-related stress. This is because investigations of war-related stress have the advantage of availing researchers of a family of stressors whose origin is beyond individual control. This is a critically important point because many researchable stressors are the product, in part, of people's own doing. Divorce, economic difficulties, and job loss, for instance, are all related to people's behavior. Even being the "victim" of an "accident" may follow from such personal factors as negligence or accident-prone behavior (e.g., drinking, tiredness). So too, while bereavement is usually not the spouse's fault, the factors that exacerbate its stressfulness (e.g., economic instability, poor relationship skills, social isolation) often are. Consequently, these stressors themselves may be the *products* of distress, as well as the cause of subsequent distress (Dohrenwend et al., 1984; Hobfoll & Walfisch, 1984; and see Chapters 1 and 3, this volume). This problem results in a confounding that is difficult to sort out either statistically or through careful experimental design, which prevents clear assignment of the causal relationship among study variables. Because war is not caused by the individuals affected, this potential confounding is avoided.

Study of war, and of other massive stressors as well, is also methodologically aided by the fact that recall of minor events may be clouded by memory and by the state of resolution of the event (Breznitz & Eshel, 1983). Favorably resolved events in particular may be subject to loss of recall as they are overshadowed by more current concerns. This makes the study of many events confounded with the degree to which the event is viewed as stressful. The relationship between perception of stressfulness and distress is removed from the question of the impact of environmental stressors on distress, because the former relates two perceptual assessments (i.e., perception of stressfulness and perception of distress) and the latter an environmental occurrence (i.e., the event) with the judged consequences of that event (i.e., perception of distress). Events surrounding war are not easily forgotten; while their magnitude is a matter of perception, the fact of their occurrence and their negative valence are not.

Finally, the psychological study of war is important because mental health professionals often treat the victims of war in both the civilian and the military population. Americans and Europeans have been able to ignore the effects of war on civilians, in part, because they have been relatively free of fear of attack and entirely free of war on or within their borders since the Second World War. The same cannot be said for the rest of the world. War is ubiquitous, its effects reverberating throughout much of the world's population. Nations also have the responsibility to care for their sons who return from war, whether their injuries are physical or psychological, and to assist in their full rehabilitation. Without research we must depend on journalists' reports or other reports by those who present their interpretation of the war and its consequences.

Israel has the unfortunate honor of being a national laboratory for research on stress resistance, thus providing rare opportunity for the study of stress and war (Breznitz, 1983a; Milgram, 1982, 1986). Israeli psychology is closely attached to its American and European counterparts, and this interchange enhances the possibility of generalizing the findings from the Israeli context. In our own work, for instance, we often utilize scales that were originally developed outside of Israel and address current questions in the English-language literature. Moreover, the population of Israel tends to be Western-oriented, with daily lives typical of many Western countries. Israelis are also the products of the same Judeo-Christian influences and democratic traditions as Western Europeans and Americans. These points do not prevent the possibility of cultural nuances affecting people's reactions, but cross-cultural comparisons are likely to reveal a common basis and few qualitative differences.

REVIEW OF THE MODELS OF ECOLOGICAL CONGRUENCE AND CONSERVATION OF RESOURCES

Before describing our studies of war-related stress, I would like to briefly review the model of ecological congruence and the model of conservation of resources. This should save the reader the trouble of having to refer back to prior chapters in which the models were described in full and crystallizes the cardinal features of the models. The function of the models is to provide a guiding framework for research and interventions, although no one study or application will be able to employ the two models in their entirety. When adopted successfully by research, however, the models should illuminate the person-environment interchange and facilitate generalization to other similar constellations of factors. For example, one journal reviewer of the study of women and war described later pointed out that this study had much in common with work on cancer and suggested that a replication of the study design using cancer patients would be of interest. This comment illustrates that the models may be used to underscore the comparative structure of the specific occurrences of the two rather different stressors.

The chief purpose of the models is to help define this intermediate region of comparisons across studies. Comparisons are typically more macro or more micro than the level of analysis I am advocating, and this limits the generalizations that may be made from investigations. On the macro level researchers often discuss the effects of all stress or the palliative effect of a single resource—say, locus of control—looking for the most global interpretation. These broad generalizations often appear inaccurate, however, when applied to other situations where different mechanisms are operating. This was the case in regard to early expectations about social support, for instance, which was envisaged as a panacea for all ills. Indeed, in reviewing the women and war study detailed below, one journal reviewer argued that if social support was not helpful then it could not be the social support defined in the literature, and this therefore was grounds for rejecting the evidence (as opposed to questioning the overly positive halo that surrounded the support concept, even in naming it social "support").

On the micro level clinicians and researchers often try to generalize from studies of the specific reactions to a given type of stressor, say cancer, again often relying on a single resource. This results in only the most limited generalizations of empirical evidence. The models I propose press the researchers and clinicians to look instead at the defining structure of their findings. What is the type of loss? What is provided by the resources at hand and what other resources might provide similar aid? How much control is optimal in the face of such stressors? By identifying the structural qualities of the person–environment interface, many commonalities will, I think, be noted among seemingly different stressors and resources. And on the contrary, many superficially similar situations will be shown to be governed by quite different operating mechanisms.

Model of Conservation of Resources

The model of conservation of resources was not used in the design of the studies we undertook, because they were based on principles evoked from the model of ecological congruence. Rather, the model of conservation of resources was derived from the studies' findings. Nevertheless I think its application promotes a richer understanding of the investigations.

The model of conservation of resources purports that people have an innate and learned desire to conserve the quality and quantity of their resources and to limit any state that may jeopardize the security of these resources. From the model a new definition of stress was devised (see Chapter 2 for a full exposition of the model). Stress is defined as a reaction to the environment in which there is (a) the threat of a net loss of resources, or (b) the net loss of resources, or (c) the lack of resource gain following the investment of resources. Resources, in turn, are defined as those objects, personal characteristics, conditions, or energies that are valued by the individual or that serve as a means for attainment of these objects, personal characteristics, conditions, or energies.

The model has a number of implications. The most salient of these are:

1. loss is central to stress,
2. people have a primary concern with the resources they possess,
3. people evaluate their environment with reference to their resources and develop resource conservation strategies,
4. people expect to obtain a net gain in resources as a consequence of their investment of resources,
5. stressful circumstances spiral to create further loss because each loss results in diminishing resources for offsetting further loss, and
6. behavior continues to be affected by loss until individuals perceive themselves in a situation of net gain of resources.

In terms of the model, individuals may counteract loss of resources in three ways. They may utilize resources to offset resource loss, such as when mastery is employed to ward off feelings of despair (loss of hope). They may alternatively reappraise resource loss as gain; an example of this occurs when individuals reinterpret failure on an examination as "the best thing that could have happened" because it spurred them to study harder and not jeopardize all their courses. On a more basic level people may reassess the value they attributed to resources they lost and those they still retain, minimizing the value of the former and maximizing the value of the latter. This occurs, for instance, when job loss is reinterpreted as tolerable because one's family is healthy. It should be emphasized, however, that each of these routes incurs costs in terms of further potential loss of resources. Those who rely on their mastery, for instance, and fail, are likely to experience a loss in their level of mastery. For this reason the act of counteracting loss (i.e., employing other resources) itself entails costs that are weighed against the potential gain of exploiting them.

Model of Ecological Congruence

The model of conservation of resources complements the model of ecological congruence. The former model outlines the nature of *stress* and the latter the elements of *stress resistance*. The model of ecological congruence is illustrated in Figure 3.3 and detailed in Chapter 3 and in other recent publications (Hobfoll, 1985a, 1986b). It states that resources will tend to either reduce, not affect, or increase strain to the extent that the combination of available resources either meets, does not meet, or interferes with task, emotional and biological demands, demands being a product of internal needs and environmental pressures. These demands are also contingent on time, both in relation to the event (e.g., recent, long past) and to the developmental state of those involved (e.g., adolescents versus mature adults, novices versus veterans). Finally, this dynamic fit of resources with demands is influenced by people's values and their perception of themselves and their situation. The six dimensions of the model then are the resource dimension, the strain dimension, the need dimension, the time dimension, the value dimension, and the perception dimension. The connective tissue of the model is conceptualized in terms of the valence of effect, which is a product of the interaction of the dimensions in the determination of the fit of resources to needs.

There are a number of implications of the model. The most cardinal of these are the following:

1. Resources interface in complex ways that may range from facilitating one another to interfering with one another.
2. Resources have innate properties and strengths, but may have varying fit with different demands. Some resources are robust, whereas others have circumscribed efficacy.
3. People will react with strains that are a product of the pressures of the situation and their own weaknesses. In the former case, failure may be particularly linked with depression; in the latter case those with high

blood pressure may be especially susceptible to coronary infarct and the aged may be particularly vulnerable to isolation and anomie.
4. The demands of a situation vary depending on peoples' internal needs and the external properties of the event, which both, in turn, change as a function of time.

Two last critical implications of the model represent how fit is determined on a psychological level, that, beyond the inherent properties of the resources and demands. Specifically,

5. individual values determine to a large part what people view as stressful and what resources may be acceptably employed to counteract stressors and
6. perceptions are seen as important in determining the strength of resources and the extent of loss.

In contrast to other recent models (cf. McGrath, 1970; Lazarus & Folkman, 1984), however, perceptions are viewed as being influential, but not overriding. This stems from the model's complementary emphasis on the objective qualities of the environment and objective resources available to the individual.

Research applications of the model should consider each of the dimensions, the more facets of the model considered the more precise the hypotheses and the greater the yield from the investigation. Minimally, two resources should be compared and their fit to the particular demands of the situation should be outlined. The requirement of two resources is based on the notion that fit is only a comparative construct, single resource designs therefore being unsuited for determining fit. In addition, the nature of the objective and perceived demands that accompany an event and how these change over time must be considered in the construction of hypotheses. Readers are referred to the previous chapter for detailed examples of studies that fulfill the essential requirements of the model.

One final point that needs to be addressed before the research is presented is the preliminary question of how researchers or clinicians are to determine the nature of resources or the demands of situations that form the basis of their ecological hypotheses. Ideally, research will focus on these prefatory questions; however, until such time applications of tangential evidence, clinical lore, and common sense must be employed. This process may be illustrated as it has occurred in the case of social support. Originally, research was based on the believed qualities of social support, based almost solely on common-sense argument and educated guesses (i.e., speculative generalization of tangential research) (Caplan, 1974; Cobb, 1976; Dean & Lin, 1977). Only later did researchers begin to tie social support theory together with empirical knowledge of social psychological and intrapsychic processes that might explain what social support provided (Shinn, Lehmann, & Wong, 1984; Shumaker & Brownell, 1984; Hobfoll, 1985b). Finally, only most recently have these principles been applied to determine whether social support actually possesses those properties attributed to it (Cohen, Sherrod, & Clark, 1986; Cutrona, 1986; Hobfoll & Lerman, 1986; Hobfoll, Nadler, & Leiberman, 1986; Sarason, Sarason, & Shearin, 1986; Stokes, 1981).

As illustrated in the progression of social support research, speculation should not be denigrated. Speculative inquiries lead to a boot-strap effect, whereby evidence bolstering the conjectures or contradictory evidence lead to renewed speculation in other directions. More is known today about social support than most other resources (see Cohen & Wills, 1985; Cohen & Syme, 1985; Gottlieb, 1981; Hobfoll, 1986a; also see Chapter 4, this volume), but even in this area there are many more unanswered questions than firm conclusions. In regard to the press of situations, in comparison, research is in an even more nascent stage (Magnussen, 1981), and bold speculation will be required to advance the field, most likely leading to more misses than hits if the history of science repeats itself.

CIVILIANS' ADJUSTMENT TO WAR

Emotional Distress of Women during War

The first study I will discuss examined the emotional distress of women during the first week of the Israel–Lebanon War, which began in June of 1982 (Hobfoll & London, 1986). The goals of this study were to illuminate how women reacted to a major, unexpected stressor that was out of their control and to examine the early phase of the stress resistance process. In this regard, few studies have investigated the immediate reactions of individuals to any kinds of stressors other than in laboratory conditions.

Traditionally, interest has focused on the more long-term reactions to stressors because researchers have been concerned with the impact of chronic stressors (Pearlin et al., 1981) or accumulation of a number of events (see Thoits, 1983, for a review). Immediate reactions are also important, however, because at such times

1. critical decisions often need to be made,
2. individuals often need to function at peak levels and undertake added responsibility,
3. failure to perform adequately may lead to long-term regret or guilt, and
4. distress at the time of crisis is experienced with extreme anguish.

In addition, long-term mental health is often affected by initial responding (Caplan, 1964). Ironically, however, because of the severity of emotional reactions at the time of events, people may actually be least able to function effectively when they most need to do so.

Background: civilian-military milieu in Israel

The model of ecological congruence urges an understanding of the social and psychological climate surrounding an event. In the current instance, it is important to describe the Israeli reserve military system. All able men from the ages of 21 to about 55 serve in the reserve army following their regular army service. The reserves are an integral part of Israel's military forces and are relied upon as experienced troops. The women in our study had close male kin (sons, husbands, brothers, or fathers) who were mobilized during the first days of the Israeli invasion of Lebanon. The conflict began with little forewarning. Orders for mobilization were received at home or at work, and men had only a few hours to arrive at arranged military meeting points. Contact with their families was restricted after this time, both officially and owing to the difficulty of communicating a message from military sites. Due to the short distances in this region between home and front lines, men could find themselves entering the battle zone within hours after being ordered into uniform.

Women whose husbands were mobilized had only a few hours to make arrangements for their work and households in response to their own transition to temporary single parent status. This meant not only increased responsibility at home but also added responsibility at work because many male coworkers were called into action. Likewise, women had only this short time to adjust themselves psychologically for the threat to their loved ones' lives and bodies that would continue over an untold number of days and weeks to come. This was further complicated by the fact that accurate information is hardest to obtain in the initial days of fighting and rumors are rampant, some of the rumors being intentional disinformation broadcast by both sides (e.g., one can turn on an Israeli television and hear the Jordanian news).

Nature of the study

Our sample consisted of women from a number of randomly selected apartment complexes in the city of Beersheva situated in the Negev desert. All women in the selected buildings (one per apartment) who were home during repeated visits throughout three days and evenings were asked to participate in the study. They were provided questionnaires that were collected two to four days after distribution. A 97 percent return rate was achieved. Respondents ranged in age from 24 to 57 years, and a majority worked full or part-time, principally in clerical, educational, or professional occupations. The exact methodology and in-depth statistical analyses of this and all other studies that I and my colleagues conducted (in this and the following chapter) may be found in the research articles referenced at the beginning of the presentation of each investigation.

Ecological rationale

Given this climate of stress we surmised that women's personal resources would be their greatest ally in resisting vicissitudes of their difficult situation. This conjecture was based on a number of arguments. First, it was thought that personal resources—we were particularly interested in self-esteem and mastery—had good fit with situational demands. Second, we reasoned that personal resources could be immediately called upon when needed and did not demand the acquisition time of external resources, which must be alerted and have time to respond. Women would do well if they told themselves they would successfully overcome their current problems and that even in the worst eventuality they would adjust as well as could be expected.

If we look a bit more closely at these resources, we see that persons who possess self-esteem resist the impulse to interpret outside events as reflecting negatively on themselves, even when they feel anxious or are functioning below their optimal level (Cronkite & Moos, 1984; Kaplan et al., 1983; Pearlin & Schooler, 1978). Those high in mastery, in turn, believe that success will follow from their own actions and that they, not outside forces, are the principal determiners of their fate (Johnson & Sarason, 1978; Pearlin et al., 1981; Sandler & Lakey, 1982). Because the current stressor resulted in demands that could not be directly confronted (i.e., women could not bring their loved ones home) and demands that had to be directly confronted (e.g., extra child-care and work responsibility), both these aspects of the self-concept were deemed important.

A secondary resource that might further mitigate the deleterious effects of stress on these women was social support. However, from the start we were suspicious of the role social support might play. Despite the widespread belief at the time of conducting our research that social support was a major external resource, we had doubts whether it would help actualize the basic resources that women needed. As discussed in Chapter 3, the effectiveness of social support is that it can provide or enhance personal resources, object resources, condition resources, or energy resources. First, we thought personal resources could provide the necessary feelings and energies that were required in this situation more quickly than could social support (the women were less likely to be in need of additional object or condition resources). Second, we were doubtful whether social support could be effectively recruited so quickly, given the sudden time of onset of the current stressor and the fact that it affected so many people.

Considering the process of providing social support led to a further dissection of this resource and emphasizes the time component of the model of ecological congruence. As illustrated in Figure 6.1 social support requires a number of phases for effective acquisition. The first phase is the recruitment phase, which requires that individuals have already decided they need support and are likely to receive it. The second stage is the response phase, when supporters must decide if they can or wish to respond given their own environmental constraints and emotional well-being. This stage also may require travel time and financial expense in terms of travel funds or taking off time at work. Ideally, a final stage of high-intensity support will follow. This phase depends on a number of factors, including recipients' clear communication of their needs, the ability of supporters to meet these needs, and the intimacy and history of the relationships between the recipient and the supporter. Each of these phases may take considerable time and often require further fine-tuning or repetition. They may also be set into motion, but still not succeed in the providing the aid required.

Given this reasoning we hypothesized that self-esteem and mastery would attenuate the emotional distress that women would feel and that social support would have a positive but more limited effect. We further predicted that this would be true for social support conceptualized in two ways, both as the actual support provided and as the level of intimacy with friends and family. These two aspects of support reflect two of the most salient aspects of support noted in the literature (see Barrera, 1986; Cohen & Wills, 1985, Chapter 4).

Moving next to the strain dimension of the model of ecological congruence we selected an indicator of emotional distress that was likely

Recruitment phase

Family ◄----   ----► Friends

Response phase

Family ◄----   ◄---- Friends

High-intensity support

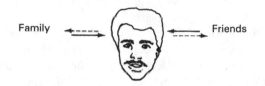

Family   Friends

FIGURE 6.1   Phases of support.

to assess the most common reactions to the current ecological mix. The strain that would follow from this kind of stressor in this kind of sample was deemed most likely to range from generalized uneasiness to severe anxiety and depressive feelings. Since this was not a clinical sample but a group of women selected from the community, we relied on two measures, one that taps recently experienced anxiety and another that taps recently experienced depression. Both measures were normed on the general population, making them especially appropriate for this sample.

Values were also considered in conceptualizing the study. In particular, we thought social support would be freely transferred given the positive Israeli attitude toward helping and the need for people to stick together during war. In more personal crises, neighbors, colleagues, and friends might be held more distant at such an initial stage of crisis, and persons would attempt to rely solely on themselves and immediate family. Such a situation would make any hypothesis about the effect of social support secondary to the question of whether social support was sought and received. Although we did not compare the level of social support directly with other situations we did find that women frequently discussed their situation and the attendant worries with family, friends, colleagues, and neighbors and that it was often the sole subject of conversation at home and at work. This can be contrasted to the behavior of women in a private crisis of illness (that will be detailed in the next chapter), who tended to exclude friends from their problems and kept the nature of their distress more private.

The last dimension of the model was not directly assessed. However, this is often the case because perceptions are an overarching facet of the model (see Chapter 3) that affects each of the other dimensions. In this case, perceptions of self-esteem, mastery, social support, the extent of risk of loss brought on by war, and emotional distress were all personal perceptions. We know that these perceptions also have a considerable objective component, but felt that what was most important was women's own assessment of the stressor, their strengths, and their distress.

Study findings and ecological implications

Earlier it was noted that we expected social support to be less well fitted to the ecology of this situation than personal resources. When we were debriefing respondents, however, it was already apparent that social support might have a dual-edged effect. Specifically, while women reported feeling comforted by social support they had received, they also reported feeling troubled by it. Spontaneous responses included, "I couldn't stand to hear her troubles too," "All we could do was talk about the war," "It [all the calls and talking] prevented me from getting anything else done," and "I kept hearing new rumors and each more horrible than the one before, so I just started avoiding everyone." This suggested a different facet of social support than had been discussed in the literature. Specifically, it was readily apparent that social support could be an additional burden both because it could increase exposure to stressors and because it interfered with other coping efforts.

When the data were analyzed it was found that both mastery and self-esteem aided in the resistance of feelings of emotional distress. Intimacy and support received, in contrast, were related to *greater* emotional distress, as we had begun to suspect upon debriefing the women. We also examined whether social support might be curvilinearly related to emotional distress, such that women who received moderate amounts of support were aided, but those receiving high or low levels of support were not. No support for such an effect was noted. Further analyzing the data we found that the negative effects of social support were only evident among women who were high in personal resources and that these effects were quite appreciable in their magnitude.

When we review these results, two processes can plausibly explain this constellation of findings. First, whereas women who possessed strong personal resources had greater stress resistance, it is likely that their particular kinds of coping style relied principally on these personal strengths. This would especially hold at the stage where their coping efforts were still successful. For them social support may have acted as a hindrance, preventing them from enacting the introspective, independent style they favored. In the second instance, women who possess more personal resources are likely to possess greater levels of social support because they are more socially attractive than women who lack these resources (Jones, 1985; Sarason et al., 1985). This possibility was borne out in this study, since both self-esteem and mastery were related to greater intimacy. Unfortunately, this leads to greater exposure to the stress of others (Riley & Eckenrode, 1986; Kessler et al., 1985) and to the rumor mills already mentioned. In addition, when groups get together they have been found to arrive at more extreme conclusions than do individuals, adding still another negative dimension to social support in a crisis situation (Myers & Lamm, 1976).

It might be possible to argue that distress led to greater receipt of support, and this might indicate that distress was causing support, and not support distress. However, it must be recalled that the women who were most likely to be negatively affected by support were those most likely to be faring well, as they were the women who possessed the personal resources. It might also be possible to argue that emotional distress and low mastery and self-esteem covaried; that is, they both were products of the stressful circumstances. If this were the case, these personal resources would be more parsimoniously viewed as further symptoms of distress. However, we have other data on the stability of the mastery and self-esteem scales that clearly support the fact that they are stable during periods of stress caused by forces outside of the individual's control (Hobfoll & Walfisch, 1984; Pearlin et al., 1981).

Nevertheless, it is important to point out that given the correlational nature of this study's findings, these arguments must rest on logic rather than empirical evidence. Conceptual replication of the process and outcome of the war study will be illustrated in the prospective study of illness to be presented in the next chapter.

Emotional Distress and Behavioral Adjustment of Students during War

Study background

One year after the Israel–Lebanon conflict began, we went back to look at the adjustment of students during the protracted war (Hobfoll, London, & Orr, in press). At this time the war was still ongoing and dissent was increasing among liberal elements of Israeli society, with students very active in antiwar activity. Israeli dead numbered over 500, which would be proportionally equivalent to about 50,000 Americans. However, this cannot be compared too closely with the Vietnam experience, since Israeli students are very often soldiers or in the family of soldiers. Students are required to enter the armed forces at age 18 before beginning university studies, and both men and women serve in the reserves while studying, after completing their service commitment. This makes the border between civilian and soldier somewhat hazy, but this is not uncommon when wars are fought close to home. Women are less likely than men to have demanding reserve duties and do not perform combat functions at any time in their military careers. Women are also excluded from service when married.

Whether or not they serve in combat roles, men have increased duty during periods of military conflict. Students often found themselves serving a month, returning home, and then being recalled for another service period. At the time of this study many male students in this sample had been at war for four to six months in a revolving door between university and military life. Many university women had volunteered to work as medics in treatment centers for the wounded. For example, all four female interviewers who were to work with me on the previously discussed project volunteered to go to the north and serve as medics. Of course female students often have close ties, friendships and love relationships, with male students or other young men who are involved in the war. Both male and female students have close kin and friends in the war, since Israel is a small, close-knit country with a large army.

Nature of the study

Questionnaires were distributed to undergraduate students in the humanities and social sciences and medicine. Male students averaged about 24 years of age and females 25 years of age. Almost a third of the women were married, some 22 percent with children, and 15 percent of the men were married, 11 percent with children. These demographics outline a sample more like the young work force in other countries than students and, indeed, a majority of students were working full or part-time in addition to studying. In addition, fully 67 percent of the men had served in Lebanon during the period of the war, and more than 90 percent of the men had served in the military with risk of entering Lebanon and with frequent detachment from their studies during the previous year.

Ecological rationale

The ecology of this situation had many elements contrasting with those of the ecology of women in the prior study and, consequently, we envisaged resources to operate differently. First, looking at the nature of the demand, we devised a list of war-related stressors ranging from being wounded or having a loved one wounded or killed, to serving in Lebanon or having the possibility of serving. Unlike typical event lists, we were isolating a particular family of stressors that were diverse but had a central theme. All of the events also shared a common underlying structure in that they were undesirable, uncontrollable, major, of clear importance to the individual, and not attributable to individuals' own actions. Only in the case of being wounded was there a possible element of fault, but this would be due to carelessness, not intentional behavior. This method can be compared with general event lists, which mix events possessing all of these underlying attributes of external demand. Furthermore, these events are not likely to be forgotten, since they are limited in number, not given to interpretation (e.g., financial problems are the product of perception, a wound is not), and flagrant.

It may also be argued that internal needs of individuals were similar, if the value dimension of the model is brought into focus. In this regard, people share a high regard for peace and for distancing themselves physically and psychologically from war. This stems from the common values for peace, personal safety, and psychological well-being (see Rokeach, 1973). In addition, there is a common desire to love and prosper. Knowing the nature of the external demand, we can assume that these are the kinds of personal needs that are evoked from this situation. Job-related stressors, in contrast, might evoke the need to achieve and to be held in esteem to a greater extent than, say the need for personal safety and safety of loved ones.

With these demands in mind, we were interested in how mastery and intimate social support might buffer the effects of war-related stress. Mastery, we thought, would have limited effect in this instance, as there were limited tasks that individuals could do vis-à-vis the war. War itself is a state of chaos, where the side with the least chaos is victor. Upon their return home, men had to incorporate their war experience and how they felt about it and had to face the anticipatory stress of future call-up. Women also had to adjust to whatever occurred and continue with their daily lives. Their task was not so much to control and master as to focus on the present and accept the past.

Social support, on the other hand, was expected to be an especially effective resource. By this time people had considerable time to enlist the aid of their social support system and to gain from such support. Moreover, intimate social contact is in many ways the phenomenological opposite of war; it testifies to life, not death. For men, their relationships at home were often what they thought most about during their period of service. For women I think it is said best in the words of a close friend, wife of a pilot in her student days: "I prayed he would be wounded, not badly, but bad enough so he could come home and be with me and so I could hold him and know he's here and safe."

In terms of strains we judged a different complex of responses to be most relevant to war-related stress. On the emotional level we predicted that war-related stress would increase recent feelings of anxiety because the events possessed components of physical threat and ego-threat (Spielberger, 1972). However, we saw a second emotion that has not received much attention, which would be of special concern here. Specifically, we thought the feeling of recent anger would be particularly relevant for war-related stress in the context of protest. Finally, although many have advocated the need for behavioral measures, few stress researchers have incorporated them in their work. We devised a measure that assessed self-reported recent adjustment to work, studies, love life, and family life. It should be noted that this behavioral measure was shown to be independent of the two emotional measures, indicating that it did not merely reflect emotional adjustment.

The perception dimension of the model of ecological congruence is thus reflected in the mastery, social support, and strain facets of this study, with events being less given to the coloring effect of perception and interpretation. The more objective measure of events allows for more confident interpretation of the relationship between events and outcome. This follows because it is unlikely that events are over- or underreported due to emotional outcome (e.g., a depressed individual reporting more hassles owing to irritability). Also, it is unlikely that the actual event occurrence was a product of emotional distress (e.g., anxiety leading to marital discord) or a symptom of distress (e.g., the perception of hassles being a symptom of depression) (see Dohrenwend et al., 1984).

Study findings and ecological implications

The findings of the study were quite different for men than for women. Once again this was because the events for men and women were actually quite different. For men, most of the events were happening to them; for women the events were happening to those they loved. Consequently, men were more likely than women to experience recent anxiety and problems in behavioral adjustment as a result of their exposure to war-related stressors. Women, in fact, showed no increased emotional distress or problems in functioning as a result of their exposure to war-related stress.

The resources affected men as predicted. Mastery was related to general well-being (i.e., less emotional distress), but it did not buffer the effect of stressors; that is, it had a similar salubrious effect on men regardless of their level of exposure to events. Social support on the other hand was found to be especially important for those men who had greater exposure to stressors during the year of the war than for men who did not. This was the case both for recently experienced anxiety and for behavioral adjustment, as may be noted in Figures 6.2 and 6.3, respectively. In fact, those with high intimate support had slightly decreasing levels of anxiety, the greater their exposure to stress. This is most probably a statistical artifact or may be related to the fact that intimacy encouraged denial. For men, possessing intimate relationships was certainly advantageous, and those who possessed them felt better emotionally and saw themselves as functioning better in their civilian lives.

For women, mastery was also related to greater well-being, but as women were relatively unaffected by war-related events there was no such stress to buffer. Interestingly, intimacy was not related to well-being or functioning among women, suggesting that intimacy may be most important when people are currently confronting stressful situations.

It was surprising that anger was not related to events surrounding the war for either sex. It is possible that at the time of the events anger was higher, but that anger levels had dissipated. More likely, however, we had erringly assumed that disdain for the war was common. Students were probably more divided on this issue than we had conjectured. Had

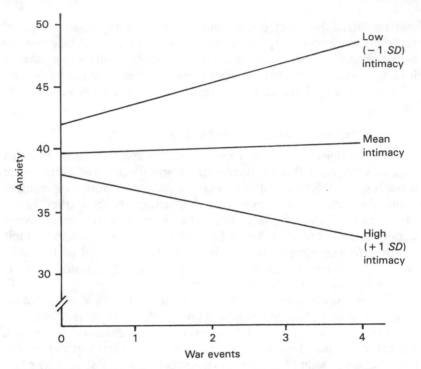

FIGURE 6.2   Effects of war-related events and intimacy on anxiety. (From Hobfoll et al., in press.)

we assessed students' attitudes toward the war we could have further analyzed this question, but we had not had the foresight.

It is interesting to compare women's reactions at the time of the war (the prior study) and one year later (the current study). At the time of the war women were deeply affected by events, as shown by their extremely high levels of anxiety and depression. Yet, even those in the student sample who were exposed to considerable war-related stressors were unaffected one year later. Considering the time dimension of the model of ecological congruence it seems plausible that stressful events are most meaningful when they are current. The events in the student sample were dispersed over a year (as in most stressful-event scales), and so fewer of them were current. For many of the events the time of adjustment was likely to have passed already. Men, in contrast, continued to live with the visions of the battlefield; these scenes are known to intrude on thinking in those exposed to war (Horowitz & Solomon,

1975). In addition, men suffered from anticipatory threat of loss (Breznitz, 1983b) because they were likely to be called up to serve once again as the labyrinth of the war became further entangled.

This leads to the suggestion that stressors lose their detrimental force as they are resolved, even if the resolution is necessarily negative. It would appear that people are principally concerned with their current problems. This raises the further possibility that the more distal events tapped by most event lists are no longer impinging on those who experienced them. This would seriously attenuate the correlation between events and outcomes. This attenuated correlation has been interpreted as indicating that stressful events are not appreciably affecting people, or that resources are moderating stress effects (Rabkin & Streuning, 1976). Rather, it may be that the principal moderator is time. The events may have been quite stressful when they occurred and may even have lasting effects in the case of the most severe events

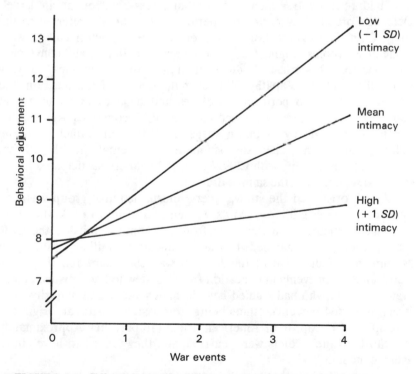

FIGURE 6.3 Effect of war-related events and intimacy on behavioral adjustment. (From Hobfoll et al., in press.)

(Lehman et al., 1987). For most stressful events, however, "time heals all wounds." Somehow this notion seems to have been lost in the romance over the all-too-easy stressful-event list methodology.

EFFECTS OF WAR ON COMBATANTS

Resisting Breakdown during Combat

Study background and design

Having considered the effects of war on the civilian population I turn now to the study of the stress of war on combatants. For these studies we had a very unusual opportunity, with access to all of the Israeli soldiers who broke down during combat in Lebanon during the Israel–Lebanon war (Solomon, Mikulincer, & Hobfoll, 1986). Specifically, every soldier who had received treatment for combat stress reaction at an Israeli Defence Force facility during the period of the war was referred to the study. Combat stress reaction (hereafter CSR) is characterized by a wide range of symptoms ranging from severe anxious agitation and conversion reactions (e.g., hysterical blindness, talking to dead comrades) to waxy immobility and acute apathy. Whatever the course of the reaction, the soldier is unable to perform his duties and behaves in an irrational manner that endangers his life and the lives of his comrades. Referral for treatment is made by battalion surgeons (physicians attached to the fighting unit), and diagnosis is made by mental health officers experienced in working with CSR. In all, 382 soldiers participated in the study (81.4 percent of the sample drawn).

As we organized the study, a very unusual control group was also devised. Through military records we selected a group of 334 soldiers who had participated in the same frontline combat units as the CSR group; they were matched for age, education, military rank, and assignment. Median age of the soldiers was 28.5 years and they were distributed fairly evenly in education from those who had finished eighth grade to those who had studied beyond high school. The majority were Israeli born (64 percent), others being from Asian or African origin (20 percent) and European or American origin (16 percent). Approximately two-thirds of the soldiers were married, and they tended to have above average income.

The threat of combat is well known through movies, but the salient features of the stressors impinging on soldiers is somewhat different. Major stressors include the threat to life and limb, the threat of having to witness horrible casualties, the threat of having to kill others, and the threat of defeat. Two other classes of less obvious stressors are also omnipresent. The first are physiological; soldiers often lack sleep, water, and food and are exposed for long periods to extremes of cold or heat, wetness, noise, insects, illness, and exertion. The second revolves around the social realm, as soldiers must confront the social disorganization that inevitably surrounds troop movement and battles and must adjust to forced intense social relationships in their immediate unit. They have not chosen these relationships, and they are often with people they would not associate with back home. Buddy systems and cliques arise and are critical for safety and comfort.

Ecological rationale

Past research has shown that the intensity of battle is a key indicator of breakdown during combat (Noy, Nardi, & Solomon, 1986; Levav, Greenfeld, & Baruch, 1979). As both the CSR and the control group were exposed to the same battles, we thought their interpretation of the intensity of combat would be the best indicator of the degree of threat of loss they encountered. This stems from the fact that although they were matched they may have experienced somewhat different actual conditions. This view of stressfulness emphasizes the perception dimension of the model of ecological congruence, but has an obvious and verifiable objective component as well.

We chose to compare two social resources, buddy support and support from noncommissioned or commissioned officers of the fighting unit (usually sergeants and lieutenants). Military folklore places the buddy system as a central factor in group cohesion, even if sound research on this question is scarce (Kellett, 1982). We also surmised, however, that support from noncommissioned and commissioned officers would be critical. The officer's function is to provide information, order, and encouragement to his men. Since loss of a sense of mastery is a key to breakdown, we suspected that support from officers would be crucial in maintaining a sense of mastery in the face of the overwhelming stressors.

The model of ecological congruence also dictates that attention be paid to the *process* by which resources act. If social support is helpful because it provides human contact and a sense of attachment, then its loss should be accompanied by an increasing sense of loneliness. For this reason we further predicted that in addition to the independent effects of battle intensity and social support on CSR, these factors would contribute to CSR via loneliness. That is, as battle intensity increased, soldiers would be likely to have increased feelings of social detachment, whereas receipt of social support would moderate this process by limiting feelings of isolation. Increased feelings of loneliness, in turn, would further contribute to likelihood of CSR.

Questionnaires that assess buddy and officer social support were administered to soldiers one year after their war experience. At the same time soldiers were asked to judge the intensity of combat and their feelings of loneliness during battle. Ratings of CSR were made jointly by combat surgeons and mental health officers at the time of occurrence, as already noted. Relatively few studies of stress or social support have obtained measures of strain by methods other than self-report, and even fewer have relied on the judgment of experienced mental health professionals. In this regard, where measures of stressors, resources, and strain are all provided by self-report, any relationship found between them may be attributable to the fact that they share a common method (with common biases). By providing experts' assessments of strain (CSR), we avoid this potential confounding, especially since diagnoses were made by experienced combat surgeons and confirmed by mental health officers.

Findings and ecological implications

Preliminary analysis indicated that ratings of battle intensity and social support were independent of one another. This is an important point because it has been suggested that the two might be confounded, such that those who are confronted with stressful circumstances report that they have less social support than those exposed to less stressful conditions (Thoits, 1982). Such a relationship would indicate that rather than being a moderator of stress, social support is itself an outcome of situational stressfulness. Being independent suggests that they separately contribute to stress resistance.

Examining the hypotheses, soldiers who experienced loneliness in combat were found to be more likely than those who did not experience loneliness to perceive themselves as lacking support for their military performance and personal support from their officers. For example, they felt that officers did not "tell soldiers when they did a good job" and did not "really care about their soldiers," respectively. Soldiers who became lonely also felt they lacked emotional support from their comrades-in-arms. For example, they did not feel that soldiers "tell each other about their personal problems," or that they were "well liked" by their comrades.

Breakdown in combat was also determined by lack of both kinds of support from officers. The felt absence of support from comrades, however, was not found to be related to CSR. Since officer support was the most important factor in determining both CSR and loneliness, we constructed a path-model to test the extent that battle intensity and officer support predicted CSR. We also tested for possible interactions of officer support and battle intensity on CSR that might indicate a stress-buffering effect, such that social support was more important under high intensity of battle than under less intense battle conditions. No support for such a stress-buffering effect was garnered. This led to the following proposed model, in which the two kinds of officer support are combined to form a single variable (see Figure 6.4).

When one examines this model, one finds that officer support and battle intensity both had modest independent effects on CSR and both contributed to CSR via their effect on loneliness (*p* values indicate the level of *independent* contribution of that path). Loneliness was also related to CSR, lonelier soldiers being more likely to develop CSR. What appears to be occurring, then, is that soldiers who are exposed to more intense battle conditions and who feel they lack officer support tend to have increased feelings of loneliness, which increases the likelihood of their developing CSR.

This does not deny that other factors also contribute to CSR. Lack of support and battle intensity also have direct effects on CSR, perhaps because they cause a feeling of extreme hopelessness or impending doom, for example. Our data suggest that the proposed model answers some of the questions about CSR, but leaves a great deal more unexplained.

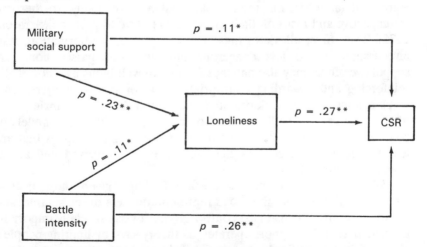

FIGURE 6.4 Path analysis of relations between battle intensity, social support, loneliness, and combat stress reactions (CSR). (Reproduced by permission from Z. Solomon et al., *Journal of Personality and Social Psychology,* the American Psychological Association, © 1986.)

In reviewing the results we were struck by the implications of the findings for attachment theory (Bowlby, 1969, 1973) and the model of conservation of resources. Attachment theory suggests that individuals are especially threatened when their attachment to principal figures is subject to loss. Officers are often perceived in parental terms; they are referred to as "the old man" and are regarded as caring, somewhat distant figures typical of many father-son relationships. In addition, officers are expected to provide answers and order and to mediate squabbles between soldiers—other attributes of paternal care. Viewed in a psychodynamic framework, combat constitutes a massive threat to ego-integrity that awakens extreme anxiety and regression. The regression is triggered by a sense of dependency, helplessness, and loss of self-confidence; the soldier returns to a more child-like state. If soldiers lack the feelings of attachment that officer support provides, they are likely to be incapable of resisting this ego-disintegration when such threat occurs. This would thus be a good example of the principle of replacement in the model of ecological congruence, such that the presence of officer support (a) prevents or replaces sense of loss and (b) makes this replacement better than buddy support, which is a less direct replacement of the loss.

The findings can also be interpreted within a cognitive framework. Without any allusion to subconscious processes it can be seen that combat represents a threat to soldiers that is likely to produce fear. Rather than focus on their task, soldiers are likely to become introspective and focus on their anxiety and failure to perform (Sarason, 1975). The officer alleviates these fears by providing information, rest, and assignment to less dangerous missions, and passes home. A supportive officer may also enhance feelings of well-being by emotionally reinforcing and rewarding appropriate behavior of the soldiers. This helps soldiers remain task oriented and inhibit feelings of anxiety that may overtake them. This is also consistent with the model of conservation of resources, as the officer is supplying resources that are lost and providing resources that minimize the perceived and actual chances of threat of loss.

We thought these were important findings, given the objective stressfulness of combat, the broad representativeness of the sample, and the use of a carefully matched control group. It was especially important to show that social support operates, as theory says, by limiting people's sense of isolation. Studies of social support have almost exclusively measured the effect of social support directly on outcome (e.g., depression, physical illness) without allusion to the mediating processes on which the theoretical models are built. The empirical questions pertaining to *process* are therefore typically ignored even though the validation of social support theory depends on verification of outcome and alleged process (Gottlieb, in press; Hobfoll & Stokes, in press).

The study was limited, however, by the use of retrospective accounts and the dependence on subjective evaluation of the very real stressor that the men faced. There was no doubt that this stressor was massive, but the actual judgments by soldiers were products of their own appraisal. For these reasons it was important to follow the course of CSR prospectively and to examine the comparative contribution of objective versus subjective determinants of intensity of combat and of social support. These points were developed in the next study.

Development of Combat Stress Reaction and Its Aftermath

Study background

CSR among combatants and its aftermath in the year thereafter was the focus of a second study of soldiers (Solomon, Mikulincer, & Hobfoll, 1987). This situation also made possible the examination of the question of the role played in stress resistance by subjective versus objective components of stressors and resources. Although perceptions are central to many of the models purporting to explain the stress-distress link (e.g., Lazarus & Folkman, 1984; Kaplan, 1983), few studies have compared the contribution of objective and subjective indicators of stressfulness or resources (Green et al., 1985). We relied on the CSR and matched control sample already detailed to investigate this question.

The model of ecological congruence emphasizes the contribution of both objective environmental circumstances and perceptions. It is difficult to study their contribution outside of the laboratory, however, for two reasons. First, outside of the laboratory it is usually unknown to any but those involved, what stressors are impinging on them. Second, when people report something as stressful they are summarizing a vast catalogue of data about the external event that no objective event list could detail (i.e., an unavoidable problem of sampling error). Divorce, for instance, may really encompass the unfolding of, say, 10 major subevents and innumerable minor hassles, whose stressfulness is also a function of their sequence. This would make comparison of the different sequences virtually impossible. This does not mean that perceptions are more important than objective determinants, only that we do not have the means for making an absolute comparison.

Our combat study could not surmount the problem of equivalent comparison of objective versus subjective determinants of outcome. However, we could study whether perceptual and objective factors each made contributions to soldiers' well-being. Specifically we isolated both objective and subjective measures of social support and combat stressfulness. We examined the contribution of these factors to CSR and to subsequent development of posttraumatic stress disorder (PTSD). Both CSR and PTSD were based on the assessments of experienced clinicians and the diagnoses of PTSD were cross-checked for reliability between clinicians. Questionnaire information was obtained as in the prior study.

Ecological rationale

CSR, as discussed in the context of the prior study, is a measure of strain consistent with the ecology of combat. PTSD is a second measure of strain that is congruent with the ecology of the reorganizational phase more distal from exposure to the stressful event. The diagnosis of PTSD was made according to clinical guidelines (DSM-III, 1980). In this disorder, the individual has been exposed to an unusually stressful event, feels a numbing of responsiveness to or reduced involvement with the external world, and displays symptoms that might include, but are not restricted to, hyperalertness, sleep disturbance, survivor guilt, difficulty concentrating, and intrusive thoughts about the event. Ratings of PTSD were made with a self-report questionnaire after it was found that such self-reports have very high agreement with the ratings of experienced clinicians. In addition, we also asked soldiers to subjectively evaluate their own functioning during combat.

Thus the study is anchored by using four highly reliable measures: (a) objective assessments of event stressfulness, (b) objective assessment of social support, (c) clinical diagnosis of CSR provided by two experienced health and combat professionals, and (d) self-ratings of PTSD verified by comparison with clinical ratings of a large subsample. Since few studies of stress or social support have a single objective measure, and almost all rely on self-report for indications of event stressfulness, resources, and outcome, we thought we could make an important contribution to the issue of the factors determining stress reactions.

In looking for objective measures we settled on four critical aspects of combat: (a) participation in front-line battles, (b) prior training preparing the soldier for his actual role during the battle (lack of training being stressful), (c) proximity to the front-line during battle, and (d) participation in the evacuation of dead soldiers. Our objective measure of support was whether they served in the same unit with others with whom they had trained or fought in the past. Many soldiers are assigned to a unit soon before battle and do not have the time to develop close social bonds with their officers or comrades. Both of these objective measures are unlikely to be influenced by perceptions; they are major events that are not likely to be lost in recall. In addition, the questionnaires were administered in official military settings and soldiers knew their reports were subject to verification.

Subjective stressfulness was measured by soldiers' global assessments of how stressful they found combat. Subjective military social support was assessed using the combined scores for support from buddies and officers already discussed. Support from officers and buddies was most congruent with preventing the development of CSR because it is related to the military environment. In the year following, however, both their ties with their military unit and family support were ecologically congruent with sorting out the personal meaning of the events surrounding the war. For this reason we also adopted a well-validated measure of family support for this phase of the study.

Findings and ecological implications

The objective and subjective measures of event stressfulness were both related to CSR and PTSD. Those who were exposed to more stressful conditions and who perceived their experiences as more stressful were more likely to develop CSR at the time of combat and PTSD following their combat experience than those who were objectively and subjectively less challenged. Contrary to expectations, objective rating of social support did not relate to CSR or PTSD; however, it did relate to soldiers' own assessment of their functioning. Specifically, soldiers who fought in units with whom they had little chance for developing attachment felt that they functioned inadequately in battle. Subjective assessment of unit support was, in contrast, related to less likelihood of CSR and PTSD.

The model of ecological congruence would further suggest that family support would also be critical in the postwar phase, because the family milieu becomes more salient in the individual's life. It was indeed found that the severity of PTSD (i.e., greater number of PTSD symptoms) was more a function of family climate than of unit support. During combat, soldiers are attempting to forestall ego-disintegration amidst the chaos around them and to preserve their physical well-being. Unit support meets both these needs. The model of conservation of resources would suggest that following war the threat would be to loss of self-esteem because of what the soldier had done or not done. Family support is critical in helping soldiers sort out what has occurred and assuring them that they are loved, esteemed, and accepted no matter what transpired under the terrible conditions of war. The soldier's family reminds him through love, affection, and understanding that whatever his losses, he has much to live for. In addition, just as unit support conveys the message that the soldier must continue to function and believe in himself because others depend on him, so does family support purvey that one is obliged to function for the sake of the family as well as oneself. In both cases, the expectations are positive that the soldier will be able to meet these obligations.

It would appear that both objective and subjective components of threat and resources are important in determining the ongoing process of stress resistance. Also, the role of stress resistance resources is a function of their congruence with the ecology of the moment. During battle, unit support is critical, but during the following months soldiers' families play a central part. Objective social support only predicted subjective functioning level and not CSR or later PTSD. As mentioned initially, however, objective measures have the handicap of coming from a limited sampling of people's full experience. A better objective measure would include, say, officers' reports of soldiers' social embeddedness in the fighting unit, since even new replacements may have made quick ties given the intensity of this experience. What is important according to the model of ecological congruence is that both subjective and objective determinants are involved in mental health outcome, and this precept is confirmed in this study.

IMPLICATIONS FOR UNDERSTANDING STRESS RESISTANCE

These studies could be narrowly interpreted just in terms of how they relate to war. It is even possible to suggest that because they were conducted in Israel that they have little application to North America or Europe. Unfortunately, such interpretations are made quite frequently. One reason for this is practical, there is so much research and theory to read carried out on North American populations that even the serious reader is taxed to look further. A second, more influential reason for this general disregard of research conducted outside the United States and Canada is based on the nonecological model that most researchers have adopted (see Triandis, 1972).

Specifically, in an ecological model one must look for the underlying principles that affect the person–situation interaction. A nonecological model, in contrast, looks for stable relationships between two or more sets of variables, even to the point of seeing culture, values, or situational demands as experimental noise disguising the true signal. This approach, too often, leads to a repetition of studies that rely principally on college students. Taking an ecological perspective, one must question whether the stressors reported by such samples are comparable to those confronted by less sheltered adult populations and whether the reported social support is representative of the deep, long-lasting relationships that adults experience and, indeed, that college students experience before their arrival on campus.

Relying, as studies do, on limited samples also obscures the "true" relationship between variables, even when "stable" relationships are noted. There are several explanations for this phenomenon. First, if a theory or model is truly robust it should generalize to various cultures (Triandis, 1972; Whiting, 1968). An excellent example of this is Piaget's theory of cognitive development (Piaget, 1973). Often, study of different cultures and different kinds of samples within a culture results in theory expansion so as to fit all of the data into a comprehensive explanation. In addition, focusing on more diverse samples increases the number of variables that one might consider as the complexity of the model expands. Fewer variables are required when only one kind of sample is repeatedly used because the full purview of the model may not be tapped. Perhaps most important, when one is repeatedly sampling a given population, it is impossible to untangle variables that aggregate in one culture, subculture, or group, but that are only artificially related to outcome. This point is illustrated in studies by Cohen et al. (1979), who by studying Japanese-Americans found that some of what were thought to be the principal components of type A behavior were part and parcel of American culture and probably unrelated to coronary disease.

My point may be illustrated in recent work on loneliness, which is one consequence of poor social support. Because the majority of samples were drawn from students and the time of questionnaire administration tended to be disregarded, studies of loneliness have confused trait loneliness with a temporary state of being alone (Rook, in press; Shaver, Furman, & Burhmaster, 1985). Shaver et al. point out that most of those who described themselves as lonely at the beginning of the school year found rewarding relationships by spring. These processes are themselves important, and may even be used as a model for adults in new environs, but this is not what was and is done. Instead, results are generalized to adult populations with almost no cross-validation according to the particular nature of the subjects. When such cross-validation is undertaken, quite different results are noted (Hansson, 1986).

With these arguments in mind, I would suggest that these war-related studies have implications for confrontation with many major stressors, especially those that share the properties of war. In particular, stressors of major impact, whose source may not be controlled but whose consequences can be influenced, may be seen as comparable.

These arguments should not be construed to mean that cultural nuances are unimportant. Indeed, the model of ecological congruence and our research suggest that underlying cultural values play an important role in the ecology of stress. However, I would argue that the Askenazi (European) Israelis in our samples have more in common with North Americans of European descent than these North Americans have in common with North American Hispanics. In fact, Israeli Sephardim (the name means of Spanish descent) have much in common with American Hispanics; both groups have large family size, prize family over individual effort, and confront similar societal prejudices. However, whereas Blacks, for instance, constitute a large percentage of the American population, a recent study of stress and social support by Dressler (1985) could cite only a handful of studies of stress among Black Americans. When the rural Blacks in his sample were studied, very different results were derived about social support than could have been learned from previous research (see also Chapter 4). The same could be said for Hispanics, Asians, and other ethnic minority groups and poor whites in America, and for Turks in Germany, Moroccans in France, and Moluccans in the Netherlands.

Cross-cultural comparisons may also help in the identification of basic psychological properties that are more resistant to cultural influences. Because of the paucity of research on disadvantaged Americans and Europeans, and for that matter the relative absence of work on any but university students, the present research also stands as a good test of the generalizability of some of the basic concepts emerging from stress research. We can see that while the particular person–situation interaction is critical, the tests and hypotheses based primarily on North American work are borne out, especially as related to personal resources. In the realm of social resources, in contrast, the environment seems to play a more important role, and cultural and value factors are more influential as well.

I would add that *how* resources affect stress resistance, as opposed to whether they *do,* also depends on cultural and situational conditions. Whether the effects of resources are direct or interactional with stress (e.g., stress-buffering) depends not only on fit in the general sense (Cohen & Wills, 1985), but on the timing, demands, values, and perceptions of those involved. These points will be further elucidated in the following chapter.

SUMMARY AND CONCLUSIONS

In this chapter research on stress resistance among civilian populations and soldiers during a time of war was detailed. The major emphasis of the chapter was to illustrate how the model of ecological resistance could be applied to stress research and how the model of conservation of resources could explain both the threat confronting people and the resistance resources likely to counteract these threats. It was illustrated how resources met the demands of certain situations and not others and how different aspects of the resource might gain predictive prominence as the situation changed.

A number of themes are highlighted in the studies presented in this section. Perhaps the most basic of these themes surrounds the issue of conducting research that tests the purported theories and models that underlie the hypotheses. Many studies of stress resistance seem to be not much more than attempts to correlate two sets of variables, one set associated with well-being and the other associated with emotional distress and illness. In contrast, I have attempted in these studies of war to delineate in greater detail why a given set of variables affect stress resistance and how the *sequence* of stress resistance will unfold.

If I have met my basic goal, then the reader has captured a sense of why mastery, for instance, would or would not be expected to limit depression in a given situation. The kind of situation, in turn, would not be limited to war or combat, but to a family of situations where individuals react to events they did not set in motion that are clearly threatening and significant. No less important, in the instances where predictions were not supported by the facts, the explanations for this should follow clearly from the model of ecological congruence and should provide a testable question for future research. Since, as discussed in Chapter 5, most studies have nonecological bases for their predictions, but use ecological arguments to explain unexpected findings, this limits the kind of progression I hope to establish. If the ecology is needed to explain complex nuances in the studies' findings, it is necessary to base studies on the same set of principles.

A second theme that emerges from this chapter is the richness that is provided by leaving the single-resource paradigm for a more complex interactive view of resources. Surely this latter method is also limited, since there are many resources that may interact to help individuals, but it will be necessary to build slowly to more complex models. It is possible to argue that the single-resource models were a necessary first research stage that must now give way to more complex interactive formulations (Cohen & Edwards, in press; Kobasa & Puccetti, 1983; Lefcourt et al., 1984). But I would add that a more macro viewpoint must also be adopted. Specifically, rather than examine all the combinations of resources that might come to mind, one should develop more overarching models of stress resistance. This would be analogous to the difference between looking for symptoms and looking for syndromes. Many illnesses have overlapping symptoms, but they tend to be distinguished by their characteristic syndromes (i.e., constellations of symptoms). Similarly, stress resistance in different situations will be explained by many overlapping resources, but particular *patterns of resources* will fit particular situational demands.

These studies were limited in being based on retrospective accounts of many of the factors of interest. Only in the case of prediction of CSR and PTSD were the objective measures clearly temporally aligned such that it could be said with confidence that the event preceded the outcome. In the next chapter, I will present applications of the models to the study of illness, another massive stressor in people's lives. These studies will follow subjects longitudinally to determine whether personal and social resources prospectively predict stress resistance. They may be used to garner support for the employment of the models of ecological congruence and conservation of resources as well.

7

STRESS RESISTANCE IN TIMES OF ILLNESS: FURTHER APPLICATIONS OF THE MODELS OF ECOLOGICAL CONGRUENCE AND CONSERVATION OF RESOURCES

*Why has thou forsaken me: and art so far from
my health and the voice of my complaint?*

(Psalms)

*Look to your health; and if you have it, praise God,
and value it next to good conscience; for health
is the second blessing that we mortals are capable
of; a blessing that money cannot buy.*

(Izaak Walton, 1593–1683)

Health is often forgotten until it is lost. Illness, however, is not so easily ignored, and being ill is one of the most ubiquitous of all stressors. Illness can poison all of the other joys of life; people often say in their most private prayers that they would trade everything they have for

Work on this chapter was made possible in part by grants from the Ford Foundation received through the Israel Foundations Trustees and Funds provided by the Faculty of Health Sciences of Ben Gurion University of the Negev. The research would not have been possible without the help of the physicians, nurses, and administrative staff of the various hospital wards at Saroka and Belinson Medical Centers.

health or to heal a sick loved one. Illness is so stressful because it can cause great physical pain, it can threaten loss of life, it can threaten loss of a loved one, and it can result in a loss of freedom that no prison could accomplish. Psychologically, illness threatens loss of one's phenomenological being in the world. Ironically, although people often become ill through no fault of their own, illness is frequently accompanied by a sense of shame and guilt (Moos, 1977).

This chapter will examine how women react to three common health problems: biopsy for potential cancer, complications in delivery, and illness of a child. These studies were designed according to the model of ecological congruence, and they represent attempts to clarify how personal and social resources interact to aid stress resistance. They improve on the war studies because they are longitudinal efforts and tap more of the facets of the ecological framework this volume has set out to illustrate.

It will be recalled that the model of ecological congruence proposes that stress resistance is a function of the fit of the constellation of resources at an individual's disposal with the instrumental and emotional tasks placed on individuals as a product of situational demands and internal needs. These tasks change as time passes and the person–environment interaction transpires. The model further states that this fit is partly a product of the innate qualities of the external demand, internal needs, and resources, and partly a product of individuals' appraisal of these same components. The model of ecological congruence does not envisage appraisal as idiographically as other stress theorists have done, however (Lazarus & Folkman, 1984; Kaplan, 1983). Rather, perceptions are seen as strongly influenced by values, many of which are shared on the cultural, group, or family level (for a more complete deliberation on the model, see Chapter 3).

The model of conservation of resources will be used, in turn, to help explain both the nature of the demands placed on women in these conditions and the meaning of the findings. Again, it is reiterated that the model of conservation of resources was based on the findings from the war and the illness studies and that the studies were not designed with this model at hand. As we interviewed men at war, women whose loved ones were in combat, and women confronted by illness, the themes that emerged repetitively were the threat of loss and the adjustment to loss.

Confronting the issue of loss I was perplexed by the difficulty of applying the accepted balance models of stress. If stress was an imbalance of threat, on one hand, and coping capacity, on the other (Lazarus &

Folkman, 1984; McGrath, 1970), how could the resources being threatened (e.g., self-esteem, mastery, hope) be the same resources that would counteract such threat? The same entity cannot exist on two sides of a scale. From this I came to see that threat is the sense of loss of resources and that these same resources or other resources are applied to counteract this sense of loss. If individuals succeed in applying their resources to counteract loss, they resist the negative effects of exposure to stressors. If they are not successful, they will continue to invest and manipulate their resources so as to thwart the continuation of loss and to enhance the probability of gain (see Chapter 2 for a detailing of the model in its entirety).

IMPORTANCE OF STUDY OF ILLNESS

The study of illness is important for applied, theoretical, and methodological reasons. The applied reasons are the most obvious. As already stated, illness is a major stressor that no one is spared. Few years pass in an individual's life without the experience of personal illness or illness of a loved one. Consequently, the more we know about stress resistance in the face of illness the more we can design preventive efforts to increase the probability that those afflicted will successfully cope. In addition, such knowledge can help identify these who are not likely to successfully manage the threats inherent in illness and the important decision making that is often needed (e.g., which treatment to choose, coordinating insurance or social services, arranging aftercare).

Theoretically, the study of illness provides a paradigm for the study of events that are not caused by individuals, that are of major importance to individuals, that are clearly undesirable, that occur unexpectedly, and that have global implications for people's lives. These characteristics have been seen as central to the type of event that is most likely to be experienced as stressful (Thoits, 1983). This avoids problems that have plagued the use of stressful-event scales, where many events are likely to be caused by those experiencing them and whose undesirability is open to interpretation. In addition, many events have limited or unknown implications for other aspects of individuals' lives, and may occur with various amounts of forewarning (Brown, 1974; Dohrenwend et al., 1984). The developmental study of some events is difficult because they have no clear starting point. Illness, however, usually has an identifiable point of beginning and often follows a chartable course.

We might compare the study of illness to the study of divorce, another very important stressor in modern life. Divorce hardly begins with the legal act of separation; rather, it has an unidentifiable starting point in marital discord or even in early interpersonal problems manifested first in youth. Nor is divorce necessarily undesirable. It may be a relief from a bad marriage, a breakup of everything one deemed important, or some mix of the two. Although often expected, it is unclear at what point people begin to psychologically prepare for the impending loss. Finally, it is a private event that may germinate and grow without any outward signs.

I have chosen divorce as an example, but it shares properties with other events that make its study theoretically vague. Marital discord, financial problems, employment difficulties, sexual problems, and parent-child conflicts are among the most common major stressful events people experience (Holmes & Raye, 1967), and they are similarly amorphous in terms of their cause, course, and meaning. Even if some illnesses are the result of peoples' personal attributes or behavior (Feuerstein et al., 1986), they tend not to be volitionally caused by people. This is especially the case if we rule out illnesses that are the product of individuals' direct behavior (e.g., lung cancer, heart disease, negligent accidents).

This is not to say that study of these other major classes of stressors should be set aside. Rather, the investigation of stress resistance and illness may theoretically serve as an anchor point. In a sense it is a simpler case than for these other stressors, and science progresses most clearly when the basic case is carefully studied and its properties delineated. Subsequently, comparisons can be made to other stressors, using illness as a marker with certain known properties.

Methodologically the study of illness is also advantageous. Although the study of major stressors is important, there are few cases where researchers have access to those experiencing these stressors. For both ethical and logistical reasons it is difficult to identify these confronting many major stressors at the time of onset or while anticipating an upcoming stressor. It would be unacceptable to enter the home of the bereaved hours after a death and, as already stated, the point of initial exposure to many stressors is obscure. When, for instance, in the case of parent-child conflict or work-related stressors did the stressor first impinge on those affected? In addition, it is difficult to acquire subjects who have not selected themselves for remediation of their problems, in the case of most stressors (e.g., those who have turned to therapy or legal assistance). This has led researchers to attempt broad-based community surveys (cf. Holahan & Moos, 1986; Pearlin et al., 1981; Williams et al.,

1981). However, even in these instances few of those sampled have been exposed to a very recent event whose course could then be followed. Instead, these studies depend on aggregating events occurring over an extended period and might follow the sample for a year. This, however, may begin at any time in relation to the onset of the stressor. So, it would not be unusual to be comparing, for instance, the first year of bereavement with the second year of bereavement, while alluding to both as the identical process (since time of onset is not typically assessed).

Illness, in contrast, is more logistically accessible to study, and such a study may be more ethically conducted than for most other major stressors. The vast majority of those with serious illness, for example, seek care and do so when the signs of the illness are emerging, which reduces the problem of self-selection (those who delay can be diverted from the study where this is not the case). In addition, they come to treatment centers, thus becoming available for study in large numbers at relatively low cost. Furthermore, we have found in our own research that even people awaiting surgery usually welcome the opportunity to talk about their feelings with a skilled interviewer. Furthermore, they seem happy to know that they can contribute to a better understanding of what they are experiencing and that their participation may save someone else some of the pain they are undergoing. In part because the medical face of hospitals is often impersonal, the individual interview is greeted warmly. Moreover, people usually have time for in-depth interviews because they often wait long hours in clinics and hospitals.

These factors combine to make the study of resisting the negative consequences of the threat of illness an important and practical arena of investigation (Moos, 1977). Its identifiable characteristics also make it especially accommodating to the investigation of the model of ecological congruence because the concept of fit can be applied best when the demands of the situation and the course of the evolving challenge are clear. Different illnesses may also be compared, thus opening the way for study of not just the interaction of resources but also the application of resources to varying circumstances. In addition, because there is little question about the stressfulness of the event, the element of perception of stressfulness is relegated to lower status, allowing more careful study of objective or widely shared subjective factors (e.g., values). In this regard, just as the study of hassles focuses attention on appraisal (Lazarus & Folkman, 1984; Kanner, Coyne, Schaefer, & Lazarus, 1981; see also Chapters 1 and 2), study of illness focuses attention on the objective components of stressors.

COPING WITH THREAT TO LIFE

Goals of Study

In the first of our investigations of stress resistance in response to illness we examined the effects on women of having to undergo biopsy (Hobfoll & Walfisch, 1984). We had a number of goals in this study. The first was to determine if personal resources and social support aid individuals in a life-threatening situation and whether they contribute independently to stress resistance. This is an important question because social support and personal resources may act independently or, on the contrary, social support may reflect character differences between people that have little to do with environmental aid. Sarason et al. (1986) argue, for example, that social support may represent a personal trait of individuals that is more stable than the changing social environment. Others have also suggested that the measures of social support may be tapping personal qualities rather than the actual behavioral exchanges they are meant to represent (Gottlieb, 1985).

Another possibility is that personal resources such as self-esteem underlie attachment to a supportive social network, and an effect of social support is really a product of the underlying self-esteem. So, for instance, individuals with high self-esteem may have more success in creating and maintaining intimate personal ties than those low in self-esteem (Hansson, Jones, & Carpenter, 1984; Jones, 1985). Consequently, any effect noted for social support could reflect on the personal attributes that contributed to social support.

An additional goal of this research was to get a closer look at the actual confrontation of stress resistance with the stressor. Most stress research begins weeks or months after exposure to the stressor, and even the literature on crisis intervention lacks empirical examinations of people's reactions close to the time of stress (Hobfoll & Walfisch, 1986; Ruch et al., 1980). As noted earlier, the initial stress period often demands peak levels of performance and is frequently experienced with intense suffering. These points make it an important area of study in its own right. In addition, initial adjustment is probably one of the best indicators of long-term adjustment, an additional reason for studying initial reactions to stressors.

A final goal was methodological in nature, but also had important theoretical implications. Specifically, our objective was to compare the same individuals under exposure to highly stressful conditions at one time and in everyday conditions at another. This allowed for prospective comparisons that are particularly suited for making causal arguments based on the findings. Researchers relying on aggregate measures of exposure to stressful events often do this by comparing the same individuals at a time of exposure to few stressful events and at a time of exposure to many stressful events. Unfortunately, exposure to many events is confounded with the outcome measures, a problem that statistical controls cannot correct. Depression, for instance, may cause marital distress even if we do not see the signs of depression until later (Gotlib & Hooley, in press). Consequently, these studies cannot untangle the event-strain-event sequence. Studies of illnesses or catastrophes, in turn, also have difficulty comparing the same individuals under high and low stress conditions; if the stressor is great enough the effect will be long-lasting, making it hard to obtain a low stress comparison. Pre-stress comparisons are no less difficult because we seldom know where fate will strike—and if we as researchers know, so do those involved.

Information on the action of resources at the time of highly stressful conditions and during everyday conditions made it possible to examine the stress-buffering question versus the direct effect. Resources might contribute to well-being independent of stressfulness (direct effect) or be especially salient under high stress conditions.

Nature of Study

A sample of women was interviewed at bedside in the hospital the day before undergoing biopsy for suspected cancer of any area of the body cavity and trunk (e.g., breast, stomach, pancreas). Women who were *not* found to have cancer were then interviewed again three months later in their own homes. The three-month period was seen as a reasonable period for recovery from the threat of cancer, since these women were found to have benign tumors or no tumors at all. In fact, almost all of the women had by this time returned to their normal routines.

The sample consisted of Israeli women from a variety of background cultures including Israel, North Africa, Asia (Iraq, Iran, Yemen), Europe, and America. Women were referred to the study randomly from a regional hospital serving a broad catchment area (e.g., all socioeconomic and ethnic groups). They averaged about 38 years of age. Those below 25 years and above 60 were not included because the event was thought to be ecologically quite different for them. Young women have a much higher rate of benign tumors, on one hand, but in a sense have more at stake, because they have more of their lives ahead of them, on the other hand. Older women are more likely to have cancerous tumors, but may feel they have less to lose because they have seen their children grow up and usually already have grandchildren. This is not to say that young and old both do not value life dearly, but age does play an important role in how one's life is evaluated. Had these women been excluded from the sample it would have been critical to examine developmental applications of the model of ecological congruence, because they would be expected to meaningfully influence women's reactions.

Ecological Rationale

In the prior chapter on war the role of mastery and self-esteem in stress resistance was discussed. War and threat of cancer have much in common. They are both largely out of the purview of people's control, are clearly of major importance to the individual, and constitute a real threat to life. At such times individuals often find themselves thinking about the possibility of death or of demeaning and debilitating physical impairment. Paradoxically, such times also evoke questions about the meaning of one's life, which threaten the core of self-esteem. Mastery may be important in such instances, as it contributes to a sense that one may control those aspects of the environment that influence one's well-being. So, for example, whereas mastery cannot act to prevent cancer, it may influence how people will live the remainder of their lives and how they will confront their deaths. It can also influence their approach to treatment. Self-esteem is likely to act by helping preserve a sense of one's worth and by preventing the current "failure" event from reflecting negatively on the self. In this regard, people may often interpret illness as somehow their fault through natural (e.g., negligence) or spiritual (e.g., sin) causes. When considering their lives, those high in self-esteem should also be more likely than those low in self-esteem to arrive at a positive self-evaluation.

These personal resources are also important because people carry them as part of their personal baggage. Because people's personal resources are integral with who they are and accompany them wherever they journey, resources may be immediately called upon. Social support, in contrast, must be recruited and have time to respond (see Chapter 6). Women may not choose to inform others of their plight when undergoing biopsy because there is little time to do so. In fact women in our study typically underwent biopsy a few days after the screening surgeon noted the possibility of a cancerous growth. In addition, many women chose not to bother friends or family with their problem. This stems in part from their feeling that illness is an embarrassment or their wish to not be a burden on loved ones.

We did judge that social support would be important at the time of biopsy, because women usually informed their more intimate kith and kin of their need for surgery. Such intimates could be spoken to on personal themes and would be likely to provide support. However, we did not think that being close was enough. Rather, we suspected that the history of interaction between the patient and her supporter was important. Specifically, we conjectured that relationships typified by sharing interests and concerns would provide fertile ground for discussing the deeply personal and far-reaching situation of these patients. Other close relationships that lacked this wider sharing were seen as having little potential benefit.

These same factors point to a direct effect of mastery and self-esteem on well-being and to a stress-buffering effect of social support. If people carry personal resources with them, these resources are available to modulate people's interaction with the environment on a moment-by-moment basis. Certainly at times of high stress the self is more taxed, but it is always working in the service of well-being—hence a direct effect on well-being. Social support, in contrast, is often dormant when not needed and is called upon when stressful circumstances occur (Cutrona, 1986). Thus social support should be especially effective under high-stress conditions, which suggests that it would have a stress-buffering effect.

In terms of a measure of strain (outcome) we chose to examine current levels of anxiety and depression using scales normed on the general population. When one is studying general populations, anxious and depressive emotions are important because they are typical expressions of emotional distress. High scores on anxiety and depression should not be confused with clinical disorders, however, because although these symptoms may cause intense suffering they may also be transient. On the other hand, they are a fair indication of who is at risk for later psychiatric difficulty. This is because they can be early signs of breakdown and because failure to cope successfully at the time of an event can cause individuals to feel they have failed, which in turn may lead to subsequent disorder.

Findings and Ecological Implications

As we suspected, the threat of cancer was met with extreme reactions. Subjects had highly elevated levels of depression and anxiety at the time of biopsy compared with three months later, when their emotional reactions fell to normal levels. Indeed, at the time of biopsy women showed levels of emotional distress similar to those evident in severely disturbed psychiatric populations. Furthermore, levels of depression were higher than those for "recent" bereavement (Radloff, 1977).

As we predicted, personal resources were related to lower levels of emotional distress both at the time of biopsy and three months later, whereas social support was related only to lower emotional distress at the time of biopsy. Those high in social support were less distressed than those lacking support. This pattern of findings is consistent with our thinking that personal resources have more of a direct effect on well-being, whereas social support has a more pronounced effect in high-stress conditions (i.e., a stress-buffering effect).

Not all types of support were helpful, however. As predicted, circumscribed relationships in which few common concerns or activities were shared did not tend to aid individuals, even at the time of biopsy. In contrast, exposure to a greater number of relationships in which a broader slice of life was shared was related to less emotional distress.

Contrary to expectations, personal resources were not more important than social resources at the time of biopsy. However, as was expected, social support did not contribute to well-being independent of the effect of the personal resources. Personal resources and social support were not very highly correlated, which suggests that those high in personal resources might be using what social support they have *more effectively* than those low in personal resources and not that they simply have *more* social support. We will look at this interaction more closely in other studies in this chapter. It should also be mentioned that as in other studies these variables accounted for only a modest amount of the total explained variance (i.e., how much of the result is accounted for by the variables).

The ecological approach also gives the flavor of what is occurring in the social interactions of these women. The data and our debriefing of women both support the contention that women sought support from those with whom they felt comfortable talking about a wide range of personal concerns and not from those with whom they had more circumscribed relationships. Mothers and children of subjects were often left out of the circle of support for these reasons, as women often reported that they either did not want to overburden these close kin or felt that they really could not talk to them. Spouses, sisters, and close women friends were most frequently cited as the major supporter. These relationships, it should be emphasized, also contained mutual trust, which suggests the two facets of self-disclosure, trust and mutual exchange (Jourard, 1971).

The value dimension emerges when one considers the differences in the two major cultures represented in the sample. Women from Asian or

North African origin are known as Sephardim or Oriental Jews. Women from European or American origin are known as Ashkenazim. Sephardim typically come from large extended families, whereas Ashkenazim tend to come from smaller more nuclear families. Ashkenazi women named family members or a friend about evenly as their main female source of support; Sephardi women, in comparison, tended to label a favorite sister as their principal female source of support. Indeed, of some 40 Sephardi women, only two named a friend as a member of their inner circle of support. One of these women had studied in Europe and lived for a period in the United States. Friends were viewed by and large by Sephardi women as having a social function, and one did not disclose personal affairs to them.

Overall, this study illustrates the value of the model of ecological congruence. Personal and social resources can be predicted to act in distinctive manners when hypotheses are based on the ecological properties of these resources. It is further demonstrated that by examining two distinct attributes of people's social networks, specific predictions can be made and are borne out by the sequence of events of a particular situation. Moreover, the more exact nature of the *resource strategies* that people choose to defend against their sense of loss emerges when the values regarding use of pertinent resources are considered.

ADJUSTMENT TO COMPLICATIONS OF PREGNANCY

In the next study we chose to examine how women adjusted to complications of pregnancy (Hobfoll et al., 1986; Hobfoll & Leiberman, 1987). Some 50 percent of all pregnancies are medically complicated, and a large, if lower, proportion have some major complication (Norbeck & Tilden, 1983; Nuckolls, Cassel, & Kaplan, 1972).

Goals of Study

Building on our prior research and the work of others, this study also had a number of specific goals. First, we were interested in verifying whether personal resources have a direct effect on stress resistance and whether social support has a stress-buffering effect. Second, we continued to have interest in examining the immediate effects of confrontation with a stressful situation.

This study also enabled us to explore some new questions. First, we were interested in how personal resources interacted with social resources. Specifically, we developed a "substitution hypothesis," which predicted that if two resources both suited situational demands, either would be sufficient and their additive value would be minimal. In other words, little would be gained by possessing the second resource. In addition, we thought it important to investigate whether resources had differing fit for differing stressful events (in the prior study we illustrated that resources had different fit with demand, which changed over time). For this reason we examined women who had different kinds of complications of pregnancy.

Nature of the Study

Our sample included women who fell into one of four groups: normal delivery with no major complications of pregnancy or delivery, premature delivery (actually defined by infant weight of under 2 kg., about 4.4 lbs.), Cesarean section, and spontaneous abortion in the second trimester (miscarriage). Women were interviewed at bedside within 20 to 30 hours after delivery or miscarriage with the use of questionnaires that tapped their resources and emotional distress. Women were again interviewed three months later at home.

Ecological Rationale

The stressfulness of these events differed. All four events carried some degree of stress at the time of initial interviews. The mothers of premature infants were stressed initially and at follow-up, because their infants generally had special needs and often were in continued danger due to their small size and poor organ development. Women delivering by C-section and those miscarrying experienced high initial stress but returned to fairly normal levels of stress three months hence. Women having uncomplicated delivery were least distressed, but more distressed initially than at follow-up. These trends mirrored the relative and changing demands of these different situations and were reflected in the women's depression levels.

Self-esteem was selected as a personal resource of particular relevance to the threats inherent in adjusting to a *fait accompli* that is usually experienced as a personal failure. In this regard women wish to have a healthy, normal delivery because it is safer and easier. Also, giving birth is phenomenologically a special part of being a woman, and being denied the opportunity to experience any facet of normal delivery is often experienced with a sense of sadness and loss. It may also elicit fantasies of rejection by one's spouse. In the case of delivering an underweight infant or miscarriage there is also the fear of possible loss and acceptance of loss, respectively. C-sections may also make the mother feel inadequate because of the difficulty in locomotion and in attending to the needs of the infant. For these reasons, women must defend against inferring that their experience was a personal failure. They must realize they are not inadequate and must not lose self-worth because of what occurred.

In addition, we found self-esteem in this and other studies we conducted to be stable over time (the same being true for mastery). This means that the external stressor is not causing changes in self-esteem and emotional distress. If it were, it would be more logical to argue that self-esteem and emotional distress covary (i.e., change together) because they both track increases and decreases in threat. Because self-esteem is stable over time, however, any correlation between self-esteem and emotional outcome must indicate that differences in self-esteem lead to differences in emotional distress. It is likely, however, that personal resources, like self-esteem or mastery, would change under chronic stressor conditions, especially if people viewed events as a consequence of their own behavior (Pearlin et al., 1981).

Intimacy with spouse was seen as a critical social resource for these women. Support from one's spouse is especially important to women (Hobfoll, 1986c), and intimacy has been determined as a critical quality of supportive relationships (Brown et al., 1975; Reis, 1984; Chapter 4). Having a child and its consequences is also an event shared by partners, and those who accept the joys and responsibilities are best prepared to support each other in adversity. A supportive husband would be quick to recognize the painful emotions experienced by his wife and would communicate to her that their relationship was strong and that nothing was her fault. He would also convey a sense of hope.

It may be noted then that self-esteem and intimate support inhibit the spread of many of the same negative thoughts and feelings. They differ, however, when the time dimension is considered. Self-esteem is likely to accompany women throughout their experience, once again evoking the "personal baggage" theme. Intimate support from spouses would wane, however. This follows because women may not continue to share lingering feelings since people expect that events of this magnitude should not be of such concern after a prolonged period. Even bereavement carries expectations, however unrealistic, that recovery should occur within weeks (cf. Lehman et al., 1987; Vachon, 1986). Spouses are likely to share these values about how long recovery should take.

In addition, intimate support can limit emotional distress only for a limited time because it is, in a sense, a temporary substitute for good self-esteem. That is, intimacy provides externally the good feelings about the self and positive self-evaluation that self-esteem provides internally. If women lack self-esteem, how long could this external inoculation effect remain? Ultimately, women who lack self-esteem will arrive at a negative self-evaluation despite support, unless their self-esteem is raised as well. During the three-month period of our study, however, we found self-esteem to be quite stable.

The model of ecological congruence dictates that the measure of strain be consistent with the demands (internal and external) of the particular stressor. Following delivery, some 15 percent of women develop clinical depression, and depressive affect is common in a much larger proportion of post partum women. Depression is likely to be associated with delivery due to stark hormonal changes, separation from loved ones at the hospital (at a time of intense need for sharing), isolation at home following delivery, and a sense of anticlimax. When medical complications occur the likelihood of depression is much more elevated. This is also consistent with the feelings of failure associated with complications, failure being associated with depression.

Study Findings and Ecological Implications

As predicted by the substitution hypothesis, having either high self-esteem or intimate support was sufficient to ward off the depression that ensued following delivery or miscarriage. This pattern is illustrated in Figure 7.1, where it can be seen that having either self-esteem or intimacy or both ensures relatively low levels of depression immediately following the event. At this time either resource is congruent with the demands of the situation. Lacking both self-esteem and an intimate spouse is, in contrast, likely to result in severe levels of depressive feelings. It may be noted in Figure 7.2 that this negative reaction is sustained at follow-up; these women remain significantly more depressed than those who possessed at least one resource.

Self-esteem was related to lower depression levels both initially and at follow-up, indicating a direct effect of self-esteem. However, further observation indicated that the effect of self-esteem was more pronounced during the formidable initial stress than three months thereafter when the stressors diminished. This would indicate a mixed direct and stress-buffering effect that has sometimes been noted in the literature (Cohen & Edwards, in press). Such mixed effects suggest that the resource generally contributes to well-being but that it has a special contribution to enhancing stress resistance.

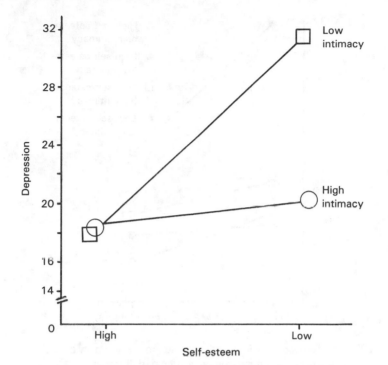

FIGURE 7.1   Effects of self-esteem and intimacy on depression among women following normal and complicated pregnancy. (Used by permission from Hobfoll & Leiberman, © 1987, American Psychological Association.)

Social support tended to be associated with a lower level of depression at the high initial stress period and had only a limited impact three months later. This is indicative of the stress-buffering effect.

More interesting findings emerge when the subgroupings are considered, however. In particular, we compared women who had an underweight infant with those who miscarried. Having an underweight infant is a prolonged stressor, continuing over the three-month period. According to our understanding of the interaction of resources only self-esteem would have a continuing positive effect on these women, however. This follows from the argument that the stress-buffering hypothesis is only partially correct. We argued, it will be recalled, that social support has a time-limited effect, depleting as individuals expect themselves to recover and as others expect this of them. We further argued that eventually low self-esteem would counteract any long-term advantage of social support. In fact, we found that social support was

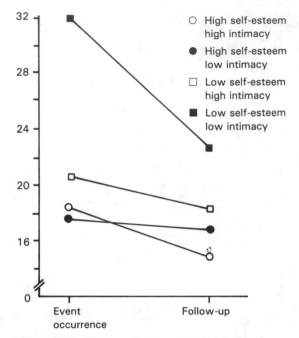

FIGURE 7.2   Effects of self-esteem and intimacy on depression among women at time of delivery or miscarriage and three months following. (Used by permission from Hobfoll & Leiberman, © 1987, American Psychological Association.)

related to lower levels of depression only at the time of initial confrontation with the stressor. These women, although still under considerable stress three months later, were no longer aided by social support (independent of self-esteem). Self-esteem, in comparison, was independently related to lower levels of depression at both times for all three pregnancy complications groups.

This may be further contrasted with the ecology of the miscarriage group. Spontaneous abortion is, in a sense, a *non*event and this point becomes clear when the values concerning miscarriage are considered. Women enter the hospital on a moment's notice, hardly have time to notify their social resources, and leave the hospital within 36 to 72 hours. It is interesting that this is one of the few events signifying loss of life that has no grief ritual associated with it. No flowers are sent, no graveyard is visited, no testimonial is made, and there is no marker of the event for future remembrance. Lay and professional reaction to the event is one of feigned lightheartedness. "You can always get pregnant again," "If it miscarried it must be for the best," "Well, you'll have fun trying again," are typical responses given to women. Women may even be telling themselves similar messages.

Notwithstanding this buoyant superficial response, the miscarriage constitutes a loss. At this stage signs of life were already evident, and women were certain to be engaging in fantasies about the child. Without social support or even the feeling that the situation deserves support, this loss is suffered in the silence of women's private thoughts. It would be expected that social support would not aid them either initially when under high stress or three months later. This is another contradiction of the stress-buffering effect and implies that if stress-buffering is to occur the event has to be congruent with the seeking and receiving of support. The finding bore out our thinking—intimate support from spouse did not aid women at the time of either interview.

Our prior biopsy study also suggested that support from intimate sources was more effective in aiding stress resistance than support from others who were considered close but not privy to personal thoughts and feelings of the individual. We examined this again on the present sample of women. Our thesis here was that social support from more superficial ties would be less likely to lead to satisfaction than would support from intimates. Our results supported our thinking; women's intimacy with spouses and closest friends were independently related to satisfaction with social support whereas mere size of one's network of others was unrelated to satisfaction. This was the case even though network members were all termed by the women to be "close" to them.

We were somewhat perplexed by finding support from family to be unimportant. Finer analysis revealed why, however. For women low in self-esteem, those who lacked intimacy with their spouse or a friend but had intimate ties with their family were least satisfied with the support they received. If, however, women possessed intimate relations with both spouse and family, or a friend and family, they were likely to be most satisfied with their support. This indicates that there is some problem with the combination of high family intimacy and low intimacy with those outside family and one's spouse. We offered two explanations for this. One possibility is that this is a sign of enmeshed family relationships wherein the intimate family inhibits or intrudes on intimacy with those outside the nuclear family (Minuchin, 1974). Alternatively, the lack of intimacy with spouse and friends may be a result of conflict in these relations that was not caused by family intimacy, but that result in seeking shelter in family relations.

This study reveals a number of striking lessons about the interaction of resources with demands. Clearly resources have general resistance properties, but they also are limited by the particular demands of the situation. As in the prior study, personal resources seem more robust than social resources. The former seem to follow the rule of "personal baggage"—available when needed. The latter seem more influenced by environmental constraints and personal traits of the individual. Considering the ecology of the event also points to how limiting is the simple thinking behind the stress-buffering hypothesis. Social support appears to especially help individuals under high stress conditions only when support is available, and support is sought or spontaneously offered. Even when these conditions are met it may only have a time-limited effect.

We also learned more about the active qualities of social support from this and the prior study. Support seems most helpful when provided by intimates, when these intimates are seen by the recipient and themselves as the likely persons to offer support, and when the intimate tie is healthy. It would appear that when relationships are conflicted or built on an unhealthy base, the effect may be deleterious rather than beneficial. Certainly these conclusions must be seen as preliminary; they are based on a few studies and may be influenced by small subsamples within these studies. Nevertheless they are attractive because they seem to clarify many of the questions that were raised in the reviews of studies of social support and personal resources presented in Chapters 4 and 5, which saw "fit" as important but which failed to indicate what the *parameters of fit* might be.

REACTIONS TO CHILDREN'S ILLNESSES

One of the greatest stressors a person can undergo is having a seriously ill child. Children are a part of their parents, and when a child is seriously ill parents are often heard to say that they wish it had occurred to them instead of the child. It is extremely difficult for parents to witness their children's suffering and to imagine the possible threat to life or future impairment. In addition, a child's illness increases the burden on parents because they must often accompany the child to frequent medical appointments if the illness is chronic and stay with the child in the hospital if the illness is acute. This results in the stress of not meeting other demands, such as with other children, work, and household chores. Furthermore, chronic illnesses often result in considerable direct and indirect cost. For all these reasons we chose this stressor as another significant major life stress that is of interest to a wide segment of the population (Hobfoll & Lerman, in press; Hobfoll and Lerman, 1986).

Goals of Study and Ecological Principles

We had a number of goals in this study. As in the prior investigations, we were interested in comparing people's reactions to acute versus chronic stressors. We also wanted to observe the course of these reactions from the time of initial confrontation with the stressor and for some period thereafter. It was deemed important to replicate our findings that

1. personal resources were more robust than social resources,
2. intimacy was more central to stress resistance than was general social support,
3. social support had a limited effect under chronic stressor conditions,
4. intimacy with spouse was more central to effective stress resistance than intimacy with friends and family, and
5. those who possessed strong personal resources would better utilize social support than those who lacked these resources.

We also raised a number of new questions. First, we wished to know how emotional distress affected social support. In this regard, we predicted that while general support would limit emotional distress, the experience of emotional distress would result in an increased demand for recent social support; that is, the more upset the individual, the more he or she will recruit aid. This feedback loop is illustrated in Figure 7.3. Second, it was seen as important to directly test how values concerning the receipt of aid might affect outcome. We predicted that the more uncomfortable people felt with seeking aid (i.e., valuing independence), the less support they would receive and the poorer would be their stress resistance. In this regard, a number of studies have indicated that people view receipt of help as a sign of weakness, but that people also differ as to how threatening they find the act of seeking help (Fisher et al., 1982; Nadler & Mayeless, 1983).

In addition, we were interested in what other factors might affect the receipt of help. Our earlier consideration of this question in Chapter 4 led to the suggestion that those who had greater personal resources would be more attractive to others and possess the requisite social skills to build strong supportive networks (Bowlby, 1973; Hansson et al., 1984; Kobasa & Puccetti, 1983; Sandler & Lakey, 1982; Sarason et al., 1987). These factors would lead to receiving more social support. People who possessed intimate ties would also gain support. This follows because intimate others are likely to respond when called upon; the recipient will feel most comfortable asking for help from those who have a shared history of intimate interaction (Clark, 1983). Intimates would also be

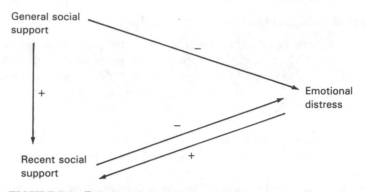

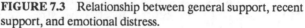

FIGURE 7.3   Relationship between general support, recent support, and emotional distress.

most likely to know what the recipient required in a given situation because of their personal knowledge of the recipient. Integrating these various processes, we predicted that individuals comfortable in receiving aid, who possessed personal resources and had intimate relationships with a few others, would receive more social support than those whose values dictated greater independence, who lacked personal resources, and who had less intimate ties.

Nature of Study

To examine these questions we interviewed three groups of women, whose children were (a) being routinely checked in a hospital clinic for a minor ailment, (b) hospitalized for an acute illness that constituted a possible threat to life or long-term impairment (e.g., meningitis; convulsions following high fever, severe asthma attack), or (c) visiting a chronic care clinic for the first time (e.g., neurological disorder, asthma, heart disease).

We used the same standardized instruments as described in the prior study of women following pregnancy complications, with the addition of two measures. To investigate the influence of women's values concerning aid we constructed and prevalidated an instrument that measured the degree to which women felt uncomfortable seeking support. A second instrument tapped the degree of *general* and *recent* support women had received. General support is the support usually received from those in one's social network. Recent support, in turn, is a measure of the actual aid acquired lately. General support is probably a good indicator of support received, but when one considers the ecology of support recruitment it becomes obvious that the promise of support may not be actualized and many factors influence the intensity of support actually achieved when needed (see also Barrera, 1986).

The mothers were interviewed on two occasions, first while waiting for care (minor illness and chronic illness groups) or within the first 48 hours of their child's hospitalization and again one year later. Almost every investigation of social support has remarked on the problem of the reliance on self-report alone in these studies. In response to this methodological weakness we administered the same measures to the women's husbands at the time of the second interview. However, instead of reporting about themselves, men reported about their wives' personal resources, social support, discomfort seeking support, and emotional distress. In this way we obtained measures of women's resources, values, and well-being from a second source with personal knowledge.

Study Findings and Ecological Implications

We had originally intended to use the physicians' diagnoses as an indicator of stress level (minor, acute, or chronic). However, upon analysis it became obvious that parents' assessment of whether the child was ill, initially and at follow-up, was a better indicator of how they would react, and so we relied on these as a measure of the child's health status. It could be argued that this supports the contention that perceptions are what matters. However, parents are not necessarily informed as to the actual nature of their child's illness. Some physicians speak in platitudes or attempt to guard the parents from the actual severity of their child's illness. Some are more straightforward, while still others are brutally honest. Given all these possibilities parents receive mixed messages and must gather objective information as they can to make their own judgments. We know that parents' assessments were generally accurate because even at the time of initial assessment parents of chronically ill children (hospitalized and in clinics) and parents of acutely ill children differed in their reactions. This suggests their ability to correctly assess the environment despite their lack of medical knowledge and their varied access to information about their child.

At the initial time of confrontation with their children's illnesses, mothers who possessed greater personal resources and who possessed greater general support experienced less emotional distress than those who lacked these resources. The greater the mother's intimacy with family, however, the greater was her emotional distress. Furthermore, the feedback loop suggested in Figure 7.3 above was also confirmed. Specifically, whereas greater levels of general support were linked to less emotional distress, more emotional distress was linked to greater levels of recent support controlling for the link between general support and emotional distress. Those interested in the complicated analysis of this question are referred to the published article (Hobfoll & Lerman, in press).

At the time of follow-up, personal resources continued to be related to less emotional distress for all three groups of mothers. In addition, intimacy with spouse was related to lower levels of emotional distress. Finer analysis indicated, however, that those most in need of support were least likely to benefit from it. Specifically, whereas those with high personal resources were further aided by receipt of intimate support and general support, those low in personal resources (who therefore were more in need of support) were actually more distressed the greater their intimacy with others. Moreover, those whose children were either well during the year or had recovered were helped by general support received, whereas mothers of chronically ill children (again most needing support) were more distressed the more general support they reported obtaining. These relationships are likely to be causally linked because ratings of emotional distress were obtained one year after ratings of support and personal resources (hence distress cannot be predicting resources).

When we examined the receipt of aid at follow-up, a number of clues emerged that helped explain why social resources were not aiding those with chronically ill children. We could see that intimacy and values about seeking aid were not influencing the receipt of aid among mothers of chronically ill children (see Figure 7.4). Intimacy and discomfort in seeking support were predictive of amount of general support received one year later among mothers of children who were well at both times or who had been ill and were now well. However, no such relationship existed between either intimacy or discomfort in seeking support and general support received.

We interpreted this to mean that the environmental demands of the continued taxing of social resources led to a leveling effect. So, for example, those who felt uncomfortable in seeking support would have to reach out for aid despite their values because their child's well-being demanded that they seek aid. In contrast, those who originally felt more comfortable seeking aid would grow more reticent to reach out due to their continued need for support. In this regard, women all tended to feel somewhat uncomfortable seeking help from others.

It is critically important to note that personal resources were more robust than social resources; they were more consistently related than social resources both to greater receipt of aid and to lower levels of emotional distress following exposure to stressful circumstances. The

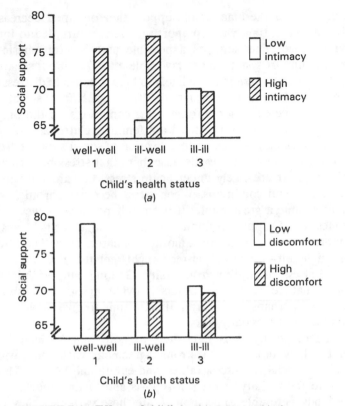

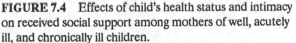

FIGURE 7.4 Effects of child's health status and intimacy on received social support among mothers of well, acutely ill, and chronically ill children.

efficacy of social resources, in contrast, was more closely tied with the situational demands. Some aspects of social support were more consequential at the time of initial reactions to stressors, for example, than during long-term stress resistance. Also as predicted, the source of support was critical; family intimacy was related to poorer stress resistance, whereas intimacy with spouse was tied with less emotional distress.

Values about receipt of aid deserve some special attention because this is a parameter that has not been previously considered. Discomfort when seeking support was related to lower levels of emotional distress; however, it primarily affected outcome through its influence on intimacy and receipt of support. It was shown that women with greater discomfort in seeking support became less intimate with their closest ties over the year's period and the amount of support they obtained decreased. As discussed above, intimacy and support received, in turn, led to improved stress resistance. This suggests a possible path whereby basic values govern the support system, more favorable attitudes about seeking help leading to a support system more likely to help in times of distress.

It may also be noted in our data that the *availability* of social support tends to be depleted under chronic stress conditions. In the only other study of this question with which I am familiar, Cutrona (1986) found that acute stress may be related to activation of social support. Together the two studies support the earlier argument that stress-buffering effects of social support are likely under acute stress, but are unlikely under continued stressful conditions. When stress becomes chronic, personal resources assume a greater role. It is entirely possible, however, that at such times social support continues to act more indirectly by sustaining personal resources. For example, mothers of chronically ill children with initially high self-esteem or mastery might feel these resources fading under the stress of continued adversity. Gaining support might boost their personal resources, as others provide emotionally supportive messages and perhaps step in from time to time to give them some time off from their arduous daily tasks.

Methodologically, it is important to note that husbands' ratings tended to show moderate to strong agreement with their wives' on personal and social resources, values, and emotional distress. This lends credence to the validity of the self-reports and further indicates that if the husbands were able to accurately rate these variables, they have an objective observable component. However, husbands' ratings did not exactly mirror their wives' self-reports. This, in turn, suggests that self-perception is an important factor; the individual is the best expert as to his or her internal state. This mix of objective and subjective factors is consistent with the model of ecological congruence, which depicts both as influencing the process of stress resistance. Outcome is not simply in the "eye of the beholder," but also in his or her acts and in the real demands of the environment.

IMPLICATIONS FOR HEALTH PSYCHOLOGY, BEHAVIORAL MEDICINE, AND PREVENTION

There has been increasing interest in the potential contribution of psychology to the study of physical health and health-related services (Feuerstein et al., 1986; Matarazzo, 1982). These studies have a number of implications for this growing area of knowledge and practice.

We and the medical personnel with whom we worked were surprised at the intense reactions of hospitalized women. It was common knowledge that biopsy and pregnancy complications were stressful, but not that they were responded to on the order of magnitude found here. Women were so distressed as to be in ranges of emotionality comparable to the most severe stressors people confront (e.g., bereavement) and at similar levels to those expressed by clinical psychiatric populations. This alerts us to the question of the degree to which they are capable of making competent decisions, since they are likely to have a distorted and narrowed frame of reference (Keinan, 1987).

The intensity of women's reactions also implies that when they inform medical staff that they're "doing O.K.," as is typical, this is a product of their perceptions of the staff's role and of whom they can legitimately "lean on." In fact, they are often in great need of someone to speak with and a shoulder to cry on. Whereas support might come instead from friends and family, visiting hours are often so constricted as to prevent the needed support that might be provided. Even when medical staff want to provide emotional support, they are often tremendously overworked in their performance of the medical services that must come first. Nurses, especially, seem in tune with the emotional needs of patients (Rand, 1986), but their heavily taxed schedules and expectations of their role may prevent them from offering more than a few calming words.

These stress levels also have implications for medical procedures. It is likely that patients expressing these levels of stress will have difficulty understanding and recalling medical instructions. In addition, the same processes that may act to limit psychological distress may work against compliance with the medical regimen (e.g., denial). For mothers of ill children this may also have the opposite effect, that is, hypervigilance. In such situations, physicians and clinics may become inundated with calls and visits in response to every minor concern of the parents. This may lead to a "cry wolf" effect, such that the physician or the parents disregard a truly serious symptom when it does occur.

Some physicians and medical staff in our studies were aware of the personal side of patients and its importance for the patient's overall physical and psychological well-being. Others were not. Nor should this be surprising, considering the nature of medical training. Few medical students, for example, learn interviewing skills, learn about cognitive impairment under stress, or are exposed to humanistic points of view. To include such topics would mean an overhaul not just of social science teaching in medical schools but of the entire study of disease (Benor, Hobfoll, & Prywes, in press). Emotional reactions are integral to an understanding of patient care, and there is a growing awareness that they are related to the etiology of many physical disorders as well.

Medicine's romance with the molecular level of disease has made more holistic approaches suspect. Yet it is unlikely that future breakthroughs will be made on the molecular level because the major medical diseases plaguing modern humankind (lung cancer, accidents, suicide, heart disease) are more clearly linked to behavior than those that earlier miracle cures redressed (polio, pneumonia) (Matarazzo, 1982). Social scientists would do well to join a coalition with psychologically knowledgeable physicians and nurses, concerned consumers, and medical educators to work to create a humanistic medical milieu that will aid patients, their families, and the ensurement of proper medical care.

IMMEDIATE VERSUS LONG–TERM STRESS RESISTANCE

The studies of war and illness presented in the past two chapters are among the few that portray the stress resistance process from a time close after the onset of a major stressor. This approach, along with the follow-up in many of these studies, allows a number of insights into this difficult area of study.

The first consistent finding that emerges is that the same factors involved in long-term stress resistance play a role in short-term stress resistance. This might appear trivial, but a number of psychological approaches would have predicted otherwise. For example, psycho-dynamic models of depression suggest that those who enlist denial may have initially not shown signs of emotional distress, but that they would have paid the price for this in greater long-term distress (Menninger, 1963; Haan, 1969). Crisis theory, in turn, might suggest few individual differences in initial reactions to such massive stressors, but rather would predict that only in the reorganizational phase do personal and social traits play a leading role (Miller & Iscoe, 1963; Caplan, 1964). This follows from one of the key principles of crisis theory; specifically, emotional distress in response to crisis is more likely to be related to environmental stimuli than to the personal and social characteristics of those involved.

In relation to this first point, we also found that initial reactions may themselves play a role in stress resistance. What I mean is that if individuals adjust well to the initial crisis phase then they attribute to themselves positive feelings about their success (e.g., "I handled that well," or "That was tough, but I didn't fall apart and was able to help my child through this difficult time"). This conclusion emerges from the fact that initial reactions were related to later reactions and from the finding that even those lacking resources did better in the long term if they did not overreact initially.

There were also important differences between immediate and long-term adjustment. Personal resources tended to aid stress resistance at both initial and follow-up periods. Social resources, in contrast, were more likely to help, depending on the particular situation at hand and the personal resources of the individual. This makes good sense because the aspects of self that we examined are quite stable; if positive, they remained so during crisis, and if negative, they were absent at all phases. Social resources, in contrast, have a general stability, but are not necessarily accessible when needed. In addition, during crisis it has been shown that even well-intentioned others often act in ways that they themselves even know to be inappropriate. Because of anxiety the translation of what they think they should do into what they actually do is distorted (Wortman & Lehman, 1985). Studies of social support have not tapped these important dynamics of the support process because most social support measures (Barrera et al., 1981; Sarason, Levine, Basham, & Singer, 1983) assess social support received over a period of time but do not attempt to match this to the needs of the individual or to any standard of what would be most appropriate given the demands being placed on the individual.

We had hoped to be able to distinguish between the effects of mastery and self-esteem, since the two traits are related but also have distinguishable characteristics. This inability to differentiate their effect was not due to redundancy of the measures either, because they were only moderately correlated. It is possible that this is another example of the substitution hypothesis—if one has mastery, self-esteem adds little more, and vice versa. Future research would do well to examine other personal resources that are even more easily separated statistically in order to determine if the substitution effect is replicable in such circumstances.

On a humanistic note, it is clear that while initial reactions to stressors are often so extreme as to be termed "the worst weeks I ever experienced," most individuals recover a few weeks or months after the crisis ends. This speaks to a marvelous resiliency of human beings. However, it should not be forgotten that these crises seem to cause prolonged psychological sequelae in a significant percentage of those exposed. From our data it would seem that anywhere from 15 to 30 percent of those exposed to massive stressors are likely to have emotional distress levels indicative of clinical disorders some three months after initial confrontation with the crisis event. Those subject to chronic stressors are likely to continue functioning but to have dulled emotionality. In personal interviews they tended to report feeling constantly worn out and seldom happy. Such responses are typical of a long-standing, low-intensity depression.

SUMMARY AND CONCLUSIONS

This chapter detailed the applications of the model of ecological congruence to research on reactions to illness. In addition, the model of conservation of resources was used to help explain the findings and the nature of the resource–situation fit. Despite the very differing nature of the threat in the three investigations, certain general findings emerged and the nature of the interaction between personal and social resources was clarified.

A number of themes concerning the issue of fit emerge from this data and the earlier war-related studies. These themes make an important contribution toward clarifying what determines "fit," until now a vague concept that has nevertheless been assigned increasing importance as a key construct in stress resistance. The problem has been that fit is usually discussed post hoc to explain unexpected findings (Cohen & Wills, 1985) or has been generally alluded to with no specific organizing principles (Billings & Moos, 1982; Mitchell & Hodson, 1986). Integrating the models of ecological congruence and conservation of resources with the findings of the studies reported in the current and prior chapters, however, leads to a number of parameters of fit.

The proposed parameters of fit are presented in Table 7.1. The first would appear to be *physical attainment.* For a resource to meet the individuals' demands during stressful situations it must be physically attainable, that is, close at hand and not occupied. If a resource is not physically available it will be of little value. This may be one reason why personal resources are more robust than social resources. Under both acute and chronic stress conditions social support may be unavailable. Benefit may still be derived from absentee support, because people may feel bolstered by their feelings of attachment to others, but such effects will probably be inadequate if not joined by actual supportive efforts and direct contact with supporters (see also Gottlieb, 1985). It should be emphasized, however, that this would also depend on which personal resources were being considered, as other personal resources have more confined effects.

The second parameter of fit is *value consistency.* Resources will meet the demands caused by stressors when those resources are consistent

TABLE 7.1 Parameters of Fit

Parameter	Key ecological question
Physical attainment	Is resource attainable?
Value consistency	Is application of resource consistent with individual societal values?
Temporal sequence	Does resource meet current environmental demands and individual needs?
Protection and replacement potential	Does resource replace resource lost, or prevent such loss?
Idiographic complementation	Does individual perceive fit between his or her needs, environmental demand, and resource?

with individual and societal values. Again the personal resources we considered have advantage here, because Western culture esteems individual effort and independence and denigrates dependency (see Rokeach, 1960). This parameter of fit also suggests why intimate support is more beneficial in major crises than support from more distant others. In this regard, while Western values denigrate dependency, the mutual support found in close relationships is deemed acceptable and appropriate and is not bound by feelings of ingratiation or careful accounting of debt (Clark, 1983). Other values may also affect utilization of other resources, as when, for example, we found in the biopsy study that women did not feel it appropriate to burden their children or parents with their health problems.

The third parameter of fit is *temporal sequence*. In this regard, resources will fit demands to varying degrees as the threatening event approaches, as it occurs, and after it transpires. Our findings suggest that the personal resources of self-esteem and mastery are more robust than social support over time. However, there is a modicum of evidence from our research and the work of others (Pearlin et al., 1981) that social resources also act to bolster flagging personal resources under chronic stressor conditions. Those high in personal resources would appear to use social support the way the desert camel uses water—they drink deeply and it sustains them for long periods. Those who lack personal resources, however, seem to rely on social support moment by moment, and support is less likely to meet either situational demands or the chronic needs of those who have a trait sense of personal inadequacy.

The next parameter of fit might be called *protection and replacement potential.* The model of conservation of resources suggests that individuals are best served when lost resources are replaced by other resources. Better yet, some resources actually prevent such loss. Illness can be seen as a threat to positive self-regard, control, and meaningful relations. As such, resources that raise sense of self-esteem, feelings of agency, and sense of attachment to others will prevent the encroachment of such loss or, in the event of loss, will help to replace the loss. Since stress is so interwoven with feelings of failure, self-esteem, mastery, and intimate support will have high general prevention and replacement potential.

However, situations make varying demands and other resources will be important as demands differ. Certain resources will have better prevention and replacement potential in, say, conditions of academic stress, economic stress, or bereavement. Given the stress of unemployment, intimate ties may, for instance, be secondary to loose, broad-based network relationships, which may best aid job search (Wellman, 1981). Our studies focused on the fit of resources to situations that constituted a major threat to individuals in conditions providing little chance to exercise direct control against the stressor. The exercising of willpower may, in contrast, be most advantageous when the event is clearly controllable (Rosenbaum & Palmon, 1984).

The last parameter of fit that emerges from this analysis is *idiographic complementation.* The intent here is to focus on what the individual judges is a good match. Such matching may not necessarily be logical but may potentially be powerful. It may be determined best by simply asking individuals whether their resources fit well with the demands placed upon them (Caplan, 1983). Unfortunately, this aspect of self will be least likely to be judged by others, since it is by definition in the individuals' own perceptual domain. I would submit that this aspect will be powerful for clinical applications on the individual level, but will hold little promise for preventive efforts with larger groups because it will vary so greatly case by case. Even on the clinical level, however, a secondary problem will emerge; individuals may express a sense of fit without being capable of pinpointing where they are lacking resources or what resources are sustaining them. This follows from the fact that this perspective on fit has been most advantageously applied when global sense of resource–demand fit is measured and not when the resources and demands are separately delineated (Caplan, 1983).

It is important, however, to accept these conclusions as preliminary leads for future research and cautious clinical applications. We have concentrated on a particular, albeit robust, combination of resources. In addition, our work was done in Israel, which, although it is similar to other Western cultures, has its own particular cultural nuances. Furthermore, our studies of reactions to illness focused on women. Men will certainly react differently than women did in many respects.

Perhaps most important, research from the laboratories of those who are advancing a model should always be suspect. I am likely to be guilty of coloring the interpretation of findings in a light favorable to my models. It will be critical for others to test these models and their consequences in their own work and to report on their findings. If the thinking underlying these models is borne out in the work of others who are less invested in seeing these points proven, firmer conclusions can be drawn. It is my hope that these studies and the models of ecological congruence and conservation of resources motivate such research and the necessary refinements of the models that will result.

8

DEVELOPMENT OF AN ECOLOGICAL LOSS THEORY OF PERSONALITY AND INTERVENTION EFFORTS

Self-preservation is the first law of nature.

(Samuel Butler, *Remains*, 1612–1680)

The model of conservation of resources and the model of ecological congruence have implications not only for an understanding of stress and stress resistance but also for a broader understanding of personality. It is my thesis that the person-environment ecology that these models illuminate leads to a comprehensive theory of personality. No one theory of personality fully addresses the complexity of the self nor predicts all aspects of behavior. On the other hand, a good personality theory should pave the way for a greater understanding of the nature of the self and aid the prediction of behavior in a broad array of contexts. In the present chapter I will attempt to illustrate how a theory of personality that meets these criteria follows from the models and will present the implications of such a theory for guiding intervention efforts.

In my consideration of a theory of personality based on a model of stress and stress resistance I originally believed such an attempt might be overgeneralizing from too limited a perspective. However, I was encouraged by two factors. First, intervention efforts that treat stress superficially (i.e., as something easily influenced) appear to have only superficial effect. This suggests that personal factors underlying stress resistance are likely to be fairly stable characteristics of individuals (see Chapter 5). Second, I was struck by the ubiquitousness of stressors in the process of living. In this there seems to be agreement not only among stress researchers (Antonovsky, 1979; Lazarus & Folkman, 1984; Moos, 1986) but also in the newspapers and everyday conversations. People are constantly talking about their problems and concerning themselves with solving the dilemmas, large and small, with which fate confronts them. Moreover, every stage in life has its own characteristic stressors as well as stressors common to other periods of life (Erikson, 1963). If stressors are so ubiquitous, then how individuals experience and react to them must be a major part of how people develop, how they see the world, how they think, and how they behave.

I will refer to the theory that I will attempt to develop as an "ecological loss theory of personality." The loss aspect follows from a thesis that will be developed, that the confrontation and resolution of loss is the primary shaper of personality. The ecological tone, in turn, is set by the argument that losses occur and are perceived as an interaction of individuals with their environments. In this regard, the theory joins a family of other theories that do not just emphasize individuals and their immediate families but concentrate equally on the individual (biologically and psychologically), the immediate environment, and the culture in which the individual lives (see Adler, 1929; Erikson, 1963; Maslow, 1968).

THEORY OF PERSONALITY BASED ON AVOIDANCE OF LOSS

A theory of personality should hold a core element so basic to the human experience that it is shared by people independent of differences in culture or upbringing (Maddi, 1972). For many theories of personality this core element is a primary motivational structure. For Freud it is the energy system generated by the id and for Maslow it is the search for human growth. The core element may vary by degree among people and may change through the lifespan. It may or may not be inborn, and it may evolve as a combination of inborn and environmental interaction. A common core element, in turn, leads to a varied set of consequences. These consequences are derived from the interaction of the basic source of motivation with the evolving self and the external environment. So, for example, Maslow proposes that the striving toward human growth interacts with both the developing personality and the external environment.

I would argue that the model of conservation of resources also leads
to such a core construct. Specifically, it follows from the model that
people are born with biological and social needs to increase pleasure,
guard against threat, and ensure the organism's and the species'
continuation. Because these needs are not always or consistently met,
there develops a secondary fear of loss. The needs are the energy "pull"
of the personality theory I will develop, and the fear of loss is the energy
"push" of the theory.

How these two forces complement or conflict with one another
creates a dynamic field for human development. On this fertile ground
the personality develops, and I am suggesting it develops on two axes.
First, the self concentrates on minimizing the possibility or continuation
of loss and on maximizing the likelihood of gain. Second, an attitude
toward the self evolves that is based on the relative success of one's
personal ability to manipulate the forces that control this loss and gain
or on having (or believing) some external agent controls them.

The baby monkey, for instance, has an inborn need for food and
warmth and clings to its mother or surrogate mother. Human infants
undoubtedly have a similar set of biological needs inborn and are likely
to have specific social needs as well. Evidence for this is difficult to
garner, but an analysis of the evolution of our species leads to the
conclusion that such encoded tendencies aid survival. Some work on
attachment in human infants also hints at the existence of such basic
social needs (Ainsworth, Blehar, Waters, & Wall, 1978; Bowlby, 1969).

Not all social or biological needs are inborn, of course. Rather, early
interactions of infants and children with their environment foster the
development of certain additional learned needs. Whether, for instance,
people feel they need one or two intimates alone or both intimates plus a
tight social group, would certainly differ for a member of a small nuclear
family and a person raised in a clan. Still, I think there is enough
evidence to support the supposition that humans have a basic need not
only for food, shelter, and heat but also for close human contact.
Furthermore, this need for human contact, just like biological needs,
appears to be stable throughout the lifespan. Only its expression
changes.

Finally, a key inference from this line of thought is that whereas
early childhood experiences would have a seminal effect on development
of personality, the personality could also be influenced throughout the
lifespan. This evolves from the logic that if needs are constant and vital
at every age, then how successfully individuals meet these needs will be
basic to how they think of themselves, how they behave, and how they
perceive their world.

Conflict Cycle

These needs cannot, however, always or consistently be met. Goal objects
are not usually available at will. Often individuals have to act to obtain
them, as when infants learn to smile for increased attention or when they
rout for the mother's breast. Furthermore, even when individuals act to
meet their needs, their aims are frequently frustrated. Mother is
unavailable, warmth does not come, and brother is interested in other
things. There are great differences in the extent to which needs are
regularly met. Some parents schedule the baby's feedings by the clock,
others feed at whim (their own or the infant's).

I have often heard parents in therapy say that the baby is crying *"just
because she wants to be held,"* or that a child is *"just* looking for
attention."* This reflects the belief that being held or given attention is
not very important or at least that it does not have to come when the
child wants it. There are parents who feed at every whimper and others
who snuggle the baby first to check if it wanted affection and attention.
We also need to remind ourselves that millions of parents in the world
are unable to meet their infants' and children's needs, due to poverty, a
state that not only makes food and shelter scarce but also separates
families and requires parents to leave their children in the care of others
who may be less attentive to their needs. It may be seen then that needs
may not be met because they are not clearly communicated, because
others are unwilling to meet the needs, or because others are unable to
meet the needs.

Whereas individuals differ as to their basic needs and environments
differ in the extent they meet these needs, I would hold that almost
everyone's needs are frequently frustrated. The more these needs are
unmet, or inconsistently met, the greater a fear of loss the individual
develops. For nearly everyone the fear of loss becomes a strong
motivating force, often superseding the pull of needs. Children or adults
who are frequently deprived of food, for instance, will become unusually
focused on aspects of their environment that are likely to lead to the
provision of food. They will become loss-oriented, and the fear of future
lack of food will be distressing. Rather than see the environment as
benign or benevolent, they will see the world as conflictual. Hence, I
would say that those who frequently experience loss become entrenched
in a conflict cycle. The conflict cycle is depicted in Figure 8.1.

It could be argued that this conflict cycle would be remedied when
the loss is remedied. So, for example, it might be expected that formerly
starved individuals would leave the conflict cycle when food is provided.
However, the experience of children in inadequate foster care shows that

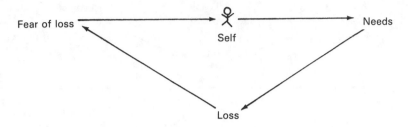

FIGURE 8.1   Ecological loss theory of personality: Conflict cycle.

many of them become food hoarders, even after food is consistently available. Likewise, refugees from the concentration camps of Nazi Germany often constructed postwar lives in a manner consistent with the conflict cycle that was a consequence of the concentration camp environment (Bettelheim, 1960). Often these behaviors led to ostracization in society or rebuke, but they may remain nonetheless. These are extreme examples, but we all are familiar with people who continue to behave defensively when others attempt to be friendly with them, for instance, although there is no need in the present environment to be so reclusive. Such people are reacting to prior loss experiences that continue in the form of current conflict cycles. Being entirely caught in a loss cycle is rare, but being predominantly preoccupied with loss is not. I would further argue that since it is impossible to entirely avoid loss, all people are in part operating within the conflict cycle.

Fulfillment Cycle

A second cycle, the fulfillment cycle, is illustrated in the upper portion of the diagram in Figure 8.2. Implied here is that people whose needs are generally met, either owing to their own actions or those of others, will become motivated to act on their desires. Desires are those resources that are not needed or required but that are wanted. One may need food, but not caviar, and one may need affection, but not a constant exchange of partners.

The fulfillment cycle is hedonistic. It operates from the desire for comfort and pleasure on both biological and social levels. It also exists, in part, as a product of the conflict cycle. That is to say, the seeking of resources that are not required is a function of the fear of loss. This point was developed in a more limited sense in Chapter 2, where it was argued that individuals seek not only to prevent or offset current loss (the conflict cycle), but they also have a primary motivation to prevent future loss. Furthermore, people seek to add resources that are not required

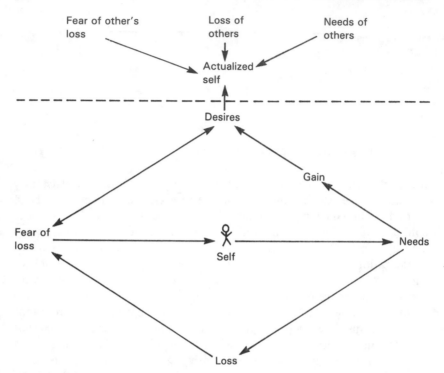

FIGURE 8.2   Ecological loss theory of personality: Conflict and fulfillment cycles.

because given the investment of other resources they expect gain of resources.

It also follows that the balance between fear of loss, which is characterized by the conflict cycle, and subsequent desire for gain, which is characterized by the fulfillment cycle, will change as environmental demands and constraints change. Indeed, this is a key point, because stressful events or circumstances enter the proposed theory here. Specifically, the environment may act to increase or decrease the likelihood of obtaining the resources that individuals require. Events or circumstances that limit the attainment of required or desired resources press individuals into the conflict cycle. They enlarge the sense of loss and the negative feelings, thoughts, and behaviors that are consistent with the conflict cycle.

For example, a woman in our pregnancy study may have been firmly oriented toward fulfillment and had only normal fears of loss. Such fears are likely to be adaptive, as in the case where fear of losing one's partner's affection leads husband and wife to be considerate and caring of one another. When confronting a serious complication of pregnancy, however, the woman becomes more loss-oriented. She is consequently more vulnerable to depression than she would be otherwise. Furthermore, if she has not developed the resources that can help her limit the conflict cycle, she is likely to remain depressed for a long time. These resources, it will be recalled, may be internal or external, and they may depend on behaviors or thoughts alone. Whereas this example is only a fabrication, the results of our study clearly support this interpretation.

A final point to be addressed here is that whether the individual is primarily operating in the conflict cycle or in the fulfillment cycle, the appraisal of loss is itself adaptive, which is also consistent with the study of stress. The appraisal process sets the stage for actions and thoughts aimed at redressing the loss, limiting the loss, or balancing the loss with gains. An individual who has never experienced loss is also unlikely to have developed adaptive resource strategies to offset loss and the subsequent maladaptive consequences if the sense of loss is sustained. Kobasa and colleagues (Kobasa, 1979; Kobasa, Maddi, & Courington, 1981; Kobasa & Puccetti, 1983) suggest, for instance, that the hardy personality is developed by a history of exposure to stressful circumstances that are not beyond the adaptive capabilities of the individual and whose consequences are meaningful for the person. Rosenbaum and Palmon (1984), and Rosenbaum and Smira (1986), in turn, have developed the concept of learned resourcefulness, which they suggest is the learned consequence of applying will power in successful attempts to adjust to challenging circumstances.

Concern for Greater Good of Humankind

Several humanistic theorists have also suggested that a few persons rise above the normal fray of events and enter a plane of functioning that is more spiritual and selfless (Maslow, 1968; May, 1958; Rogers, 1961). I would argue that there are few people who achieve this unusual state—a Mahatma Gandhi or Mother Theresa is extremely rare. However, many people possess a spark of this higher element. Some portray this spark more consistently, others express it in fleeting instances in their lives. This level is depicted in the uppermost portion of Figure 8.2 and is separated from the fulfillment and conflict cycles.

Anything said about persons who operate on this level or about instances in which many people perform an act of greater good must be based on speculation, as there is no sound research to indicate the forces at work here. There is at least theoretical convergence on the point that reaching this level requires a great deal of introspection. Those who frequently act in this self-actualized manner are said to be somewhat reclusive (Maslow, 1968). Yet they are at the same time sensitive to the needs of others. I would suggest that these individuals are detaching themselves from their own concerns of gain and loss and accepting a responsibility for the gains and losses of others. This detachment seems to be a conscious decision to step back from the day-to-day world into a more spiritual domain.

People whom we call self-actualized, such as Mahatma Gandhi, and acts of selflessness such as devoting one's life to an orphanage or a nation's birth, are also involved in a desire to maximize gain and minimize loss. The loss and gain are not, however, the person's own, but that of those others who will beneffit from his or her selfless actions. Such people have a deeply developed empathy for the suffering of others, and it might be said that they feel the losses as if they were their own. I am aware that these are speculations that help complete the personality theory I am proposing but that are difficult to support empirically. Perhaps, however, such selfless people are so rare that it is just as well to propose that they are touched with the spirit of God, since we may never have access to enough self-actualized individuals to test my suppositions.

Dominant Sphere of Influence

Personality will also be determined to a large extent by whether psychological loss or biological loss are the dominant spheres of influence. In this regard, the development of personality can be depicted as in Figure 8.3. In this diagram the motivational forces can be seen to spin like compass needles on two axes, a social axis and a biological axis. In this way, the principal forces shaping people's personalities and style of reacting to the world will be a function of the degree to which biological or social losses have primarily occurred or have been successfully countered.

The biological and social spheres of influence are encountered, for example, in threats to life from war and illness. Such events bring to the fore both biological and psychological fears. Other events are more exclusively psychological, such as rejection from a lover, and would spin the axes in a way that accentuated this aspect of the self. In everyday life the dominant sphere may in part be a function of economics. As Maslow (1968) has suggested, the preoccupation of the poor and the disenfranchised is more biological. The poor must concentrate their energies on gaining resources such as shelter and food. Those who have

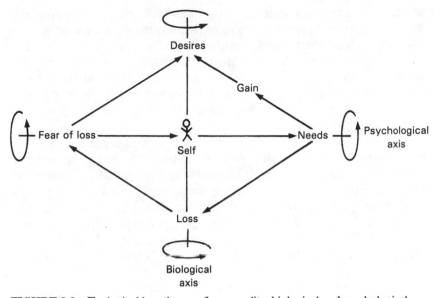

FIGURE 8.3   Ecological loss theory of personality: biological and psychological dominance.

more economic opportunity, in turn, also have the luxury of becoming more psychologically oriented and motivated.

The ecological loss model suggests, however, that events may quickly change the orientation of individuals and the dominant sphere of influence. This may occur subtly, as in the aging process, when people become increasingly concerned with their physical health, or more abruptly, as when illness suddenly erupts.

Personality Types

Maddi (1972) suggests that a good theory of personality should not only have a core element but should also lead to certain personality types. A number of personality types have emerged from the stress literature, and the ecological loss theory of personality leads to a way of providing structure to these types.

Types stemming from conflict cycle

One controversy in the literature, for example, is whether learned helplessness necessarily leads to depression and whether depression is always preceded by a sense of helplessness (Abramson, Seligman, & Teasdale, 1978). It follows from the above discussion that learned helplessness may occur when one's own behavior does not meaningfully decrease the probability of losing resources nor the likelihood of gaining resources. When this occurs, individuals will either learn to become dependent on others to gain their protection or become entirely apathetic. Such a profile is characteristic of those with learned helplessness. Since further behavior that might offset the loss is not believed to be effective, the sense of loss would be so pervasive as to produce depression.

The depression that develops as a consequence of learned helplessness, however, might appear more moderate than some reactive depressions, because those with learned helplessness learn to buffer the depression with apathy—"not feeling" being preferred to "feeling bad." In addition, passive acceptance of the protection of others, a common ploy of those who feel helpless, may also limit depression. These two processes, apathy and social support, might help explain why helplessness does not necessarily lead to depression; that is, it alone is not sufficient to produce depression.

A second personality type that may also follow from the experience of loss is the compensatory personality. Individuals with this personality type continue to make attempts to offset their losses. However, their attempts are likely to be strategically inadequate. This follows because if they had succeeded in counteracting loss, they would have moved into the fulfillment cycle and be less influenced by the conflict cycle. Such individuals are likely to exhibit inappropriate anger and hostility and self-defeating behavior rather than helplessness. Such compensation then would fall under the rubric of neurosis, that is, a style of behavior that does not follow from the objective circumstances and that results in sustaining the feelings of loss. The compensatory type could also be associated with depression, but it would not be associated with helplessness. This may help explain why helplessness is not necessary for producing depression.

Some indirect evidence for these two conflict-centered types is in the finding that learned helplessness and anger are both related not only to psychological distress but also to physical disease (Feuerstein et al., 1986). Indeed, a review of the literature on behavioral medicine suggests that these are two of the traits most commonly associated with physical disease. This is especially interesting because the two reactions are quite opposite in terms of activity or activation level. I am not aware that they have ever been commonly related to a core element that would suggest why their effect would be so similar.

A third type of personality results from constant frustration at not having one's needs met. If the sense of loss is so profound and all-encompassing as to reduce any hope of even partially meeting the need for basic psychosocial or biological resources and if the reason for this inability to meet needs is a result of random or bizarre "rules," individuals are likely to exit from the cycle into nonparticipation. Such nonparticipation is typified by schizophrenic reactions in which the rules that govern gain and loss in everyday affairs are abandoned. Obviously, to the extent schizophrenia is genetically determined there is no need to devise any such route to schizophrenia. However, much of what is thought of as schizophrenia and the more moderate borderline behavior could well be a consequence of the inability to meet basic social–psychological needs, especially owing to double-binding or conflicting signals as to what is expected of the individual. So, for example, parents who demand a constantly changing pattern of behaviors from the child or a pattern so bizarre or complex as to be uninterpretable, will be schizophrenogenic (i.e., producing schizo-phrenia). Such thinking is consistent with double-bind theories of schizophrenia (Bateson, Jackson, Haley, & Weakland, 1956) and family models of schizophrenia (Ackerman, 1958; Lidz, Fleck, & Cornelison, 1965).

Types stemming from fulfillment cycle

Whereas the conflict cycle may lead to personality types that are either active or passive, the fulfillment cycle necessitates an active posture. A similar point was also made by Adler (1929), who posited that the healthy personality could only be linked with an active stance. The fulfillment cycle is associated with activity because offsetting loss and enhancing gain both require action.

Two major personality types follow from entry into the fulfillment cycle. When people's needs are met and they move toward fulfilling their desires, they develop either a mastery approach to life or an active religious stance. Both approaches are associated with self-esteem. The mastery approach is typified by such traits as sense of mastery, resourcefulness, hardiness, and internal locus of control, and portends a bias toward active coping. The active religious stance shares its internal locus of control with an acceptance that control is also exerted by a powerful outside force. This may take the form of a firm belief in God or a more secular belief that the world is usually fair and favorable.

An example of the religious type can be seen in our own studies. In the investigation of parents of ill children, for instance, we found that the ultra-orthodox Jews in the study were no more psychologically distressed than their secular counterparts, despite their view that God controls all things. Nor were they significantly lower than their secular counterparts in their sense of mastery or self-esteem. Rather, in-depth discussion with some of them revealed that they felt that even though God ruled, humans should care for themselves spiritually and materially to the best of their abilities. Other religions are typified by a more passive approach; that is, it all rests in God's hands.

An example of the secular form of belief in shared control may be seen among baseball players. Baseball players often construct superstitious rituals that they follow during a winning streak. They might not change their socks, or they might touch their hats in a certain way or swing with their "lucky bat." This belief in supernatural forces does not for a moment cause them to practice less, let up on their concentration, or allow their state of conditioning to slide. Similarly, boxers from Catholic countries can be observed to cross themselves in the Olympic games before a match; but they do not subsequently let down their guard!

Frankl (1963) suggests that the most resilient people may have a combination of a strong sense of mastery and a powerful belief in the meaningful order of the world and their part in it. He found that persons with such an approach were especially resilient in the concentration camps. Maslow (1968) also suggests that the most resilient individuals are high on mastery and possess a spirituality that sustains and guides them. Studies of extreme situations suggest that mastery has a limited domain of effectiveness; events may in reality be so distressing and overpowering as to make mastery wholly inadequate. At such times, a sense of meaningfulness seems to help sustain individuals (Bulman & Wortman, 1977). Still, one's sense of mastery may help individuals make the best of the current situation or at least result in imagining a future time when actions may limit loss or increase gain of resources.

It is important to reiterate here that people remain loss-motivated even if their behavior usually results in gaining resources, except in the case of truly self-actualized individuals. Again, this is a result both of early childhood experiences and of the nature of stressful circumstances. During childhood and when stressors erupt, individuals realize that the world was not created to meet their needs and fulfill their desires. The experience of loss or the threat of loss motivates them to seek gains that will buffer them from future losses or compensate for past loss.

The direction an individual takes may also be construed as an aspect of personality. It follows from the ecological loss theory of personality that people direct themselves to where they feel they are most likely to experience gain and avoid loss. Individuals with fear of losing intimacy would be likely to become involved in business or work, say, and would avoid marriage. If married, they would tend nonetheless to avoid intimacy and the potential loss threatened by having intimacy. Those who have found they can meet their needs and fulfill their desires through social contact, in contrast, are likely to invest energies and resources toward building strong social ties.

Other aspects of the self may develop as a consequence of the behavior styles that increased gains and limited losses. Traits such as introversion–extroversion and rigidity–flexibility, for instance, may be explained by the path that was most likely to lead to gain and avoid loss. If, for example, a flexible style was rewarded, flexibility would become a trait of the individual.

Random and Culture-Bound Relationships

Some aspects of personality will develop as a product of random or cultural factors that result in behaviors, feelings, or thoughts aggregating. Individuals may falsely perceive, for instance, that a certain style of behavior results in obtaining resources and avoiding loss of resources. This association may be cultural and, in fact, unrelated to any cause-and-effect link. So, for example, independence may be fostered because it is esteemed, regardless of its consequences. The cultural forces may be so powerful as to obscure the actual relationship between independence and loss and gain of resources. The association may also be reinforced because a trait esteemed by society will be repeatedly highlighted when it is, in fact, associated with success. When independence is associated with failure (e.g., not being a team member), in contrast, this may be glossed over or seen as a special case.

Random associations between one's actions and outcome also occur and may even result in "streaks," where, say, an association between an action and loss repeats itself. These streaks may be noted as salient by individuals and result in their adopting a trait or style of behaving that they believe is causally associated with achieving positive and avoiding negative outcomes. For example, a child may cry frequently at preschool. On two or three such occasions her father might come early to pick her up, which may result in her adopting a whining, teary style. Nor would the behavior be easily extinguished, because he may also appear randomly to pick her up on other occasions, when once again she will be likely to be crying. Such infrequent reinforcement is very powerful.

Shaping of Personality

Whereas the model of conservation of resources outlines the factors of loss and gain, it does not fully clarify why personalities are shaped differently and how changes in personality might occur through the life span. The model of ecological congruence may be applied in this regard, because it specifically details the major factors shaping personality. This follows from the premise that personality is largely the product of the way stressful circumstances are resolved, the model of ecological congruence outlining the principal parameters affecting that resolution.

The first principle that may be derived from applying the model of ecological congruence is that personality is dynamic, changing in the life span. Early childhood experiences with loss, how the child responds to such loss, and how the child's environment helps in his or her responding will be critical. However, challenges and threats continue throughout people's lives, and the process of stress resolution, by which personality is shaped, also continues its course.

This brings us to the second principle that follows from applying the model of ecological congruence, and more specifically, from the time dimension of the model. Personality develops as a function of the special crises characteristic of the different stages of development in the life span. In this regard, people confront qualitatively different kinds of stressors during different developmental periods (Datan & Ginsberg, 1975; Erikson, 1963). As a consequence, personality would be marked by periods of developmental "jumps." These jumps would occur as a product of confronting the qualitatively different crises of a given period of life (e.g., sacrificing one's own needs for those of one's child; job retirement).

In addition, personality would also be shaped by the special stressors that might confront individuals, with no relation to development but perceived in relation to a person's developmental stage. The death of a loved one, for instance, will signify different kinds of loss for a child and an adult, but will be a major shaping event for both. In emphasizing the developmental facet, however, it should not be lost that these qualitative advances occur in addition to the more linear process of development that follows from confrontation with everyday stressors that do not markedly change over the life span.

Such thinking is clearly consistent with the theoretical contributions of Erikson (1963) who postulated that at each stage of development there exist characteristic stressors that must be overcome in order that the individual mature. Each stage of development had one global stressor that was to be mastered, such as resolving the identity crisis during adolescence. Erikson grasped the tenor of each stage, but may have overshadowed the fact that the stages were composed of minor and major events and circumstances that were the actual tasks to be mastered. In addition, his theory differs from the present one in that what he calls crises are more phenomenological than I am suggesting. Moreover,

Erikson does not emphasize what motivates individuals to continue the upward progression through the life span. In this regard, I would suggest that to avoid net loss and enhance the possibility of net gain, individuals are constantly motivated to enhance their position. Since challenges and stressors constantly confront individuals, to cease resolving crises would be to accept increasing loss.

A third principle follows from applying the perception and value facets of the model of ecological congruence. Here it is reasoned that people will note, appraise, and interpret their losses and gains because of idiosyncratic tendencies and as a function of commonly held values. Consequently, people will develop resource conservation strategies that are consistent with their world view. These resource strategies tend to be applied in many different situations, causing individuals to react in a fairly stable manner. Such tendencies may be so stable as to reach the level of a personality trait (e.g., aggressiveness, timidity, dogmatism).

It is also likely that perceptions will result in individuals developing a limited number of approaches to a finite set of categories of events. In other words, individuals do not evaluate the environment in its full complexity (Kruglanski, 1980; Tversky & Kahneman, 1974), but neither do they simplistically apply the same trait approach to all situations. An aggressive businesswoman may be socially timid, and a liberally minded father may be an authoritarian boss. Trait theories of personality have tended to lose sight of this middle ground, not entirely flexible nor entirely rigid, that probably represents the complex way most individuals approach the world.

An additional point also follows from the perception facet of the model. Specifically, we know from punishment experiments that the organism increases behavior that will lead to avoidance of punishment. This fact suggests that the experience of loss will increase the tendency to attend and be sensitive to aspects of the environment that are contextually related to loss. Such sensitivity is a salient aspect of personality, such as when people are sensitive to criticism or rejection.

Finally, the model of ecological congruence emphasizes that resources also interact with one another. Consequently, aspects of personality that develop to offset resource loss and facilitate resource gain will develop in relation to other traits that complement one another. Similarly, traits that are inconsistent will tend not to occur in the same individual. Moreover, personal traits and ways of approaching the world will have a developmental quality. That is, there will be a natural progression of resource strategies, where mastery may lead to greater self-esteem, greater sociability, and a generally positive mood, for example.

One of the few researchers who have tried to derive such a constellation of traits empirically is Kobasa (1979), and the present theory suggests that others would do well to follow her lead. This suggestion is also consistent with comprehensive reviews of the literature on the effectiveness of personality resources in confronting stress (see Cohen & Edwards, in press, Chapter 5), which show that studying single traits has obscured the extent to which these traits overlap or are independent of one another.

Biological Influences and Limitations

Personality is also affected by inborn dispositions and tendencies that are molded in early stages of biological development. Degree of emotional arousal and the characteristics of that arousal have, in particular, been associated with biological determinism. Such traits as the emotional response to events, for example, have been attributed in part to biological predisposition (see Larsen et al., 1986; Fiske & Maddi, 1961). In this regard, the optimal level of stimulation or the characteristic level of response to environmental stimuli is envisaged as related to biological factors either independent of or interacting with psychological processes. For example, Larsen et al. attribute the degree to which people strongly react to external events as a function of the excitability of the nervous system.

If we merge these concepts with the ecological loss theory, we see that the extent of reactivity to loss may be a function of activation tendencies. Those who tend to react strongly may experience their losses and gains as more extreme. This might give them a greater sense of hopelessness or mastery, respectively. The objective experience, then, would be only one indicator of the degree to which losses challenge people, since their biological predispositions would affect the intensity of the psychological reaction.

In addition to activity or arousal level, how much people fear loss and feel confident that they can fulfill their needs and desires will be a function of their physical constitution. Those who are physically ill will have heightened fears of loss because they naturally must be more dependent on others and because their physical state makes the experience of loss more likely. This line of thought was discussed at length by Adler (1956), who saw it as the core of the inferiority complex. This does not mean, however, that those who have a physical handicap, say, are predestined to be loss-oriented. Rather, the challenges facing them are more substantial and will require greater effort and investment of resources to overcome. This investment must come originally from outside sources such as parents, siblings, and institutions. Later, it must come from the individuals themselves.

I have witnessed a touching example of this in children with Down's syndrome. In my occasional contact with these children in different settings I have become acquainted with a number who seem to have risen to strong levels of self-esteem and mastery. Their achievements seem to follow directly from having parents who treated them with compassion, in consideration of their problem, and with challenge, in consideration of their future. They were treated as normal family members with special needs and given frequent opportunity to achieve and excel. Rather than accentuate their loss by making them dependent, their parents enhanced their sense of mastery and self-esteem by providing an environment that fitted both their strengths and their weaknesses.

Exactly how biologically based predispositions affect personality is not currently known. Indeed, we know precious little about this aspect of personality development. However, it can be said that where biologically set tendencies occur, they seem to influence personality by interacting with environmental factors. Future research, especially developmental investigations, will be necessary to sort out the nature of this interaction and how they affect the reaction to loss.

Loss and Awareness

A final question about the ecological loss theory of personality is whether people are aware of the losses and gains and strategies for applying resources. Given my own cognitive bias, I suggest that for the most part they either occur within the purview of awareness or come into awareness if individuals turn their attention in the right direction. As to this second point, learning may be mechanical, but if individuals stop to think about how and why they are reacting in the way they are, the answers will generally become apparent.

Some learning, however, may also be precognitive and occur without awareness. Even the most extreme cognitive stance must accept the fact that biological aspects of personality may occur without awareness. I would argue that attachment needs are also biological in origin (see also Bowlby, 1969; 1973), as are the needs for security, sex, shelter, nutrients, and procreation. It is only a next step that the fulfillment of these needs may occur without awareness and that the experience of social loss, say, may affect individuals without their awareness. In this sense it would be consistent both with psychodynamic notions and with principles of learning theory that a defensive structure of self can develop containing elements that are both conscious and unconscious. Likewise, personality traits that enhance the possibility of gain may occur with or without awareness.

I would choose to take issue with a major aspect of psychodynamic theory, however. Other than fear of losing attachment and need to meet basic biological and social drives, there is no evidence for the existence of any predetermined conflicts that are biological or instinctual in origin. An Oedipus complex may be a consequence of children interacting with parents in a given society, but there is no reason to believe it is inborn.

It also follows that if conflicts are not inborn, then the solutions or modes of resolution will not be predetermined. Rather, the methods by which the loss–gain conflict is resolved will be a function of social modeling, chance learning, and cognitive "puzzle solving." Particular social conflicts that are common in a society, however, will likely elicit typical solutions that can be interpreted psychodynamically. For this reason, the ecological loss theory of personality places considerable emphasis on family dynamics and early childhood experience. However, I take issue with the proposition that instinct is strongly involved in this process.

IMPLICATIONS FOR INTERVENTION

The model of conservation of resources and the model of ecological congruence may also be used to guide intervention efforts. In formulating stress interventions, we must emphasize two critical points. First, resource conservation strategies are integral to the formation of personality, as this chapter has attempted to argue. Second, natural coping strategies are likely to be maintained by a complex person–environment interaction; that is, they are created and sustained because they meet individuals' needs in a given environment. From these two basic tenets it follows that superficial attempts to assist people, or to change how they resist stress, will have only minimal effect because neither personality nor environment is easily given to change. Only concentrated intervention efforts, often including environmental manipulation, will have any significant or lasting impact. Unfortunately, such superficial stress resistance efforts have already proliferated in the form of stress workshops. These workshops have potential as starting points, but may lead to disenchantment with the potential of other change agents that more comprehensively apply the principles garnered from stress resistance research.

Having stated this caveat I will now suggest some basic principles for potentially effective interventions. In keeping with the format of this volume, I will organize them around the principles of the model of conservation of resources and the model of ecological congruence. I will also attempt to speak to the likelihood of success and limitations of the intervention strategies in existing research.

Model of Conservation of Resources and Intervention

From the model of conservation of resources, five basic principles for intervention efforts may be derived. These principles should be considered as primary considerations in any intervention.

Principle 1

As was argued in Chapter 2, the research strongly suggests that loss of resources is a major form of stress. I have argued more strongly that it is the central core of stress. Consistent with either viewpoint, the first principle of stress intervention is that interventions should be directed at helping people to confront or prevent loss of resources and to enhance gain of resources. This may be done in several ways. The most direct way to limit loss is to change the environment. Interventionists may change the environment for individuals who are threatened by loss or have experienced loss. Alternatively, intervention may be directed at increasing others' potential for inducing environmental change. Thus, for example, intervention may consist of legal aid to battered women or of helping them utilize their resources to gain such aid. This class of intervention may be operationalized through such varied efforts as teaching social, managerial, or employment skills, providing financial assistance, or offering marital or occupational counseling. The common focal point of such interventions is to change those elements of the environment that are causing or perpetuating the resource loss and to enhance those elements of the environment that might help facilitate resource gain.

Probably the largest stress intervention effort ever implemented was based on this principle. I am referring here to the veterans benefits for American military personnel returning from World War II. I first heard this program analyzed on social and psychological grounds by Ira Iscoe, a leading community psychologist. Dr. Iscoe pointed out that these men and women had missed an education by going to war or had found their job skills outdated by the new technologies that the war created. This might have led to a national tragedy if not for the educational benefits that paid for training in a wide variety of professions and skills, while at the same time providing a living stipend. Concurrently, veterans were offered housing loans so they could enter the housing market with their young families. These resources allowed them to enhance their skills, sense of mastery, and self-esteem, in circumstances where the threat to loss could have presaged an inevitable acceptance of fatalism and loss. Millions of veterans benefited from this program, which remained in effect until only recently. The strength of the program was to change the environment such that people could apply their own resources to exploit their potential.

A second direction for intervention efforts also follows from Principle 1. Intervention can be aimed at assisting individuals to reevaluate the nature of the threat to their loss of resources. This strategy is aimed at cognitive rather than environmental change. If one can convince people that what they see as a threat to loss may actually be a challenge to other gains, this strategy will be successful. Care should be taken here, however, not to minimize real concerns about loss. Certain losses must be mourned, and to minimize their meaning would be destructive (Janis, 1958; Lindeman, 1944; Parkes, 1970).

There exist, however, several categories of loss whose meaning is easy to exaggerate or whose consequences are overestimated owing to lack of information. Many work stressors are of this type, as when a boss's lack of acknowledgment for workers' accomplishments is taken as a sign of disapproval. A frank discussion may reveal that the boss felt that he or she communicated approval in end-of-the-year raises or did not even realize that dissatisfaction was being communicated. Even job loss may portend a more positive future than first imagined, as when an employee had stuck to a job that he had outgrown years earlier.

The third corollary that follows from Principle 1 is that interventions can focus on changing the underlying values that individuals assign to losses and gains. Financial loss may be reevaluated as more minor when the focus is changed to health. As discussed in Chapter 2, however, this is a path fraught with problems. When individuals challenge their values it should not be for expedience. This argument follows from the notion that when values are changed, past gain and loss balance is also subject to reinterpretation and individuals risk increasing their total sense of loss. So, for example, if an executive is challenged to reevaluate his esteem for financial gain, as a strategy to ameliorate the stress following some recent financial debacle, he risks seeing many years of his life as spent for nought. On the other hand, there are times when the principal cause of repeated distress is precisely the individual's value hierarchy, and in such cases this may need attention.

Principle 2

As already mentioned, the strategy that people develop to minimize resource loss and maximize resource gain may be deeply ingrained and part and parcel of personality. This leads to Principle 2, that intervention efforts will need to be sustained and must have sufficient depth to counter habit-strength and the personal investment people have in being a certain way.

It follows then that intervention aimed at any of the three corollaries of Principle 1 must proceed in a way that (a) introduces new resistance strategies, (b) provides meaningful examples for the individual, (c) allows individuals to test the strategy, (d) encourages feedback following application, and (e) includes follow-up for weeks and months after the main body of the intervention is completed. Stress workshops typically only include the first two points.

The work of Meichenbaum and colleagues in what they call stress inoculation (see Meichenbaum & Jaremko, 1983) is an excellent example of putting all five of these corollaries of principle to work and has proven to be one of the most successful stress intervention approaches. After the source of stress is identified, stress inoculation includes cognitive rehearsal of new ways to manage the stressor, which are then tried out in the "real world." Those that are successful are further reinforced by the therapist through further cognitive rehearsal and actual practice.

Principle 3

It also follows from the model of conservation of resources that intervention strategies must prove successful to the individual in both minimizing loss and maximizing gain, or they will eventually be rejected. People develop complex resource utilization strategies that are like diplomatic treaties between the conflicting needs of the self and the demands of the environment. A woman may feel that her husband is not providing affection, but may nevertheless reject intervention aimed at challenging him on this issue because she also fears loss of economic security. Likewise, assertiveness training may help a man deal with social stress, but he will reject this training if he fears that a new posture will threaten job loss.

Interventionists must consider fully why a particular inadequate stress resistance strategy has been adopted and sustained. Intervention must focus not only on adoption of a strategy that will increase resource gain but also on secondary or hidden purposes of the strategy to be corrected. Learning theory, upon which much of the thinking of the model of conservation of resources is based, suggests that most if not all resource conservation strategies are learned because they provide some reinforcement through resource gain or avoidance of punishment via resource loss. Paradoxically, if a strategy seems particularly self-defeating, the forces perpetuating the strategy must be that much more powerful to have sustained it.

Principle 4

Because people develop their resource conservation strategies over long periods of time and because these become integral to personality, the strategies and the traits behind them will normally be resistant to change. However, I would state as Principle 4 that during crises people are likely to be especially amenable to stress interventions. This follows from the tenets of crisis theory, which suggest that crises provide fertile ground for personal change (Caplan, 1964). The logic is that during crises people find their normal coping strategies and personal resources unsuitable for meeting the demands of the crisis. Because of this they are willing to try alternative approaches, whereas normally they might resist change. In addition, the crisis itself acts as a testing ground for the new approach, where success will provide ample reinforcement for the newly adopted strategy. At other times people may not be exposed to stressors that challenge their proven methods of stress resistance, and so they have less motivation for exerting effort toward change.

Felner et al. (1983) point out that the focus of intervention should be on adaptive behavior during transitional periods. This also implies that during such periods interventionists may meet a less resistant target, because individuals are likely to feel overwhelmed and therefore more open to intervention efforts.

In an ongoing intervention effort, Jason (1986, and personal communication) has developed a stress intervention program that illuminates both this principle and those already cited. Children in the 3rd to 5th grades who have moved to a new school are targeted as being "at risk." Indeed, early evaluation has shown that they are in greater academic and behavioral difficulty than others identified as "problem children" in the same schools. Children are assigned an older student buddy who has already successfully undergone such a transition. In addition, they are matched with a class peer who is encouraged to guide them around the classroom and schoolyard for a period of months. They are assigned a tutor-advocate who helps them increase their academic skills and keeps the school posted as to their ongoing needs. In addition, children attend a group discussion, which allows them to disclose their problems, receive reinforcement, and receive feedback as to alternative ways of handling problems. This program is being carefully evaluated with strict controls and large numbers of subjects, and we look forward to the results. However, this program is likely to succeed because it exploits the moment of crisis with a comprehensive intervention that targets the child's mastery, academic abilities, social skills, and social needs.

Principle 5

The fifth principle for intervention that follows from the model of conservation of resources is that minimizing certain losses is beyond the power of individuals. The stressors of poverty, single parenthood, teenage pregnancy, and regional job layoffs may require that intervention seek to directly offset or correct the actual loss. Such intervention may be wholly outside of the realm of individuals' power.

Psychology and psychiatry have both been guilty at times of relying on intervention strategies that inherently blame the victim, if not for their problems then for the solution. Some circumstances, however, can only be approached when it is accepted that those involved are victims and that intervention must act in their behalf. Western society and the United States, in particular, have historically adopted a model of "rugged individualism," whereby the individual is expected to "stand on his own two feet," and this has been strongly reflected in human service planning (Attkisson & Broskowski, 1978).

This point is illustrated in our own work on the needs of skid row residents (Hobfoll, Kelso, & Peterson, 1980, 1981). For these individuals we found that a two-tiered system of care might best meet their needs. The first tier would be for individuals who might benefit from rehabilitation efforts. A lower tier, however, was most ecologically congruent with the needs of a large percentage of the homeless who were interviewed. For these more debilitated men and women, the primary needs were medical care, shelter, food, and hygienic facilities. Rehabilitation was a pretense, likely to meet the needs of agencies or the demands of taxpayers, but not the needs of the target group.

Model of Ecological Congruence and Intervention

A number of principles for intervention also follow from the model of ecological congruence. These may be organized according to the dimensions of the ecological congruence model.

Resource dimension: personality

Stress researchers suggest a number of resources that can be enhanced or developed to facilitate stress resistance (see Cohen & Edwards, in press; Chapter 5). These include mastery, self-esteem, internal locus of control, hardiness, resourcefulness, flexibility, social prowess, and private self-consciousness. Alternatively, interventions may aim at helping people rid themselves of some traits that inhibit resource acquisition or increase the probability of resource loss. Examples of these include type A behavior, anger, and trait anxiety. Personal skills may also be enhanced and those lacking these skills may be directed to learn new skills.

The factors that underlie the development of the mastery-related aspects of personality (e.g., mastery, internal locus of control, hardiness, and helplessness) (Abramson & Martin, 1981; Kobasa, 1979; Lefcourt et al., 1984) and self-esteem (Maslow, 1968; Rogers, 1961) are better understood than some other personal attributes (e.g., resourcefulness, private self-consciousness, flexibility, anger proneness). Mastery-related resources may be enhanced by interventions that encourage individuals to test newly acquired skills or abilities already in their repertoire, on increasingly difficult tasks. It is important that the new challenge not be too difficult and that success be accompanied by ample reinforcement. There are five aspects of such interventions to enhance mastery:

1. learning new skills that fit better with environmental and personal demands than preintervention approaches,
2. receiving incentives for investing resources in these new strategies,
3. applying new skills successfully in a program of graduated difficulty or complexity,
4. receiving reinforcement for the new skill acquisition, and
5. follow-up to further reinforce generalization of feelings of mastery and to prevent slippage.

Mastery enhancement may be focused on a given task, say, managing supervisory stress. This might include learning to deal with increased responsibility and the feeling that one is responsible for other people, and having to be sensitive to the stress experienced by employees, both at home and at work. Such focused (not to be confused with short-term) interventions may be conducted in individual or group format, and participants either may be identified through self-referral in response to solicitation or may be referred on the basis of being at risk. So, new managers or those experiencing staff problems might be referred. More generalized mastery can also be enhanced in individual or group formats. It can be expected that participants in the latter kinds of programs will have experienced a more general set of problems and will be more debilitated than participants in the groups focusing on a single problem.

Resource dimension: social support

Many resources are provided or actualized through social support. Social support intervention efforts may be divided into those aimed at the individual, the dyad, or the larger group. In general, there is an explosion of knowledge from studies of social support and loneliness that may be cautiously applied to stress interventions.

Beginning with interventions targeted at the individual level, Rubenstein and Shaver (1982) note that a sad-passive reaction to loneliness was the most debilitating strategy people could adopt. Their research further suggests that interventions may meet with success if they encourage lonely individuals to actively cope with their solitude (e.g., through a hobby, reading, or exercise) or more actively seek social contact. The latter approach might be intuitively obvious, but interventionists may not have thought of the former alternative, which suggests that there are skills related to solitude.

Other research suggests that people can be trained to be more socially adept, to react to stressful events in ways that encourage support, and to better understand their role in their failure to achieve close social contact (Rook, in press). Work by Eckenrode (1983), for example, suggests that changing people's attitudes about the potential effectiveness of social support will increase support-seeking during times of crisis. Work by others also indicates that if individuals can be encouraged to display a problem-solving mode of coping, this is likely to attract support from others (Dunkel-Schetter, Folkman, & Lazarus, 1987). Specifically, squarely confronting a problem may have the counterintuitive effect of eliciting further informational support, and positive reappraisal may encourage expressions of emotional support. Here it may be that those who distance themselves from the problem have been subtly telling potential supporters not to interfere or that the subject is taboo.

Another paradoxical intervention strategy follows from the findings of Lehman, Ellard, & Wortman (1986). Their research suggests that it is important for the distressed individual to cue the behavior of the helper. This means that *those in need of help must aid the helper.* By informing helpers that their approach is working or by cueing them on how they could help more effectively, helpers' own debilitating anxiety may be

lowered. In this regard, Lehman et al. found that helpers have good
intent and precrisis judgment about what they should do, but they act
inappropriately because of anxiety. Because their anxiety stems in part
from their inexperience in this role, it is very possible that lowering their
anxiety level enhances their performance.

Individual and dyadic efforts may also be directed at enhancing
capacity for intimacy and the intimacy in a relationship. There is ample
evidence that intimacy, in particular, is a key to effective social support
(Hobfoll, 1985b; Sarason et al., 1987; Chapter 4), and intervention
designed to enhance the ability to create and sustain intimate
relationships may be a primary focus for interventionists. It should be
pointed out, however, that achieving intimacy depends on one's fear of
loss if one were to become intimate, on social attractiveness, and on a
wide array of complex social skills. Individuals may need to learn
appropriate self-disclosure skills (Jourard, 1971) and to become
sensitized to the importance of empathy. They may also have to learn in
certain situations to sacrifice their own needs to the needs of their
partner. This may be the work of intensive psychotherapy rather than of
any workshop.

Perhaps the most promising area for social support intervention is
helping people derive maximum benefit from existing relationships. For
a couple whose relationship is not too disturbed, for instance, modest
efforts to draw them more closely together may revitalize intimacy and
consequent support. These efforts might include having them work on
some of the above-mentioned skills and having them consider and
vocalize what they want from the relationship, how they can help their
partner, and how they can reshape their lives to allow time for intimacy.

Working within existing relationships can also be effective because
people are quick to feel that they are a burden to others, especially if
there is not a history of mutual aid and obligation with the supporter. In
our work with parents of ill children and with subjects who themselves
were under health-related stress, we found this repeatedly. It is
interesting, however, that in developing a measure of the degree to which
people felt uncomfortable in seeking support, people consistently
responded that they felt very comfortable in supporting a close friend or
family member. This may be one key to intervention—to help individuals
empathize with the feelings of the helper so they can see that an intimate
other feels it is a sign of love to be asked to help. Obviously, such
reciprocal feelings are most likely to occur in close relationships.

Another class of social support interventions designed to reduce
stress emerges from research on the dyadic level among individuals
involved in more seriously impaired marital relationships. In particular,

the research on expressed emotion suggests that for those vulnerable to depression, having a partner who tends to express negative emotions exacerbates the problem (Gotlib & Hooley, in press). It is not clear whether this kind of negative expressed emotion is a primary cause of depression, but given the data it is reasonable to begin to investigate how interventions designed to lower the expressed emotion of the nondepressed partner may affect the depressed partner's emotional distress and the marital satisfaction of both. It should be emphasized, however, that the partners' expressions of anger may be a way to conserve other resources (e.g., their own self-esteem) and to ward off their own depression. With this in mind, interventionists should concentrate on offering substitute methods of resource conservation that meet the needs of both the depressed and the nondepressed partner.

Social support interventions may be especially effective during crisis. This follows, in part, from Principle 4 above, that during crisis individuals are more willing to try new approaches to solve their problems because "tried and true" strategies are failing. For this reason, grafting relationships or providing support groups to widows (Vachon, Lyall, Rogers, Freedman-Letofsky, & Freeman, 1980), to the recently divorced (Bloom, Hodges, & Caldwell, 1982), and to the children of the divorced (Stolberg & Garrison, 1985) may prove effective, even among people who normally would not consider seeking aid from strangers or sharing personal problems. Such relationships may prove helpful even if they do not reach levels of deep intimacy or if they are used only for a brief period during crisis. Evidence for this comes from the experience of soldiers, in which support from buddies and officers sustains men during extreme stress (Solomon, Mikulincer, & Hobfoll, 1987), despite the fact that these men may never be contacted after leaving the service. The reason that such efforts are successful is that a brief but intense level of intimacy is often gained when high levels of stress are encountered.

In a currently ongoing intervention study, Hofien (1986) is applying the principles of crisis and of social support intervention between partners. Specifically, he has begun work with the wives of men with serious back injuries. The intervention is designed to teach them social support skills, encourage the use of skills they already possess, and help them gain support from others, in realization that they too are under significant stress. His strategy relies on repeated individual meetings tailored to the women's situational needs and to their doubts about their supportive potential. Unlike many stress intervention strategies, Hofien's considers fully the ecological principles that others have observed to be important in natural stress resistance (e.g., Hobfoll &

Walfisch, 1984; Hobfoll & Leiberman, 1987; Holahan & Moos, 1986; Pearlin et al., 1981; Chapters 5, 6, & 7).

When members of the target group are not in particular crisis, artificial attempts at support may not prove effective. In one study, for example, McGuire and Gottlieb (1979) attempted to facilitate adjustment to parenthood among new parents. Their effort met with little success. In another study, Chapman and Pancoast (1985) attempted to strengthen elderly clients' informal helping networks, but met with resentment for the implied encroachment into the personal world of those whom they intended to help. Both these programs may have been unsuccessful because the target population were only assumed to be open to supportive attempts. In fact, they were not threatened enough to change their ingrained resource conservation strategies. This interpretation is also consistent with research discussed in Chapter 2 in which transitions themselves may not be as stressful as some argue because most people have natural adaptive capabilities.

Before leaving a discussion of social support interventions it is important to note that interventions on the group level or systems level may also enhance social support and thereby aid stress resistance. For instance, many hospitals have made visitation more accessible, and spouses are being encouraged to participate in prenatal preparation and in delivery. Felner et al (1983) illustrated that changing students' class schedules to encourage attachment to a homeroom teacher and to peers facilitated social support and resulted in psychological and academic gains. Holahan, Wilcox, Burnam, and Culler (1978) also illustrated that more distance from meeting grounds resulted in lower social satisfaction of college dormitory residents. The availability of midwives to pregnant and delivering women has also been shown to increase their satisfaction with care, in contrast with cases where gynecologists (male or female) are the primary hospital contact (Rand, 1986). In still another study, Glidewell, Tucker, Todt, and Cox (1982) noted that teachers were more likely to share support in a resource center that encouraged "experience swapping," than in hierarchical instruction (which implies lower status of the helpee).

It also follows from the resource dimension of the model of ecological congruence that constellations of resources will be the most profitable target for intervention. By working on a complex of naturally aggregating resources, interventionists can change aspects of the self that facilitate stress resistance in a wide spectrum of circumstances. Because these are aspects of personality, however, they may not be easily amenable to change outside of times of crisis or with younger people. One encouraging area of intervention in this regard is illustrated by the work of Cowan and associates with young children (Cowen, Dorr, Trost, & Izzo, 1972; Weissberg et al., 1981). Aiming to enhance children's problem-solving skills and their view of their own potential for success, such interventions also affect a wide range of stress resistance resources such as mastery, self-esteem, and sense of meaningfulness.

Time dimension

The time dimension of the model of ecological congruence suggests principles that follow from its developmental aspects and from the issue of time vis-à-vis an event's occurrence. Stress interventions should be suited for the developmental stage of the individual. Hansson (1986), for example, illustrated that the needs of the young-old and the old-old differ very much. For the old-old, isolation may not be so distressing if other needs are being met. At this time of life, a principal concern may be the relationship with God. For the young-old, in contrast, social stressors are still salient and isolation is still very threatening.

Likewise, with adolescents, for example, there exist stressors that are shared by many and can be targeted in interventions to large groups. Fear of pregnancy, fear of AIDS, fear of not finding a good job, or fear of not being accepted to college are common adolescent fears of future loss that may be approached in group or individual settings. For younger children, working with parent-child dyads may be especially effective, as the parent and the child are at a developmental state where they must work together to help support the child's stress resistance.

Time in relation to the event is also important. Whereas stage theory has not exactly characterized the phases that people follow either in anticipation of an event or subsequent to its occurrence, there do exist likely sequences of reactions to stressful events (Silver & Wortman, 1980). Care must be taken here not to generalize that all individuals follow the same sequence or that any stage in the sequence must necessarily be "worked through," as was thought earlier. This suggests a combination normative-individual approach that may be applied to individuals or groups in which specific stages are expected and prepared for but in which it is also acknowledged that there is no one "right course" to stress resistance.

An example of this can be seen in the social support applications of self-help groups for widows (Vachon et al., 1980; Bankoff, 1986). The supportive widow may share what she went through six or nine months after the death of her spouse but also emphasizes that she never experienced a certain phase that she heard others in the group describe.

We may be confident in suggesting, however, that initial confrontation with crisis is typically accompanied by extreme reactions that tend to diminish over time (Hobfoll & Walfisch, 1984; Hobfoll & Leiberman, 1987; Chapter 7). Although individuals should gradually recover from initial severe reactions, we also have good evidence that that mourning or emotional distress follows for a prolonged period (Vachon, 1986; Lehman et al., 1987). We probably know little more about the time dimension than did those who initiated and codified the Jewish ritual of grief following the first year of mourning, but it seems reasonable that functioning at work and with family should be expected a week or so after even severe events and that a steady upswing should follow. This does not imply that bouts of depression will not occasionally occur or that setbacks will not emerge. A year following severe crisis nearly full functioning should be expected, although it may still be difficult for people two to six years after the event to feel like their "old selves."

After a prolonged period, interventionists must begin to ask what resources are being gained and what losses are being offset that prevent people from abandoning prolonged distress reactions. This will seem paradoxical to those who are set on believing that no one would suffer intentionally. However, even without evoking concepts of denial or repression, it can be seen that emotional distress and physical illness may have reinforcement potential because of their tendency to attract secondary gain and diminished expectations (Merton, 1957).

The time dimension is also highlighted in the aforementioned comprehensive school intervention by Jason. Rather than assume that at-risk children may be characterized by stages of stress during their transition to the new school, Jason's intervention monitors the students' weekly progress and setbacks and adjusts the intervention accordingly. Other programs would also benefit by keeping their hands on the "pulse" of the problem, as this can aid more generalized efforts.

Strain dimension

The strain dimension of the model of ecological congruence presses interventionists to look for particular outcomes rather than for generalized outlets of strain. This may be done on two levels. The first level is outcomes that are likely caused by the nature of the stressful circumstances. The second is outcomes that are likely caused by individuals' own characteristics.

An example of the first case is in work by Cutrona (1986), who reported that although loneliness was very common during the first semester of college, a majority of students who were originally lonely recovered by the spring term. This suggests that the loneliness experienced so painfully during transitions may be limited by interventions that enhance the circumstances for social contact. In our own studies of war, reported in Chapter 6 (Solomon et al., 1987), loneliness was also seen as an indicator of the likelihood to develop combat stress reactions. Here, early identification of loneliness and special attempts on the part of officers and buddies to provide support would be in order.

While studies of type A behavior have focused on the individual (Friedman & Rosenman, 1959; Glass, 1977), the setting may also be implicated in the interplay between type A behavior and heart disease. Specifically, organizations that encourage or require executives to meet impossible schedules under unrelenting demands are also inviting health hazards. Interventions aimed at helping employees structure the schedules efficiently, limiting Saturday work and evening work, and allowing more flexible schedules may increase worker satisfaction, decrease the likelihood of heart attacks, and even enhance decision making. As a recent study has illustrated, when stress levels increase, decisions tend to be based on a more limited field of options (Keinan, 1987). If stress researchers can illustrate to senior executives the payoff of such interventions, these payoffs may be able to offset the attraction of short-term gains made by excessive demands.

Interventions will also be more effective if they approach individual tendencies to experience certain kinds of strain. Recent work by Chesney et al. (1984) illustrates this principle. These researchers show that anger and how it is expressed may be a sign of emotional strain that, in turn, results in secondary health strains. Those susceptible to frequent bouts of anger may be identified and referred to programs that teach them more effective styles of coping. Since anger and hypertension seem to be particularly highly correlated, hospitals and clinics may be ideal settings for identifying high-risk individuals.

Values dimension

The values dimension of the model of ecological congruence is the most neglected in intervention strategies. Underlying this problem may be an attitude in America that cultural background is not a salient factor. To speak of different values, in a sense, is to divide Americans and is antithetical to the "melting pot" ideal that is itself a basic American value.

If we are to consider values in our intervention strategies we must attend to the fact that different cultures and subcultures have different accepted styles for dealing with stress. In our own research in Israel we found, for example, that Sephardic Israelis felt uncomfortable in seeking support from outside the family. There was a value placed on honor that was so central that even if seeking aid had proved helpful such a route would mean dishonoring the self and the family. Many Hispanics and Orientals share this idealization of honor, and this will need to be addressed in formulating any approach that might expose people's problems.

There exists a more general value in many societies for independence and privacy. Many group approaches or attempts to identify individuals who have not sought help may be seen as encroaching on one or both of these values. The study reported by Chapman and Pancoast (1985) that was mentioned earlier is a good example. The elderly people in the study may even have been particularly sensitive to attempts by young people to encroach on their independence.

Since self-esteem is also highly valued, interventionists would be advised to emphasize the strengths of target populations instead of their weaknesses. "Selling" intervention as mastery-enhancing or skill training may be more attractive than addressing the problem. Similarly, during early phases of the intervention it would be advised to highlight the positive strategies individuals are already using and why they are positive before spotlighting ineffective or self-defeating strategies. A general rule here is to apply to intervention some of the principles of empathic support that psychologists, psychiatrists, and social workers practice with individual clients and patients (Rogers, 1961; Truax and Carkhuff, 1967).

Still other values are related to sex. Mitchell and Hodson (1986) show, for example, that women with traditional attitudes about women's roles are more passive in the face of a physically abusive partner. Women with nontraditional attitudes are more likely, in contrast, to cope actively as physical threats increase. When one considers intervention, any attempt to change coping behaviors will interact with natural tendencies. Women with traditional sex-role orientations may resist interventions that encourage their action orientation. If interventionists are cognizant both of the need for an action orientation in certain circumstances and of the conflict this may have with values, a dual-pronged intervention that targets change in both values and behavior may be devised.

Stressful medical procedures, especially those surrounding pregnancy and gynecological problems, may be targeted for intervention when one considers the growing number of women who are placing value on feminist principles. Women who express these values, or those who prefer female caregivers, may choose midwives or female gynecologists. And some women, for example, do not want their husbands present at the delivery because this crosses their values concerning modesty. Few solutions are good for everyone, and differential values are likely to be one dividing line on which person- or group-specific treatments are organized.

Before leaving the issue of sex differences and values, it should also be pointed out that men may as a group be less comfortable with social support than are women (Hobfoll & Stokes, in press; Kessler et al., 1985). This is probably a reflection of male values about showing weakness and being dependent. For many men it is better to suffer than to expose a sign of insecurity or doubt about a problem. One solution to this problem was already mentioned above, when it was suggested that interventions emphasize strengths and mastery, rather than those weaknesses or problems that are being addressed. Another avenue of intervention is through working with married couples or opposite-sex partners. Women often act as the emotional conduits for their partners and are more likely to be able to disclose personal issues. This may be used as a model for men if it is encouraged by sensitive group leaders. In such groups the group leaders may also be an opposite-sex dyad, and the male interventionist may model self-disclosure and sharing of problems and relying on social support. Since many stressors affect married couples, this is a natural strategy for marital and personal interventions. It would be particularly appropriate to focus on dual-career couples, who are particularly suitable to shared stressors (Aneshensel, 1986; Vanfossen, 1986).

Perception dimension

The perception dimension of the model of ecological congruence emphasizes that stressors have both objective and subjective components. The first principle that I would suggest from this dimension is that stress interventionists should not overemphasize perceptions. Even when perceptions are part of the problem, overemphasizing them may be interpreted by people as minimizing their plight, or worse, as calling them delusional. Attempts by supporters to minimize reactions as "only feelings" have been shown to be very distressing when practiced by natural supporters (Wortman & Lehman, 1985). People do not want to hear that their problems are "all in their minds" or "not so bad."

This raises a dilemma for interventionists, however, because research clearly indicates that appraisal is an important aspect of the stress and stress resistance process (Lazarus & Folkman, 1984). For instance, lonely students were shown to attribute their loneliness to being rejected by others, although they were not evaluated differently by nonlonely students (Jones, 1985). In general, interventionists may help people become aware of ways in which they exaggerate negative aspects of the environment or underestimate the chance of positively influencing events. Research on persons who naturally possess these characteristics suggests that pessimism leads to avoidance of problem-solving, whereas a more optimistic attitude leads to the feeling that positive actions help solve problems (Carver & Scheirer, 1983).

It is somewhat ironic that focusing on perceptions and emotion-focused coping (e.g., looking for a silver lining) can actually facilitate action-oriented coping. This has been shown to be the case because emotion-focused coping gives a period of rest so that one can remobilize resources and may prevent a self-defeating action approach for insoluble problems. At a later phase of the same stressor sequence, an action orientation may be more successful. Both Gentry and Kobasa (1984) and Scheier et al. (1986) support this contention. There is no right or wrong way to cope, only ways that have better or poorer fit to individual and situational constraints and tendencies. However, there is increasing evidence that possessing the ability to flexibly switch from emotion-focused to action-focused modes, as the situation demands, is important in stress resistance (Wheaton, 1983). Individuals must learn to focus on solutions, while realizing that sometimes actions will distance them from solutions. Moreover, some solutions may need to be internal (e.g., resolving grief), and emotion-focused coping may be the only beneficial approach.

Another important area for intervention regarding perception is revealed by research on what has been called "self-handicapping" (Baumgardner, Lake, & Arkin, 1984; Jones & Berglas, 1978; Pyszczynski & Greenberg, 1983; Smith, Snyder, & Perkins, 1983). Self-handicapping people justify applying less effort to a problem because of some handicap, in order that their failure not be attributed to lack of ability. So, for example, interventionists can help individuals see that their alcohol abuse or adoption of the sick role are extreme strategies to hide their fear of failure should they try to confront their problems. Such efforts will also have to enhance self-confidence, and perhaps this could be done by working directly on acquisition of skills. With new skills and a modicum of self-confidence, these individuals may be more willing to take small risks without resorting to self-handicapping. These small wins could be reinforced by supportive family or friends or by group member who share the problem.

Overall, perceptions are an important area for intervention. However, it should not be forgotten that these perceptions preserve positive self-regard or ward off unacceptable interpretations of events. Thus there will be resistance to change. Nor are perceptual biases necessarily in the realm of awareness. Whether due to early conditioning and modeling or to psychodynamic defenses, they are likely to be deeply ingrained. I am suggesting in a number of these interventions that if individuals are allowed to test new strategies with little risk and if they are reinforced for their successes, they will be increasingly willing to accept the interventionist's interpretation of their behavior and its consequences.

Valence of effect

When one considers the valence of effect, it is obvious that the five dimensions of the model of ecological congruence must be enjoined to determine the complex nature of the fit between resources and threat. To help organize intervention efforts, the following model-based intervention checklist is provided.

1. What is the nature of the loss?
   a. Is environmental intervention or personal intervention called for?
   b. Is the loss one that may be re-evaluated as other than a loss?
   c. Are the individual's or group's values predisposing them to unnecessary sense of loss that may be minimized by altering values?
2. Does the intervention carry sufficient intensity and depth to counteract habit-strength and/or environmental causes of stress?
3. Will the intervention "appear" successful to the target individuals?
4. Is there a particularly stressful time when intervention may be conducted, so that individuals are experiencing the crisis when intervention takes place?
5. Is the intervention likely to cause the victims of circumstances beyond their control to feel "blamed" for their plight? Would direct environmental intervention on the part of the interventionist therefore be more suitable?
6. Resources.
   a. What are the natural resources (internal and external) at the individual's command and which among these may be reinforced?
   b. What resources (lacking or weak) are particularly congruent with the type of loss experienced or anticipated?
   c. Does the resource enhancement strategy consider the full development and maintenance of the resources?
   d. Are there constellations of resources involved?

    e. Are there aspects of the person's self, values, or circumstances, or characteristics of the group that may lead to resistance to the type of intervention effort or the resulting resources?

    f. Is the intervention best suited at the individual, dyadic, group, or systems level?

7. Time.

    a. How does the event-resource interaction affect the individuals when developmental status is considered?

    b. What are the stages vis-à-vis the event that need to be considered; how does resource-demand fit evolve in the particular circumstances or milieu?

8. Strain.

    a. Do the target individuals have a "weak-link" that provides a key to the direction of intervention?

    b. Are the situational demands likely to lead to a particular strain?

    c. Do the individual's weaknesses, in interaction with situational demands, lead to a particularly likely strain?

    d. May this strain be used in its early manifestations as an indicator for risk so that prevention efforts can be mobilized?

9. Values.

    a. what are the individual and cultural values that may impact the change or adoption of new stress resistance strategies? Will these, in fact, lead to greater stress?

    b. Are there notable sex or ethnic differences that need to be considered? What about values that change over the life span?

10. Perception

    a. May the emphasis on perception overshadow the objective nature of the stressor or the resources?

    b. May perceptions be highlighted without affronting the target individual's "belief" in the reality of the situation, i.e., will intervention be seen as minimizing plights or belittling viewpoints?

    c. May emotion-focused coping be used to enhance later action-focused coping (e.g., allowing time-out to rest or design new stress resistance approaches, choosing a more advantageous "battlefield" on which stress may be challenged).

    d. Is emotion-focused coping the ideal strategy to overcome the particular loss involved?

11. Valence of effect. When resources, needs/demands, strains, time, values, and perceptions are considered together, do particularly likely interactions emerge and might these affect the outcome of intervention in a meaningful fashion? May this be most efficiently

considered by comparing a finite number of reasonable interventions?

Those considering stress interventions will need to face the complexity of the problems they are trying to solve, problems that are tied with deeply ingrained personality traits and styles of behavior and that are set in environments that are not particularly malleable. One can avoid the issue of values, the environmental context, or the evolving nature of the person-event interaction, for example, but this will only restrict the populations with whom stress interventions can be applied. The limitations that have been shown to constrain individual therapy should be a lesson (Lorion, 1973). By paying heed to the ecological nature of stress, we can develop models that are not limited to young, educated, verbal, attractive, and white individuals (as are many individual psychotherapy models) that are blueprints for change in the widest variety of cases and situations.

I would further suggest that an in-depth consideration of this checklist invites the realization that a successful intervention program should be planned with the aid of allied professionals (sociologists, anthropologists, physicians, nurses), clergy, and key informants (lay experts). The particular consultants would depend on the target of intervention and on the familiarity of the primary interventionist with the relevant social milieu. In fact, the stress literature itself is one of the few research areas in which physicians, nurses, psychologists, psychiatrists, social workers, sociologists, anthropologists, educators, and organizational behaviorists have shown common interest. Interventionists need to become acquainted with work outside of their own narrow disciplines. The more we share one another's knowledge and special expertise, the more likely we are to meet the complex challenge of counteracting stress.

SUMMARY AND CONCLUSIONS

In this chapter the model of conservation of resources and the model of ecological congruence were developed toward what was termed an ecological loss theory of personality. The models and the resultant personality theory were applied to a blueprint for interventions designed to aid stress resistance. Where possible, empirical evidence drawn from our own research or the work of others was cited to support the admittedly speculative propositions developed in the current chapter. I have purposely attempted here to be bold, but in each case to present ideas that are eminently testable.

Calling on the thinking of Popper (1959), this endeavor offers a theory, models, and hypotheses that are all open to being shown false and that may be seen as alternatives to many of the current modes of thinking about stress. As Kuhn's (1962) arguments suggest, I have also attempted to expose the "theory ladenness of facts" that follows from contemporary conceptualizations of stress dominated by an overwhelmingly cognitive perspective. In addition, I have strived to offer, if not a completely different paradigm, then an alternative approach for analyzing the nature of stress and stress resistance.

Ecological Loss Theory of Personality

It was proposed that people are born with biological and social needs that are not consistently met. This results in the development of a fear of loss that is basic to personality. To offset this loss, the infant, child, and adult develop resource conservation strategies to minimize resource loss and maximize resource gain. When stress researchers have considered particular situations, they have used a snapshot approach to understanding these resource conservation strategies. When we look at people, however, we can see that they naturally develop styles of resource conservation that they rely on in a variety of situations. The styles may vary in their flexibility, but they are always finite. These strategies are reinforced if they meet individuals' complex needs, and thus they become incorporated in the individual's personality.

It was further postulated that when individuals' own inadequate efforts or the environment press them toward resource loss, they become involved in a conflict cycle in which their primary concern is avoiding loss. Contrariwise, it was held that when individuals can generally meet their needs they become secondarily motivated toward meeting their desires. Even in this fulfillment cycle, however, fear of loss plays a principal role, since many of the desires are designed to prevent future loss of resources. An example of this is wishing to be popular with everyone, a desire that is motivated out of the fear of being unloved. The healthier approach would be to concentrate on a few intimate bonds; even this, however, is partially motivated by the fear of being alone.

Consistent with the thinking of Maslow and Rogers I also postulated that a few individuals rise above this deficiency motivation. They substitute fear of loss for others in place of their own fears of loss, it was argued. Such individuals as Mahatma Gandhi and Mother Theresa are examples of those with deep empathy for the loss of others. Few individuals were seen as reaching this plane, although many individuals occasionally reach this level of functioning. Many parents, for example, become truly concerned for their children's welfare, over and above any thought of their own gain. Particular acts of kindness are also examples.

The chapter went on to consider whether biological loss or psychological loss is the dominant sphere of influence. This relative dominance was seen as dependent on the particular kinds of losses individuals encounter. The predominant sphere of compensation, aimed at counteracting the loss, can be seen on one hand as developmentally set by early or prolonged life events. On the other hand, the sphere of influence may change rapidly, for example when disaster or illness strikes.

Next, the ecological loss theory of personality led to a number of personality types. Learned helplessness, for instance, was depicted as following from the conflict cycle in cases where individuals' efforts failed to have a pervasive effect on consequences. The conflict cycle was also seen as potentially fostering a much more active compensatory style, characterized by inappropriate, self-defeating, or hostile attempts to correct for losses. Such a style might follow when attempts to counteract loss are occasionally successful but the general trend of events is pressing the individual toward loss or threat of loss.

Whereas the conflict cycle may lead to an active or passive personality type, the fulfillment cycle was envisaged as necessarily leading to an active posture. Two basic personality types followed from primary involvement in the fulfillment cycle. The first of these is a mastery type, which is characterized by an action orientation and a belief that one's own behavior is likely to lead to success or, at least, to the best possible outcome. The second personality style is an active religious stance. This does not necessarily imply religion in the clerical sense; it may also include a firm belief in a fair or just world that is likely to react favorably to one's actions.

It was suggested that the direction individuals take in life is also influenced by the areas of life in which they feel they can maximize resource gains and those in which they feel they are most likely to experience resource loss. Consistent with learning principles, people tend to construct their world in order to be exposed and directed toward the favorable areas and will avoid the others.

An additional corollary to the ecological loss theory of personality was suggested. Specifically, it was argued that culture and chance may both confront individuals with apparent cause and effect relationships between their strategy and outcome, when in actuality the resource outcome is a product of the culture or happenstance. Because individuals attribute the effect to their own actions or thoughts, they are likely to incorporate aspects of their personality or styles of approaching circumstances that are, in fact, unrelated to resource loss or gain. These will be reinforced, however, because their cultural or chance association is likely to be repeated sporadically.

A number of principles regarding the shaping of personality were seen as following from the model of ecological congruence.

1. Personality is dynamic and changes throughout the life span
2. Personality develops as a function of the special crises characteristic of the different stages of development throughout the life span and of crises unrelated to the normal course of development
3. People develop resource strategies that are consistent with their world view
4. Personality will develop such that the traits and strategies designed to offset resource loss and to enhance resource gain are consistent or complementary
5. Traits and strategies may also be limited by, interact with, and be predetermined by biological dispositions.

Intervention Principles

The model of conservation of resources, the model of ecological congruence, and the ecological loss theory of personality were next integrated to suggest interventions for aiding stress resistance. The primary thesis derived from the ecological loss theory of personality is that natural resource strategies and personality traits are deeply ingrained and resistant to change. Within the constraints of this important caveat, a number of principles followed from the two models.

First, it was suggested that interventions should help people to confront or prevent the loss of resources and enhance the potential for resource gain. This is possible by assisting in direct efforts to change the environment, by encouraging reevaluation of the nature of potential or past losses and gains, or by affecting individuals' underlying evaluation of resources and gains. Second, it follows from the model of conservation of losses that any effort to make these changes will need to be sustained and have sufficient depth. Third, any new strategy for conserving resources must prove effective to the individuals involved. Here it was highlighted that resource strategies often have secondary effects, for example, when passivity may ensure security even though it is self-defeating in many other respects.

Despite the fact that natural stress resistance approaches are deeply ingrained, during crises people may be particularly amenable to interventions designed to change their approach and the underlying personality traits. This followed from thinking that during crises and some transitions, individuals find their own strategies inadequate and have ample opportunity to test a new style or approach. This, in turn, allows interventionists the opportunity to provide reinforcement and to help individuals tailor new ways of thinking or behaving to their particular needs.

A final principle that follows from the model of conservation of resources is that for many people the environment dictates their losses. For the poor, the underprivileged ethnic minorities, the handicapped, and any disempowered group, person-focused interventions may be a way of blaming the victim. Many stressor situations can only be remediated through the interventionist's direct action on the individual's or group's behalf. Such interventions may at times be political or societal, since this is the level on which much of stress operates.

The model of ecological congruence was seen to fine tune the general principles that follow from the model of conservation of resources. In so doing, it guides interventionists with more specific recommendations for enhancing stress resistance.

The resource dimension of the model highlighted a number of resources on which research has focused. Two classes of resources about whose development we know more are related to mastery and social support. Specific examples of how intervention efforts could maximize the positive applications of these resources were discussed. It was shown that research on natural uses of these may guide interventionists to those areas of the self, behavior, and social interaction that are critical for avoiding resource loss and to areas likely to lead to maximizing meaningful gain. In particular, suggestions for social support intervention were made, because this has been the most productive area of stress resistance research to date.

Next, the time dimension of the model of ecological congruence was applied to thinking about intervention. Here it was noted that people undergo special stressors and have particular resources depending on their developmental stage. For stress interventions to be successful, more attention should be directed to the changing needs and demands that come at different times in people's lives, owing to environmental and internal factors. Development should also affect whether efforts be directed at the individual, the dyad, or the larger group, because at different times during the life span these different social levels are the more naturally approachable target.

Time was also considered in terms of the stressful event or circumstances. Because the demands and needs exerted on individuals change from the time of anticipating a stressor event, during event sequences, and following exposure to stressors, interventions should also be tailored to meet this evolving process. Here it was also emphasized that an approach that anticipates people's reactions but that also meets their inevitable idiosyncratic variations will be most successful. Moreover, what is helpful at one stage may be detrimental if applied when individuals are experiencing different kinds of demands or have themselves changed from their exposure with stress.

The model of ecological congruence also highlighted that environmental pressures and individuals' weaknesses tend to produce characteristic strains. These strains may be pinpointed as "red flags" for early intervention, before more serious reactions evolve, to the extent that we gain knowledge regarding the natural course of the disease or psychological reaction. Individuals or situations may be identified as high risk so that preventive efforts can be used.

The interrelated value and perception dimensions of the model of ecological congruence were discussed next. Successful efforts at changing natural systems must take into account individuals' values and their personal perceptions of the problem. However, it was argued that this idiosyncratic approach be tempered by an understanding that people share many values and perceptions because they live in societies that uphold common value systems. Also, objective factors play a major role in determining perceptions. Discussion followed on how commonly held values and perceptions may be capitalized on for directing research.

The full model of ecological congruence was then integrated in a discussion cf the interactive valence of effect. Researchers and interventionists were encouraged to consider the entire ecology in designing ways to aid people's natural stress resistance tendencies. These interactions are necessarily complex, but if attention is not directed to the ecological level interventions might be limited and quite possibly detrimental.

Present and Future

At the current time there is a special need to integrate practical intervention efforts with research. It will be important to attempt model programs that have a sound research base including a longitudinal design and appropriate control and comparison groups. If such efforts are successful, we will learn much more about the active components of stress, since applying interventions will tease out causal trends more easily than would be possible when one studies events as they naturally occur. An added dividend will be that such research will reveal many insights into personality and how the self absorbs and counteracts the daily challenges and all-too-frequent major stressors that confront it.

People live in a complex and oftentimes stressful world. Indeed much of philosophy, literature, religion, and everyday talk is about how stress is confronted and how it causes pain and anguish. Yet, even when exposed to the most stressful of circumstances, the human spirit usually predominates. This volume pays tribute to this spark of life and to the fact that it exists within a complex ecology. Hopefully, some of the ideas generated in this book will aid the inevitable human effort involved in stress resistance. As researchers we can never be fully satisfied with the applicability of the findings of our imperfect science. Nevertheless, I firmly believe that the explosion of research on stress and stress resistance can be applied with increasing sophistication and confidence, while at the same time we strive always to improve our efforts.

REFERENCES

Abramson, L. Y., & Martin, D. J. (1981). Depression and the causal inference process. In J. H. Harvey, W. Ickes, & R. E. Kidd (Eds.), *New directions in attribution research* (Vol. 3, pp. 117–168). Hillsdale, NJ: Lawrence Erlbaum.

Abramson, L., Seligman, M. E. P., & Teasdale, J. P. (1978). Learned helplessness in humans: Critique and reformulation. *Journal of Abnormal Psychology, 87* 49–74.

Ackerman, N. W. (1958). *The psychodynamics of family life.* New York: Basic Books.

Adler, A. (1929). *Problems of neurosis: A book of case histories.* London: Kegan Paul, Trench, Truebner & Co.

Adler, A. (1956). *The individual psychology of Alfred Adler.* New Jersey: Basic Books.

Adorno, T. W., Frenkel-Brunswik, E., Levinson, D. J., & Sanford, R. N. (1950). *The authoritarian character.* New York: Harper.

Ainsworth, M. D. S., Blehar, M. C., Waters, E., & Wall, S. (1978). *Patterns of attachment.* New Jersey: Lawrence Erlbaum.

American Psychiatric Association (1987). *Diagnostic and statistical manual of mental disorders* (3rd ed., revised). Washington, DC: Author.

Andrews, G., Tennant, C., Hewson, D. M., & Schonell, M. (1978). The relation of social factors to physical and psychiatric illness. *American Journal of Epidemiology, 108,* 27–35.

Andrews, G., Tennant, C., Hewson, D. M., & Vaillant, G. E. (1978). Life event stress, social support, coping style and risk of psychological impairment. *The Journal of Nervous and Mental Disease, 166,* 307–316.

Aneshensel, C. S. (1986). Marital and employment role-strain, social support and depression among adult women. In S. Hobfoll (Ed.), *Stress, social support, and women* (pp. 99–112). Washington, DC: Hemisphere.

Aneshensel, C. S., & Frerichs, R. R. (1982). Stress, support, and depression: A longitudinal causal model. *Journal of Community Psychology, 10,* 363–376.

Antonovsky, A. (1979). *Health, stress, and coping.* San Francisco: Jossey-Bass.

Argyle, M. (1983). *The psychology of interpersonal behavior* (4th ed.). Harmondsworth, Great Britain: Penguin Books.

Argyle, M. & Henderson, M. (1985). The rules of relationships. In S. Duck & D. Perlman (Eds.), *Understanding personal relationships: An interdisciplinary approach* (pp. 63–84). Beverly Hills, CA: Sage.

Attkisson, C., & Broskowski, A. (1978). Evaluation and the emerging human services concept. In C. Attkisson, W. A. Hargreaves, M. J. Horowitz, & J. E. Sorenson (Eds.), *Evaluation and the emerging human service concept* (pp. 3–26). New York: Academic.

Auerbach, S. M. (1976). Trait-state anxiety and adjustment to surgery. *Journal of Consulting and Clinical Psychology, 44,* 809–818.

Bandura, A. (1964). The stormy decade: Fact or fiction? *Psychology in the Schools, 1,* 224–231.

Bandura, A. (1977). *Social learning theory.* Englewood Cliffs, NJ: Prentice-Hall.

Bandura, A., Ross, D., & Ross, S. (1961). Transmission of aggression through imitation of aggressive models. *Journal of Abnormal and Social Psychology, 63,* 572–582.

Bandura, E. A., Walters, R. H. (1959). *Adolescent aggression: A study of the influence of child-training practices and family interrelationships.* New York: Ronald Press.

Bankoff, E. A. (1986). Peer support for widows: Personal and structural characteristics related to its provision. In S. Hobfoll (Ed.), *Stress, social support, and women* (pp. 207–220). Washington, DC: Hemisphere.

Barrera, M., Jr. (1986). Distinctions between social support concepts, measures, and models. *American Journal of Community Psychology, 14,* 413–445.

Barrera, M., Jr., Sandler, I. N., & Ramsey, T. B. (1981). Preliminary development of a scale of social support: Studies on college students. *American Journal of Community Psychology, 9,* 435–447.

Basowitz, H., Persky, H., Korchin, S. J., & Grinker, R. R. (1955). *Anxiety and stress.* New York: McGraw-Hill.

Bateson, G., Jackson, D. D., Haley, J., & Weakland, J. (1956). Toward a theory of schizophrenia. *Behavioral Science, 1,* 251–264.

Baumgardner, A. H., Lake, E. A., & Arkin, R. M. (1984). *Claiming depression as a self-handicap.* Unpublished manuscript, University of Missouri, Columbia.

Benor, D. E., Hobfoll, S. E., & Prywes, M. (in press). Community-oriented medical education. In M. Lipkin, J. Greep, H. G. Schmidt, & M. DeVries (Eds.), *Education for tomorrow's medicine today.* New York: Springer-Verlag.

Beres, D. (1961). Character formation. In S. Lorand & H. I. Schneer (Eds.), *Adolescents: Psychoanalytic approach to problems and therapy.* New York: Hoeber.

Berkman, L. G., & Syme, S. L. (1979). Social networks, host resistance and mortality: A nine-year follow-up of Alameda County residents. *American Journal of Epidemiology, 109,* 186–204.

Bernard, J. (1971). *Women and the public interest: An essay on policy and protest.* Chicago: Aldine.

Bettelheim, B. (1960). *The informed heart.* Free Press.

Billings, A. G., & Moos, R. H. (1981). The role of coping responses and social resources in attenuating the stress of life events. *Journal of Behavioral Medicine, 4,* 2, 139–157.

Billings, A. G., & Moos, R. H. (1982). Stressful life events and symptoms: A longitudinal model. *Health Psychology, 1,* 99–118.

Billings, A. G., & Moos, R. H. (1984). Coping, stress, and social resources among adults with unipolar depression. *Journal of Personality and Social Psychology, 46,* 877–891.

Blau, P. M. (1964). *Exchange and power in social life.* New York: Wiley.

Bloom, B. L., Hodges, W. F., & Caldwell, R. A. (1982). A preventive intervention program for the newly separated: Initial evaluation. *American Journal of Community Psychology, 10,* 251–264.

Bowlby, J. (1969). *Attachment and loss (Vol. 1): Attachment.* London: Hogarth Press.

Bowlby, J. (1973). *Attachment and loss (Vol. 2): Separation and anger.* New York: Basic Books.

Bowlby, J. (1980). *Attachment and loss (Vol. 3): Loss.* New York: Basic Books.

Breznitz, S. (1967). Incubation of threat: Duration of anticipation and false alarm as determinants of the fear reaction to an unavoidable frightening event. *Journal of Experimental Research in Personality, 2,* 173–179.

Breznitz, S. (1983a). The noble challenge of stress. In S. Breznitz (Ed.), *Stress in Israel* (pp. 265–274). New York: Van Nostrand Reinhold.

Breznitz, S. (1983b). Anticipatory stress reactions. In S. Breznitz (Ed.), *The denial of stress* (pp. 225–255). New York: International Universities Press.

Breznitz, S. (1983c). The seven kinds of denial. In S. Breznitz (Ed.), *The denial of stress* (pp. 257–280). New York: International Universities Press.

Breznitz, S., & Eshel, Y. (1983). Life events: Stressful ordeal or valuable experience. In S. Breznitz (Ed.), *Stress in Israel.* New York: Van Nostrand Reinhold.

Brown, G. W. (1974). Meaning, measurement, and stressful life events. In B. S. & B. P. Dohrenwend (Eds.), *Stressful life events: Their nature and effects* (pp. 217–243). New York: Wiley.

Brown, G. W., Bhrolchrain, M., & Harris, T. (1975). Social class and psychiatric disturbances among women in an urban population. *Sociology, 9,* 225–254.

Brown, G. W., & Harris, T. (1978). *The social origins of depression: The study of psychiatric disorder in women.* New York: Free Press.

Bulman, R. J., & Wortman, C. B. (1977). Attributions of blame and coping in the "real world": Severe accident victims react to their lot. *Journal of Personality and Social Psychology, 35,* 351–363.

Burda, P. C., Jr., Vaux, A., & Schill, T. (1984). Social support resources: Variation across sex and sex role. *Personality and Social Psychology Bulletin, 10,* 119–126.

Burgess, A. W., & Holstrom, L. L. (1979). *Rape, crisis and recovery.* Bowie, MD: Bradie.

Burke, D. J., & Weir, T. (1978). Sex differences in adolescent life stress, social support, and well-being. *Journal of Psychology, 98,* 277–288.

Cannon, W. B. (1932). *The wisdom of the body.* New York: Norton (2nd ed., 1939).

Caplan, G. (1964). *Principles of preventive psychiatry.* New York: Basic Books.

Caplan, G. (1974). *Support systems and community mental health: Lectures on concept development.* New York: Behavioral Publications.

Caplan, R. D. (1983). Person-environment fit: Past, present, and future. In C. L. Cooper (Ed.), *Stress research* (pp. 35–77). New York: Wiley.

Caplan, R. D., Tripathi, R. C., & Naidu, R. K. (1985). Subjective past, present, and future fit: Effects on anxiety, depression, and other indicators of well-being. *Journal of Personality and Social Psychology, 48,* 180–197.

Carver, C. S., & Scheirer, M. F. (1983). A control theory model of normal behavior and implications for problems in self-management. In P. C. Kendall (Ed.), *Advances in cognitive behavioral research and therapy* (Vol. 2, pp. 127–194). New York: Academic.

Chapman, N. J., & Pancoast, D. L. (1985). Working with the informal helping networks of the elderly: The experiences of three programs. *Journal of Social Issues, 41,* 47–64.

Chesney, A. P., Gentry, W. D., Gary, H. E., Kennedy, C., & Harburg, E. (1984). *Anger-coping style as a mediator in the relationship between life strain and blood pressure.* Unpublished manuscript.

Chiriboga, D. A. (1977). Life event weighting systems: A comparative analysis. *Journal of Psychosomatic Research, 21,* 415–422.

Clark, M. S. (1983). Reactions to aid in communal and exchange relationships. In J. D. Fisher, A. Nadler, & B. M. DePaulo (Eds.), *New directions in helping* (Vol. 1, pp. 281–304). New York: Academic.

Cobb, S. (1976). Social support as a moderator of life stress. *Psychosomatic Medicine, 3,* 300–314.

Cohen, F., & Lazarus, R. S. (1973). Active coping processes, coping dispositions, and recovery from surgery. *Psychosomatic Medicine, 35,* 375–389.

Cohen, F., & Lazarus, R. S. (1979). Coping with the stresses of illness. In G. S. Stone, F. Cohen, & N. E. Adler (Eds.), *Health psychology* (pp. 217–254). San Francisco: Jossey-Bass.

Cohen, J. B., Syme, S. L., Jenkins, C. D., Kagan, A., & Syzanski, S. J. (1979). Cultural context of Type A behavior and risk CHD: A study of Japanese-American males. *Journal of Behavioral Medicine, 106,* 375–384.

Cohen, L. H., McGowan, J., Fooskas, S., & Rose, S. (1984). Positive life events and social support and the relationship between life stress and psychological disorder. *American Journal of Community Psychology, 12,* 567–587.

Cohen, S. (1980). Aftereffects of stress on human performance and social behavior: A review of research and theory. *Psychological Bulletin, 88,* 82–108.

Cohen, S., & Edwards, J. R. (in press). Personality characteristics as moderators of the relationship between stress and disorder. In R. W. J. Neufeld (Ed.), *Advances in the investigation of psychological stress.* New York: Wiley.

Cohen, S., & Hoberman, H. M. (1983). Positive events and social supports as buffers of life change stress. *Journal of Applied Social Psychology, 13,* 99–125.

Cohen, S., Kamarck, T., & Mermelstein, R. (1983). A global measure of perceived stress. *Journal of Health and Social Behavior, 24,* 385–396.

Cohen, S., & McKay, G. (1984). Interpersonal relationships as buffers of the impact of psychological stress on health. In A. Baum, J. E. Singer, and S. E. Taylor (Eds.), *Handbook of psychology and health* (Vol. 4, pp. 253–267). Hillsdale, NJ: Lawrence Erlbaum.

Cohen, S., Sherrod, D. R., & Clark, M. S. (1986). Social skills and the stress-protective role of social support. *Journal of Personality and Social Psychology, 50,* 963–973.

Cohen, S., & Syme, S. L. (1985). Issues in the study and application of social support. In S. Cohen & S. L. Syme (Eds.), *Social support and health* (pp. 3–207). New York: Academic.

Cohen, S., & Wills, T. A. (1985). Stress, social support, and the buffering hypothesis. *Psychological Bulletin, 98,* 310–357.

Cooke, D. J. (1981). Life events and syndromes of depression in the general population. *Social Psychiatry, 16,* 181–186.

Cooke, D. J., & Green, J. G. (1981). Types of life events in relation to symptoms at the climacterium. *Journal of Psychosomatic Research, 25,* 5–11.

Cowen, E. L., Dorr, D. A., Trost, M. A., & Izzo, L. D. (1972). Follow-up study of maladapting school children seen by nonprofessionals. *Journal of Consulting and Clinical Psychology, 39,* 235–238.

Coyne, J. C. (1976). Toward an interactional description of depression. *Psychiatry, 39,* 28–40.

Coyne, J. C., Aldwin, C., & Lazarus, R. S. (1981). Depression and coping in stressful episodes. *Journal of Abnormal Psychology, 90,* 439–447.

Crandall, J. E. (1984). Social interest as a moderator of life stress. *Journal of Personality and Social Psychology, 47,* 164–174.

Cronkite, R. C., & Moos, R. H. (1984). The role of predisposing and moderating factors in the stress-illness relationship. *Journal of Health and Social Behavior, 25,* 372–393.

Croog, S. H., Shapiro, D. S., & Levine, S. (1971). Denial among male heart patients: An empirical study. *Psychosomatic Medicine, 33,* 385–397.

Crozier, M. (1964). *The bureaucratic phenomenon.* Chicago: The University of Chicago Press.

Cutrona, C. E. (1986). Behavioral manifestations of social support: A microanalysis investigation. *Journal of Personality and Social Psychology, 51,* 201–208.

Datan, N. (1975). *Life-span developmental psychology.* New York: Academic.

Datan, N., & Ginsberg, L. H. (1975). *Normative life crisis.* New York: Academic.

Davidson, L. M., & Baum, A. (1986). Chronic stress and posttraumatic stress disorder. *Journal of Consulting and Clinical Psychology, 54,* 303–308.

Dean, A., & Lin, N. (1977). The stress-buffering role of social support: Problems and prospects for systematic investigation. *Journal of Nervous and Mental Disease, 165,* 403–417.

DeLongis, A., Coyne, J. C., Dakof, G., Folkman, S., & Lazarus, R. S. (1982). Relationships of daily hassles, uplifts, and major life events to health status. *Health Psychology, 1,* 119–136.

Diener, E., Larsen, R. J., Levine, S., & Emmons, R. A. (1985). Intensity and frequency: Dimensions underlying positive and negative affect. *Journal of Personality and Social Psychology, 48,* 1253–1265.

DiMatteo (Ed.), *Interpersonal issues in health care* (pp. 69–100). New York: Academic.

Dohrenwend, B. S., & Dohrenwend, B. P. (Eds.) (1974). *Stressful life events: Their nature and effects.* New York: Wiley.

Dohrenwend, B. S., & Dohrenwend, B. P. (1981). Socioenvironmental factors, stress, and psychopathology. *American Journal of Community Psychology, 9,* 128–159.

Dohrenwend, B. S., Dohrenwend, B. P., Dodson, M., & Shrout, P. E. (1984). Symptoms, hassles, social support, and life events: Problem of confounded measures. *Journal of Abnormal Psychology, 93,* 222–230.

Dohrenwend, B. S., & Martin, J. L. (1979). Personal versus situational determination of anticipation and control of the occurrence of stressful events. *American Journal of Community Psychology, 7,* 453–468.

Doyle, J. A. (1983). *The male experience.* Dubuque: Wm. C. Brown Company.

Dressler, W. W. (1985). Extended family relationships, social support and mental health in a southern black community. *Journal of Health and Social Behavior, 26,* 39–48.

Duck, S., & Perlman, D. (1985). The thousand islands of personal relationships: A prescriptive analysis for future explorations. In S. Duck & D. Perlman (Eds.), *Understanding personal relationships: An interdisciplinary approach* (pp. 1–15). Beverly Hills, CA: Sage.

Dunkel-Schetter, C., Folkman, S., & Lazarus, R. S. (1987). Social support received in stressful situations. *Journal of Personality and Social Psychology, 53,* 71–80.

Dunkel-Schetter, C., & Wortman, C. B. (1982). The interpersonal dynamics of cancer: Problems in social relationships and their impact on the patient. In H. S. Friedman & M. R. DiMatteo (Eds.), *Interpersonal issues in health care* (pp. 69–100). New York: Academic Press.

Durlak, J. A. (1979). Comparative effectiveness of paraprofessional and professional helpers. *Psychological Bulletin, 86,* 80–92.

Eaton, W. W. (1978). Life event, social support and psychiatric symptoms: A re-analysis of the New Haven data. *Journal of Health and Social Behavior, 19,* 230–234.

Eckenrode, J. (1983). The mobilization of social supports: Some individual constraints. *American Journal of Community Psychology, 11,* 509–528.

Erikson, E. (1963). *Childhood and society*. New York: Norton.

Erikson, E. H. (1968). *Identity: Youth and crisis*. New York: Norton.

Erikson, S. A. (1984). *Human presence: At the boundaries of meaning*. Macon, GA: Mercer University Press.

Eysenck, H. J. (1952). The effects of psychotherapy: An evaluation. *Journal of Consulting Psychology, 16,* 319–324.

Eysenck, H. J. (1957). *The dynamics of anxiety and hysteria*. London: Routledge and Kegan Paul.

Eysenck, H. J. (1961). *Handbook of abnormal psychology*. New York: Basic Books.

Fanshel, S. (1972). A meaningful measure of health for epidemiology. *International Journal of Epidemiology, 1,* 319–337.

Fausteau, M. F. (1974). *The male machine*. New York: McGraw-Hill.

Felner, R. D. (1985). Vulnerability in childhood: A preventive framework for understanding children's efforts to cope with life stress and transitions. In M. C. Roberts and L. Peterson (Eds.), *Prevention of problems in childhood: Psychological research and applications* (pp. 11–56). New York: Wiley-Interscience.

Felner, R. D., Farber, S. S., & Primavera, J. (1983). Transitions and stressful life events: A model for primary prevention. In R. D. Felner, L. A. Jason, J. N. Moritsugu, & S. S. Farber (Eds.), *Preventive psychology: Theory, research and practice* (pp. 199–215). New York: Plenum.

Feuerstein, M., Labbe, E. E., & Kuczmierczyk, A. R. (1986). *Health psychology: A psychobiological perspective*. New York: Plenum.

Figley, C. R. (Ed.) (1978). *Stress disorders among Vietnam veterans: Theory, research and treatment*. New York: Brunner/Mazel.

Figley, C. R., & Leventman, S. (Eds.) (1980). *Strangers at home: Vietnam veterans since the war*. New York: Praeger.

Fisher, J. D., Nadler, A., & Whitcher-Alagna, S. (1982). Recipients' reactions to aid. *Psychological Bulletin, 91,* 27–54.

Fiske, D. W., & Maddi, S. R. (1961). A conceptual framework. In D. W. Fiske and S. R. Maddi (Eds.), *Functions of varied experience* (pp. 11–56). Homewood, IL: Dorsey.

Fleming, R., Baum, A., Gisrel, M., & Gatchel, R. (1982). Mediating influences of social support on stress at Three Mile Island. *Journal of Human Stress, 8,* 14–22.

Folkman, S., & Lazarus, R. S. (1985). If it changes it must be a process: Study of emotion and coping during three stages of a college examination. *Journal of Personality and Social Psychology, 48,* 150–170.

Folkman, S., & Lazarus, R. S. (1986). Stress processes and depressive symptomology. *Journal of Abnormal Psychology, 95,* 107–113.

Folkman, S., Lazarus, R. S., Dunkel-Schetter, C., DeLongis, A., & Gruen, R. J. (1985). Dynamics of a stressful encounter: Cognitive appraisal, coping, and encounter outcomes. *Journal of Personality and Social Psychology, 50,* 992–1003.

Folkow, B., & Neil, E. (1971). *Circulation*. New York: Oxford University Press.

Frankl, V. E. (1963). *Man's search for meaning*. Boston: Beacon.

French, J. R. P., Jr., Caplan, R. D., & Harrison, R. V. (1982). *The mechanisms of job stress and strain.* London: Wiley.

French, J. R. P., Rodgers, W. L., & Cobb, S. (1974). Adjustment as person-environment fit. In G. V. Coelho, D. A. Hamburg, & J. E. Adams (Eds.). *Coping and adaptation* (pp. 316–333). New York: Basic Books.

Freud, A. (1958). Adolescence. *Psychoanalytic Study of the Child, 13,* 255–278.

Freud, S. (1905). Three essays on the theory of sexuality. *Standard Edition, 7,* 135–243. London: Hogarth Press.

Freud, S. (1916–17). Introductory lectures on psychoanalysis, *Standard Edition, 15–16.* London: Hogarth Press.

Freud, S. (1920). Beyond the pleasure principle. *Standard Edition, 18.* London: Hogarth Press.

Freud, S. (1926). Inhibitions, symptoms, and anxiety. *Standard Edition, 20.* London: Hogarth Press.

Freud, S. (1931). *The interpretation of dreams.* New York: Carlton House.

Friedman, M., & Rosenman, R. H. (1959). Association of specific overt behavior pattern with increases in blood cholesterol, blood clotting time, incidence of arcus senilis and clinical coronary artery disease. *Journal of the American Medical Association, 169,* 1286–1296.

Ganellen, R. J., & Blaney, R. H. (1974). *Type A behavior and your heart.* New York: Knopf.

Gaudry, E. (1971). *Anxiety and educational achievement.* New York: Wiley.

Gentry, W. D., Foster, S., & Haney, T. (1972). Denial as a determinant of an anxiety and perceived health status in the coronary care unit. *Psychosomatic Medicine, 33,* 39–44.

Gentry, W. D., & Ouellette Kobasa, S. C. (1984). Social and psychological resources mediating stress-illness relationships in humans. In W. D. Gentry (Ed.), *Handbook of behavioral medicine* (pp. 87–116). New York: Guilford Press.

Glass, R. C. (1977). *Behavior patterns, stress, and coronary disease.* Hillsdale, NJ: Lawrence Erlbaum.

Glidewell, J. C., Tucker, S., Todt, M., & Cox, S. (1982). Professional support systems: The teaching profession. In A. Nadler, J. P. Fisher, & B. M. DePaulo (Eds.), *Applied research in help-seeking and reactions to aid* (pp. 189–212). New York: Academic.

Goffman, E. (1959). *The presentation of self in everyday life.* New York: Doubleday.

Goodhart, D. E. (1985). Some psychological effects associated with positive and negative thinking about stressful events: Was Pollyanna right? *Journal of Personality and Social Psychology, 48,* 216–232.

Goplerud, E., & Depue, R. A. (1985). Behavioral response to naturally occurring stress in cyclothymia and dysthymia. *Journal of Abnormal Psychology, 94,* 128–139.

Gore, S. (1985). Social support and styles of coping with stress. In S. Cohen & S. L. Syme (Eds.), *Social support and health* (pp. 263–278). New York: Academic.

Gotlib, I. H., & Hooley, J. M. (in press). Depression and marital distress. In S. Duck, D. F. Hay, S. E. Hobfoll, B. Ickes, & B. Montgomery (Eds.), *The handbook of research in personal relationships*. London, New York: Wiley.

Gotlib, I. H., & Robinson, L. A. (1982). Responses to depressed individuals: Discrepancies between self-report and observer-related behavior. *Journal of Abnormal Psychology, 91,* 231–240.

Gottlieb, B. (in press). Support interventions: A typology and agenda for research. In S. Duck, D. F. Hay, S. E. Hobfoll, B. Ickes, & B. Montgomery (Eds.), *The handbook of research in personal relationships*. London, New York: Wiley.

Gottlieb, B. H. (1978). The development and application of a classification scheme of informal helping behaviours. *Canadian Journal of Behavioral Science, 10,* 105–115.

Gottlieb, B. H. (Ed.). (1981). *Social networks and social support*. Beverly Hills, CA: Sage.

Gottlieb, B. H. (1985). Social support and the study of personal relationships. *Journal of Social and Personal Relationships, 2,* 351–375.

Green, B. L. (1982). Assessing levels of psychological impairment following disaster. *Journal of Nervous and Mental Disease, 17,* 544–552.

Green, B. L., Grace, M. C., & Gleser, G. C. (1985). Identifying survivors at risk: Long-term impairment following the Beverly Hills Supper Club fire. *Journal of Consulting and Clinical Psychology, 53,* 672–678.

Grinker, R. K., & Spiegel, J. P. (1945). *Men under stress*. New York: McGraw-Hill.

Haan, N. (1969). A tripartite model of ego-functioning: Values and clinical research applications. *Journal of Nervous and Mental Disease, 148,* 14–30.

Habif, V. L., & Lahey, B. B. (1980). Assessment of the life stress-depression relationship: The use of social support as a moderator variable. *Journal of Behavioral Assessment, 2,* 167–173.

Hackett, J. P., Cassem, N. H., & Wishnie, H. A. (1968). The coronary-care unit: An appraisal of its psychological hazards. *New England Journal of Medicine, 279,* 1365–1370.

Hammen, C., Mayol, A., DeMayo, R., & Marks, T. (1986). Initial symptom levels and the life-event-depression relationship. *Journal of Abnormal Psychology, 95,* 114–122.

Hansson, R. O. (1986). Relational competence, relationships, and adjustment in old age. *Journal of Personality and Social Psychology, 50,* 1050–1058.

Hansson, R. O., Jones, W. H., & Carpenter, B. N. (1984). Relationship competence and social support. In P. Shaver (Ed.), *Review of personality and social psychology* (Vol. 5, pp. 265–284). Beverly Hills, CA: Sage.

Harlow, H. F. (1961). The development of affectional patterns in infant monkeys. In B. M. Foss (Ed.), *Determinants of infant behaviour* (Vol. 1, pp. 3–33). New York: Wiley.

Harrison, R. V. (1978). Person-environment fit and job stress. In C. L. Cooper & R. Payne (Eds.), *Stress at work* (pp. 333–355). New York: Wiley.

Henderson, S. (1981). Social relationships, adversity and neurosis: An analysis of projective observations. *British Journal of Psychiatry, 138,* 391–398.

Henderson, S., Byrne, D. G., Duncan-Jones, P., Scott, R., & Adcock, S. (1980). Social relationships, adversity and neurosis: A study of associations in a general population sample. *British Journal of Psychiatry, 136,* 574–583.

Hetherington, E. (1979). Divorce: A child's perspective. *American Psychologist, 34,* 851–858.

Hinde, R. A. (1966). *Animal behavior: A synthesis of ethology and comparative psychology.* New York: McGraw-Hill.

Hinkle, L. E., Jr. (1974). The effects of exposure to culture change, social change and changes in interpersonal relationships to health. In B. S. Dohrenwend & B. P. Dohrenwend (Eds.), *Stressful life events: Their nature and effects* (pp. 7–44). New York: Wiley.

Hirsch, B. J. (1979). Psychological dimensions of social networks: A multimethod analysis. *American Journal of Community Psychology, 7,* 263–277.

Hirsch, B. J. (1980). Natural support systems and coping with major life changes. *American Journal of Community Psychology, 8,* 159–172.

Hirsch, J. (1967). *Behavior-genetic analysis.* New York: McGraw-Hill.

Hobfoll, S. E. (1982). *Observations on the mechanics of social support.* Paper presented at the 1982 Meetings of the American Psychological Association, Washington, DC.

Hobfoll, S. E. (1985a). The limitations of social support in the stress process. In I. G. & B. R. Sarason (Eds.), *Social support: Theory, research, and application* (pp. 391–414). The Hague, The Netherlands: Martinus Nijhoff.

Hobfoll, S. E. (1985b). Personal and social resources and the ecology of stress resistance. In P. Shaver (Ed.), *Review of personality and social psychology* (Vol. 6, pp. 265–290). Beverly Hills, CA: Sage.

Hobfoll, S. E. (Ed.). (1986a). *Stress, social support, and women.* Washington, DC: Hemisphere.

Hobfoll, S. E. (1986b). The ecology of stress and social support among women. In S. E. Hobfoll (Ed.), *Stress, social support, and women* (pp. 3–14). Washington, DC: Hemisphere.

Hobfoll, S. E. (1986c). Social support: Research, theory, and applications from research on women. In S. Hobfoll (Ed.), *Stress, social support, and women* (pp. 239–254). Washington, DC: Hemisphere.

Hobfoll, S. E., Kelso, D., & Peterson, W. J. (1980). The Anchorage skid row. *Journal of Studies on Alcohol, 41,* 94–99.

Hobfoll, S. E., Kelso, D., & Peterson, W. J. (1981). Agency usage of skid row persons. *Journal of Alcohol and Drug Education, 26,* 832–838.

Hobfoll, S. E., & Leiberman, Y. (1987). Personality and social resources in immediate and continued stress resistance among women. *Journal of Personality and Social Psychology, 52,* 18–26.

Hobfoll, S. E., & Lerman, M. (1986). *Predicting receipt of social support: A longitudinal study of parent's reactions to their child's illness.* Unpublished manuscript, Tel Aviv University.

Hobfoll, S. E., & Lerman, M. (in press). Personal relationships, personal attitudes, and stress resistance: Mother's reactions to their child's illness. *American Journal of Community Psychology.*

Hobfoll, S. E., & London, P. (1986). The relationship of self concept and social support to emotional distress among women during war. *Journal of Social & Clinical Psychology, 12,* 87–100.

Hobfoll, S. E., London, P., & Orr, E. (in press). Mastery, intimacy and stress resistance during war. *Journal of Community Psychology.*

Hobfoll, S. E., Nadler, A., & Leiberman, J. (1986). Satisfaction with social support during crisis: Intimacy and self-esteem as critical determinants. *Journal of Personality and Social Psychology, 51,* 296–304.

Hobfoll, S. E., & Stokes, J. P. (in press). The process and mechanics of social support. In S. Duck, D. F. Hay, S. E. Hobfoll, B. Ickes, & B. Montgomery (Eds.), *The handbook of research in personal relationships.* London, New York: Wiley.

Hobfoll, S. E., & Walfisch, S. (1984). Coping with a threat to life: A longitudinal study of self-concept, social support, and psychological stress. *American Journal of Community Psychology, 12,* 87–100.

Hobfoll, S. E., & Walfisch, S. (1986). Stressful events, mastery, and depression: An evaluation of crisis theory. *Journal of Community Psychology, 14,* 183–195.

Hofien, D. (1986). *Social support as a learned behavior.* Doctoral proposal, Tel Aviv University.

Holahan, C. J., & Moos, R. H. (1986). Personality, coping and family resources in stress resistance. A longitudinal analysis. *Journal of Personality and Social Psychology, 51,* 389–395.

Holahan, C. J., & Moos, R. H. (1987). Risk, resistance, and psychological distress. A longitudinal analysis with adults and children. *Journal of Abnormal Psychology, 96,* 3–13.

Holahan, C. J., Wilcox, B. L., Burnam, M. A., & Culler, R. E. (1978). Social satisfaction and friendship formation as a function of floor level in high rise student housing. *Journal of Applied Psychology, 63,* 529–531.

Holmes, T. H., & Rahe, R. H. (1967). The social readjustment rating scale. *Journal of Psychosomatic Research, 11,* 213–218.

Homans, G. C. (1961). *Social behavior: Its elementary forms.* New York: Harcourt, Brace & World.

Horney, K. (1937). *The neurotic personality of our time.* New York: Norton.

Horowitz, M. J., & Solomon, G. F. (1975). Delayed stress response syndromes in Vietnam Veterans. *Journal of Social Issues, 31,* 67–80.

House, J. S. (1981). *Work stress and social support.* Reading, MA: Addison-Wesley.

Hughes, M., & Gove, W. R. (1981). Living alone, social integration and mental health. *American Journal of Sociology, 87,* 48–74.

Hulka, B. S., Cassel, J. C., Kupper, L. L., & Burdette, J. A. (1976). Communication, compliance, and concordance between physicians and patients with prescribed medications. *American Journal of Public Health, 66,* 847–853.

Husaini, B. A., Newbrough, J. R., Neff, J. A., & Moore, M. C. (1982). The stress-buffering role of social support and personal competence among the rural married. *Journal of Community Psychology, 10,* 409–426.

Isen, A. M. (1970). Success, failure, attention, and reaction to others: The warm glow of success. *Journal of Personality and Social Psychology, 15,* 294–301.

Jahoda, M. (1958). *Current concepts of positive mental health.* New York: Basic Books.

Janis, I. L. (1958). *Psychological stress: Psychoanalytic and behavioral studies of surgical patients.* New York: Wiley.

Janis, I. L. (1971). *Stress and frustration.* New York: Harcourt Brace Jovanovich.

Janis, I. L. (1983). The role of social support in adherence to stressful decisions. *American Psychologist, 38,* 143–160.

Jason, L. A. (1986). *A preventive intervention for high risk transfer children.* NIMH Grant Application.

Jenkins, C. D. (1979). Psychosocial modifiers of response to stress. In J. E. Barret et al. (Eds.), *Stress and mental disorder* (pp. 265–278). New York: Raven Press.

Jensen, A. R. (1969). How much can we boost I.Q. and scholastic achievement? *Harvard Educational Review Monograph, 39,* 1–123.

Jensen, A. R. (1980). *Bias in mental testing.* New York: Free Press.

Johnson, J. H., & Sarason, I. G. (1978). Life stress, depression, and anxiety: Internal-external control as a moderator variable. *Journal of Psychosomatic Research, 22,* 205–208.

Jones, E. E., & Berglas, S. (1978). Control of attributions about the self through self-handicapping strategies: The appeal of alcohol and the role of underachievement. *Personality and Social Psychology Bulletin, 4,* 200–206.

Jones, W. H. (1985). The psychology of loneliness: Some personality issues in the study of social support. In I. G. Sarason & B. R. Sarason (Eds.), *Social support: Theory, research, and applications* (pp. 225–241). The Hague, The Netherlands: Martinus Nijhoff.

Jones, W. H., & Briggs, S. R. (1983). *Shyness and Interpersonal Behavior.* Unpublished manuscript, The University of Tulsa.

Jourard, S. M. (1971). *The transparent self.* New York: Van Nostrand Reinhold.

Kamin, L. J. (1976). Heredity, intelligence, politics, and psychology. In N. J. Block, & G. Dworkin (Eds.), *The IQ controversy* (pp. 242–264). New York: Pantheon.

Kanner, A. D., Coyne, J. C., Schaefer, C., & Lazarus, R. S. (1981). Comparisons of two modes of stress measurement: Daily hassles and uplifts versus major life events. *Journal of Behavioral Medicine, 4,* 1–39.

Kaplan, H. B. (1983). Psychological distress in sociological context: Toward a general theory of psychosocial stress. In H. B. Kaplan (Ed.), *Psychosocial stress: Trends in theory and research* (pp. 195–264). New York: Academic.

Kaplan, H. B., Robbins, C., & Martin, S. S. (1983). Antecedents of psychological distress in young adults: Self-rejection, deprivation of social support, and life events. *Journal of Health and Social Behavior, 24,* 230–244.

Keinan, G. (1987). Decision making under stress: Scanning of alternatives under controllable and uncontrollable threats. *Journal of Personality and Social Psychology, 52,* 639–644.

Kellett, A. (1982). *Combat motivation: The behavior of soldiers in combat.* Boston, Kluwer Nijhoff.

Kelly, K. E., & Houston, B. K. (1985). Type A behavior in employed women: Relation to work, marital, and leisure variables, social support, stress, tension and health. *Journal of Personality and Social Psychology, 48,* 1067–1079.

Kennedy, C. D., Chesney, A. P., Gentry, W. D., Gary, H. E., & Harburg, E. (1984). *Anger-coping style as a mediator in the relationship between hostility and blood pressure.* Unpublished manuscript.

Kessler, R. C. (1983). Methodological issues in the study of psychological stress. In H. B. Kaplan (Ed.), *Psychosocial stress: Trends in theory and research* (pp. 267–341). New York: Academic.

Kessler, R. C., & Essex, M. (1982). Marital status and depression: The importance of coping resources. *Social Forces, 61,* 484–507.

Kessler, R. C., & McLeod, J. D. (1985). Social support and mental health in community samples. In S. Cohen & S. L. Syme (Eds.), *Stress and anxiety* (pp. 219–240). New York: Academic.

Kessler, R. C., McLeod, J. D., & Wethington, E. (1985). The costs of caring: A perspective on the relationship between sex and psychological distress. In I. G. & B. R. Sarason (Eds.), *Social Support: Theory, research, and applications* (pp. 491–506). The Hague, The Netherlands: Martinus Nijhoff.

Klein, M. (1932). *The psychoanalysis of children.* London: Hogarth.

Kobasa, S. C. (1979). Stressful life events, personality, and health: An inquiry into hardiness. *Journal of Personality and Social Psychology, 37,* 1–11.

Kobasa, S. C., Maddi, S. R., & Courington, S. (1981). Personality and constitution as mediators in the stress-illness relationship. *Journal of Health and Social Behavior, 22,* 368–378.

Kobasa, S. C., Maddi, S. R., Donner, E. J., Merrick, W. A., & White, H. (1984). *The personality construct of hardiness.* Unpublished manuscript.

Kobasa, S. C., Maddi, S. R., & Zola, M. A. (1983). Type A and hardiness. *Journal of Behavioral Medicine, 6,* 41–51.

Kobasa, S. C., & Puccetti, M. C. (1983). Personality and social resources in stress resistance. *Journal of Personality and Social Psychology, 45,* 839–850.

Krause, N. (1985). Stress, control beliefs, and psychological distress: The problem of response bias. *Journal of Human Stress, 11*(1), 11–19.

Kruglanski, A. W. (1980). Lay epistemological process and contents. *Psychological Review, 87,* 70–87.

Kuhn, T. S. (1962). *The structure of scientific revolutions.* Chicago: University of Chicago Press.

Kulka, R. A., Klingel, D. M., & Mann, D. W. (1980). School crime and disruption as a function of student school fit: An empirical assessment. *Journal of Youth and Adolescence, 9,* 353–370.

Kuo, W. A., & Tsai, Y. M. (1986). Social networking, hardiness and immigrants' mental health. *Journal of Health and Social Behavior, 27,* 133–149.

Larsen, R. J., Diener, E., & Emmons, R. A. (1986). Affect intensity and reactions to daily life events. *Journal of Personality and Social Psychology, 51,* 803–814.

Latene, B., & Darley, J. M. (1970). *The unresponsive bystander: Why doesn't he help?* New York: Appleton-Century-Crofts.

Lazarus, A. A. (1971). *Behavior therapy and beyond.* New York: McGraw-Hill.

Lazarus, R. S. (1966). *Psychological stress and the coping process.* New York: McGraw-Hill.

Lazarus, R. S. (1983). The costs and benefits of denial. In S. Breznitz (Ed.), *The denial of stress* (pp. 1–30). New York: International Universities Press.

Lazarus, R. S., & Folkman, S. (1984). *Stress, appraisal, and coping.* New York: Springer.

Lazarus, R. S., DeLongis, A., Folkman, S., & Gruen, R. (1985). Stress and adaptational outcome: The problem of confounded measures. *American Psychologist, 40,* 770–779.

Lefcourt, H. M., Martin, R. A., & Selah, W. E. (1984). Locus of control and social support: Interactive moderators of stress. *Journal of Personality and Social Psychology, 47,* 378–389.

Lefcourt, H. M., Miller, R. S., Ware, E. E., & Sherk, D. (1981). Locus of control as a modifier of the relationship between stressors and moods. *Journal of Personality and Social Psychology, 41,* 357–369.

Lehman, D. R., Ellard, J. H., & Wortman, C. B. (1986). Social support for the bereaved: Recipients' and providers' perspectives on what is helpful. *Journal of Consulting and Clinical Psychology, 54,* 438–446.

Lehman, D. R., Wortman, C. B., & Williams, A. F. (1987). Long-term effects of losing a spouse or child in a motor vehicle crash. *Journal of Personality and Social Psychology, 52,* 218–231.

Levav, I., Greenfield, H., & Baruch, E. (1979). Psychiatric combat reactions during the Yom Kippur War. *American Journal of Psychiatry, 136,* 637–641.

Levi, L. (1972). Introduction: Psychosocial stimuli, psycho-physiological reactions, and disease. In L. Levi (Ed.), *Stress and distress in response to psychosocial stimuli* (pp. 11–27). Oxford: Pergamon.

Lewis, R. A. (1978). Emotional intimacy among men. *Journal of Social Issues, 34,* 108–121.

Lidz, T., Fleck, S., & Cornelison, A. R. (1965). *Schizophrenia and the family.* New York: International Universities Press.

Lin, N., Ensel, W. M., Simeone, R. S., & Kuo, W. (1979). Social support, stressful life events, and illness: A model and empirical test. *Journal of Health and Social Behavior, 20,* 108–119.

Lindemann, E. (1944). The symptomatology and management of acute grief. *American Journal of Psychiatry, 101,* 141–148.

Loehlin, J. C., Lindsey, G., & Spuhler, J. N. (1975). *Race differences in intelligence.* San Francisco: Freeman.

Lorion, R. P. (1973). Patient and therapist variables in the treatment of low-income patients. *Psychological Bulletin, 79,* 263–270.

Maddi, S. R. (1972). *Personality theories: A comparative analysis.* Homewood, IL: Dorsey.

Magnussen, D. (1981). *Toward a psychology of situations: An international perspective.* Hillsdale, NJ: Lawrence Erlbaum.

Marlowe, D. H. (1979). *Cohesion, anticipated breakdown, and endurance in battle: Considerations for severe- and high-intensity combat.* Unpublished manuscript, Division of Neuropsychiatry, Walter Reed Army Institute of Research, Washington, DC.

Maslow, A. H. (1968). *Toward a psychology of being.* New York: Van Nostrand Reinhold.

Matarazzo, J. D. (1982). Behavioral health's challenge to academic, scientific, and professional psychology. *American Psychologist, 37,* 1–14.

May, R. (1950). *The meaning of anxiety.* New York: Ronald Press.

May, R. (1957). *Existence: A new dimension in psychiatry and psychology* (pp. 3–37). New York: Basic Books.

May, R. (1958). Contributions of existential psychotherapy. In R. May, E. Angel, & H. F. Ellenberger (Eds.), *Existence: A new dimension in psychiatry and psychology* (pp. 37–91). New York: Basic Books.

McFarlane, A., Norman, G., Streiner, D., & Roy, R. (1983). The process of social stress: Stable, reciprocal, and mediating relationships. *Journal of Health and Social Behavior, 24,* 160–173.

McGrath, J. E. (1970). A conceptual formulation for research on stress. In J. E. McGrath (Ed.), *Social and psychological factors in stress* (pp. 10–21). New York: Holt, Rinehart & Winston.

McGuire, C., & Gottlieb, B. H. (1979). Social support groups among new parents: An experimental study in primary prevention. *Journal of Child Clinical Psychology, 8,* 111–116.

Meichenbaum, D. (1977). *Cognitive behavior modification: An integrative approach.* New York: Plenum.

Meichenbaum, D., & Jaremko, M. E. (Eds.), (1983). *Stress reduction and prevention.* New York: Plenum.

Menaghan, E. G. (1983). Individual coping efforts: Moderators of the relationship between life stress and mental health outcomes. In H. B. Kaplan (Ed.), *Psychosocial stress: Trends in theory and research* (pp. 157–191). New York: Academic.

Menninger, K. (1963). *The vital balance: The life process in mental health and illness.* New York: Viking.

Merton, R. K. (1957). *Social theory and social structure: Toward the codification of theory and research.* New York: Free Press.

Milgram, N. A. (1982). A general introduction. In C. D. Spielberger, & I. G. Sarason (Eds.), & N. A. Milgram (Guest Ed.), *Handbook of stress: Theoretical and clinical aspects.* Washington, DC: Hemisphere.

Milgram, N. A. (1986). An attributional analysis of war-related stress: Modes of coping and helping. In N. A. Milgram (Ed.), *Stress and coping in time of war* (pp. 9–25). New York: Brunner/Mazel.

Miller, K., & Iscoe, I. (1963). The concept of crisis: Current status and mental health. *Human Organization, 22,* 195–201.

Miller, R. S., & Lefcourt, H. M. (1983). The stress buffering function of social intimacy. *American Journal of Community Psychology, 11,* 127–139.

Minuchin, S. (1974). *Families and family therapy.* Cambridge, MA: Harvard University Press.

Minuchin, S., Baker, L., Rosaman, B. L., Liebman, R., Milman, L., & Todd, T. C. (1975). A conceptual model of psychosomatic illness in children: Family organization and family therapy. *Archives of General Psychiatry, 32,* 1031–1038.

Mitchell, R E. (1982). Social networks of psychiatric clients: The personal and environmental context. *American Journal of Community Psychology, 10,* 387–432.

Mitchell, R. E., Cronkite, R. C., & Moos, R. H. (1983). Stress, coping and depression among married couples. *Journal of Abnormal Psychology, 92,* 433–448.

Mitchell, R. E., & Hodson, C. A. (1983). Coping with domestic violence: Social support and psychological health among battered women. *American Journal of Community Psychology, 11,* 629–654.

Mitchell, R. E., & Hodson, C. A. (1986). Coping and social support among battered women: An ecological perspective. In S. E. Hobfoll (Ed.), *Stress, social support, and women* (pp. 153–168). Washington, DC: Hemisphere.

Monroe, S., & Steiner, S. C. (1986). Social support and psychopathology: Interrelations with preexisting disorders, stress, and personality. *Journal of Abnormal Psychology, 95,* 29–39.

Moos, R. H. (1977). *Coping with physical illness.* New York: Plenum.

Moos, R. H. (1984). Context and coping: Toward a unifying conceptual framework. *American Journal of Community Psychology, 12,* 5–25.

Moos, R. H. (1986). *Coping with life crises: An integrated approach.* New York: Plenum.

Moos, R. H., & Schaefer, J. A. (1986). Life transitions and crisis: A conceptual overview. In R. H. Moos (Ed.), *Coping with crises: An integrated approach* (pp. 3–28). New York: Plenum.

Mowrer, O. H. (1950). *Learning theory and personality dynamics.* New York: Ronald Press.

Mueller, D., Edward, D. W., & Yarvis, R. M. (1977). Stressful life events and psychiatric symptomatology: Change or undesirability. *Journal of Health and Social Behavior, 18,* 307–316.

Murrell, S. A., & Norris, F. H. (1984). Resources, life events, and changes in positive affect and depression in older adults. *American Journal of Community Psychology, 12,* 445–464.

Myers, B. G., & Lamm, N. (1976). The group polarization phenomenon. *Psychological Bulletin, 83,* 602–627.

Nadler, A., & Mayeless, O. (1983). Recipient of self-esteem and reactions to help. In J. D. Fisher, A. Nadler, B. M. DePaulo (Eds.), *New directions in helping* (Vol. 1, pp. 167–188). New York: Academic.

Nasby, W., & Yando, R. (1982). Selective encoding and retrieval of affectively valent information: Two cognitive consequences of children's mood states. *Journal of Personality and Social Psychology, 43,* 1244–1253.

Nelson, D. W., & Cohen, L. H. (1983). Locus of control and control perceptions and the relationship between life stress and psychological disorder. *American Journal of Community Psychology, 11,* 705–722.

Norbeck, T., & Tilden, V. (1983). Life stress, social support and emotional disequilibrium in complications of pregnancy: A prospective, multivariate study. *Journal of Health and Social Behavior, 24,* 30–46.

Norris, F. A., & Murrell, S. A. (1984). Protective function of resources related to life events, global stress, and depression in older adults. *Journal of Health and Social Behavior, 25,* 424–437.

Noy, S., Nardi, C., & Solomon, Z. (1986). Battle and military unit characteristics and the prevalence of psychiatric casualties. In M. A. Milgram (Ed.), *Stress and coping in time of war* (pp. 73–78). New York: Brunner/Mazel.

Nuckolls, K. G., Cassel, J., & Kaplan, B. H. (1972). Psychosocial assets, life crisis and the prognosis of pregnancy. *American Journal of Epidemiology, 95,* 431–441.

Pagel, M. D., Erdly, W. W., & Becker, J. (in press). Social networks: We get by with (and in spite of) a little help from our friends. *Journal of Personality and Social Psychology.*

Parkes, C. M. (1970). "Seeking" and "finding" a lost object: Evidence from recent studies of the reaction to bereavement. *Social Science and Medicine, 4,* 187–201.

Parkes, C. M. (1971). Psychosocial transitions: A field for study. *Social Science and Medicine, 5,* 101–115.

Parkes, C. M. (1972). *Bereavement.* New York: International Universities Press.

Parry, G. (1986). Paid employment, life events, social support, and mental health in working class mothers. *Journal of Health and Social Behavior, 27,* 193–208.

Parsons, T. (1949). *Essays in sociological theory.* Glencoe, IL: Free Press.

Paykel, E. S. (1974). Life stress and psychiatric disorder: Applications of the clinical approach. In B. S. Dohrenwend and B. P. Dohrenwend (Eds.), *Stressful life events: Their nature and effects* (pp. 135–149). New York: Wiley.

Paykel, E. S., Emms, E. M., Fletcher, J., & Rassaby, E. S. (1980). Life events and social support in puerperal depression. *British Journal of Psychiatry, 136,* 339–346.

Pearlin, L. I. (1983). Role strains and personal stress. In H. B. Kaplan (Ed.), *Psychosocial stress: Trends in theory and research* (pp. 3–32). New York: Academic.

Pearlin, L. I., Leiberman, M. A., Menaghan, E. G., & Mullan, J. T. (1981). The stress process. *Journal of Health and Social Behavior, 22,* 337–356.

Pearlin, L. I., & Schooler, C. (1978). The structure of coping. *Journal of Health and Social Behavior, 19,* 2–21.

Peplau, L. A., & Perlman, D. (Eds.), (1982). *Loneliness: A sourcebook of current theory, research and therapy.* New York: Wiley-Interscience.

Perls, F. (1969). *Gestalt therapy verbatim.* Lafeyette, CA: Real People Press.

Pfeffer, J. (1981). *Power in Organizations.* Boston: Pitman.

Piaget, J. (1973). Need and significance of cross-cultural studies in genetic psychology. In J. Berry and P. Dasen (Eds.), *Culture and cognition: Reading in cross-cultural psychology* (pp. 299–309). London: Methuen.

Popper, K. R. (1959). *The logic of scientific discovery.* New York: Basic Books.

Pyszczynski, T., & Greenberg, J. (1983). Determinants of reduction in intended effort as a strategy for coping with anticipated failure. *Journal of Research in Personality, 17,* 412–422.

Rabkin, J. G., & Streuning, E. L. (1976). Life events, stress, and illness. *Science, 194,* 1013–1020.

Radloff, L. S. (1977). The CES-D scale: A self-report depression scale for research in the general population. *Applied Psychological Measurement, 1,* 385–401.

Rand, C. S. (1986). The stress of childbearing: Nurse-Midwives as a source of social support. In S.E. Hobfoll (Ed.), *Stress, social support, and women* (pp. 173–183). Washington, DC: Hemisphere.

Rehm, L. P. (1978). Mood, pleasant events, and unpleasant events: Two pilot studies. *Journal of Consulting and Clinical Psychology, 46,* 854–859.

Reis, H. T. (1984). Social interaction and well-being. In S. Duck (Ed.), *Personal relationships, Vol 5: Repairing personal relationships* (pp. 21–45). London: Academic.

Reis, H. T., Senchak, M., & Solomon, B. (1985). Sex differences in the intimacy of social interaction: Further examination of potential explanations. *Journal of Personality and Social Psychology, 48,* 1204–1217.

Rhodewalt, F., Hays, R. B., Chemers, M. M., & Wysocki, J. (1984). Type A behavior, perceived stress, and illness: A person-situation analysis. *Personality and Social Psychology Bulletin, 10,* 1, 149–159.

Rhodewalt, F., & Agustsdotter, S. (1984). On the relationship of hardiness of the Type A behavior pattern: Perception of life events versus coping with life events. *Journal of Research and Personality, 18,* 212–223.

Rich, A. R., Sullivan, J. A., & Rich, V. L. (1986). *Hardiness, social support, and depression in college students.* Paper presented at the annual meeting of the Midwestern Psychological Association, Chicago, Illinois.

Riley, D., & Eckenrode, J. (1986). Social ties: Subgroup differences in costs and benefits. *Journal of Personality & Social Psychology, 51,* 770–778.

Rogers, C. R. (1961). The loneliness of contemporary man as seen in "The case of Ellen West." *Annals of Psychiatry, 137,* 22–27.

Rokeach, M. (1960). *The open and closed mind.* New York: Basic Books.

Rokeach, M. (1973). *The nature of human values.* New York: Free Press.

Rook, K. S. (1984). The negative side of social interaction: Impact on psychological well-being. *Journal of Personality and Social Psychology, 46,* 1097–1108.

Rook, K. S. (1985). The functions of social bonds: Perspectives from research on social support, loneliness, and social isolation. In I. G. Sarason & B. R. Sarason (Eds.), *Social support: Theory, research, and applications* (pp. 243–267). The Hague, The Netherlands: Martinus Nijhoff.

Rook, K. S. (in press). Toward a more differentiated view of loneliness. In S. Duck, D. F. Hay, S. E. Hobfoll, B. Ickes, & B. Montgomery (Eds.), *The handbook of research in personal relationships.* London, New York: Wiley.

Rosenbaum, M., & Palmon, N. (1984). Helplessness and resourcefulness in coping with epilepsy. *Journal of Consulting and Clinical Psychology, 52,* 244–253.

Rosenbaum, M., & Smira, K. B. (1986). Cognitive and personality factors in the delay of gratification of hemodialysis patients. *Journal of Personality and Social Psychology, 51,* 357–364.

Rosentiel, A., & Roth, S. (1981). Relationship between cognitive activity and adjustment in four spinal-cord-injured individuals: A longitudinal investigation. *Journal of Human Stress,* March, 35–43.

Ross, C. E., & Mirowski II, J. (1979). A comparison of life event weighting schemes: Change, undesirability and effect-proportional indices. *Journal of Health and Social Behavior, 20,* 166–177.

Rubenstein, C. M., & Shaver, P. (1982). *In search of intimacy.* New York: Delacorte Press.

Ruch, L. D., Chandler, S. M., & Harter, R. A. (1980). Life change and rape impact. *Journal of Health and Social Behavior, 21,* 248–260.

Ruch, L. D., & Leon, J. L. (1986). The victim of rape and the role of life change, coping, and social support during the rape trauma syndrome. In S. E. Hobfoll (Ed.), *Stress, social support, and women* (pp. 137–152). Washington, DC: Hemisphere.

Ryff, C. D. (1979). Value transition and adult development in women: The instrumentality-terminality sequence hypothesis. In M. Rokeach (Ed.), *Understanding human values: Individual and societal* (pp. 148–153). New York: Free Press.

Salmon, T., and others. (1929). In Medical Department of the U.S. Army, *Neuropsychiatry in the World War* (Vol. 10). Washington, DC: U.S. Government Printing Office.

Sandler, I. N., & Lakey, B. (1982). Locus of control as a stress moderator: The role of control perceptions and social support. *American Journal of Community Psychology, 10,* 65–80.

Sarason, B. R., Sarason, I. G., Hacker, T. A., & Basham, R. B. (1985). Concomitants of social support: Social skills, physical attractiveness and gender. *Journal of Personality and Social Psychology, 49,* 469–480.

Sarason, B. R., Shearin, E. N., Pierce, G. R., & Sarason, I. G. (1987). Interrelationships between social support measures: Theoretical and practical implications. *Journal of Personality and Social Psychology, 52,* 813–832.

Sarason, I. G. (1975). Test anxiety, attention, and the general problem of anxiety. In C. D. Spielberger and I. G. Sarason (Eds.), *Stress and anxiety* (Vol. 1, pp. 165–187). Washington, DC: Hemisphere.

Sarason, I. G., Levine, H. M., Basham, R. B., & Singer, B. R. (1983). Assessing social support: The social support questionnaire. *Journal of Personality and Social Psychology, 44,* 127–139.

Sarason, I. G., & Sarason, B. R. (1985). Social support: Insights from assessment and experimentation. In I. G. Sarason and B. R. Sarason (Eds.), *Social support: Theory, research and applications* (pp. 39–51). The Hague, The Netherlands: Martinus Nijhoff.

Sarason, I. G., Sarason, B. R., & Shearin, E. N. (1986). Social support as an individual difference variable: Its stability, origins and relational aspects. *Journal of Personality and Social Psychology, 5,* 845–855.

Sarason, S. B. (1974). *The psychological sense of community: Prospects for a community psychology.* San Francisco: Jossey-Bass.

Schacter, S., & Singer, J. E. (1962). Cognitive, social and physiological determinants of emotional states. *Psychological Review, 69,* 379–399.

Schaefer, C., Coyne, J. C., & Lazarus, R. S. (1981). The health-related functions of social support. *Journal of Behavioral Medicine, 4,* 139–157.

Scheier, M. F., Weintraub, J. K., & Carver, C. S. (1986). Coping with stress: Divergent strategies of optimists and pessimists. *Journal of Personality and Social Psychology, 51,* 1257–1264.

Schönpflug, W. (1985). Goal directed behavior as a source of stress: Psychological origins and consequences of inefficiency. In M. Frese & J. Sabini (Eds.), *The concept of action in psychology* (pp. 172–188). Hillsdale, NJ: Lawrence Erlbaum.

Schur, M. (1958). The ego and the id in anxiety. *Psychoanalytic Study of the Child, 13,* 190–220.

Sears, R., Macoby, E., & Levin, H. (1957). *Patterns of child rearing.* Evanston, IL: Row, Peterson.

Segal, B., Huba, G. J., & Singer, J. L. (1980). *Drugs, daydreaming, and personality.* Hillsdale, NJ: Lawrence Erlbaum.

Seidman, E., & Rappaport, J. (1974). The educational pyramid: A paradigm for research, training, and manpower utilization in community psychology. *American Journal of Community Psychology, 2,* 119–130.

Selye, H. (1950). *The physiology and pathology of exposure to stress.* Montreal: Acta.

Selye, H. (1951–1956). *Annual report of stress.* New York: McGraw-Hill.

Shaver, P., Furman, W., & Buhrmaster, D. (1985). Aspects of a life transition: Network changes, social skills and loneliness. In S. Duck and D. Perlman (Eds.), *The Sage series in personal relationships* (pp. 193–219). London: Sage.

Shils, E. A., & Janowitz, M. (1948). Cohesion and disintegration in the Wehrmacht in World War II. *Public Opinion Quarterly, 3,* 281–282.

Shinn, M., Lehmann, S., & Wong, N. W. (1984). Social interaction and social support. *Journal of Social Issues, 40,* 55–76.

Shumaker, S. A., & Brownell, A. (1984). Toward a theory of social support: Closing the conceptual gaps. *Journal of Social Issues, 40,* 11–36.

Silver, R., & Wortman, C. B. (1980). Coping with undesirable life events. In J. Garber & M. E. P. Seligman (Eds.), *Human helplessness* (pp. 279–375). New York: Academic.

Silverman, L. H., & Weinberger, J. (1985). Mommy and I are one: Implications for psychotherapy. *American Psychologist, 40,* 1296–1308.

Skinner, B. F. (1938). *The behavior of organisms.* New York: Appleton-Century-Crofts.

Smith, T. W., Snyder, C. R., & Perkins, S. C. (1983). The self-serving function of hypochondriacal complaints: Physical symptoms as self-handicapping strategies. *Journal of Personality & Social Psychology, 44,* 787–797.

Solomon, Z., & Benbenishty, R. (1986). The role of proximity, immediacy and expectancy in frontline treatment of combat stress reaction among Israelis in the Lebanon war. *American Journal of Psychiatry, 143,* 613–617.

Solomon, Z., Mikulincer, M., & Hobfoll, S. E. (1986). Effects of social support and battle intensity on loneliness and breakdown during combat. *Journal of Personality and Social Psychology, 51,* 1269–1276.

Solomon, Z., Mikulincer, M., & Hobfoll, S. E. (1987). Objective versus subjective measurement of stress and social support: Combat related reactions. *Journal of Consulting and Clinical Psychology, 55,* 577–583.

Solomon, Z., Weisenberg, M., Schwarzwald, J., & Mikulincer, M. (1985). *Post-traumatic stress disorder among soldiers with combat stress reaction: The 1982 Israeli experience.* Unpublished manuscript.

Somes, G. W., Garrity, T. F., & Marx, M. B. (1981). The relationship of coronary-prone behavior pattern to the health of college students at varying levels of recent life change. *Journal of Psychosomatic Research, 25,* 565–572.

Spielberger, C. D. (Ed.). (1966a). *Anxiety and behavior.* New York: Academic.

Spielberger, C. D. (1966b). The effects of anxiety on complex learning and academic achievement. In C. D. Spielberger (Ed.), *Anxiety and behavior* (pp. 361–398). New York: Academic.

Spielberger, C. D. (Ed.) (1972). *Anxiety: Current trends in theory and research* (Vols. 1 & 2). New York: Academic.

Spielberger, C. D. (1986). *Stress and emotion.* Paper presented at the International Conference on Stress and Emotion. Visegrad/Budapest.

Spielberger, C. D., Johnson, E. H., Russell, S. F., Crane, R. J., Jacobs, G. A., & Worden, T. J. (1985). The experience and expression of anger: Construction and validation of an anger expression scale. In M. A. Chesney & R. H. Rosenman (Eds.), *Anger and hostility in cardiovascular and behavioral disorders* (pp. 5–29). New York: Hemisphere.

Srole, L., Langner, T. S., Michael, S. T., Opler, M. K., & Rennie, T. A. (1962). *Mental health in the metropolis: The Midtown Manhattan study.* New York: McGraw-Hill.

Star, R. P. (1973). *The discarded army: Veterans after Vietnam.* New York: Charterhouse.

Stein, C. H., & Rappaport, J. (1986). Social network interviews as sources of etic and emic data: A study of young married women. In S. E. Hobfoll (Ed.), *Stress, social support, and women* (pp. 47–66). Washington, DC: Hemisphere.

Stokes, J. P. (1983). Predicting satisfaction with social support from social network structures. *American Journal of Community Psychology, 11,* 141–152.

Stokes, J. P., & Wilson, D. G. (1984). The inventory of socially supportive behaviors: Dimensionality, prediction, and gender differences. *American Journal of Community Psychology, 12,* 53–69.

Stolberg, A. L., & Garrison, K. M. (1985). Evaluating a primary prevention program for children of divorce. *American Journal of Community Psychology, 13,* 111–124.

Sullivan, H. (1953). *The interpersonal theory of anxiety.* New York: Norton.

Suls, J., & Fletcher, B. (1985). Self-attention, life stress and illness: A prospective study. *Psychosomatic Medicine, 47,* 469–481.

Suls, J., Gastorf, J. W., & Witenburg, S. H. (1979). Life events, psychological distress and the Type A coronary-prone behavior pattern. *Journal of Psychosomatic Research, 23,* 315–319.

Swann, W. B., & Predmore, S. C. (1985). Intimates as agents of social support: Sources of consolation or despair? *Journal of Personality and Social Psychology, 49,* 1609–1617.

Taylor, A. J., & Frazer, A. G. (1982). The stress of post disaster body handling and victim identification work. *Journal of Human Stress, 8,* 4–12.

Taylor, S. E. (1983). Adjustment to threatening events: A theory of cognitive adaptation. *American Psychologist, 41,* 1161–1173.

Thoits, P. (1982). Conceptual, methodological, and theoretical problems in studying social support as a buffer against life stress. *Journal of Health and Social Behavior, 23,* 145–159.

Thoits, P. A. (1983). Dimensions of life events that influence psychological distress: An evaluation and synthesis of the literature. In H. B. Kaplan (Ed.), *Psychosocial stress: Trends in theory and research* (pp. 33–103). New York: Academic.

Thoits, P. A. (1986). Social support as coping assistance. *Journal of Consulting and Clinical Psychology, 54,* 416–423.

Tinbergen, N. (1951). *The study of instinct.* London: Oxford University Press.

Triandis, H. C. (1972). *The analysis of subjective culture.* New York: Wiley.

Triandis, H. C., & Brislin, R. W. (1984). Cross-cultural psychology. *American Psychologist, 39,* 1006–1016.

Tripathi, R. C., Caplan, R. D., Naidu, R. K. (1986). Accepting advice: A modifier of social support's effect on well-being. *Journal of Social and Personal Relationships, 3,* 213–228.

Truax, C. B., & Carkhuff, R. R. (1967). *Toward effective counseling and psychotherapy: Training and practice.* Chicago: Aldine.

Tversky, A., & Kahneman, D. (1974). Judgement under uncertainty: Heuristics and biases. *Science, 185,* 1124–1131.

Tversky, A., & Kahneman, D. (1981). The framing of decisions and the psychology of choice. *Science, 24,* 453–458.

Ulman, L. P., & Krasner, L. (1969). *A psychological approach to abnormal behavior.* Englewood Cliffs, NJ: Prentice-Hall.

Vachon, M. L., Lyall, W. A., Rogers, J., Freedman-Letofsky, K., & Freeman, S. J. (1980). A controlled study of self-help interventions for widows. *American Journal of Psychiatry, 137,* 1380–1384.

Vachon, M. L. S. (1979). *Identity change over the first two years of bereavement: Social relationships and social support in widowhood.* Unpublished dissertation, University of York (Canada).

Vachon, M. L. S. (1986). A comparison of the impact of breast cancer and bereavement: Personality, social support and adaptation. In S. E. Hobfoll (Ed.), *Stress, social support, and women* (pp. 187–202). Washington, DC: Hemisphere.

Vanfossen, B. (1981). Sex differences in the mental health effects of spouse support and equity. *Journal of Health and Social Behavior, 22,* 130–143.

Vanfossen, B. E. (1986). Sex differences in depression: The role of spouse support. In S. Hobfoll (Ed.), *Stress, social support, and women* (pp. 69–83). Washington, DC: Hemisphere.

Vinokur, A., & Selzer, M. L. (1975). Desirable versus undesirable events: Their relationship to stress and mental distress. *Journal of Personality and Social Psychology, 32,* 329–337.

Visotsky, H. M., Hamburg, D. A., Goss, M. E., & Lebovitz, B. Z. (1961). Coping behavior under extreme stress. *Archives of General Psychiatry, 5,* 423–443.

Walker, K. N., MacBride, A., & Vachon, M. L. S. (1977). Social support networks and the crisis of bereavement. *Social Science and Medicine, 11,* 35–41.

Walster, E., Walster, G. W., & Berscheid, E. (1978). *Equity: Theory and research.* Boston: Allyn & Bacon.

Warheit, G. J. (1979). Life events, coping, stress, and depressive symptomatology. *American Journal of Psychiatry, 136,* 502–507.

Watson, J. B. (1928). *Psychological care of infant and child.* New York: W. W. Norton.

Watson, J. B. (1970). *Behaviorism.* New York: W. W. Norton.

Weissberg, R. P., Gesten, E. L., Rapkin, B. D., Cowen, E. L., Davidson, E., Flores de Apodaca, R., & McKim, B. J. (1981). Evaluation of a social problem-solving training program for suburban and inner-city third-grade children. *Journal of Consulting & Clinical Psychology, 49,* 251–261.

Weissman, M. M., & Klerman, G. (1977). Sex differences and the epidemiology of depression. *Archives of General Psychiatry, 34,* 98–111.

Weisz, J. R., Rothbaum, I. M., & Blackburn, T. C. (1984). Standing out and standing in: The psychology of control in America and Japan. *American Psychologist, 39,* 955–969.

Wellman, B. (1981). Applying network analysis to the study of support. In B. H. Gottlieb (Ed.), *Social networks and social support* (pp. 171–200). Beverly Hills, CA: Sage.

Wethington, E., & Kessler, R. C. (1986). Perceived support, received support, and adjustment to stressful life events. *Journal of Health and Social Behavior, 27,* 78–89.

Wheaton, B. (1983). Stress, personal coping resources, and psychiatric symptoms: An investigation of an interactive model. *Journal of Health and Social Behavior, 24,* 208–229.

Wheeler, L., Reis, H. T., & Nezlek, J. (1983). Loneliness, social interaction, and sex roles. *Journal of Personality and Social Psychology, 45,* 943–953.

Whiting, J. (1968). Methods and problems in cross-cultural research. In G. Lindzey & E. Aronson (Eds.), *Handbook of Social Psychology* (Vol. 2, pp. 693–728). Reading, MA: Addison-Wesley.

Wiebe, D. J., & McCallum, D. M. (1986). Health practice and hardiness as mediators in the stress-illness relationship. *Health Psychology, 5,* 425–438.

Wilcox, B. (1981). Social support in adjusting to marital disruption: A network analysis. In B. Gottlieb (Ed.), *Social networks and social support* (pp. 97–115). Beverly Hills, CA: Sage.

Wilcox, B. L. (1986). Stress, coping, and the social milieu of divorced women. In S. E. Hobfoll (Ed.), *Stress, social support, and women* (pp. 115–133). Washington, DC: Hemisphere.

Wildman, R. C., & Johnson, P. R. (1977). Life-change and Langner's 22-item mental health index: A study and partial replication. *Journal of Health and Social Behavior, 18,* 179–188.

Williams, A. W., Ware, J. E., & Donald, C. A. (1981). A model of mental health, life events, and social supports applicable to general populations. *Journal of Health and Social Behavior, 22,* 324–336.

Williams, R. M. (1979). Change and stability in values and value systems: A sociological perspective. In M. Rokeach (Ed.), *Understanding human values and value systems: A sociological perspective* (pp. 15–46). New York: Free Press.

Wolff, P. H. (1987). *The development of behavioral states and the expression of emotions in early infancy.* Chicago: University of Chicago Press.

Wortman, C. B., & Lehman, D. R. (1985). Reactions to victims of life crisis: Support attempts that fail. In I. G. Sarason and B. R. Sarason (Eds.), *Social support: Theory, research and applications* (pp. 463–489). The Hague, The Netherlands: Martinus Nijhoff.

Zajonc, R. B. (1980). Feeling and thinking: Preferences need no inferences. *American Psychologist, 35,* 151–175.

Zajonc, R. B. (1984). On the primacy of emotion. *American Psychologist, 39,* 117–123.

Zuckerman, M. (1976). Sensation seeking and anxiety, traits and states, as determinants of behavior in novel situations. In I. G. Sarason & C. D. Spielberger (Eds.), *Stress and anxiety,* (Vol. 3, pp. 141–170). New York: Wiley.

Zuckerman, M. (1979). Sensation seeking and risk taking. In C. Izard (Ed.), *Emotions in personality and psychopathology* (pp. 163–197). New York: Plenum.

Zuckerman, M., Bone, R. N., Neary, R., Mangelsdorff, D., & Brustman, B. (1972). What is the sensation seeker? Personality trait and experience correlates of the Sensation Seeking scales. *Journal of Consulting and Clinical Psychology, 39,* 308–321.

INDEX

Abramson, L., 292, 306
Academic fit and strain, 67
Achievement and high school students, 68
Ackerman, N. W., 162
Acts of greater good, 289–290
Adcock, S., 145
Adjustment to stressors, 86, 101, 203–205
Adler, A., 167, 203, 284, 299
Adolescence, 162–163
Adorno, T. W., 168
Affect intensity and life events, 179
Aggregate model, 89
Agustsdottir, A., 175, 177
Ainsworth, M. D., 285
Aldwin, C., 157
Andrews, G., 125, 194
Aneshenel, C. S., 80, 125, 141, 145, 315
Anger:
    and evolution, 104
    and war-related stress, 234–235
Antonovsky, A., 18, 81, 85, 95, 164–166,
        284
Anxiety, functions of, 49–51
Appraisal:
    cognitive, 10
    component, 13
    process, 37–39
    process of loss, 289
    of threat and demand, 84
Argyle, M., 77
Arkin, R. M., 316

Attachment, 134
    absence of, 139
    early long term effects, 34, 104
    theory, 242
Attkisson, C., 305
Auerbach, S. M., 9

Balance model, 16–18
Bandura, A., 163, 168
Bankoff, E. A., 158, 311
Barrera, M., 228, 271, 277
Baruch, E., 239
Basham, R. B., 78, 144, 277
Basowitz, H., 171
Bateson, G., 293
Baum, A., 89, 130
Baumgardner, A. H., 316
Becker, J., 149
Behaviorism, 114
Benbenishty, R., 50
Benor, D. E., 275
Beres, D., 162
Berkman, L. G., 145
Bernard, J., 145
Berscheid, E., 76, 140, 151
Bettelheim, B., 287
Bhrolcrain, M., 127, 133, 135
Billings, A. G., 193, 194, 278, 296
Biological and biophysical systems,
        31–33, 35

Biological determinism and personality, 298
Biological process, 52
Biological responses, description, 103
Blackburn, T. C., 96
Blaney, R. H., 175, 199
Blau, P. M., 147
Blehar, S., 285
Bloom, B. L., 309
Bowlby, J., 49, 51, 104, 133, 242, 269, 285, 299
Breznitz, S., 48, 88, 95, 196, 219, 220, 237
Briggs, S. R., 138
Brown, G. W., 53, 117, 125, 133, 135, 253, 263
Brown, R. J., 28
Brownell, A., 121, 225
Browski, A., 305
Bulman, R. J., 178, 214, 294
Burda, D. C., Jr., 144
Burgess, A. W., 34, 190
Burke, D. J., 143
Burnam, M. A., 310
Byrne, D. G., 145

Caldwell, R. A., 309
Cancer biopsies as stressors, 61, 90, 99, 190, 256–261
Cannon, W., 5, 14, 22
Caplan, G., 6, 12, 47, 120, 276, 304
Caplan, R. D., 67, 101, 106, 224, 226, 280
Carkhuff, R. R., 116, 314
Carpenter, B. N., 256
Carver, C. S., 194, 195, 316
Cassel, J., 82, 117, 121, 261
Cassem, N. H., 196
Chandler, S. M., 90, 218
Chapman, N. J., 310
Chemers, M. M., 176, 177
Chesney, A. P., 179, 180, 313
Children's health, 207
Children's illness, 268–274
Chiriboga, D. A., 28
Clark, M. S., 35, 76, 140, 185, 270, 279
Cobb, S., 66, 120, 224
Coconut Grove fire, 6
Coff, S., 118
Cognitions, 41

Cognitive and subconscious systems, 33–35
Cognitive appraisal, 10
Cohen, F., 65, 196
Cohen, J. B., 145, 177
Cohen, L. H., 144, 174
Cohen, S., 45, 66, 121, 123, 127–129, 157, 167, 174, 175, 185, 187, 225, 228, 247, 248, 250, 264, 278, 298, 306
Combat stress, 10–12, 170–171, 218, 238–246
Conditions, definition, 72
Conflict cycle, 286–287
Control, 173
    cultural differences in, 95–96
Cooke, D. J., 191
Coping, 10, 26
    vs. appraisal, 64–65
    conceptualization of, 188–189
    definition, 16
    with paralysis, 178–179
    personality characteristics as, 201–202
    prior experience and, 189–191
    stressful encounters, 103
    styles, 65–66
    transformational, 62, 65–66
Courington, S., 62
Cowen, E. L., 310
Cox, S., 310
Coyne, J. C., 53, 98, 157, 186, 255
Crandall, J. E., 184
Crane, R. J., 178
Crisis theory, 6–7
Cronkite, R. C., 182, 188, 196, 197, 206, 207, 227
Croog, S. H., 154
Crozier, M., 76
Culer, R. E., 310
Cultural differences in reactions to stress, 260–261
Cutrona, C. E., 225, 259, 274, 312

Dakof, G., 98
Darley, J. M., 139
Datan, N., 87, 296
Davidson, L. M., 89
Dean, A., 118, 224
Death, 27

DeLongis, A., 88, 98
Demands:
    definition of, 83
    on individuals, measurement of, 69
    vs. threat, 84
DeMayo, R., 98
Depression:
    coping with, 192–193
    functions of, 51
Depue, R. S., 98
Diener, E., 179
Dodson, M., 13, 54
Dohrenwend, B. P., 13, 45, 54, 69, 76, 98,
    117, 166, 253
Dohrenwend, B. S., 13, 45, 54, 69, 76, 98,
    117, 166, 219, 234, 253
Dominant spheres of influence, 290–291
Donald, C. A., 81, 125
Donner, E. J., 194
Dorr, D. A., 310
Dressler, W. W., 154
Duck, S., 132
Duncan-Jones, P., 145
Dunkel-Schetter, C., 88, 142, 307
Durlak, J. A., 116

Eckenrode, J., 231, 307
Ecological loss theory, 284–300
Ecological model of stress, 21
    vs. nonecological models, 246–247
Edward, D. W., 28
Edwards, J. R., 66, 123, 174, 175, 187,
    250, 264, 298
Eigenwelt, 162
Ellard, J. H., 307
Emmons, R. A., 179
Emms, E., 82, 127, 133, 135
Emotional distress:
    and behavioral adjustments during war,
        232–238
    during war, 225–231
Emotions:
    and arousal states, 41
    and cognitions, 41, 105
    and the core model, 41
    and men, 96
    men's vs. women's, 102
Energies, definition of, 75

Ensel, W. M., 125
Environment, appraisal of, 84
Environmental pressures, categorization
    of, 69
Environmental theories, 114
Erdly, W. W., 149
Erickson, E. H., 26, 284, 296
Eschel, M., 219
Essler, M., 136
Eustress, 43–45
Evaluative systems, 31–35
Event stressfulness measures, 244–246
Events:
    and psychopathology, 113
    relevance of, 85
    and roles, 88
    sensitivity to, 85–86
    and stress, 28, 117–118
    study of, 253–254
Experiences, early childhood, 34
Eysenck, H. J., 117

Factors vs. process distinction, 62, 64
Fanshel, S., 166
Farber, S. S., 30, 45, 68
Fausteau, M. F., 144
Felner, R. D., 30, 45, 68, 150, 304, 310
Feuerstein, M., 35, 81, 254, 274, 292
Fight-or-flight reaction, 14
Figley, C. R., 218
Films, themes of stress in, 4
Fisher, J. D., 152, 269
Fiske, D. W., 298
Fit theory, 129–130
Fleming, R., 130
Fletcher, J., 82, 127, 133, 135
Folklow, B., 14
Folkman, S., 9, 13, 16, 26, 62–66, 69, 84,
    88, 98, 188, 191–194, 212, 243,
    252, 253, 255, 307
Fooskas, S., 144
Foster, S., 154
Frankl, V. E., 14, 85, 168, 294
Frazer, A. G., 50
French, J. R. P., 66, 67, 101, 106
Frenkel-Brunswik, E., 168
Frerichs, R. R., 125
Freud, A., 162

Freud, S., 47, 48, 51, 113, 133–134
Friedman, M., 176, 313
Fulfillment cycle, 287–289

Ganellen, R. J., 175, 199
Garrison, K. M., 309
Garrity, T. F., 178
Gary, H. E., 179, 180
Gastof, J. W., 177
Gatchel, R., 130
General adaptation syndrome, 6
Gentry, W. D., 62, 105, 150, 179, 316
Ginsberg, L. H., 296
Gisrel, M., 130
Glass, R. C., 313
Gleser, G. C., 99, 218
Glidewell, J. C., 310
Goffman, E., 156, 198
Goodhart, D. E., 37, 180
Goplerud, E., 98
Gore, S., 129
Goss, M. E., 119
Gotlib, I. H., 98, 257
Gottlieb, B. H., 78, 167, 225, 243, 256,
    278, 309
Grace, M. C., 99, 218
Green, B. L., 13, 99, 218, 243
Green, J. G., 191
Greenberg, J., 316
Greenfeld, H., 239
Grinker, R. R., 151, 171
Grove, W. R., 137
Gruen, R. J., 88
Guernica, 168

Haan, N., 195, 276
Habif, V. L., 136
Hackett, J. P., 196
Haley, J., 293
Hamburg, D. A., 119
Hammech, C., 98
Haney, T., 154
Hansonn, R. O., 138, 246, 256, 269, 311
Hardiness, 63–65, 174–176
Harlow, H. F., 133
Harris, T., 28, 127, 133, 135
Harrison, R. V., 67
Harter, R. A., 90, 218

Hays, R. B., 176, 177
Health:
    conceptualization of , 164–166
    services, implications of stress research
        for, 275–276
Henderson, S., 77, 127, 144
Hetherington, E., 30
Hewson, D. M., 125, 194
Hinde, R. A., 104
Hinkle, L. E., 190
Hirsch, B. J., 21, 143, 148
Hoberman, H. M., 45, 127
Hobfoll, S. E., 20, 21, 37, 54, 61, 69, 70,
        74, 75, 77, 86, 95, 99, 106, 121,
        125, 129, 130, 132, 133, 135, 136,
        141, 143, 149, 150, 152, 155, 167,
        190, 218, 219, 231, 243, 256, 261,
        263, 268, 272, 276, 305, 308, 309,
        311, 315
Hodges, W. F., 309
Hodson, C. A., 21, 69, 145, 204, 278, 314
Hofien, I., 309
Holmes, T. H., 29, 53, 78, 112, 190, 254
Holmstrom, L. L., 34, 190
Holocaust, effects of, 27–28
Holohan, C. J., 206, 254, 309, 310
Hooley, J. M., 257, 309
Horney, K., 14, 113
Horowitz, M. J., 237
House, J. S., 121
Houston, B. K., 177
Hughes, M., 137
Hulka, B. S., 76
Humanism, 115
Husaini, B. A., 136, 145, 201

Illness, 251–253
Information hoarding, 76
Intervention, 301–319
    checklist, 317–319
    and conservation of resources model,
        301–305
    and ecological congruence model,
        305–319
Intimacy:
    and evolution, 104
    development of, 133–135
    during war, 230
    importance of, 135

Intimacy (*Cont.*):
  research on, 135–137
  sexual, 134
  and social support, 132–137, 146–147
Iscoe, I., 276
Isen, A. M., 41
Israel-Lebanon War, 225, 232, 238
Izzo, L. D., 310

Jackson, L. D., 310
Jacobs, G. A., 178
Jahoda, M., 163, 166
Janis, I. L., 9, 150, 196, 302
Janowitz, M., 119
Jaremko, M. E., 79, 188, 303
Jason, L., 304
Jenkins, C. D., 177, 185
Jenson, A. R., 114
Johnson, E. H., 178
Johnson, J. H., 53, 65, 78, 95, 100, 173, 227
Johnson, P. R., 190, 191
Jones, W. H., 137, 154, 157, 231, 256, 315
Jourard, S. M., 260, 308

Kagan, A., 177
Kahneman, D., 198, 297
Kamarck, T., 186
Kamin, L. J., 114
Kanner, A. D., 53, 255
Kaplan, B. H., 82, 117, 121, 227
Kaplan, G., 118
Kaplan, H. B., 19, 20, 23, 182, 203, 243, 252, 261
Keinan, G., 103, 275, 313
Kellet, A., 11, 12, 119, 239
Kelly, K. E., 177
Kennedy, C., 179, 180
Kessler, R., 54, 89, 129
Kessler, R. C., 81, 128–129, 136, 141, 144, 214, 231, 315
Klein, M., 133
Klerman, G., 144
Klingel, D. M., 67
Knowledge as energy resource, 76–77
Kobasa, S. C., 37, 38, 45, 62, 63, 65, 69, 77, 81, 95, 100, 105, 117, 156, 157,
    175, 194, 201, 250, 269, 289, 298, 306
Korchin, S. J., 171
Krasner, L., 114
Krause, N., 174
Kruglanski, A. W., 103, 198, 297
Kuczmierszyk, A. R., 35
Kuhn, T., 320
Kulka, R. A., 67
Kuo, W. A., 125, 175

Labbe, E. E., 35
Lagner, T., 165
Lake, E. A., 316
Lakey, B., 65, 92, 136, 173, 201, 227, 269
Lamm, N., 151, 231
Larsen, R. J., 179, 298
Latene, B., 139
Lazarus, R. S., 8–10, 12, 13, 16, 17, 20, 22,
    23, 26, 38, 48, 52, 53, 62–66, 69,
    84, 88, 98, 105, 114, 157, 188,
    191–194, 196, 212, 243, 252, 255,
    284, 315
Learning theory, 132–134
Lebovitz, B. Z., 119
Lefcourt, H. M., 65, 77, 95, 99, 100, 157,
    173, 201, 202, 250, 306
Lehman, D. R., 74, 89, 132, 142, 158, 224,
    238, 263, 277, 307
Leon, J. L., 69
Lerman, M., 69, 268, 272
Levav, I., 239
Levi, L., 82
Levin, H., 168
Levine, H. M., 78
Levine, S., 154, 179, 277
Levinson, D. J., 168
Lewis, R. A., 96, 144
Lidz, I., 293
Lieberman, J., 132, 136
Lieberman, M. A., 127, 130
Lieberman, Y., 54, 69, 77, 88, 135, 261
Life event survey approach, 53
Lindemann, E., 6, 22, 27, 102, 196, 302
Lindsey, G., 114
Linn, N., 118, 125, 224
Literature, themes of stress in, 3
Loehlin, J. C., 114
London, P., 75, 130, 133, 150

Loneliness:
  definition, 137
  during war, 239–240
  and social support, 137–139
Lorion, R. P., 319
Loss, 27–31, 157–158
Lyall, W. A., 309

Maccoby, E., 168
Maddi, S. R., 62, 194, 284, 291
Magnussen, D., 225
Major events vs. minor hassles, debate,
  13–16
Mann, D. W., 67
Marks, T., 98
Marlow, D. H., 151, 170, 171, 218
Martin, R. A., 65
Martin, S. S., 182
Marx, M. B., 178
Maslow, A. H., 44, 169, 284, 289, 290,
  294, 306
Mastery, 227–228, 230–231, 233, 235,
  293–294, 306
Matarazzo, J. D., 274, 276
May, R., 162, 172, 181, 289
Mayeless, O., 269
Mayol, A., 98
McCallum, D. M., 175
McCleod, J. D., 144
McFarlane, A., 174
McGowan, J., 144
McGrath, J. E., 16–20, 23, 26, 43, 45, 52,
  224, 253
McGuire, I., 310
McKay, G., 121, 129, 157
McKleod, J. D., 128, 141
Meichenbaum, D., 79, 188, 303
Menaghan, E. G., 18, 54, 127, 130
Menninger, K., 185, 276
Mermelstein, R., 186
Merrick, W. A., 194
Merton, R. K., 141, 312
Michael, S. T., 165
Mikulnicer, M., 20, 238, 309, 243
Milgram, N. A., 170, 220
Miller, K., 276
Miller, R. S., 99, 173
Minuchin, S., 82, 147, 149, 267
Mirowski, J., 28

Miscarriage, 266
Mitchell, R. E., 21, 69, 116, 145, 188, 193,
  204, 206–208, 278, 314
Mitwelt, 162
Models, need for, 220–221
Monroe, S., 52
Moore, M. C., 136, 145
Moos, R. H., 17, 21, 24, 84, 150, 188, 194,
  196, 197, 206, 207, 213, 231, 252,
  254, 255, 278, 284
Mowrer, O. H., 172
Mueller, D., 28
Mullan, J. T., 54, 127, 130
Murrel, S. A., 99, 201
Myers, B. G., 151, 231

Nadler, A., 132, 136, 152, 269
Naidu, R. K., 67
Nardi, C., 239
Nasby, W., 41
Needs, definition, 83
Needs dimension, 83–87
Neff, J. A., 136, 145
Neil, E., 14
Nelson, D. W., 174
Newbrough, J. R., 136, 145
Norbeck, T., 82, 127, 261
Norman, G., 174
Norris, F. H., 99, 201
Noy, S., 239
Nuckolls, K. G., 82, 117, 121, 261

Object resources, definitions, 72
Old Testament:
  themes of stress in, 2–3
  compensation in, 102
Opler, M. K., 165
Orr, E., 130

Pagel, M. D., 149
Palmon, N., 108, 280, 289
Pancoast, D. L., 310
Paraprofessionals, 116–117
Parkes, C. M., 7, 27, 30, 302
Parry, G., 203
Parsons, T., 145
Paykel, E. S., 7, 82, 127, 133, 135

Pearlin, L. I., 18, 30, 54, 69, 87, 127, 130, 208–210, 213, 225, 227, 231, 263, 279, 309
Peplau, L. A., 137
Perception, 37–39, 48, 97–100
Perception dimension, 97–101
Perkins, S. C., 316
Perlman, D., 132, 137
Persky, H., 171
Personal characteristics, 74–75
Personality development, 295, 296, 298, 300
    dominant spheres, effects of, 290
    effects of childhood experiences, 285, 294
    interaction of resources, 297–298
    perceptions, effect of, 297
    stressors and values, 296, 297
Personality theory, 283–285
Personality types, 291–293, 295
Pfeffer, J., 76
Physical sciences, concept of stress in, 5
Piaget, J., 247
Pierce, G. R., 135
Popper, K. R., 319
Post traumatic stress disorder, 244–246
Predmore, S. C., 156, 198
Primavera, J., 30, 45, 68
Prywkes, M., 276
Psychodynamic theory, and loss, 48–50
Puccetti, M. C., 37, 77, 156, 157, 201, 250, 269
Pyszynski, T., 316

Rabkin, J. G., 113, 117, 166, 237
Radloff, L. S., 260
Rahe, R. H., 29, 53, 78, 112, 190, 254
Rand, C. S., 275, 310
Rappaport, J., 117, 141, 148
Rassaby, E. S., 82, 127, 133, 135
Reactions to victims, 139–140
Rehm, L. P., 88
Reis, H. T., 263
Rennie, T. A., 165
Research, 88–90
Resource dimension, 72–80
Resources, 77–80
    accumulation of, 43, 287–288
    conditions as, 72
    conservation of, 25–57, 304
    definition, 26
    and developmental stages, 90
    energies as, 75
    evaluated, 31
    external and internal, 77–78
    investment of, 35–37, 42
    knowledge as, 76–77
    loss of, 26–31, 35, 38, 42–45, 48, 287–288, 301
    net gain of, 35
    objects as, 72
    personal, 74, 227, 231, 256, 258, 260
    raw, 31, 33–34
    reassessing, 38–39
    resistance of, 117–118
    risking, 42
    and social support, 155–157
    traits and characteristics of, 75
    and transitions, 30–31
    utilization strategies, 302, 303
    values of, 78–81
Rhodewalt, F., 175–177
Rich, A. R., 144
Rich, J. L., 144
Ries, H. T., 145
Riley, D., 231
Risk taking, 39–41
Robbins, C., 182
Robinson, L. A., 98
Rogers, J., 309
Rogers, W. L., 66, 289, 306, 314
Rokeach, M., 92, 93, 168, 233, 279
Roles, 87
Rook, K. S., 131, 148, 149, 247, 307
Rose, S., 144
Rosenbaum, M., 95, 100, 180, 181, 280, 289
Rosenman, R. H., 176, 313
Rosentiel, A., 196
Ross, C. E., 28
Ross, D., 168
Ross, S., 168
Roth, S., 196
Rothbaum, I. M., 96
Roy, R., 174
Rubenstein, I., 307
Ruch, L. D., 69, 90, 190, 191, 218, 256
Russell, S. F., 178

Salmon, T. W., 11, 12
Sandler, I. N., 65, 92, 173, 201, 227, 269
Sanford, R. N., 168
Sarason, B. R., 34, 132, 135, 144, 231, 269
Sarason, I. G., 34, 53, 65, 78, 95, 100, 132,
        135, 144, 167, 173, 186, 225, 241,
        277, 308
Sarason, S. B., 119
Schacter, S., 41
Schaefer, C., 53, 255
Schaefer, J. A., 84
Scheirer, M. F., 194, 195
Schill, T., 144
Schonell, M., 194
Schönpflug, W., 26, 42
Schooler, C., 30, 227
Schur, M., 49
Scott, R., 145
Sears, R., 168
Selah, W. E., 65
Self, 162
Self-actualization, 44, 169, 289–290
Self-confidence and coping, 206
Self-denigration, 182
    and social support, 203
Self-disclosure, 185–186
Self-esteem, 227–228, 230–231, 263, 293
    and stress resistance, 182
Seligman, M. E., 292
Selye, H., 5–8, 22, 26
Selzer, M. L., 30
Senchak, M., 145
Sensation seeking, 39–41
Sensation seeking scale, 40
Shapiro, D. S., 154
Shaver, F., 247
Shearin, E. N., 34, 132, 135, 225
Sheier, I., 316
Sheirer, M. F., 316
Sherk, D., 173
Sherrod, D. R., 185
Shils, E. A., 119
Shinn, M., 224
Shrout, P. E., 13, 54
Shumaker, S. A., 121, 225
Siedman, E., 117
Signal theory, 51
Silver, R., 88, 142, 311
Silverman, L. H., 104
Simeone, R. S., 125

Singer, B. R., 78, 277
Singer, J. E., 41
Sireuning, E. L., 237
Skinner, B. F., 114
Smira, K. B., 95, 100, 180, 181, 289
Smith, T. W., 316
Snyder, C. R., 316
Social adjustment rating scale, 29
Social factors, influence of, 36
Social interest, 184–185
Social support, 77, 227–231, 307–311
    absence of, 139
    definition, 120–121
    factors limiting effectiveness of, 149
    functionalist theory, 145–146
    and loss, 157–158
    intervention, 146–147
    in marriage, 145–146
    negative social interactions and, 148
    personality factors, 151–153
    reasons for offering and withholding,
        141–143
    research on, 117–123
    resources and sense of self, 155–156
    sex differences, 143–147
    situational factors, 149–151
    stress buffering and direct effects of,
        123–132
    of unhealthy behaviors, 148
Solomon, B., 145
Solomon, G. F., 237
Solomon, Z., 12, 50, 238, 239, 243, 309,
        312
Somes, G. W., 178
Spielberger, C. D., 8–10, 17, 20, 22, 38,
        104, 151, 178, 234
Spuhler, J. N., 114
Srole, L., 165
Star, R. D., 218
Stien, C. H., 141, 148
Stokes, J. P., 121, 132, 143, 144, 152, 225
Stolber, A. L., 309
Strain, 16, 81–83
Strain dimension, 81–83
Streiner, D., 174
Stress:
    concepts in physical science, 5
    definitions, 10, 16–17, 19–20, 26
    ecological models of, 21
    events and anger, 179–180

Stress (*Cont.*):
  illness and, 255
  inoculation, 303
  intervention program, 304–305
  mid- and long-term behavior, 47–48
  models of, categorization, 61
  optimism and, 180
  problem specific, 82
  psychological vs. physical, 81
  vs. psychopathology, 52–54
  reactions, 45, 49–52
  research, 117–118
  response and evolutionary develop-
      ment, 8–9, 14–15, 35
  sociological perspectives of, 18–19
Stress process, 9, 87
Stress resistance, 246–249
  definition, 16
  immediate vs. long-term, 277
  and personality traits, 66
  strategies, 303–304
Stress resistance models:
  cognitive-behavioral, 63–65
  ecological congruence vs. factor-
      process and person-
      environment models, 70
  factor-process, 62
  hardiness, 62–63, 65–66
  necessity of, 60–61
  person-environment fit, 66–69
  transactional, 63
Stressors:
  aggregate measures of, 129
  characteristics of, 99–100
  definition, 16
  effects vs. neurosis, 13–14
  environmental, Cannon-Selye tradition,
      5
  major vs. minor, 13, 15–16
  war-related, 233
Streuning, E. L., 113, 117, 166
Student-school fit, 68
Subconscious processes, 52
Subliminal exposure, 104
Sullivan, H., 49, 136
Sullivan, J. A., 144
Suls, J., 177, 183
Swann, W. B., 156, 198
Syme, S. L., 145, 177, 225
Syzanski, S. J., 177

Tasks, 83, 86
Taylor, A. J., 50
Taylor, S. E., 86
Teasdale, J. P., 292
Tennant, C., 125, 194
Thoits, P., 74, 30, 31, 44, 54, 103, 125,
      150, 225, 240, 253
Threat, 27
  definition, 84
  ego, 17
  perceptions of, 28, 30, 37, 38
  physical vs. ego, 8
Three Mile Island, 89
Tilden, V., 82, 127, 261
Time dimension, 87–91
Tinbergen, N., 104
Todt, M., 310
Transactional model, 63–65
Triandis, H. C., 246, 247
Tripathi, R. C., 67
Trost, M. A., 310
Truax, C. B., 116, 314
Tsai, Y. M., 175
Tucker, S., 310
Tversky, A., 198, 297

Ullmn, L. P., 114
Umwelt, 162

Vachon, M. L. S., 150, 205, 263, 309, 311
Vaillant, G. E., 125
Valence of effect, 101–102, 317–319
Valence of fit, definition of, 72
Value dimension, 91–97
Value of resources, 78–79
Values, 33, 95–96
  cultural and family, 92
  Frankl's, 168–169
  in Kaplan's model, 19
  and parental advice, 102
  personal, 93
  sources of, 92–93
  and stress buffering, 130
Vanfossen, B., 78, 134, 141, 145, 315
Vaux, A., 144
Victims, auto accident, 89
Vinokur, H. M., 30
Visotsky, H. M., 119, 158, 172

Walfisch, S., 7, 61, 99, 125, 190, 256
Walker, K. N., 150
Wall, S., 285
Walster, E., 76, 140, 151
Walster, G. W., 76, 140, 151
War:
    reactions to, 235–237
    study of, 218–220
Waraheit, G. J., 133
Ware, E. E., 173
Ware, J. E., 81, 125
Waters, M. C., 285
Watson, J. B., 114
Weinberger, J., 104
Weintraub, J. K., 195
Weir, T., 143
Weisz, J. R., 96
Weithington, E., 81
Wellman, B., 280
Wethington, E., 129, 141
Wheaton, B., 174, 194, 316
Whichter-Alagna, S., 152
White, H., 194
Whiting, J., 247
Wiebe, D. J., 175
Wiesberg, R. D., 310

Wiessman, M. M., 144
Wilcox, B. L., 21, 30, 81, 88, 127, 310
Wildman, R. C., 190, 191
Williams, A. F., 47
Williams, A. W., 81, 125, 254
Williams, R., 92
Wills, T. A., 127, 145, 167, 225, 228, 278
Wilson, D. G., 144
Wishnie, H. A., 196
Witenburg, S. H., 177
Wolff, P. H., 51
Wong, N. W., 224
Worden, T. J., 178
Worlman, C. B., 142
Wortman, C. B., 47, 88, 130, 132, 142,
        178, 214, 277, 294, 315
Wothington, E., 144
Wysocki, J., 176, 177

Yando, R., 41
Yarvis, R. M., 28

Zajonc, R. B., 105
Zuckerman, M., 39–40